The Politics of War Trauma

STUDIES OF THE NETHERLANDS INSTITUTE FOR WAR DOCUMENTATION

1 Ralf Futselaar — *Lard, Lice and Longevity. The standard of living in occupied Denmark and the Netherlands 1940-1945*
ISBN 978 90 5260 253 0

2 Martijn Eickhoff (translated by Peter Mason) — *In the Name of Science? P.J.W. Debye and his career in Nazi Germany*
ISBN 978 90 5260 327 8

3 Johan den Hertog & Samuël Kruizinga (eds.) — *Caught in the Middle. Neutrals, neutrality, and the First World War*
ISBN 978 90 5260 370 4

4 Jolande Withuis & Annet Mooij (eds.) — *The Politics of War Trauma. The aftermath of World War II in eleven European countries*
ISBN 978 90 5260 371 1

The Politics of War Trauma

The aftermath of World War II in eleven European countries

Jolande Withuis & Annet Mooij
(eds.)

aksant
Amsterdam
2010

ISBN 978 90 5260 371 1

Cover design: Jos Hendrix, Groningen
Lay out: Hanneke Kossen, Amsterdam
Printed in the Netherlands

Aksant Academic Publishers, PO Box 2169, NL-1000 CD Amsterdam, www.aksant.nl
in co-operation with Transaction Publishers, www.transactionpub.com

Contents

Acknowledgements

On the occasion of the publication of this book we would like to thank all who have contributed to this comprehensive and complex international project.

First of all, of course, our eight authors, who, with enormous dedication and resourcefulness, have opened up a new area of research. We retain very good memories of our collaboration, and in particular of our work conference in Amsterdam on 10 October 2008. The active and inspirational contribution of our oldest author, Polish psychiatrist and family therapist Maria Orwid, on that day is still vivid in our minds. We deeply regret that she is not here to see the publication of this book, but we consider ourselves fortunate that our work could profit from her valuable knowledge and insights. Maria Orwid passed away in February 2009, at the age of 78.

Furthermore we thank Julia Suchar. Had it not been for her kind offices we never would have been able to include Poland in this project. We also received assistance from historian Karel Berkhoff, sociologist Tom de Ridder and psychotherapist Kees van der Velden, who provided, each in his own field, essential contributions. Thanks are also due to the scientific supervisory committee, consisting of dr. Eveline Buchheim, dr. Conny Kristel and prof. dr. Peter Romijn of the Netherlands Institute for War Documentation, and prof. dr. Pieter Lagrou of the Université Libre de Bruxelles. Their close and thorough reading has benefited the book.

With the exception of the chapters on Germany and Austria, that were translated by James Fearns (Germany) and Mel Greenwald (Austria), Maggie Oattes translated or corrected the entire book with great care and commitment.

The title 'project coordinator' does not do justice to the importance of Anne Helfrich. She kept the project going, took care of all correspondence, paid the bills, gave the authors the warmest welcome, and remained cheerful throughout. She has been invaluable for the successful conclusion of this project and for keeping up our job satisfaction.

Last but not least, we want to thank our subsidizer, the Ministry of Health, Welfare and Sport, Department of Victims and Remembrance World War II. Their generous grant made this pioneering project possible. We owe a debt of gratitude to Puck Huitsing in particular for her inspiring interest and her confidence in our work.

Annet Mooij, Jolande Withuis
September 2009

List of Abbreviations

AIVG	Aide aux Israélites Victimes de la Guerre (Aid to Jewish War Victims)
AK	Armia Krajowa (Home Army)
ANED	Associazione Nazionale Deportati (National Association of Deportees)
ANEI	Associazione Nazionale Ex Internati (National Association of Ex-Internees) [military deportees]
ANMIG	Associazione Nazionale Mutilati e Invalidi di Guerra (National Association of Mutilated and Disabled Veterans)
ANPI	Associazione Nazionale Partigiani Italiani (National Association of Italian Partisans)
APA	American Psychiatric Association
CDEC	Centro di Documentazione Ebraica Contemporanea (Centre for Contemporary Jewish Documentation)
CDJ	Comité de Défense des Juifs (Jewish Defense Committee)
CEGESOMA	Centre for Historical Research and Documentation on War and Contemporary Society
CFLN	Comité Français de la Libération Nationale (French Committee of National Liberation)
CLN	Comitato di Liberazione Nazionale (Committee of National Liberation)
CLNAI	Comitato di Liberazione Nazionale per l'Alta Italia (National Committee for the Liberation of Upper Italy)
CMP	Centre Médico-Psychologique (Medical Psychological Centre)
CMR	Conseil Médical de la Résistance (Medical Committee of the Resistance)
CNPPA	Confédération Nationale des Prisonniers Politiques et Ayants-droit (National Confederation of Political Prisoners of Belgium)
CNR	Conseil National de la Résistance (National Council of the Resistance)
Comintern	Communist International
COR	Conseil de l'Ordre de la Résistance (Council of Order of the Resistance)
DSM	Diagnostic and Statistical Manual of Mental Disorders
ESTSS	European Society for Traumatic Stress Studies
Expogé	= NVEPG: Nederlandse Vereniging van Ex-Politieke Gevangenen uit de bezettingstijd (Dutch Association of Ex-Political Prisoners)
Fiapp	Fédération Internationale des Anciens Prisonniers Politiques (International Federation of Former Political Prisoners)

Fildir	Fédération Internationale Libre des Déportés et Internés de la Résistance (Free International Federation of Deportees and Resistance Internees)
Fir	Fédération Internationale des Résistants (International Federation of Resistance Fighters)
FLN	Front de Libération National (National Liberation Front)
FNACA	Fédération Nationale des Anciens Combattants en Algérie, Maroc et Tunisie (National Federation of Ancient Combattants of the Algerian, Moroccan and Tunisian wars)
FNDIR	Fédération Nationale des Déportés et Internés de la Résistance (National Fédération of Déportées and Internées of the Résistance)
FRG	Federal Republic of Germany
GD	Groupement (Patriotique et) Démocratique (Patriotic and Democratic Group)
GDR	German Democratic Republic
GRPF	Gouvernement Provisoire de la République Française (Provisional Government of the French Republic)
ISTSS	International Society for Traumatic Stress Studies
IV-INIG	Institut des Vétérans – Institut National des Invalides de Guerre, Anciens Combattants et Victimes de Guerre (Institute for Veterans – National Institute for War Disabled, War Veterans and War Victims)
KOVG	Kriegsopferversorgungsgesetz (War Victims Care Provision Law)
KPÖ	Kommunistische Partei Österreichs (Austrian Communist Party)
KZ	Konzentrationslager (concentration camp)
LPPD	Ligue Luxembourgeoise des Prisonniers Politiques et Déportés (Luxembourg League of Political Prisoners and Deportees)
MdE	Minderung der Erwerbsfähigkeit (reduced earning capacity)
MGV	Maandblad Geestelijke volksgezondheid (Monthly on Public Mental Health)
NAC	Nederlands Auschwitz Comité (Netherlands' Auschwitz Committee)
NATO	North Atlantic Treaty Organization
NKVD	Narodnyj Komissariat Vnoetrennich Djel (People's Commissariat for Internal Affairs)
NSDAP	Nationalsozialistische Deutsche Arbeiterpartei (National Socialist German Workers' Party)
OAS	Organisation de l'Armée Secrète (Secret Army Organization)
OBSI	Official Belgian Scale for the establishment of the degree of Invalidity
OFG	Opferfürsorgegesetz (Victims Care Provision Law)
ÖVP	Österreichische Volkspartei (Austrian People's Party)
OVRA	Organizzazione per la Vigilanza e la Repressione dell'Antifascismo (Organization for Vigilance and Repression of Anti-Fascism) [secret police]
PCF	Parti Communiste Français (French Communist Party)
POW	Prisoner of war
PTSD	Post-Traumatic Stress Disorder

RAD	Reichsarbeitsdienst (Reich Labour Service)
RSI	Repubblica Sociale Italiana (Italian Social Republic)
SA	Sturmabteilung (Storm troopers)
SED	Sozialistische Einheitspartei Deutschlands (Socialist Unity Party of Germany)
SFAP	Société Franco-Algérienne de Psychiatrie (Franco-Algerian Psychiatric Society)
SIP	Società Italiana di Psichiatria (Italian Psychiatric Society)
SPÖ	Sozialdemokratische Partei Österreichs (Social Democratic Party of Austria)
SS	Schutzstaffel (Protection Squad)
SSJ	Service Social Juif (Jewish Social Service)
STO	Service de Travail Obligatoire (Compulsory Work Service)
UNRRA	United Nations Relief and Rehabilitation Administration
VdB	Volksdeutsche Bewegung (Ethnic German Movement)
VdH	Verband der Heimkehrer, Kriegsgefangenen und Vermisstenangehörigen (Association of Returnees, Prisoners of War and Families of Missing Persons)
VOS	Vereinigung der Opfer des Stalinismus (Association of the Victims of Stalinism)
WBP	Wet Buitengewoon Pensioen (Extraordinary Pensions Act)
WHO	World Health Organization
WUBO	Wet Uitkeringen Burger-Oorlogsslachtoffers 1940-1945 (Benefit Act for Civilian War Victims 1940-1945)
WUV	Wet Uitkeringen Vervolgden (Benefit Act for Victims of Persecution)
WVF	World Veterans Federation

Introduction: The Politics of War Trauma

» *Jolande Withuis*

Today it is as self-evident as the importance of vitamins: the idea that intensely emotional negative experiences can leave us with late, protracted and even permanent mental and physical health damage, i.e.: that healthy, mentally stable adult persons can become 'traumatized'. This is actually a relatively recent notion. The term trauma may be common in large parts of the world at the start of the 21st century, but it was unusual when World War II drew to a close. Whereas in most Western countries 'trauma' is now automatically associated with a psychological injury, at that time the term trauma referred simply to a physical injury. This shift in meaning represents something larger: it illustrates the radical changes in how we feel severe adversity affects our lives and health, and in how people assess others and themselves as being victims.

In 1945, after the Allied victory over Nazi Germany, Europe had to come to terms with its devastating losses. Millions of people had lost their lives; even more millions had to live on without their loved ones; many were to suffer uncertainty about the fate of their nearest and dearest for a long time. Others were ill, starved and haunted by their own experiences in camps and in hiding, during combat and bombardments. The material damage was immense. The joy of liberation was accompanied by sadness, fear and anger. It is estimated that more than 150 million people died; more than half were civilians.

People returned from deportations, violence and imprisonment, and resumed life as best they could. But how was their health and how did medical professionals see their future?

Nowadays in Western countries like Denmark, France, Great Britain, the Netherlands and the USA (but notably not in Austria, Belgium, Italy or Poland), a disaster like World War II would be met with an army of psychotraumatologists, diagnosing people as potential or even probable future sufferers of the symptoms of PTSD. Survivors and soldiers, widows and witnesses, persecuted and perpetrators would be seen as victims who, through immediate psychotherapeutic treatment and medical monitoring, might be prevented from developing a chronic, invalidating mental disorder.

This development towards immediate and intensive care was strongly stimulated by the inclusion in 1980 by the American Psychiatric Association (APA) of Post Traumatic Stress Disorder (PTSD) in its official Diagnostic and Statistical Manual of Mental Disorders, DSM III. The diagnosis of PTSD requires the presence of at least three symptoms which must all occur over a longer period of time: intrusive flashbacks; avoidance of situations and emotions associated with the war; and a persistent state of physical hyperarousal. In a weaker form these phenomena are part of normal everyday life; if they are serious they make a normal life practically impossible.

The acceptance of PTSD meant that from 1980 on, the medical profession recognized the possibility that even a mentally stable adult could be traumatized by an exterior experience like war. This possibility had not been officially acknowledged before. In some histories of medicine PTSD is therefore described as the final outcome of 35 years of thinking about mental war damage, or even as the radiant light after a century of dwelling in darkness. This is too simplistic a view. PTSD was not 'discovered' like, for instance, penicillin, and contrary to usual assumptions the change in psychiatric paradigm from 1980 was not purely the result of medical progress.

Here we will not discuss the medical, psychological and philosophical critique the PTSD approach has met with.[1] Instead we will focus on the historical developments from the end of World War II to PTSD. The recognition of PTSD in 1980 was the result of heavy lobbying to integrate into psychiatry three experiences and discoveries that had a major impact in the 1970's. First, there were the veterans of the Vietnam War, many of whom fell victim to violent and addictive behavior and depression. No less influential were the discoveries of feminism concerning how many women suffered life-long psychological wounds as a consequence of crimes like incest, rape and other forms of (often domestic) violence. Before the recognition of PTSD such women and soldiers had often been wrongly diagnosed as suffering from schizophrenia or personality disorders and subsequently had not been adequately treated. Last but not least, at the same time that these observations on veterans and women were made, reports from the United States as well as from Europe increasingly mentioned the phenomenon of so-called 'late consequences' of World War II. It became clear that although this war had been over for more than a quarter of a century, camp survivors, resistance fighters and other victims still often suffered depressing and invalidating symptoms, symptoms that showed a remarkable likeness to those of the traumatized women and veterans.

The way in which the period from 1939 to 1945 is remembered, has been the object of ample historical studies. From this 'history of memory' we learn that what is remembered is in no way a simple reflection of what happened. Neither the

1 Cf. McNally, *Remembering trauma*; Rosen, *Posttraumatic stress disorder*; Shephard, 'Risk factors', 'Why the psychiatry of war is too important'; Summerfield, 'The invention of post-traumatic stress disorder'; Withuis, *Erkenning*, 'Does PTSD really exist?'; Young, *The harmony of illusions*.

individual's memory, nor the collective rituals of commemorating provide pure representations of what was experienced. Both social memory and individual memory are dynamic processes of continuous change and development. Furthermore, memory is divided and the subject of controversy and conflict, dominance and hegemony, neglect and forgetting.[2]

'Coming to terms' not only means rituals, monuments, remembrance and memory; it also means mourning and recovery. Physical and mental exhaustion can result in temporary or chronic illness. This aspect of the aftermath of war is what this book focuses on: did survivors become ill; how were these illnesses perceived by the survivors themselves, their doctors and their societies; and which categories of war patients were supported by their national states?

The Politics of War Trauma compares the attitudes and policies towards the health consequences of World War II in eleven European countries: Austria, Belgium, Denmark, East-Germany, France, Italy, Luxembourg, the Netherlands, Norway, Poland and West-Germany. In a truly interdisciplinary way the book connects aspects of the aftermath of World War II that are not usually analyzed together. Changes in medical and psychological thinking about the consequences of the war and the prevalence of war-related health problems are analyzed in the context of post-war political history, in particular the rise and decline of the Cold War. In the 35 years between the victory over Nazism and the inclusion of PTSD in DSMIII, the medical approach to the survivors developed remarkably asynchronously in the countries we studied. It often took time and considerable persistence before symptoms were recognized as consequences of World War II experiences.

The Politics of War Trauma is the result of a three year project by a team of one psychologist, two psychiatrists, three sociologists and four historians of various nationalities who all worked with the same research questions. Every author had to do pioneering work. As there was very little research on which to build, they had to find new sources. They had to combine the (pre-)history of World War II, the history of memory, political and medical history, pension laws and statistics, an understanding of trends in psychology and national and international psychiatric traditions. In addition they needed an understanding of the cultural and social peculiarities of 'their' countries.

The project was a follow-up on earlier research by the two editors into the role of psychiatry in Dutch World War II-memory. Surprised about the differences in the mental climate and culture of remembrance of World War II between the Netherlands and neighboring Belgium, which has no trauma culture and certainly not with regard to World War II, we realized that the post-war European medical

2 Cf. Bessel and Schumann (eds.), *Life after death*; Lebow et al. (eds.), *The politics of memory*; Van Lingen, *Kriegserfahrung*; Moeller, *War stories*.

care for the victims of World War II had never been inventoried. Obviously the question why the views and welfare provisions in each country were so different had also never been analyzed.

In the Netherlands the relatively new concept of psychotrauma became part of the general societal body of knowledge within a few decades. This development, that has culminated in today's mental climate in which people who did not win the lottery claim to suffer a PTSD and therefore think of themselves as deserving compensation, is not matter-of-course. Elsewhere developments after World War II were very different. But how, and why? These are new and ambitious questions.

The Politics of War Trauma consists of two sections.

In the extensive first section ten authors in nine chapters provide an overview of the medical approaches to the victims in eleven countries. The chapters on Germany and Scandinavia each address two countries. Ralf Futselaar analyzes the two Northern pioneers of the *KZ syndrome*, Denmark and Norway; Svenja Goltermann compares the former Federal Republic of Germany and the German Democratic Republic.

All nine chapters furthermore provide a summary of the relevant war and post-war history as a context for the medical-sociological facts. We link the care for the sick to the war history in order to determine to what extent choices in post-war policy were based on the actual historical weight of the fate of particular categories of civilians and soldiers. For all countries we have tried to inventory which groups of war victims were defined as victims or heroes, and which were neglected; which victim hierarchies were observable in, for instance, the sequence of the legislation; and what influence pressure groups like concentration camp *amicales* and associations of veterans and former political prisoners had. Did the differences in pace in providing care parallel the incongruence that was already observed in earlier research into the way in which World War II was commemorated, for example the relatively late attention for the genocide of the Jews?

In the second part of *The Politics of War Trauma*, based on the previous separate chapters, the countries are compared on several aspects.

Chapter 10, 'The Aftermath of World War II: A comparison', lists the main differences between the countries with regard to culture of remembrance, legislation and victim groups.

Chapter 11, 'The Management of Victimhood. Long-term health damage from Asthenia to PTSD', compares medical-psychological thinking in the eleven nations and reconstructs the routes along which the asynchronous recognition of the 'late consequences' spread across Europe. This 'tour' clearly shows that the recognition of war trauma started with the investigations into the health of ex-political prisoners by physicians who had themselves been part of the resistance. For a long time the main actors were not so much the national governments, but rather *trans-*

national organizations of, for example, resistance and prisoners of war, though always operating within the context of the various national legislations.

Although the nation state certainly is not the only or most important variable to explain the variety in attitudes towards mental illness or the possible development towards a trauma culture (culture, religion, degree of individualization and prosperity are at least as important), we still decided in favor of a comparison between nations. With regard to coming to terms with World War II the nation state does seem to make the logical unit of research. Matters such as decorations, compensation and benefit regulations, medical care, pension schemes (all of which play a role in the coping process) are almost always organized within national boundaries, and they turned out to differ strongly along national lines indeed.

The selection of the eleven countries presented here was based on both practical and theoretical considerations.

Two Western allies are missing, although PTSD is booming business in both countries: the United Kingdom and the United States. We did not include these two countries because we were specifically interested in the post-war fate of deported population groups such as Jews and political prisoners. Unlike the hostilities – the fighting – in which British and American allies were involved, the experience of deportation and imprisonment in concentration camps and extermination camps of groups of people was new, also in a medical-psychological sense. Both *combat fatigue* and the post-war experiences of British and American soldiers have already been described.

Research in Hungary, Bulgaria, Czechoslovakia, the former Soviet Union and former Yugoslavia was outside the bounds of possibility, no matter how much we would have liked to include these countries. Nevertheless we are very pleased that we were able to include in our study the main Western and Southern European countries from which sections of the population were carried away, and that in one case we managed to overcome the language problems that so complicate research in Eastern Europe: *The Politics of War Trauma* contains an interesting chapter on Polish post-war psychiatry, a chapter that perfectly illustrates the title of our book.

The war histories of the studied countries are complex. We wanted to incorporate this complexity in the study, because it implies as many options regarding the groups the state could provide assistance for. After the Allied victory, did the national heart in Austria, Luxembourg and Italy go out to the defeated native *Wehrmacht* soldiers, or to those who had deserted, fled, or engaged in resistance, or who, because they were Jews, had ended up in camps? What type of care did these choices result in? Did victims themselves appeal for medical assistance or financial support, and if so to what state? To Germany, to their countries of origin, or to the country where they had chosen their domicile after 1945? And how did the then still two German states respond to requests for compensation? As these questions belonged in this project, both East and West Germany are also included in our book.

The subject of benefit or pension provisions for war victims is not often addressed in books on the welfare state. It is nevertheless obvious that they do go to the heart of the modern welfare state. State interests play a role in benefits for sick and disabled soldiers and the surviving relatives of those who have perished. In order to attract recruits, future soldiers must be sure that in case of illness or death they or their surviving relatives will be taken care of. Wounded soldiers need to recover their health in order to return to the battlefield or be able to work after the war. And the schemes need to remain affordable.

The situation in Germany and Great Britain following World War I is a case in point.

The German law of 1920 in principle offered room for a benefit on psychic grounds. But only on the condition that causality could be proved, which is always difficult. German psychiatry, however, increasingly viewed war neurosis as a 'pension neurosis': a quasi-illness that not only heavily burdened the government budget, but was also thought to lead to a lazy society. Pensioners themselves were often weighed down by the stigma of being profiteers unwilling to work, all the more so in view of the lack of reintegration schemes. After the Weimar Republic came to an end the situation worsened. A decree in 1934 formally excluded mental disorders from the right to compensation. The war disabled were increasingly declared public enemies, regardless of whether their condition was psychological or somatic.[3]

The United Kingdom after World War I pursued a relatively kind-hearted policy, and as a result the costs of the epidemic 'shell shock' had mounted considerably by the end of the 1930's. In what Ben Shephard in his much-praised *A War of Nerves* analyzed as a back-and-forth movement between tough and tender that was observable throughout the twentieth century, the pendulum in 1940 had swung back to tough. The shell shock policy had seduced people to stay ill at the state's expense. The realization that in the most extreme circumstances even the strongest can break, was worsted by the political decision and medical policy intention to never again start such a money guzzling, difficult to control scheme. 'Determined not to incur such a bill again', the War Office made sure that as early as 1939 'the medical policy machine was locked into a very restrictive definition of war neurosis'.[4]

3 See Neuner, 'The effects of compensation policy'.
4 See Shephard, *A war of nerves*, 165-6.

Interesting common ground with our study is also found in Theda Skocpol's historical-sociological study into the origin of the American welfare state.[5] She contrasts the early European schemes with the American provisions. Whereas in Europe the first schemes, organized between 1870 and 1910 under pressure from trade unions, were destined to categorically protect employees and the economically needy against the risks of illness and poverty, the United States had had a pension program since 1862, that was intended for Civil War veterans and their (surviving) relatives. These – generous – pensions reflected the national sentiment of the Northern states, and were furthermore necessary to encourage volunteers to enlist. Initially many of the people who were eligible did not actually apply for a pension. People had an aversion against accepting money from the state, did not need it, or wanted to forget the war. In later years the number of applications increased. In the long run the disability program in effect functioned as an old-age pension, but one exclusively reserved for the 'morally deserving': for those who had earned this reward by enlisting in the army. And there were many. Because the pension followed political rather than economic lines, it cut across the boundaries of class and race. Also, it was relatively easy to gain access. After the law was amended in 1890, applicants were not even obliged to prove they suffered from injuries or illness caused by the war. Anyone who had served for a period of ninety days received a pension purely on the basis of age. Those who had fought for the other side, or had evaded military service, however, were excluded from the provision no matter what.

Scokpol does not view this system as an early type of welfare state, but rather as an expression of public care for a specific group of people: 'Legitimate Civil War pensions were idealized as that which was justly due to the righteous core of a generation of men (and survivors of dead men) – a group that ought to be generously and constantly repaid by the nation for their sacrifices.' It should not be necessary for this generation to have to turn to charity or poor relief in their old age or in case of illness. This was considered shameful and humiliating, unlike the honorable pension. Apart from that the legacy of this generosity was a permanent wariness of 'open-ended public spending, especially for military veterans ...'.

Related dilemmas are addressed in the following chapters. Who are the schemes intended for? Is a causal relationship between the war and later health complaints a precondition for eligibility? Is it an illness benefit, is it damages for endured suffering, or is it an honorary pension for courage and sacrifice?

One of the methodological tasks we faced was that the diseases and complaints that were the object of the public debates, conflicts and developments we have studied, are often vague and are not always recorded in the statistics as conse-

---

5 Skocpol, *Protecting soldiers and mothers.* Especially 102-115, 148-151, quotations 149, 533.

quences of war. The type of complaints that today would result in a diagnosis of PTSD, half a century ago, as long as life remained livable, would be interpreted as characterological idiosyncrasies rather than complaints that a doctor could treat. If the anxieties, irritability, compulsive actions and re-experiencing the trauma became too serious to lead a relatively normal existence and the person had to be hospitalized, the patient data were often 'hidden', for instance under the heading of schizophrenia. In this way the incorrect impression could arise that the war did not have any detrimental consequences. In the occasional fortunate circumstance a meticulous analysis of medical files can result in a reconstruction of the true situation. However, this approach, as carried out by Goltermann in Germany, is rarely feasible due to, among other things, privacy laws or the destruction of medical files.

Even when war diseases were kept up to date in the statistics, the methodological problems are not solved. In the Netherlands the number of treatments and benefits for complaints attributed to wartime experiences, increased dramatically after about 1970. But that still does not tell us which complaints and symptoms those 'recognized' patients had, and since when.

For those reasons we approached the subject from three different directions. We looked at the schemes established by the authorities. We focused on the activities and desires of victim groups and on the symptoms presented by the patients. And we analyzed medical debates, especially in the field of psychiatry, assuming that they will provide an idea of the types of patients and medical problems doctors encountered in their daily practice.

These medical debates actually built largely on pre-war discussions. Even if no single doctor had dealt with this type of total war, genocide and concentration camps before, the fact that psychiatry decided, hesitated and held different views about possible long-term consequences of extreme events was not new.[6] A condition with the romantic name *soldier's heart* was known from the aftermath of the American Civil War. Its symptoms were concentration disorders, fatigue, apathy, sweating and palpitations. Because of the latter symptom the condition was also called *irritable heart*, although there was nothing wrong with patients' hearts. The complaints that accompanied soldier's heart used to be classified under the broad concept of 'neurasthenia', and today are considered anxiety disorders.

The symptoms of the war disabled after World War I were more flamboyant than soldier's heart: *shell shock* could lead to deafness, dumbness, blindness, amnesia, strange physical contortions, compulsive movements, exhaustion, paralysis, tremors, and overall maladjustment. In the nineteenth century such 'conversions' were placed in the category of 'hysteria'; today they are referred to as somatoform disorder.

6 For the history of thinking about possible permanent health consequences of war, see especially Shephard, *A war of nerves*. Also: Jones and Wessely, *Shell shock to PTSD*; Lerner, 'Psychiatry and casualties of war', *Hysterical men;* Lerner and Micale, 'Trauma, psychiatry, and history'.

Both soldier's heart and shell shock were conditions in people who remained ill after their original wounds had healed, or who became ill when no physical injuries were apparent. The term 'shell shock' illustrates this confusion. The name 'shell' refers to a grenade, outcome of the fact that the symptoms initially were considered the effect of shrapnel, air pressure, noise, or poison. However, doctors quickly discovered that some of the soldiers who suffered from shell shock had not been anywhere near an exploding grenade. For that reason the complaints were also diagnosed as the disease GOK, *God Only Knows.*

Shell shock proved to be the result of psychological phenomena like intense fear. Even men with nerves of steel broke down as they waited helplessly for death to descend arbitrarily upon them, without ever having seen the enemy; they turned into trembling wrecks tormented by nightmares. The 'management of fear' became one of the main themes of the famous Great War literature.

In any event, the late psychic consequences of war are complaints whose course was difficult to predict, for which until recently there was no effective therapy and for which no organic substrate can be found in accepted medical research. This therefore leaves the physician with lots of room for his own opinion – *and* for the fear that he is being told a tale.

The role of physicians in the diagnosis was and remains crucial. Freud referred to the military physicians of World War I as the 'machine guns behind the front line', because it was their job to declare the soldiers fit again as quickly as possible so they could return to the front. In that same war soldiers who today would be defined as ill were executed as deserters. Even recently, almost a century later, one executed English soldier was rehabilitated because, according to current understanding, he had suffered from PTSD. On the other hand the famous poet Siegfried Sassoon, who was opposed to the British participation in the war on principle, did not want to take advantage of the possibility of being exempted from military service on medical grounds. As an officer he did not want to abandon his men. This exemption opportunity was one of the reasons that military physicians generally treated their patients with distrust.

Wars were not the only cause of the phenomenon that some people did not recover after a serious accident, even when their injuries had long healed. As early as the mid nineteenth century – with its rapid industrialization and mechanization on the one hand, and a budding social security legislation on the other – the well-known railway and factory accidents had occupied physicians. At the same time Charcot, Freud, and Janet studied the (sexual) traumas that were supposedly hidden behind hysteria.[7]

7 Herman, *Trauma en herstel.*; Leys, *Trauma*; McNally, *Remembering trauma.*

In the Interbellum there were intense debates in the entire field of psychiatry about the influence of emotions on people's state of health. In countries that had not been involved in World War I the insurance physicians in particular discussed the 'traumatic neuroses' (with trauma referring to physical injury). In Belgium the workplace accidents expert doctor M. Moreau was to play a role in the discussions on what the assistance schemes should look like after World War II ended. The medical key question with regard to accidents as well as shell shock and *Kriegsneurosen* was always whether a mentally healthy adult could be permanently affected by an external cause without organic consequences, i.e. merely on the basis of psychological stress.

There are two recurring issues in these disputes.

Firstly, if a person, for example as a result of the scare, remained anxious and unstable after an accident, did this not mean that he was already anxious and unstable before the accident? The relevance of this question for awarding benefits is evident. For in that case the accident was not the actual cause of his problems. The patient's illness was then a consequence of his personality or vulnerability, as it had been formed before the event (in medicalese: 'pre-existing personality'). The term that was and is commonly used in this case is 'premorbidity'.

A second point of doubt was whether material and immaterial kindness did not in fact sustain traumatic neurosis. Was recovery not hampered by awarding a benefit or exemption from finding a job? In cases like these physicians spoke of 'pension neurosis'; Freud, and in his slipstream medical sociologists, talked about 'secondary gain', or also 'flight into illness'.

Although the two are often confused, secondary gain is not synonymous with malingering. In the case of secondary gain actual symptoms exist, in the case of malingering they are feigned by the patient. As soon as he is out the door with the coveted sick note in his pocket, he can go on his merry way. The question of how to recognize malingerers was prominent in the pre-war debates.

On the eve of World War II neurologists and psychiatrists in general were convinced that psychic symptoms were the expression of a disease in the structure or working of the brain. The disorder was thought to have an organic basis, even if these defects were generally impossible to detect in the brain. With such a wide variety of difficult to explain complaints, it was tempting for a physician to think of malingering or 'pension neurosis', or a degenerative or hereditary condition that predisposed individuals to mental illness. That is not to say that they ignored environmental factors altogether. But for a change in a person's mental health to be acknowledged as permanent, organicity was a required precondition. In its absence, the condition was supposed to be of a passing nature.

Psychoanalysts, who did not share this exclusively organically oriented perspective on psychiatric illnesses, nevertheless thought that a trauma could not do permanent damage in a mentally healthy adult. If it did, so they felt, it had to be based on traumatic childhood experiences.

The following chapters describe how, starting from these ideas, medical-psychological care developed in confrontation with the many thousands who attempted to resume their lives after the disastrous 1939-1945 episode – injured, anxious and desperate, after having suffered horrifying experiences and massive personal losses.

PART I

Eleven Nations

I A Nation of Victims

How Austria dealt with the victims of the authoritarian *Ständestaat* and national socialism

» *Helga Embacher and Maria Ecker*

After World War II, the Federal Republic of Germany (FRG) had to face up to its responsibility for National Socialism. Austria, on the other hand, succeeded all the way up to the 1980's in portraying itself as a victim of National Socialist aggression. The Moscow Declaration issued by the Allies in 1943 served as a basis for this stance. In it, the governments of the United Kingdom, the Soviet Union and the United States of America declared the annexation (*Anschluss*) imposed on Austria by Germany on March 12, 1938 as null and void, and stated that they wished to see re-established a free and independent Austria. The Declaration also characterized Austria as 'the first free country to fall a victim to Hitlerite aggression' and stated that it had to be liberated from German domination. Nevertheless, Austria was also called upon to accept responsibility for having fought in World War II on the side of Nazi Germany, and to contribute to its own liberation.[1] From the Allies' point of view, the Moscow Declaration was above all a propaganda instrument meant to encourage Austrian resistance, but Austrian politicians used this document from 1945 until well into the 1980's to support the so-called 'victim thesis' (also known as the 'victim myth'). The passage referring to shared responsibility for World War II was omitted from consideration and the role as victim was emphasized. In pursuing this course, Austria hoped not only to conclude a State Treaty as quickly as possible but also to avoid any sort of reparations payments for which, in the view of Austria's political leaders, the FRG bore sole responsibility. The Allies knew better, but as a result of the Cold War they agreed to the Austrian victim thesis. Another factor that proved to be helpful to the Austrian cause was the position of Israel, which, pursuant to *realpolitische* considerations, concurred with the victim thesis and renounced claims

1 The literal wording: 'Austria is reminded, however, that she has a responsibility, which she cannot evade, for participation in the war at the side of Hitlerite Germany, and that in the final settlement account will inevitably be taken of her own contribution to her liberation.'

to compensation payments as a state.[2] The State Treaty signed in 1955 by the four Occupation Powers omitted any reference to Austria's shared blame.[3] Despite the numerous contradictions inherent in the victim thesis, it could essentially be maintained until well into the 1980's. Since then, Austrian scholars in contemporary history have generally reached a consensus that the occupation of the State of Austria in 1938 did indeed contravene international law; nevertheless, a majority of the population, for a variety of reasons, welcomed the *Anschluss*, and Austrians were involved in the crimes of National Socialism.

In this paper, we will show that the victim thesis also determined how Austria dealt with the various groups of victims of the authoritarian *Ständestaat* (corporative state) and National Socialism, as well as with the perpetrators and fellow travelers. Furthermore, the *Opferfürsorgegesetz*, the chief piece of legislation regulating the treatment of and care provided for victims of the Nazis and resistance fighters living in Austria (and the more than sixty amendments enacted since its original passage), have to be evaluated in the historical context of the victim thesis.

1933-1938: Victim versus victim

To this day, historians and political scientists are divided by disagreement on the proper designation of the authoritarian system that prevailed in Austria from 1934 to 1938. Austrofascism, Christian corporative state, clerical fascism, semifascism, fascism from above – this multiplicity of terms is indicative of the problems raised by the effort to undertake an exacting scholarly assessment, and thus of research gaps as well.[4] The First Republic, which emerged from the collapse of the Hapsburg Monarchy in 1918, collapsed itself in the wake of grave political and economic crises with the so-called 'self-elimination of the Parliament' on March 4, 1933.[5] The Communist (KPDÖ) and National Socialist (NSDAP) parties were banned. On May 1, 1934, Chancellor Engelbert Dollfuss enacted 'in the name of God the Almighty, from Whom all law proceeds', an authoritarian, corpora-

2 Austria played a key role above all as a way station for Eastern European Jewish Holocaust survivors. Vienna, as the last outpost on the Western side of the Iron Curtain, had tremendous importance for Israeli diplomacy since official diplomatic relations with the FRG were not established until 1965. After having been granted a 30 million Schilling loan by Austria and successfully concluded reparations negotiations with the FRG, the Israeli Government officially renounced claims to reparations payments from Austria. See Embacher, 'Restitutionsverhandlungen', 70 ff.

3 On the subject of the victim thesis, see Bischof, 'Die Instrumentalisierung', 345-366; Stourzh, *Um Einheit und Freiheit*, 11-27.

4 The standard work in this field is Tálos/Neugebauer, *Austrofaschismus* (currently in its 2nd edition).

5 The 'May Constitution' preceded the 'self-elimination of the Parliament' (March 4, 1933), which was in fact a breach of the constitution by the Dollfuss Government in league with the *Heimwehr* paramilitary organizations.

tive constitution. The Dollfuss Regime then proceeded to govern on the basis of the Monarchy's Wartime Economy Enabling Act, which served as the basis for restricting fundamental rights such as freedom of the press, freedom of association and freedom of assembly. Functioning as the essential pillar of this system was the Catholic Church, which had also been represented up to 1933 by clerics holding political offices. The Concordat signed with the Vatican on May 10, 1933 by Minister of Justice Kurt Schuschnigg granted the Catholic Church a series of extraordinary rights – for example, on August 16, the government made secession from the Church more difficult by demanding a formal examination of the mental and emotional state of the individual wishing to do so.

Right from the outset, the government saw itself as being confronted by two political opponents: Austromarxism and National Socialism.[6] In an attempted rebellion by the Social Democrats on February 12, 1934, armed workers battled the forces of the *Heimwehr* (paramilitary organizations closely aligned with the Christian Social Party), the military and the police. This civil war claimed hundreds of lives and led to the arrest of approximately 10,000 Social Democrats. Responsibility for this was in the hands of the government. The Social Democratic Party and its subsidiary organizations were outlawed, whereby the left wing of the political spectrum was almost totally decimated and forced into a state of illegality. Leading functionaries had to flee the country posthaste; others ended up in the Wöllersdorf Detention Camp that had originally been set up to hold Nazis. Once the authoritarian corporative state had put the left virtually out of commission, it concentrated its political struggle on the right. In July 1934, Chancellor Dollfuss was murdered during an attempted National Socialist putsch. Thereafter, conservative circles stylized the man as a martyred resistance fighter; the left, on the other hand, saw Dollfuss as the dictator who had set these evil events in motion. After 1933, Austria's authoritarian *Ständestaat* was serving on one hand as a land of exile for refugees from Nazi Germany; on the other hand, even prior to 1938, victims of political persecution as well as individual Jewish intellectuals were already leaving the country. The approximately 1,700 *Spanienkämpfer* who went to Spain in 1936 with the aim of carrying on the struggle for democracy that had been lost in Austria represented the largest national contingent in the Spanish Civil War measured as a proportion of the source country's total population. Out of this group, 220 died and, after the Spanish Republic was crushed, many ended up in German concentration and extermination camps.[7]

For a time, the authoritarian *Ständestaat* had had a prominent advocate in Mussolini, but he ultimately succumbed to pressure from Hitler once Italy's conquest of Abyssinia betokened closer relations between that country and Nazi Germany.

---

6 In 1932, the Nazi Party (NSDAP) garnered up to 16% of the vote in certain districts.

7 DÖW, The Documentation Centre of Austrian Resistance, 1986; Landau, *Lexikon*.

By 1936, Austria was already being forced to accept infiltration by National Socialists and, thus, its own increasing powerlessness. On March 11, 1938, Austrian Chancellor Kurt Schuschnigg gave in to the pressure and took his leave from the population in a radio address that concluded with the words 'God protect Austria!' As a VIP, he was accorded special treatment in the Dachau concentration camp; many of his regime's functionaries arrived in his wake, though their stay was under much less favorable conditions.

Representatives of the authoritarian *Ständestaat* were without question among the first victims of National Socialism; nevertheless, their shared responsibility for the elimination of Austrian democracy and the persecution of political dissenters – the victims of 1933-34 – cannot be overlooked. The Social Democrats, as victims of the authoritarian *Ständestaat* and of National Socialism, must, in turn, face the fact that, following the Austrian Civil War of 1934, many of its members and sympathizers defected to the Nazi camp, and Karl Renner (chancellor in 1918; first president of the Second Republic in 1945), despite all the distance he maintained to National Socialism, had publicly advocated the *Anschluss*. Nor did anti-Semitism have to be imported from Germany. Since 1920, Austria had been governed by parties with openly anti-Semitic platforms. The Social Democrats and the Catholic Church were by no means free of anti-Semitism, though, prior to 1938, there were still essential differences between this and the annihilationist anti-Semitism of the Nazis.[8] The populace's meager Austrian consciousness proved to be the greatest dilemma. With the collapse of the Habsburg Monarchy, its German-speaking former subjects has sought their salvation in *Anschluss* to Germany, which was forbidden by the victorious powers. Nevertheless, advocacy of annexation remained more or less alive across the political spectrum, and the authoritarian *Ständestaat* failed in its attempt to establish a new Austrian identity on the basis of German national character, customs and traditions. It was not until the 1950's that an Austrian identity gradually began to take shape, whereby the country's effort to distance itself from Germany as National Socialist aggressor was one of the elements that played a role in this process.[9]

1938-1945: Adjustment, persecution and resistance

On March 12, 1938, the German *Wehrmacht* marched into Austria, cheered on by large segments of the population, many of whom hoped that the *Anschluss* would

8 Pulzer, *The rise of political antisemitism*; Lichtblau, 'Antisemitismus', 454-471.

9 In initial polls conducted in 1946, 46% of Austrians still declared themselves to be members of the German people and only 49% professed an Austrian identity. In 1980, 67% affirmed an Austrian nation. See Botz, *Eine Deutsche Geschichte*, 19-38.

lead to a brighter economic future.[10] Among the first 151 prisoners sent to Dachau were sixty prominent Jews, representatives of the *Ständestaat*, Communists and Social Democrats. Immediately following German annexation, many Austrians already began launching their careers as perpetrators and profiteers of the new system. Acts of violence and 'wild Aryanization' were already breaking out on the night before the *Anschluss*, particularly in Vienna, where the vast majority of the approximately 206,000 Austrian Jews lived.[11] Jews were forcibly recruited into 'scrubbing details' to cleanse anti-Nazi slogans from the sidewalks.[12] In contrast to Germany, where the passage of numerous laws had excluded the Jewish population from many areas of society and social life gradually during the first five years on Nazi rule, the persecution in Austria commenced immediately after March 12 and to an extent that was unprecedented up to then. The November 1938 pogrom was the next climax in the ongoing radicalization of persecution measures, making it crystal clear that life in Austria had become impossible for Jews. Their possibilities to flee, few to begin with, were reduced even further by the outbreak of World War II on September 1, 1939. The deportations to concentration and extermination camps began in Fall 1941. 135,000 Jewish men and women were able to save themselves via emigration; 65,000 were murdered; a mere 5,816 survived to experience liberation in Austria.[13] Only a handful of Austrians put up resistance against the persecution of Jews.[14] The Catholic Church – with only a few exceptions – maintained a persistent silence. Scant attention was paid to the voices that warned against anti-Semitism – for instance, Irene Harrand, who analyzed the roots of Christian hate for Jews even before 1938.[15]

On the whole, anti-Nazi *resistance* in Austria has to be characterized as meager and ineffective, though we cannot fail to mention in this connection that the labor movement had already been driven into illegality in 1933-34 and was almost totally powerless. In contrast to other countries, there was neither a broad-based national resistance movement in Austria nor an Austrian government in exile. The biggest share of the resistance that was put up came from Communists, whose Free Austrian Movement was able to organize exiles in many countries. They were the first to come out strongly for an Austrian identity. Other activists included Social Democrats and leftist splinter groups like the Revolutionary Socialists, former Christian Socials and members of the *Heimwehr*, Monarchists and Catholics. A total of approximately 2,700 Austrians were sentenced to death as active resis-

10 Haas, 'Der Anschluss'; Botz, *Machtübernahme.*

11 25,000 of whom were reclassified as Jews once the Nürnberg Racial Laws went into effect. See Moser, *Demographie.*

12 Safrian and Witek, *Und keiner war dabei.*

13 Moser, *Demographie.*

14 Weinzierl, *Prüfstand; Zu wenig Gerechte.*

15 Pauley, *From prejudice to persecution*, 253-258.

tance fighters; more than 500 partisans fell in action; and about 32,000 men and women – the majority of Jewish descent – died in concentration camps and prisons and during Gestapo incarceration, whereby archive material makes it impossible to differentiate between resistance fighters and victims. The number of those arrested is estimated at 100,000; by way of comparison, there were 700,000 Austrian members of the Nazi Party.[16]

The Catholic Church, an institution that functioned as an opinion leader primarily in rural areas, played an ambivalent role during the Nazi Era.[17] After having lost its political patron, the authoritarian *Ständestaat*, it sought to come to an arrangement with the ideological foe, the National Socialists. The Church's support for the war against their common enemy, Soviet communism, has to be seen as a major error. Nevertheless, despite the 'pro-*Anschluss* declaration' published by Austrian bishops on March 18, 1938, an anti-ecclesiastical campaign was already being launched in the fall of that year. This was by no means limited to expropriations,[18] enforced political conformity and outlawing the Catholic press; more than 800 priests were sent to prisons or concentration camps, fifteen were executed and more than 1,500 were forbidden to preach or give instruction in schools.[19] Indeed, many of these victims of persecution felt that they had been left in the lurch by the Church establishment.

The Protestant Church, as a reaction to the authoritarian *Ständestaat* as well as for the sake of its traditionally close ties to its coreligionists in Germany, welcomed the *Anschluss* and had congenial relations with National Socialism. Prior to 1938, whole sectors of its hierarchy served as Nazi cover groups, and two-thirds of its clergymen were proud of their illegal membership in the NSDAP. Even so, the Protestant Church also had to accept expropriations and the dissolution of its associations. In individual communities in the Province of Burgenland, confiscations of schools and other real property utterly paralyzed community life. Nevertheless, due to its small membership (about 300,000), the socio-political significance of the Austrian Protestant Church was rather negligible.[20]

In addition to those who were persecuted for political reasons and as members of the Catholic Church, the National Socialists' victims included Romany and Sinti (gypsies), Jehovah's Witnesses, homosexuals, victims of euthanasia, as well as the

16 Neugebauer, *Der österreichischer Widerstand.*
17 Moritz, *Grüß Gott und Heil Hitler.*
18 Bandhauer-Schöffmann, *Entzug und Restitution.*
19 Weinzierl, 'Kirchlicher Widerstand'.
20 Jabloner et al., *Schlussbericht*, 221-22.

extremely heterogeneous category of asocial elements ranging from prostitutes and 'loafers' to the so-called *Schlurfs*, young long-hairs who listened to banned music.[21] Of Austria's 11,000 Romany and Sinti, many of whom were long-term residents of Burgenland, a mere 1,500 to 2,000 survived the persecution.[22]

Of the approximately 500 Jehovah's Witnesses, 445 were imprisoned and 145 died.[23] The group had already been banned by the authoritarian *Ständestaat* in 1936. Based on a strict interpretation of the Bible, they rejected any form of support for warfare; many even refused to take part in the *Volksabstimmung*.[24]

As a victim group, the situation of the homosexuals was unique, since the law[25] on the basis of which they were persecuted was in effect both prior to 1938 and after 1945. Throughout Austria, more than 3,000 people were prosecuted on account of homosexuality, almost 700 in Viennese courts alone. Although in Austria – in contrast to Germany – women as well faced sanctions under this law, the victims were predominantly men. It can be assumed that 'sexual deviance' by women tended to be classified as asocial and punished under that category.[26]

In Austria, thousands of people were victims of Nazi euthanasia. Between 1940 and 1945 at Spiegelgrund, the 'pediatric department' of the Am Steinhof Sanatorium, 700-800 sick, handicapped and retarded youngsters were killed. This was supervised by the head of the neonatal department, Dr. Heinrich Gross. So-called racial hygiene was the primary motive; medical research was only a secondary consideration. In conjunction with Operation T4 carried out at sanatoriums and clinics throughout the Third Reich between 1940 and 1941, more than 18,269 persons were surreptitiously murdered in gas chambers at Hartheim Castle in Upper Austria. More than 5,000 persons underwent forced sterilization in Austria. As recent interdisciplinary publications have shown, this system of 'psychiatric extermination' was based upon a widely branching network that extended throughout the entire social welfare system and was rooted in the 'black pedagogy' of that time. Whereas the Catholic Church remained silent about the annihilation of the Jews, protests by the German Episcopate and individual clergymen forced the termination of this purported euthanasia, although so-called 'wild euthanasia' went on covertly until 1945.[27]

---

21 Gerbl et al., 'Die "Schlurfs"', 243-268.

22 Steinmetz, *Österreichs Zigeuner.*

23 DÖW, 1998; Rammerstorfer, *Nein statt Ja und Amen.*

24 Aigner, 'Die Verfolgung der Zeugen Jehovas', 9-21.

25 § 129 lit.b of the *Österreichisches Strafgesetzbuch* of 1852.

26 Wahl, *Verfolgung und Vermögensentzug Homosexueller*; Pfanzelter, 'Homosexuelle und Prostituierte', 75-97; Müller und Fleck, 'Unzucht wider die Natur'.

27 Gabriel/Neugebauer, *Vorreiter der Vernichtung.*; Jabloner et al., *Schlussbericht*, 182-187; Berger, 'Verfolgte Kindheit'.

In Austria, ethnic minorities were also among the victims of the Nazis. The persecution of the Slovenian-speaking population of the southern part of the Province of Carinthia – a group of 20,000-30,000 that had been subjected to strong assimilation pressure long before 1938 – began with the German *Wehrmacht's* invasion of Yugoslavia. Officers and members of Slovenian cultural facilities as well as priests were arrested. Three died in concentration camps. The Nazis had developed a deportation plan even prior to the invasion of Yugoslavia; afterwards, it was implemented. In 1942, 1,975 Carinthian Slovenes were given short notice to pick up and go. 917 were resettled to camps for ethnic Germans in the so-called Altreich. Their abandoned farms were originally to have been turned over to resettled peasants from Kanaltal and South Tyrol as well as local Nazi big-shots. These Carinthian Slovenes had had a fundamentally conservative, Catholic orientation and were not necessarily negatively disposed to the *Anschluss*;[28] nevertheless, the resettlement plan drove many of them into the arms of Tito's partisans. This resulted in even more deaths and led to yet another wave of resettlement in 1944. A total of 612 Carinthian Slovenes were interned, 298 sent to concentration camps and twelve sentenced to death. The victims included women who were by no means strongly committed to a political cause and young girls who – often involuntarily – supported their husbands and brothers in the forests and were not always entirely aware of the consequences of their deeds.[29] In addition to the Slovenes, other ethnic groups – Czechs, 30,000-40,000 Hungarians and 35,000 Croatians in Burgenland – were subjected to forced assimilation and expropriations.[30]

Analysts long ignored the fact that Austrian industry and agriculture profited massively from the exploitation of approximately one million forced laborers.[31] This was an extremely heterogeneous group, and the treatment accorded to its members depended on the particular individual's ethnic origins. In general, it can be said that the majority did not voluntarily report for their labor detail in Austria. A special case was the labor 250,000 POW's were forced to do in violation of the Geneva Convention. Closely related to the problematic issue of forced labor and one widely omitted from consideration is the fate of 'German' women who were persecuted for having intimately fraternized with forced laborer (so-called 'sex criminals')[32] It took pressure from abroad for Austria to finally agree in 2000 to

28 Slovene associations recommended a 'yes' vote in this plebiscite.

29 Sima, 'Die Deportation', 63-68; Malle et al., *Vermögensentzug, Rückstellung und Entschädigung*; Embacher and Reiter, 'Partisanin aus christlicher Nächstenliebe', 553-579.

30 Jabloner e.a, *Schlussbericht*, 170-175.

31 Feichtlbauer, *Zwangsarbeit*, 45; Hornung, Ela et al., *Zwangsarbeit in der Landwirtschaft*; Karner and Ruggenthaler, *Zwangsarbeit in der Land- und Forstwirtschaft*; Rathkolb and Freund, *NS-Zwangsarbeit in der Elektrizitätswirtschaft*; Bischof, Karner and Stelz-Marx (Hg.), *Kriegsgefangene des Zweiten Weltkrieges*.

32 Nußbaumer, 'Osteuropäische Frauen'; Hauch, 'Ostarbeiterinnen'; *Industrie; Frauen in Oberdonau*.

set up a Reconciliation Fund[33] to provide compensation to former forced laborers. To this day, however, a sense of injustice in this context is absent among many segments of the population, who reject compensation being paid to forced laborers with the argument that 'our people' had to work too.

1945: The Austrian nation as victim

In 1945, the Austrian population was very relieved indeed that the war was over; nevertheless, the Allied liberation that turned into a ten-year occupation was accompanied by ambivalent feelings. It was not the events of 1945 but rather the conclusion of the State Treaty with which Austria regained full sovereignty in 1955 that is inscribed as 'liberation' in the Austrian collective consciousness.[34]

World War II, the bottom line: massive destruction, above all in Eastern Austria (though this was by no means comparable to the utter devastation of certain German cities); 80,000 bombed-out homes, famine, pestilence, looting and rape (mostly in the Russian Occupation Zone); a total of 120,000 dead as a result of arrest, imprisonment in concentration camps and euthanasia programs; 247,000 military dead and 25,000-30,000 civilians killed by warfare conducted in the air and on the ground. Of approximately 1.2 million Austrian *Wehrmacht* soldiers, 170,000 finished the war as permanent invalids. About 480,000 became POW's. To put these numbers into perspective: according to the 1939 census, the total population of Austria was 6,653,000. Practically every single village mourned young men who fell in combat.[35] Moreover, Austria was confronted by a gigantic wave of refugees. In 1945, the country accommodated 1.65 million foreigners, including 900,000 of non-German ethnic origins. Of these, 20,000-30,000 were liberated Jewish concentration camp prisoners. Between 1945 and 1948, thousands of Jewish refugees from Eastern Europe passed through Austria or spent time in camps here.[36] Very few Austrian Jews survived the camps, and only a few thousand – mostly the elderly and sick – returned from emigration. Many felt political allegiance to the Social Democrats (SPÖ) or the Austrian Communist Party (KPÖ); their relationship to Jewry and Judaism was highly ambivalent in many cases.[37] The presence of Jewish refugees, the return of those who had been driven out and initial demands for compensation payments were already producing anti-Semitic

33 Slave laborers each received a one-time, lump-sum payment of, respectively, 20,000 schillings (agricultural workers) and 105,000 schillings (concentration camp inmates).

34 Uhl, '1994 – Erinnern und Vergessen'; 'Transformationen des österreichischen Gedächtnisses'.

35 Bruckmüller, *Wiederaufbau in Österreich.*

36 Albrich, *Exodus durch Österreich.*

37 Embacher, *Neubeginn ohne Illusionen.*

incidents even in the immediate wake of the Holocaust. Caught up in their own suffering, the Austrian populace was incapable of sympathy for those who had been persecuted and murdered. In many circles, concentration camp survivors had the image of ex-criminals. Veterans and soldiers who had fallen in action were regarded as the true victims. Army deserters and returning emigrants were seen as traitors to the Fatherland, whereby the latter group was frequently accused of having led a cushy life abroad while Austrians were suffering at home.[38] Austrian officialdom launched no initiatives to facilitate the return of these exiles, aside from a few who had performed particularly 'meritorious service' abroad.

And then there was the problematic issue of the denazification of 700,000 former members of the NSDAP, 540,000 of whom complied with the order to officially register. 23% of these registered National Socialists were summarily dismissed from public service jobs and 36,000 from positions in the private sector. With the passage of the 1948 law providing for amnesty for lesser offenders, most ex-Nazis were rehabilitated, though this political camp regarded itself as a victim of the new system. For them, the end of the war had meant that their world had collapsed.[39] Austrian People's Courts tried 137,000 cases: 17% of defendants were convicted, 43 of them sentenced to death. The People's Court trials of the physicians and staff personnel who had been involved in the murder of handicapped persons took place in 1946-47. The People's Courts were confronted with a large number of those who had denounced their fellow citizens to the Nazi authorities. With the conclusion of the State Treaty, the People's Courts were dissolved and their duties taken over by courts with juries,[40] some of which made international headlines in the 1960's when numerous jury trials of Nazi criminals ended in acquittal. In the mid-1970's, Austria closed the books on the prosecution of Nazi criminals; the protests of Jewish organizations and, above all, by Simon Wiesenthal, proved unsuccessful.[41]

On the governmental level, the two political camps that had been mortal enemies in 1934 now saw themselves forced to cooperate. Once Red Army troops took Vienna on April 13, 1945, representatives of the SPÖ, the Austrian People's Party (ÖVP) and the KPÖ formed a provisional government of April 27. The two major parties, SPÖ and ÖVP, emerged as the winners of the first postwar elections in November 1945. The KPÖ, the party that had put up active resistance and suffered the greatest losses in doing so, received only 5.4% of the vote and was excluded

38 Embacher, 'Eine Heimkehr gibt es nicht?'

39 Reiter, *Die Generation danach.*

40 Kuretsidis-Haider and Garscha, 'Nationalsozialistische Verbrechen vor Gericht.'; http://www.nachkriegs-justiz.at.

41 In 1966, Simon Wiesenthal confronted the Austrian federal government with a 'Blame and Atonement Memorandum' in which he called attention to the high proportion of Austrians among Nazi perpetrators.

from the government in 1947. The SPÖ and ÖVP ruled in the form of a coalition until 1966; the ÖVP ruled alone from 1966 to 1970, then, the SPÖ ruled alone from 1970 to 1983 under Chancellor Bruno Kreisky, a man who personally symbolized the ambivalence of Austrian victimhood. Of Jewish descent, a Social Democrat who was arrested in 1934 and interned in Wöllersdorf, Kreisky succeeded in fleeing to Sweden. Like many leftist Austrian Jews, he saw himself as having been primarily a victim of political persecution and rejected a Jewish identity being ascribed to him. In fact, as federal chancellor, he was accused of treating former National Socialists too indulgently.[42]

As already mentioned, Austrian politicians instrumentalized the Moscow Declaration after 1945 to underpin the victim thesis in their pursuit of the country's concrete interests. The Declaration of Independence dated April 27, 1945, another essential document in the founding of the Second Republic, also defined the *Anschluss* as an act that had been forced upon Austrians 'deprived of their power and will.' World War II was interpreted as a 'senseless and hopeless war of conquest that no Austrian had ever wanted.' The persecution of the Jews and the theft of their property had been ordered by the German authorities, which is also why the FRG would have to make restitution payments to the Austrian victims. Austria rejected not only the obligation to make financial reparations but also any form of admission of moral guilt. With respect to compensation payments, it was argued that Austria did not exist as a state in 1938 and thus could not have caused damages to anyone. This assertion was underpinned with references to Austrian resistance (which, in reality, had been slight on the whole), whereas there was silence about the people's overwhelming approval of the *Anschluss*, their involvement in Nazi crimes and, by no means least of all, the role of Austrian soldiers in the German *Wehrmacht*.[43] Leading politicians were aware of the inconsistencies inherent in the victim thesis, but they hoped that this would pave the way to a State Treaty and exemption from restitution and reparations payments to victims of the Nazis and the State of Israel.[44]

What also emerged in Austria in addition to the 'half-truth of the victim thesis' was the myth of the so-called 'spirit of the concentration camp road,' whereby the members of the various mutually hostile political factions interned in Dachau were said to have set aside their ideological differences and, under the motto 'Never Again War,' gotten together to build a new, democratic Austria. In fact,

42 Reiter, *Unter Antisemitismusverdacht*.

43 *Rot-Weiss-Rot Buch*, 1946.

44 On the subject of restitution, see, for example: Jabloner et al., *Schlussbericht*; Bailer, *Die Entstehung der Rückstellungs- und Entschädigungsgesetzgebung*; Embacher, *Restitutionsverhandlungen mit Österreich*, Forster, *Wiedergutmachung*.

this readiness to build a consensus was rather more attributable to the difficult postwar economic situation and pressure from the occupation powers. On the whole, the influence of concentration camp survivors and resistance fighters was minimal and, in any case, they were quickly ousted from leadership positions and candidate lists. The SPÖ as well as the ÖVP showed little interest in facilitating the return to Austria of those who had done meritorious service to the party before they had been driven into exile. Recent scholarship has shown that the SPÖ, which had lost a major proportion of its intellectuals through the expulsion of the Jews, concentrated its efforts to recruit its new elite among *Ehemalige* circles (former Nazis).[45] In addition to the 'spirit of the concentration camp road,' another myth that has been eagerly overworked has to do with postwar reconstruction – it is said that everyone from top engineers all the way down to common laborers all got down to work and jointly rebuilt the state. Indeed, without massive financial subsidies from the Marshall Plan (1948-1952), postwar reconstruction would have proceeded much less successfully.[46]

The Catholic Church, still one of the pillars of society after 1945, also continued to play an ambivalent role. In the view of political scientist Anton Pelinka, the church had indeed learned its lesson from history in that it took leave of political Catholicism and declared its allegiance to democracy, but it never really faced up to its own history and responsibility. It has neither openly distanced itself from the *Ständestaat* nor expressed regret about its bishops' attitude towards the *Anschluss* and the silence it maintained about the persecution of the Jews. On one hand, church leaders have stressed Catholic resistance and the Catholic Church as victim by focusing on the courageous resistance fighters in their own ranks; on the other hand, what is often left out of consideration is the fact that these very acts of the victims had only too often not been condoned by the establishment church.[47] Probably the most famous case was that of Franz Jägerstätter, a Catholic who refused induction into the *Wehrmacht* and was executed in 1943 in Brandenburg.[48] In 1947, a Catholic newspaper in Linz rejected an article about Jägerstätter because, according to church leaders, publishing it would have been an affront to former soldiers and prisoners of war.[49] As has been shown by the discussions surrounding the canonization and beatification of Catholic resistance fighters, the deeds of these men and women were rather an embarrassment to the establishment church and, as such, particular attention was not to be called to them. This attitude took a long time to change – for instance, Sister Restituta (née Helene Kafka), a

45 Neugebauer and Schwarz, *Der Wille zum aufrechten Gang.*
46 Bischof, Pelinka and Stiefel, 'The Marshall Plan in Austria'.
47 Pelinka, 'Paradigmenwechsel', 43-55; Liebmann, 'Katholischer Widerstand'.
48 Zahn, *Solidarity Witness;* Putz, *Ernst Jägerstätter.*
49 Bailer, *Wiedergutmachung.*

nun and nurse who had been executed in 1943, was not beatified until 1998.[50] Franz Jägerstätter was finally beatified in 2007, though the driving force behind this initiative was the Pax Christi movement and not the Linz Diocese.[51] It is interesting to note that the Vatican, in what was the numerically largest beatification in its history, simultaneously honored 498 Catholics who died fighting against the militias of the democratic government during the Spanish Civil War.[52] As with the political parties, the Catholic Church's primary concern was the integration of former National Socialists and soldiers. Resistance fighters proved to be a disruptive influence in this effort. Nor was there ever a call during the postwar years for prayers of thanks for the end of the criminal National Socialist system; thanks were expressed only for the end of the war.[53]

In the late 1940's, it was already possible to observe a paradigm shift in Austrian commemoration culture and the collapse of the anti-fascist consensus that had been in place until then, at least among the political elite, as the anti-fascist monuments that had dominated commemoration – above all in Vienna – in the immediate postwar years began to be overshadowed by memorials to fallen soldiers.[54] It became all too clear that soldiers who had served in the *Wehrmacht* and died in battle were considered the war victims who were uppermost in Austrian consciousness. The *Heimkehrer* (returning POW's) were on one hand trumped by the war heroes and on the other hand left up to their own devices since the reconstruction effort called for men who were fit and industrious. Psychological care programs were largely nonexistent[55] and, in comparison to the post-World War I years, the psychological consequences of the war were accorded significantly less attention after 1945. Instead, these men were advised to knuckle down and get to work rebuilding Austria. In this vacuum, veterans' organizations became primary care providers – certainly a politically questionable development.[56] The Austrian veterans association, the *Kameradschaftsbund*, was officially founded in 1952. It erected memorials to fallen soldiers or adapted monuments from prior wars to commemorate those who died in World War II. The group strictly rejected jointly memorializing soldiers and concentration camp victims.[57] Thus, the *Kameradschaftsbund*, which had strong support from both major political parties and, above all, the Catholic Church, exercised interpretational sovereignty over the commemoration of the war and its victims for decades.

50 Kunzenmann, *Sr. Maria Restituta Kafka*; Beinhauer, 'Selige Sr. Restituta'.
51 Conversation with Linz theologian Dr. Helmut Wagner in March 2008.
52 *Der Standard*, October 29, 2007.
53 See '*Grüß Gott statt Heil Hitler*,' ORF 2, April 2008.
54 Uhl, *Steinernes Bewusstsein*; Gärtner and Rosenberger, *Kriegerdenkmäler*.
55 Czech, 'Fahnenflucht in die Krankheit?', 24-26.
56 Embacher, '...daß die Ehre der Kameraden', 96-132.
57 Uhl, 'Transformationen', 112.

In summary, it can be maintained that the victim thesis, which, despite its international recognition, always stood on a shaky foundation after 1945, did bring together the once-hostile political camps as well as the Catholic Church, though in doing so it completely excluded considerations of responsibility for the authoritarian *Ständestaat* and the at least partial consent given to National Socialism. There was also general agreement on the integration of former Nazis, marginalization of the victims of National Socialism, and rejection of compensation payments. Only under pressure – above all from the USA – did Austria in 1953 declare its readiness to negotiate with Jewish organizations,[58] whereby this was primarily a matter of the settlement of material losses (Restitution Laws), the restitution of unclaimed, mostly Jewish property, as well as individual forms of aid provided to victims living abroad. Whereas Austria only grudgingly consented to compensation payments and instituting measures to aid victims of National Socialism, the state unhesitatingly enacted the *Kriegsopferversorgungsgesetz* (War Victims Care Provision Law, KOVG) and thus assumed responsibility for providing care to returning veterans of the German *Wehrmacht* (and, later, the *Waffen-SS* too) who, according to the logic of the victim thesis, had gone to war on behalf of a foreign state.[59] Emil Maurer, president of the Jewish Community of Vienna, brought up this contradiction in 1953 when he pointed out that Austria, as a victim, should not have to pay the pensions of *Wehrmacht* soldiers, who, after all, had not been fighting for freedom.[60] To this day, measures to benefit the Nazis' victims have always been legislated in tandem with measures for the various victims of the war in order to avoid what politicians called 'giving preferential treatment to the victims of National Socialism.' Furthermore, we will show that the KOVG constituted the basis for the *Opferfürsorgegesetz* (Victims Care Provision Law OFG).

The Waldheim Affair and the end of the lie Austria had been living

1986 is considered the turning point in the way Austria dealt with its recent past.[61] 'In the war, I didn't do anything different than what hundreds of thousands of other Austrians did – namely, my duty as a soldier.' With these words, Kurt Waldheim, the ÖVP's candidate in the 1986 presidential election, defended himself against charges of having hushed up his wartime service in the Balkans in his official autobiography.[62] Waldheim did indeed go on to win that election following

58 Embacher, *Restitutionsverhandlungen*.
59 Manoschek and Sandner, 'Die Krieger als Opfer', 109-144.
60 Embacher, *Neubeginn ohne Illusionen*, 143-144.
61 Dachs, 'Von der "Sanierungspartnerschaft"', 290-303.
62 Botz and Sprengnagel, *Kontroversen*; Gehler, '... eine grotesk überzogene Dämonisierung', 614-665.

a campaign featuring anti-Semitic 'slips of the tongue,' mostly from the ranks of the ÖVP. But in its aftermath, he was confronted by a newly-awakened civil society. In 1991 in the Austrian Parliament, Chancellor Franz Vranitzky (SPÖ) made the first public acknowledgment of Austria's shared responsibility for National Socialism. In an effort to do damage control, leading politicians from across the political spectrum orchestrated high-profile diplomatic efforts that included numerous trips to Israel.[63]

The highly emotional debate about Waldheim's war service record certainly did make an impact. The Waldheim Affair and the Commemorative Year 1988 (50th anniversary of the *Anschluss*) also provided an occasion to take a closer look at the victims of National Socialism. Scholars in the field of contemporary history, who had been slowly approaching the subject of fascism, National Socialism and resistance since the 1960's,[64] could observe a paradigm shift: whereas attention had previously been focused on victims of political persecution and prominent, predominantly male exiles, the perspective now began to be expanded to include Jewish victims, Romany and Sinti, homosexuals (due to active efforts by gay and lesbian groups), Jehovah's Witnesses, victims of Nazi euthanasia and, gradually, even deserters from the German *Wehrmacht*. In the early 1980's, more attention started to be paid to the role of women in the Austrian resistance and in the concentration camps, though this was less an upshot of the Waldheim Affair and more directly attributable to the feminism that had became widespread in the 1970's.[65] Expanding the focus of resistance research to include women was a by no means insignificant factor in modifying the very concept of resistance and thus the concept of victimhood as well, in that, in addition to politically organized resistance, consideration also started to be given to individual strategies of refusal and forms of protest situated in a gray area between resistance and conformity.[66] The publication in 1988 of '*Ich bin dafür, die Sache in die Länge zu ziehen*' (I'm in favor of dragging this thing out as long as possible) by British historian Robert Knight triggered a public debate about Austrian indemnification policies. Ten years later, the Austrian government set up a Historians Commission charged with the task of looking into the Nazis' seizure of property within the territory of the Republic of Austria as well as subsequent restitution and compensation. In addition to the final report,[67] more than 40 individual studies were published.

63 Embacher and Reiter, *Gratwanderungen*.

64 Neugebauer, 'Zwanzig Jahre Dokumentationsarchiv'; 'Widerstandsforschung in Österreich'; *Der österreichischer Widerstand*; Malina/Spann, *Bibliographie*; Hanisch, 'Der Ort des Nationalsozialismus'.

65 Karin Berger et al., *Der Himmel ist blau; 'Ich geb Dir einen Mantel'*.

66 Botz, 'Methoden- und Theorieprobleme'.

67 Jabloner e.a, *Schlussbericht*.

In the 1980's, Austrian writers[68] and filmmakers gave a voice to certain victims of the Nazis, whereby the reactions to such works included over-identification with the victims.[69] More and more victims went public with their stories, either as subjects of autobiographies or in the role of 'contemporary eyewitness to history.' Most were victims of political persecution; almost all were secular Jews.[70] The so-called *Wehrmacht* Exhibition that was shown in Vienna in 1995 and then in other Austrian provinces triggered the next debate about what happened during World War II. For the first time, the spotlight was focused on the role of the 1.3 million Austrians who served in the German *Wehrmacht*, as well as on the question of desertion.[71]

A new conception of self also manifested itself in the Austrian culture of commemoration. Aside from a very few exceptions, the first memorials for Jews, Romany and Sinti, and victims of euthanasia were erected in the 1980's. In 2000 the central Holocaust Memorial was unveiled on *Judenplatz* (Jews' Square) in Vienna – an initiative undoubtedly influenced by the corresponding debate in Germany. Nevertheless, the discussions of a planned memorial to homosexual victims on Vienna's Morzinplatz, the former site of Gestapo Headquarters, show that the commemoration of certain groups is still not a matter that can be taken completely for granted.[72] On the whole, though, a multifaceted sense of awareness of the various groups of victims of National Socialism is evident in Austria. In conjunction with the rehabilitation of deserters in recent years, private initiatives have even succeeded in erecting plaques commemorating deserters.[73] Such efforts can increasingly be observed in rural communities as well. Especially interesting is the trend towards 'integrative commemoration' now being manifested by soldiers' memorials that – mostly in connection with a redesign or renovation – are expanded to include all groups of victims.[74]

---

68 Mitgutsch, *Haus der Kindheit*; Gstrein, *Die englischen Jahre*; Hackl, *Abschied von Sidonie*; Schindel, *Gebürtig; Ohneland*; Rabinovici, *Papirnik'; Suche nach M.*; Beckermann, *Unzugehörig*; Kerschbaumer, *Der weibliche Name.*

69 Embacher, 'Literatur der Gefühle', 148-166.

70 Stojka and Berger (ed.), *Wir leben im Verborgenen*; Busch/Winhab, *Jelka*; Prusnik, *Gämsen auf der Lawine*; Heger, *Die Männer mit dem rosa Winkel.*

71 Manoschek, 'Österreichische Opfer', 87-111.

72 In March 2008, Viennese municipal authorities announced that due to architectural and urban planning considerations, the monument – which had already been approved – would nevertheless not be able to be erected.

73 See, for example, the article that appeared on p. 10 of the September 25, 2007 edition of the Austrian daily newspaper *Der Standard* describing the unveiling of a plaque mounted on the wall of the parish church in St. Gallus to commemorate a man who refused induction in the military and was subsequently executed at Berlin Plötzensee in 1941.

74 For example, the redesign of the soldiers' memorial in Puchkirchen am Trattberg, Upper Austria; see http://www.dioezese-linz.at/redaktion/index.php?action_new=Lesen&Article_ID=23606 (September 3, 2006); also see Ecker, 'Spätes Gedenken'.

The *Opferfürsorgegesetz* and the role of the victims' associations

The *Bund der politisch Verfolgten – Österreichischer Bundesverband* (Association of Victims of Political Persecution, in short: KZ Verband) was officially founded in September 1946.[75] In contrast to its predecessor organizations like *Volkssolidarität* in Vienna and smaller aid committees in the other provinces, the KZ Verband saw its role not only as a charitable organization but also as political instrument and moral authority. To accomplish this, resistance fighters were to occupy political and social leadership positions. As *Volkssolidarität* had done before them, the KZ Verband was made up of representatives of the three political parties (SPÖ, ÖVP and the Austrian Communist Party, KPÖ) and 'persons who had been persecuted on account of their descent.' At first, though, members of The Action Committee of Jewish Concentration Camp Survivors[76] that was founded in 1946 and later the Association of Those Persecuted on Account of Their Descent had to fight for admission to the KZ Verband, which was originally open only to victims of political persecution and excluded all other groups of victims. Simon Wiesenthal had criticized the KZ Verband for having thus maintained after 1945 the so-called Aryan paragraph that had been part of the bylaws of anti-Semitic associations.[77] And at a convention in Graz in 1947, Jewish survivors accused the KZ Verband of carrying on the inmate hierarchy that the Nazis had sought to enforce in the concentration camps. Even to this day, many 'Aryan' survivors just cannot seem to get over certain feelings of superiority towards other groups of victims.[78]

The KZ Verband assumed a significant role due to its advisory function in formulating federal and provincial legislation dealing with the Nazi era and the influence it exerted on the implementation of the OFG.[79] The first OFG, as the central piece of legislation regulating the treatment to be accorded to Nazi victims living in Austria and resistance fighters, was already passed in 1945 and generally corresponded to its West German counterpart, the *Bundesentschädigungsgesetz* (Federal Indemnification Law). As the Austrian law's very name implies, Austria – in accordance with its conception of self as the first victim of National Socialism – regarded

75 Bailer, *Wiedergutmachung*, 42 ff; Embacher, *Neubeginn ohne Illusionen*, 107ff.

76 Immediately after it was founded, the association, with 1,670 members already, launched a campaign to reform the OFG.

77 Letter dated June 8, 1946 from Simon Wiesenthal to Dr. Sobek, chairman of the KZ Verband, S.W-C., M-9/10, Yad Vashem, Jerusalem.

78 Embacher, *Neubeginn ohne Illusionen*, 106.

79 The OFG advisory groups included the Victims Care Commission set up in the Social Welfare Ministry and the Pension Commission installed at the various provincial governments. Both commissions were made up of government officials and representatives of the victims associations (proportionally, based on party membership). Beginning in 1949, with the dissolution of the KZ Verband, the ÖVP, SPÖ and KPÖ named their representatives. Beginning in 1976, the three victims associations and the Jewish Community of Vienna each had the right nominate a representative. See Pfeil, *Die Entschädigung von Opfern*, 68 ff, 204 ff.

its obligation as providing care to victims and not compensation, which was up to the FRG. Particularly for the majority of the surviving Austrian Jews, it was a big disadvantage that the services to be provided under the OFG were exclusively for recipients with Austrian citizenship, and were not available to those who were living abroad and, after having been deprived of their Austrian citizenship in 1938, had become citizens of their new country. Of the approximately 130,000 Jews who had been driven out of Austria, only a few thousand returned.[80] It was only pressure from American Jewish organizations and, above all, the USA that brought Austria around to accepting responsibility and doing something for this group as well.

The OFG and its amendments provide a good indication of how society regarded the various victim groups. The original intention of the law provided only for the indemnification of active resistance fighters, whereby it had to be demonstrated that such activities were carried out either 'with weapon in hand' or constituted 'total commitment in word and deed' on behalf of an 'independent, democratic Austria, conscious of its historical mission.' The timeframe during which such acts of resistance had to have occurred – no doubt as a compromise between the SPÖ and the ÖVP, the two parties of the governing coalition – was 1933-1945. Thus, persecution by the authoritarian *Ständestaat* – an issue that had been socially taboo – was included and equated with persecution by the Nazis. Nevertheless, this view proves to be historically untenable. Explicitly excluded from these provisions were National Socialists, who were also persecuted in 1933-34. As legal scholar Walter Pfeil concluded in his assessment of the OFG, even for experts, this legislation is difficult to read, incomprehensible and thus subject to interpretation. The amendments can be given a positive evaluation to the extent that they – often in response to the efforts of victims associations – expanded the group of persons entitled to take advantage of the services provided.

The first amendment was already passed in 1947; this expanded piece of legislation is the actual OFG (Federal Law 'governing care for the victims of the fight for a free, democratic Austria and the victims of political persecution') that, as further amended, remains in force today.[81] Nevertheless, due to its differentiation between 'active' and 'passive' victims and their entitlement to different forms of

80 A satisfactory solution with respect to citizenship was not instituted until 1993, when it became possible to reacquire Austrian citizenship without having to give up subsequently acquired foreign citizenship. Nevertheless, all that former Austrians could claim was compensation for time spent in incarceration as provided in OFSG 1952/53 be. The first concrete measure was taken in 1956 when, under pressure from the USA, Austria set up an Aid Fund endowed with $21 million to help needy ex-Austrians. Then, in 1961, lump-sum payments were made to those who were forced into hiding and for having to wear the Star of David on outer garments and for having been deprived of education. It was not until 2005 that Austrian citizenship was dropped as a requirement to receive a pension (*Rentenfürsorge*). See Burger/Wendelin, *Die Praxis der Vollziehung.*

81 The most notable works on this issue are: Bailer, *Wiedergutmachung*; Pfeil, 'Die Entschädigung von Opfern'; Jabloner et al., *Schlussbericht*, 146-450; DÖW, 1992; Bailer-Galanda/Blimlinger, *Vermögensentzug.*

indemnification, this law too is based on a selective, hierarchical concept of victimhood. Ever since 1945, recognition was accorded to the 'active victims' – resistance fighters and the politically persecuted (victims of fighting); to this category was added the 'passive victims' – those who were persecuted for political, national and religious reason and because of their 'descent' (victims of political persecution). The different treatment manifested itself above all in the fact that recognition as a resistance fighter – regardless of whether one had fought against the authoritarian *Ständestaat* or against the Nazis – entitled the individual to an *Amtsbescheinigung* (official attestation) whereas the other victims only received an *Opferausweis* (victim ID). The *Amtsbescheinigung* constituted ongoing entitlement to all service provided under the OFG, including pensions that were sometime quite generous and corresponded to those granted to war victims. Holders of the *Opferausweis*, on the other hand, were entitled only to minimal aid to provide the bare necessities and a small annual tax deduction. Moreover, the guidelines governing recognition as a victim for purposes of the OFG were strict and formalistic, so that it was difficult to achieve recognition for acts of resistance beyond the realm of conventional political resistance. Many victims of National Socialism went home empty-handed. Following her return from Auschwitz, physician Ella Lingens applied for an *Amtsbescheinigung* but was turned down with the explanation that 'having hidden Jews is a private matter and not a form of resistance.'[82] Women who gave food to POW's or helped them to escape were also excluded; the line of argumentation was that they had not thereby done anything on behalf of a free, democratic Austria.[83] Jehovah's Witnesses, who had not defined themselves as political opponents of National Socialism and had not even received recognition for their acts of resistance from their own religious community until the 1990's, were also often excluded from receiving the benefits of the OFG. For example, a Jehovah's Witness from Salzburg was turned down for both the *Amtsbescheinigung* and the *Opferausweis* in 1947 on the grounds that having been in a concentration camp was insufficient; one had to have 'committed clear acts on behalf of a free Austria, and not merely had attitudes that were basically hostile to National Socialism.'[84] A similar argument was invoked in 1947 to deny a pension under the OFG to the widow of Franz Jägerstätter. The Social Welfare Ministry argued that her husband had not fought for a 'free, democratic Austria'; rather, 'his actions were motivated by melancholy and religious reasons.'[85] In a 1956 letter to Mahnruf, the official publication of the KZ Verband, a representative of the Carinthian KZ Verband complained that numerous Carinthian Slovenes who had survived the resettlement camps and

82 Lingens, 'Jüdische Schicksale', 634.
83 Bailer, *Wiedergutmachung*, 165-166.
84 Maislinger, 'Andere religiöse Gruppen', 323.
85 Putz, *Ernst Jägerstätter*, 277.

were now living on the verge of poverty were denied an *Amtsbescheinigung*; what they had received, an *Opferausweis*, 'wasn't worth much at all.' This letter also went on to say that the process of assignment to a particular category was the job of police officials who were not fluent in the victims' mother tongue, Slovenian, and many of these men's attitudes towards National Socialism were far from objective and distant. The author quite justifiably asked why the interview was conducted by policemen and not by community officials as was the case with war victims.[86]

The gradual decline of the anti-fascist consensus and growing anti-communism had an impact on the KZ Verband. Once the last Communist had been ousted from the Austrian government at the height of the Cold War in November 1947, Minister of the Interior Oskar Helmer (SPÖ), with the approval of his party and the ÖVP, dissolved the KZ Verband. The official justification given for this step was irregularities in the Viennese KZ Verband; in reality, though, it was designed to break the dominance of the Communists who, due to their disproportionate involvement in the resistance movement, were strongly represented in the KZ Verband. For the rank-and-file members as well as the functionaries of the KZ Verband, this step came as a complete surprise. Ultimately, the representatives of the Nazi's victims followed the dictates of their respective parties and each party founded its own association: the SPÖ had its *Verband der sozialistischen Freiheitskämpfer* (Association of Socialist Freedom Fighters), the ÖVP's group was named *Kameradschaft*, and the KPÖ retained the name KZ Verband. Only in Tyrol did the members refuse to split up. Survivors who belonged to no political party were left up to their own devices.[87] It was not until 1970 that the *Arbeitsgemeinschaft der KZ Verbände und Widerstandskämpfer Österreichs* merged the individual associations.[88]

A certain degree of progress could be achieved for some survivors with the 3rd amendment to the OFG in 1949, which came at the same time compensation for war victims was improved. Now, in addition to political persecutees, 'passive' victims who had been subjected to particularly severe persecution or whose health had been ruined were also granted an *Amtsbescheinigung* and thus had a claim to a pension. In addition to Jews, Romany and Sinti benefitted from this change – at least for a short time. In 1950, things got worse again: the authorities began to demand documentary proof of having been interned in a concentration camp; eyewitness testimony was deemed unreliable. The victims had to present proof that they had been persecuted for racial reasons and had not been arrested as

86 Letter to the editor of *Mahnruf* dated March 2, 1956 from Herr Nieschelwitzer; personal property of Helga Embacher.

87 In Carinthia, the communist-oriented KZ Verband was the only organization actively committed to advocating the interests of surviving Austrian Slovenes. For these people, though, representation by the KZ Verband was not always grounds for unmitigated joy since it tended to reinforce the widespread prejudice that the Slovenes were 'proponents of Tito.'

88 Bailer, *Wiedergutmachung*; Embacher, *Neubeginn ohne Illusionen*.

'asocials,' who were still excluded from receiving OFG benefits. Another major problem was the fact that the OFG excluded individuals with a criminal record, and some Romany and Sinti had neglected to have convictions for minor offenses (for instance, failure to have a fixed address) expunged from the record. Even the compensation for incarceration that was a provision of the 7th amendment of the OFG (1952) benefited only those Romany and Sinti who had survived a concentration camp. A stay in the 'detention camp' in Lackenbach and Salzburg was considered merely a restriction of ones freedom, which was compensated to a much lesser extent and not until the passage of the 12th amendment to the OFG in 1961.[89] Jewish victims who had survived in ghettos such as in Shanghai or in hiding (under 'inhuman conditions') and had been forced to wear a Star of David did not receive compensation until 1961 with the 12th amendment to the OFG. 1961 was also the year in which the resettled Carinthian Slovenes – even those who had not been arrested as resistance fighters and those whose health had been severely damaged – received a small amount of compensation.[90]

Whereas Jews, Carinthian Slovenes and Romany were at least officially acknowledged as victims, other groups – those without a lobby – remained excluded from the care provisions of the OFG: the victims of Nazi medical crimes until 1995[91], 'asocials'[92] and homosexuals[93] until 2005. Since homosexuality remained punishable by law in Austria until the repeal of § 129 in 1974, the provisions of the ASVG (General Social Security Law) whereby years of incarceration were taken into consideration for pension computation purposes were also not applied to homosexual victims of the Nazis. Whereas 'war years' counted towards the pensions of Nazi perpetrators and *Wehrmacht* soldiers, for example, a homosexual's six years in the Sachsenhausen and Flossenbürg concentration camps did not, as historian Gabriele Anderl has shown.[94] Victims of military justice – above all deserters, many of them Jehovah's Witnesses – were also confronted by numerous problems.[95]

As previously mentioned, the various amendments made to the OFG over time also constitute an ongoing indicator of society's cognizance of responsibility for National Socialism. The improvements made during the Commemorative Year 1988 have to be interpreted as a reaction by the Austrian government to the inter-

89 Jabloner et al., *Schlussbericht*, 427 ff, 156-165; Freund/Baumgartner/Greifeneder, *Vermögensentzug*.
90 Bailer, *Wiedergutmachung*,174 f.
91 The revision occurred pursuant to a parliamentary motion by the Greens and a conserted campaign by scholars.
92 See, for example, Kreitner, '*Öffentliche "Jugendfürsorge"*'; Bailer-Galanda/Blimlinger, *Vermögensentzug*, 66; also see Elisabeth Scharang's documentary film '*Meine liebe Republik*' (My Dear Republic), a portrait of Nazi victim Friedrich Zawrel.
93 Bunzl, *Symptoms of Modernity*.
94 Gabriele Anderl in: *Profil*, 15.4.1997
95 Manoschek, 'Opfer der Militärjustiz'.

national pressure it was subjected to as a result of the Waldheim Affair, but these changes were also attributable to a climate that was gradually becoming more liberal – and not only in Austria – and, last but not least, the emergence of a new, global Holocaust consciousness.[96] In 1988, Austria set up a fund for '*Ehrengaben*' (honorary gifts), whereby recipients – still categorized hierarchically according to *Amtsbescheinigung* and *Opferausweis* – were compensated with a lump-sum payment. Furthermore, there was a cash infusion to the Aid Fund that had been set up in 1956 and a one-time payment was made to victims living abroad. At the same time, the OFG was amended to enable all those who had been incarcerated for at least a year to receive an *Amtsbescheinigung* and thus be able to apply for a pension. The prime beneficiaries were Romany and Sinti as well as Carinthian Slovenes who survived in assembly or transit camps following their forced resettlement.[97]

The establishment in 1995 of the National Fund of the Republic of Austria for the Victims of National Socialism meant that, for the first time, compensation (in the form of a lump sum of approximately 5,000 euros) would be paid to all victims of persecution including members of those group who had previously been discriminated against. The National Fund law not only expanded the circle of those entitled to indemnification; its wording – in accordance with the new historical consciousness of the 1990's – for the first time explicitly expressed in a piece of Austrian legislation the country's 'full responsibility to the victims.' Chancellor Franz Vranitzky, in his previously-mentioned 1991 address before Parliament, had already more precisely defined the victim concept by specifically referring to, alongside war victims, resistance fighters and political persecutees, 'Jews, Gypsies, the mentally and physically handicapped, homosexuals, members of ethnic minorities, and political and religious dissenters.' In 1993 during a state visit to Israel, Vranitzky apologized to the Israeli population and the whole world for the crimes committed by Austrians in World War II. He rejected collective guilt but accepted moral responsibility. It is also interesting to note that amendments to the OFG and other indemnification measures for victims of the Nazis were increasingly instituted in response to pressure from civil society, whereas the victims associations (due, among other factors, to their members' advanced age) lost much of their political power.[98] As Walter Pfeil noted critically, the influence of the Austrian victims associations – each of which, as previously mentioned, was affiliated with a political party – proved to be rather problematic since this led to a system in which the interests and problems of the smaller and/or less 'well-established' groups of victims were not adequately taken into account in both the writing and

96 Ecker, *Tales of edification and redemption?*

97 Forster, *Wiedergutmachung*, 166f.

98 The 1995 amendment that granted recognition to those who had been persecuted on account of their handicaps was also the result of a parliamentary initiative of the Greens and a campaign by scholars.

enforcement of legislation. The situations of victims who did not fit into 'conventional patterns' were thus given only limited consideration by the OFG and its implementation regulations.[99] As scholars in this field are well aware, social biases survived the concentration camps and lived on after 1945 in the victims associations.

The acknowledgment of psychological consequences

(The lack of) social recognition and sources

Demonstrating the impact that persecution had on an individual's mental health also proved to be problematic in a number of respects, despite the fact that physicians – though almost exclusively outside of Austria – began dealing with this issue almost immediately after the end of the war.[100] The first works were eyewitness reports that already began to appear in the late 1940's and early 50's; the authors were trained psychiatrists, psychologists and sociologists who had themselves been in prisons and concentration camps. An example is the first-person account that Austrian psychotherapist Viktor Frankl published in 1947. In a chapter entitled 'Psychology of Inmates Liberated from Concentration Camps,' Frankl cautioned against the fallacious assumption that concentration camp survivors needed no psychological care.[101] Emanuel Edel and Ella Lingens were among the physicians who confronted issues connected with psychological consequences of persecution in articles and speeches. Ludwig Popper, an officially recognized expert with years of experience in the field of psychological care of victims, published a brief essay on these issues in 1973.[102]

Aside from these isolated activities, though, the prevailing opinion during the decades immediately after the war was that 'psychological consequences of injuries or other aftereffects had to have subsided by two years at the very latest.'[103] Cases in which this did not occur were referred to as so-called 'pensioners' neurosis,' a diagnosis that had been in common use since World War I. It was applied to soldiers who remained neurotically fixated on their symptoms and thus, as recipients of invalid pensions, constituted a 'long-term drain' on the state's finances.[104] Popper reported on his scientific debates held over the course of many years with

99 Pfeil, *Die Entschädigung von Opfern.*
100 Bailer-Galanda, 'Entschädigung für seelisches Leid?', 216.
101 Frankl, ... *Trotzdem*; Grubrich-Simitis, 'Extremtraumatisierung', 211.
102 Bailer, *Wiedergutmachung*, 217. The study to which Bailer refers here is: Francesconi, *Extremtraumatisierung.*
103 Cited in: B. Bailer-Galanda, 'Verfolgungsbedingte Gesundheitsschäden'.
104 Berger/Dimmel/Forster/Spring/Berger, *Vollzugspraxis*, 209.

Hans Hoff, Austria's foremost psychiatrist at the time. The position that ultimately gained acceptance held 'pensioner's neurosis' to be conceptually inadequate.[105] Thus, it is not surprising that up to the 1960's in Austria, clinical psychological evaluations submitted by consulting experts in cases having to do with the OFG came to the conclusion that such individuals' percentage reduction in their ability to carry on gainful employment (*Minderung der Erwerbsfähigkeit*, MdE) as a result of the mental consequences of persecution was minimal to absolutely nonexistent. It was not until 1965 that mental illness was officially recognized for purposes of determining MdE.[106]

The extent to which and in which form psychological consequences actually were included in applications for benefits under the OFG is a subject that has been only partially researched. A relevant study published in 2004 by the Austrian Historians Commission is probably the most important milestone in this effort. The authors of this analysis concluded that 'no broad-based investigations of the disabilities of those who were persecuted by the Nazi regime in Austria have been conducted.'[107] They also mentioned that, although 25 conferences on the subject of such health consequences were held between 1954 and 1985, not one of them took place in Austria. Furthermore, there was never a public discussion of potential uncertainties with respect to expert opinions and evaluations.[108] (As to the results of this study, see below.)

Initiatives of individuals

During this time when the discussion of the psychological consequences of persecution largely took place outside of Austria, what was done in this country was the result of the committed involvement of individual men and women. These efforts were indeed discussed abroad, though little to no public notice of them was taken in Austria. For examples, Hermann Langbein, an Austrian survivor of Auschwitz, was already making an effort in the 1960's to provide what would be referred to today as psychosocial care to former concentration camp inmates. He was active as an observer at the so-called Auschwitz Trials in Frankfurt (1963-65). In his detailed and comprehensive account of the proceedings, he described how many of the survivors who gave eyewitness testimony broke down under this pressure. 'The arrival of the first Polish witnesses made it obvious that immediate steps had to be taken.

105 Bailer-Galanda, *Die Entstehung der Rückstellungs*, 220.
106 Bailer-Galanda,'Entschädigung für seelisches Leid?', 216.
107 Berger et al., *Vollzugspraxis*.
108 Between 1951 and 1961 alone, 16 conferences and 21 symposia were held by the *Gesellschaft der Gutachterärzte* (Society of Physicians Providing Expert Opinions), though the published annals do not include a single article about the consequences of incarceration in a concentration camp and the physical effects of the diverse forms of Nazi persecution. Berger et al., 'Vollzugspraxis', 211-212.

Besides the mental pressure – which, needless to say, was overwhelming – came the fact that, during the first weeks, these individuals had not a pfennig of German currency in their pockets, were unfamiliar with the country and often brought many misconceptions about it with them, were not fluent in the language, and hadn't made hotel reservations. All of this was a severe burden on these people.' In the beginning, these witnesses were left completely on their own. It took some time until the Red Cross finally got involved and sent over women, who then displayed 'touching sympathy' in caring for these poor souls.[109] According to accounts by Langbein's daughter, he played a key role in organizing this initiative.[110]

Ella Lingens, herself a concentration camp survivor, summed up the situation in Austria on the occasion of a 1967 symposium in Cologne dedicated to assessing 'Health Impairment as a Result of Incarceration and Persecution.' At the time, Lingens worked at the Ministry for Social Administration, where she dealt with OFG matters in the form of appeals of application rejections. 'My job was to medically evaluate [these claims] on the basis of new expert opinions, possibly having the individuals examined in a clinic or obtaining the assessment of a medical school professor.'[111] In her address, she expressed understanding for the fact that experts felt overwhelmed by the task of delivering opinions on health impairments, but at the same time she complained about the 'shocking' latitude that they had in going about this. Time and again, claims were rejected on the basis of 'the most incredibly bizarre grounds,' though this was indeed said to have become less frequent and a shift could be said to have occurred, albeit one that was 'gradual and unfortunately by no means pervasive.'[112] Lingens leveled her sharpest criticism at the opinions of Austrian psychiatric experts outside of Vienna, many of whom were unfamiliar with the corresponding literature and the transformation of attitudes towards the mentally ill. As Lingens wrote in 1967, what implementation of the OFG called for was 'not only the collaboration of psychiatric experts with a genuine democratic orientation and high moral scruples, but also those who have acquired the necessary specialized knowledge in this field.'[113]

The hurdles of the Opferfürsorgegesetz (OFG)

The various versions of the OFG as well as the way they were implemented in everyday practice constituted a perfidious reflection of the Austrian culture of

109 Langbein, *Der Auschwitz-Prozess*, 45. See also: Langbein, *Menschen in Auschwitz*, 536, 553. Here, Langbein recollects encounters with survivors he attempted to convince to testify as witnesses for the prosecution, and who turned him down out of fear of what the stress would do to their nerves.

110 As discussed in a conversation between Lisa Langbein and Maria Ecker on March 3, 2008.

111 Lingens, 'Die Situation in Österreich', 22-23.

112 Lingens, 'Die Situation in Österreich', 24.

113 Lingens, 'Die Situation in Österreich', 28.

commemoration – the lack of understanding for psychological consequences in general but especially when it came to concentration camp survivors, whose very existence contradicted Austria's treasured victim myth. According to the OFG, the extent of the damage to an individual's health was measured in stages of disability until 1957; thereafter, as previously mentioned, in MdE (percentage diminishment of the capacity to engage in gainful employment). What had to be proved was not only the existence of a health impairment but also the causality (i.e. a connection between the persecution to which the person had been subjected and the impairment of the person's health).[114] Gradually, the evaluating experts had to acknowledge the fact that many of the injuries that resulted from persecution were proving to be very persistent and/or that they sometimes even took many years to manifest themselves, so that physicians and even the patients themselves had difficulty believing that injuries suffered in connection with persecution were the original cause of these health issues. In her study of the everyday practice of indemnification in Austria, Brigitte Bailer provided detailed descriptions of cases in which applications were – demonstrably unjustly – rejected by evaluating experts on the grounds of lack of causality, and the applicants were even accused of feigning disability. An international exchange of experiences that began to take place within the framework of medical symposia is what launched a process of clarification of the connection between health impairment and persecution.[115] Because the problem of proving causality repeatedly led to difficulties, the victims' associations began in the late 60's to demand that victims of pensionable age (women 55 and over; men 60 and over) be acknowledged as exhibiting 100% MdE for purposes of receiving a victim's pension without having to prove causality. West Germany dealt with this issue by instituting the so-called 'concentration camp assumption' in the final version of the 1965 Federal Indemnification Law. According to this provision, in the case of someone who had spent at least a year in a concentration camp and whose MdE was at least 25%, it was to be assumed without further ado that the MdE resulted from persecution. Austria did not adopt a clause of this sort in the OFG.[116]

Moreover, applicants were all too often confronted by physicians who were inadequately informed about the character of Nazi persecution. Ludwig Popper, an expert in psychiatric evaluation and himself a victim of Nazi persecution, concluded in 1973: 'It is regrettable that (...) no effort has been made up to now to convene a meeting of the evaluating experts who deliver opinions for purposes of administering the *Opferfürsorgegesetz* and to train them as is done in conjunction with other problems on a regular basis in continuing professional education

114 See Bailer-Galanda, 'Verfolgungsbedingte Gesundheitsschäden', 216.

115 Bailer, *Wiedergutmachung*, 117, 222 ff.

116 Bailer, *Wiedergutmachung*, 222.

courses for official physicians. Over the entire time that I've been involved with caring for victims, I've never heard of such a training course having been held. And as a result, the evaluating experts are inadequately inform.'[117] Here, it must also be recalled that many Austrian physicians had sympathized with National Socialism and most Jewish physicians had not returned to Austria from emigration. As a recent exhibition about Nazi euthanasia in Egg in Vorarlberg showed, all 10 doctors in the Bregenzerwald region of that province who had been involved in culling out handicapped persons for liquidation were again granted contracts by health insurance providers after 1945, despite the fact that two of them had even been head of their local Nazi Party organization.[118] Things did not improve until the 1980's and 90's, partially as the result of the arrival of a new generation of physicians with no historical baggage.[119]

The applicants themselves referred over and over again to what they saw as a highly inappropriate claims evaluation practice, the lack of expert knowledge on the part of those doing the assessment and, above all, the equating of war victims and persecution victims that they perceived as humiliating. In 1980, an applicant complained that the evaluating experts were following medical opinions that were obsolete, and especially that they were unfamiliar with the delayed consequences of persecution. Furthermore, he criticized the equal treatment accorded to OFG and KOVG applicants: 'Every person seeking payment under § 1 KOVG 1957 took to arms to fight against the re-establishment of the Republic of Austria and for the victory of the Third Reich, fought – whether consciously or not – against the group of persons described in § 1 OFG, and not only with permitted weapons but also by means of point-blank execution, murder in gas chambers, slow starvation and experiments of all sorts that led to death.'[120]

Moreover, there was no shortage of evaluating experts who failed to display the 'genuine democratic orientation and high moral scruples' that Ella Lingens had called for. In some cases, applicants even encountered physicians who had made quite a name for themselves during World War II as zealous Nazis. This can be illustrated in depth by the well-documented cased of Gerhart Harrer. Harrer was born in 1917 in Innsbruck and studied medicine in Vienna. He was already an enthusiastic follower of National Socialism in high school and joined the Nazi Students Association in 1932. In February 1938 and thus even before the *Anschluss* that merged Austria into the Third Reich, Harrer became a member of the SS,

117 Cited in Bailer-Galanda,'Verfolgungsbedingte Gesundheitsschäden', 218.
118 Jutta Berger, 'Ein Drama, über das man nicht redet' in: *Standard*, April 11, 2008, 11.
119 Bailer-Galanda, 'Verfolgungsbedingte Gesundheitsschäden', 218.
120 Berger et al., *Vollzugspraxis*, 197. The KOVG governed care provided to those who had taken part in the war – thus, veterans of the *Wehrmacht*. On the equating of OFG and KOVG applicants, also see: Manoschek and Sandner, 'Die Krieger als Opfer'.

and in 1940 was accepted for membership in the Nazi Party. At about the same time, he became an assistant professor at the Institute for Hygiene and Psychiatric Clinic of the University of Vienna. Furthermore, he was a member of the university's SS Study Group, whose mission included propagandistic efforts that were the particular favorites of Nazi ideologists: genetic biology and racial hygiene. After the war, Harrer's career continued unabated despite his activities during the Nazi years. He wrote his post-doctoral thesis in 1950 at the University of Innsbruck. In 1962, he took over as medical director of the Psychiatric Clinic of the Province of Salzburg, a post that he held until 1984. In 1971, he was appointed to the chair in forensic psychiatry at the University of Salzburg School of Law. As head of the Department of Neurology at the Hospital of the Province of Salzburg, he was called in as a consultant by the Salzburg Department of Public Health to evaluate OFG cases. Thus, it was a former SS doctor and expert in racial hygiene who was charged with assessing the persecution-related disabilities of victims of the Nazis. In one case involving a woman who had been imprisoned on 'racial' ground in a series of concentration camps from October 1940 to April 1945, Harrer came to the conclusion that her seizures were 'not an illness subject to compensation under the OFG' since her years spent in concentration camps 'had surely had no influence' upon the course of her condition.[121] In 2007 on the occasion of Harrer's 90th birthday, the Christian Doppler Clinic in Salzburg erected a plaque on the facility's grounds in honor of its former director.[122] In April 2008, Gerhart Harrer's name still appeared on the official list of physicians authorized to give expert testimony in courts of law.[123] He has never made a public statement about these matters. With respect to the case of Harrer and other such experts with incriminating pasts, historian Brigitte Bailer remarked that they can 'hardly (have) brought forth the necessary empathy for the situation of the victims of National Socialism.'[124]

Experts with demonstrably incriminating pasts were not the only problem; there were continually irregularities involving government bureaucrats too. Some officials dragged their feet in handling applications; others simply used their own discretion in applying a particularly narrow interpretation of the OFG. For those who were victimized in this way, the problems already began with the filing of an application. Each and every service to be provided under the OFG had to be applied for separately, which means that the victims had to be very well informed about the legal possibilities open to them to even be able to take advantage of their rights. Furthermore, the only simple way for victims to get access to information

121 See Neugebauer and Schwarz, *Der Wille zum aufrechten Gang*, 241-247.

122 Bettina Fernsebner-Kokert, 'Kritik an der Ehrentafel für Klinik-Chef', in: *Der Standard*, August 25-26, 2007, 11.

123 http://www.edikte1.justiz.gv.at/edikte/sv/svliste.nsf/0/91FDEE8B2B8C4334C1256F9A0056E2D2!OpenDocument (April 2, 2008).

124 See Neugebauer and Schwarz, *Der Wille zum aufrechten Gang*, 246.

about the currently prevailing legal situation was if they were members of one of the victims associations or the Jewish Community of Vienna and subscribed to these organizations' publications, which reported on amendments and application requirements. Reportage about the OFG in mainstream media was scant to nonexistent. Thus, it is highly probable that many members of the very groups of victims that this legislation was meant to aid had no idea that they were even entitled to these benefits. This applies especially to victims who had no official organization to advocate their interests. Plus, numerous victims opted not to appeal a rejection of their application due both to the arduous nature of the process and to the enormous psychological stress it represent[125]

In a 1990 address, Erhard Busek, then a cabinet minister, uttered critical words about the hurdles placed in the paths of people seeking aid under victim care legislation: 'What derision has been heaped upon victims of war criminals in our Austria by representatives of the judiciary, what humiliations have "respectable" officials of the Second Republic inflicted upon survivors of the Holocaust when they sought indemnification (...): Could human beings have done this without first wrapping their consciences in sleevelets?'[126]

Milestones: The founding of ESRA and the studies of the Historians Commission

Busek's statement reflects a self-critical consciousness of and multifaceted way of looking at the victims and perpetrators of National Socialism. Together with heightened acceptance with respect to the (delayed) psychological consequences of the traumas that victims had gone through, this paved the way for the establishment of the first psychosocial institution designed specifically to deal with Holocaust survivors. Whereas a psychosocial outpatient clinic for survivors had already been opened in the Netherlands in 1960, such a facility was not set up in Austria until 1994 with the founding of ESRA.[127] ESRA is meant to serve 'all victims of Nazi persecution, their immediate family and descendants whose personality development took place under the impact of the consequences of their parents' suffering during the Shoah.'[128] Nevertheless, non-Jewish victims have only very hesitatingly taken advantage of the services offered by this organization. At first, very few Sinti and Romany came; it was not until the word got out in their families that effective aid was available at ESRA that it became the go-to facility for many Gypsies living in Vienna. Moreover, subsidies from the National Fund have made it possible

125 Bailer-Galanda, 'Entschädigung für seelisches Leid?', 229ff.
126 Bailer-Galanda, 'Entschädigung für seelisches Leid?', 229ff.
127 www.esra.at. The organization's website provides a lot of information about this 'psychosocial center' but no explanation of what the name ESRA means.
128 Vyssoki, 'Trauma bei den Opfern der NS-Verfolgung', 201.

in recent years to increasingly provide counseling and care to clients outside of Vienna. Since 1999, care is also available for victims at the *Am Spiegelgrund* facility. In 2002, the National Fund sent a letter to all victims of Nazi persecution living in Austria and abroad of whom it had records to advise them of what ESRA does; since then, more and more political persecutees have taken advantage of its services.[129]

In 2004, the time was ripe for the previously-mentioned study by the Historians Commission, the first large-scale critical examination of how the OFG was implemented in actual practice. Its analysis included a survey of all illnesses cited by applicants over the course of their proceedings: cardiovascular disease, 12.1%; damage to muscular-skeletal system, 9.6%; gastrointestinal dysfunction, 8.4%; nervous system disorders, 7.3%; mental illness, 7.2%. Thus, taken together, psychological and neurological disorders – whose clinical pictures cannot always be clearly differentiated from each other – far outnumber cases of cardiovascular disease.[130] The symptoms most frequently cited by those suffering from psychological and neurological disorders were exhaustion, crying fits, depression, sleep disorders and various types of obsessive-compulsive behavior.[131] However, this project's pragmatic constraints necessitated selecting and reviewing only a representative sample (1,200 applications) of the estimated 100,000 OFG files on hand, whereby no material could be examined from the provinces of Upper Austria, Salzburg, Tyrol and Lower Austria.[132] Nor has there ever been a survey that breaks down applicants by victim group, gender and age.

The discussions currently taking place in conjunction with the 2008 Commemorative Year provide interesting insights into the current state of the public perception of the psychological consequences of persecution. On one hand, they show heightened acceptance; on the other hand, they also reveal a discrepancy when the victims themselves put up resistance against the trend to *Pathologisierung* (in which they are regarded as pathologically unstable). Following the launch of the Letter to the Stars initiative that aimed to invite survivors living abroad to visit Austria, a discussion flared up in the Austrian daily newspaper Der Standard about 'the right way' to care for these survivors during such a trip, whereby the most interesting aspect of this debate was its 'psychological dimension.' ESRA, by this point established as the 'official ombudsman' of the psychological aspects of persecution, explicitly warned about the danger of possibly 're-traumatizing' the victims, something indicative of an increasing 'psychologization' of the discourse surrounding the issue of how to deal with the victims of National Socialism.

129 See Vyssoki, 'Trauma bei den Opfern der NS-Verfolgung', 201.
130 See Berger e.a, 'Vollzugspraxis', 193.
131 See Berger e.a, 'Vollzugspraxis', 195.
132 A representative sample from the provinces of Vienna, Burgenland, Carinthia, Vorarlberg, and Styria was examined for the project's report. See Berger, 'Vollzugspraxis', 29.

Among those who had a say in this discussion was American psychologist Dorit Whiteman, a native of Vienna and herself a victim of Nazi persecution. She summarized the fears of the initiative's critics in the following terms: 'The young hosts and hostesses, in their naivety and ignorance, would endanger the survivors' psychological equilibrium (...) by subjecting them to greater psychological pressure than they could handle. The organizers of this initiative have failed to consider that their guests would have to be accompanied by professional care-givers because, due to the survivors' psychological make-up, it is to be expected that emotional outbursts and awkward scenes will occur.' Whiteman went on to vehemently reject these ascriptions, and responded to the critics in the following terms: 'Both as a survivor and as a psychologist, I find your commentary completely out of place. We're not pale wrecks who need protection.'[133]

Summary

This discussion about the 'right' way to deal with victims of Nazi persecution is an expression of increasing sensitivity towards the psychological consequences of persecution that has been apparent since the 1990's, but it is also indicative of the fact that even the children and grandchildren of the war generation, despite their well-meaning intentions, often have a hard time dealing 'normally' with victims. It is not always easy to identify the boundary between necessary acceptance and/ or recognition of psychological consequences and *Pathologisierung*. Interviews and conversations with survivors of the Shoah have made us aware of the fact that many survivors have remained silent about their psychological problems out of fear of *Pathologisierung* and the accompanying fear of no longer being taken seriously. Regrettably, no studies have been conducted in Austria about survivors who have undergone therapy, and rules protecting clients' right of privacy prohibit ESRA from giving out information. We know from statements of members of the second generation that very many survivors kept silent and only rarely sought medical attention. According to psychiatrist David Vyssoki, many symptoms remain dormant for a long time before emerging in old age. Individuals who go into retirement have not only more time on their hands; their long-term memories – and thus their recollections of traumatic experiences – become more present. Some ask why they were the ones who happened to survive and develop guilt feelings.[134]

133 On the subject of this discussion, see, for example, the following articles in *Der Standard*: 'Event mit "Kirtagscharakter"', December 15, 2007; 'Letter to the Stars: Stolpersteine der Erinnerung', December 15, 2007; 'Letter to the Stars: Der Fluch der guten Erinnerung', December 15, 2007.

134 'Im Alter wird das Langzeitgedächtnis präsenter', in: *Der Standard*, June 9, 2008, M1.

The skepticism in Austria towards psychiatric help also has to be traced back to the role that physicians and psychiatrists played in National Socialism. A large proportion of Austria's physicians were driven out during the Nazi years, while others remained active while the Nazis held sway, and showed scant sensitivity towards their victims after 1945. For instance, Auschwitz survivor Mali Fritz was told by a doctor that it couldn't have been so bad or she wouldn't still be here.[135]

Up to now, there have been very few studies on the subject of continuity among government officials, physicians and psychologists. Whereas greater acceptance of the various different victims groups has been evident in Austria above all since the 1980's, it is still difficult even to this day to name names and call attention to perpetrators and accomplices.[136] For example, the Vienna Psychoanalytic Society that had been founded by none other than Sigmund Freud only recently began the process of coming to terms with its Nazi past. As Andrea Bronner, Elisabeth Braining and Samy Teicher have shown, psychoanalysis was liquidated in one fell swoop in 1938; most of the members were forced to flee; a few were murdered. Those who re-installed psychology and psychoanalysis in Austrian clinics and universities after 1945 and were also in charge of education and training frequently had incriminating pasts. Few psychologists and psychoanalysts have indicated a readiness to openly confront the role they played in the National Socialist system. Even those like Heinz Strotzka, who as a youth joined the Nazi Party while it was still illegal in Austria but turned into a convinced democrat after 1945, had a hard time dealing with Jews.[137] The discussion about the Nazi past of celebrated Salzburg psychologist Igor Caruso – one that did not get underway until Spring 2008 – might impart a powerful impetus to additional projects to close the gaps that still exist in research.[138]

The biographies of Austrian officials, physicians and psychologists just might contain an explanation for the scant understanding that those outside of the survivor community (Langbein, Lingens, Frankl) brought with them to their encounters with victims. And this is another possible explanation for the fact that there are still no Austrian publications to speak of on the subject of psychological problems and delayed consequences. As we have shown, the discussion about psychological harm and the definition of these conditions was carried out predominantly by physicians who were themselves victims and thus brought the necessary sensitiv-

135 Fritz, *Essig gegen den Durst*, 136.

136 A recent example comes from Bregenzerwald, where the decision about a commemorative plaque referring to the victims and perpetrators of euthanasia is being kicked back and forth among the affected communities. See Jutta Berger, '"Ein Drama, über das man nicht redet." Veranstaltungsreihe im Bregenzer Wald über NS-Morde an Kranken und Behinderten', in: *Der Standard*, April 11, 2008, 11.

137 See Bronner, *Vienna Psychoanalytic Society*; Brainin and Teicher, 'Die Wiener Psychoanalytische Vereinigung', 274-297.

138 *Ö1 Dimensionen*, May 15, 2008: 'Verdrängung oder Verleugnung? Lücken in der Biografie'.

ity with them to this task. With respect to post-traumatic stress disorder and the concept of trauma, it must be assumed that these were imported into the Austrian discussion. In fact, it is unlikely that a country-specific discourse can be identified in any of the other countries whose citizens took part in this debate; rather, this has to be analyzed in an international context (also as the result of international meetings and symposia). The internationalization of the debate can also probably be traced back to the expulsion of numerous psychologists and physicians from Germany and Austria and their research studies conducted on survivors in many different countries.

In summary: research has been done in Austria only on some individual points having to do with the physical and mental consequences of Nazi persecution; there is still much work to do. As for the perpetrators and fellow-travelers, we still lack detailed and comprehensive research about numerous people who climbed the career ladder to great heights after 1945. With regard to the victims, it will take intensive research in the *Opferfürsorge* files to arrive at multifaceted conclusions. In our view, this ought to be an interdisciplinary effort involving collaboration among historians, psychologists and physicians.

2 A Kaleidoscope of Victimhood

Belgian experiences of World War II

» *Sonja van 't Hof*

Writing about wartime and post-World War II Belgium is no easy task. There is hardly a national, Belgian perception of its history; the perception varies according to regional, lingual, religious and political background. This is paralleled by the fragmented political situation in Belgium, officially a federalized state. The federalization process between 1970 and 1993 aimed to solve the long-standing social and political conflicts between the Flemish and francophone population. For the Flemish these were of a cultural nature, for the Walloons predominantly economic. In response to the economic issues, increasing autonomy has been granted to the *regions* Flanders, Walloon and the capital, Brussels. Three *communities* guarantee cultural autonomy for the Flemish, the francophone and the German-speaking populations.[1] In Walloon, there are two governments and parliaments, one for the region and one for the community. Flanders has one government and one parliament for both. In addition, the German-speaking community and the Brussels region each have a government and parliament. The federal government and parliament are not hierarchically placed above them, but have different competences, such as military defense. The result is a labyrinth of six political arenas and civil service facilities.

The old antagonism between the Flemish and francophone population still permeates every aspect of social and political life. The inhabitants have a regional-cultural identity first, and a Belgian identity second. The Flemish and francophone populations watch different television channels, read different papers, discuss different political topics and have a different outlook on the present and the past.[2] This dates back a long time.

Until World War II, the predominantly Catholic and conservative Flemish population lived in a predominantly rural economy. It was subordinate to the Catholic Church as well as to the francophone-dominated Belgian state. The francophone population dominated the political, economic and cultural elite, and French was

1 Beyens, 'Federalisering op z'n Belgisch', 5-9.
2 Beyens, 'Federalisering op z'n Belgisch', 5-9.

the official language in all public life, from politics to the army. The francophone region was more anticlerical than the Flemish, and the Catholic Church was less influential in the political and social life. The francophone elite voted predominantly liberal, the laborers mostly socialist (the communist party was quite small). Because of their elite position, the francophones developed more affinity with the Belgian nation-state than the Flemish. The different affinities and the separate cultural, political and religious worlds played an important role in the two World Wars and resulted in divergent memories and historiographies of both wars.

During World War I and II, the Flemish cooperated and collaborated more with the Germans than the francophones. However, there was also francophone collaboration. After World War II, the Flemish Catholics retrospectively started to portray their collaboration in both wars as 'understandable idealism'. It had been a reaction to the unjustified anti-Flemish attitude of the Belgian state. The purge after World War II is still referred to by some extreme nationalist Flemings as 'the oppression'. In turn, this distortion and simplification has served the Walloon interest in maintaining its mythical identity of collective resistance. The mythical identities, politically instrumental to both sides, keep each other alive. These caricatures still dominate the social debates in Belgium.[3]

Remarkably, the scholarly debates about World War II and its aftermath demonstrate great sophistication and global consensus about historical processes.[4] Obviously, in brief historical descriptions such as the present one, sophistication is easily lost. The reader is therefore kindly requested to keep in mind that any undue generalizations in this text result mainly from trying to be concise.

World War I and the Interbellum[5]

The experiences during World War I would prove to be of importance for those during the next war. In 1839, the European powers had confirmed Belgium's independence in the Treaty of London. The treaty also guaranteed Belgium eternal neutrality. Hence, when Germany invaded Belgium in 1914, the French and British armies were obligated to intervene.

The front stabilized at the river Yser in Flanders and from there south to Ypres. In the small coastal area behind it, the Belgian government and King Albert I resided. The King had personally taken command of the army, which yielded him

3 De Wever, 'De collaboratie in Vlaanderen', 39-49; De Schaepdrijver, 'Een eeuwig soort heden', 12-17.

4 Interview Kesteloot. For sophisticated descriptions and analyses of collaboration in Flanders and Walloon, and the post-war representations by the parties of themselves and the other, see Gotovitch and Kesteloot, *Collaboration, répression,* or the Dutch translation of 2003.

5 This section is mainly derived from Dumoulin et al., *Nieuwe geschiedenis van België,* 685-1118.

the honorary title ‘le roi-soldat’. The German-speaking region around Eupen and Malmédy, north-west of Luxemburg, was annexed by the Germans. In the intermediate territory, a strict military regime was installed. The resistance in this region mainly entailed clandestine press and military espionage for the English. The Belgians were so successful at these activities that some organizations would be revived during World War II.

For the francophone population, World War I predominantly meant losses: oppression, persecution, plundering, devastation and German atrocities. For the Flemish population the experiences were more ambivalent, since the occupation also entailed a degree of emancipation and offered sudden social and occupational possibilities. The German *Flamenpolitik* granted the Flemish some autonomy and gave them cultural rights which the Belgian state had withheld.

After the war, citizens who in varying degrees had cooperated or collaborated with the Germans were punished, but not harshly. The collective punishment for the Flemish population was more severe: the *Flamenpolitik* of the Germans was reversed and the promises by the Belgian governments to grant the Flemish provinces bilingualism remained unfulfilled. This caused resentment and severely compromised Flemish loyalty to the Belgian state. The francophone population remained dominant, even though during the 1930’s the economic and demographic balance shifted in favor of the Flemish.

The Interbellum was a period of growing political instability and polarization, with 22 cabinets in 22 years. Both king Leopold III and the majority of the Belgian population grew dissatisfied with parliamentary democracy. Flemish nationalist movements gained electoral success and in addition, because of the conservative Catholic influence, a large part of the Flemish population was receptive to fascist ideologies. This was less the case for the francophone population, although it should be emphasized that the francophone catholic-fascist movement *Rex* was at the height of its popularity around 1936-1937. The situation at the eve of World War II was politically complex. Both resistance and collaboration during the war could have several origins.

World War II[6]

When Germany again violated Belgium’s neutrality on 10 May 1940, British and French troops assisted the Belgian army. The cabinet fled to France and set up a government in exile; it would travel to London in October 1940. Large parts of the general population, remembering the German atrocities of World War I, also tried

6 Mostly derived from Dumoulin et al., *Nieuwe geschiedenis van België*, 1137-1223.

to flee. King Leopold III, however, refused to leave. Following his father's example, he assumed command of the army.

After two weeks, the French supreme command ordered a retreat. Without consulting his cabinet, king Leopold III requested an armistice. The cabinet responded by officially depriving him of his powers. This caused a rift that would deepen during the war and would remain a problem until 1950. The army capitulated on 28 May and the Nazis imprisoned Leopold III in his Brussels' palace. He enjoyed relative freedom, however. He visited Hitler in November 1940, pleading for a role for himself in a civil government, but to no avail.

The Nazis installed a military government with Alexander von Falkenhausen at its head. Hitler would not decide to install a civil government until the end of the war. Upon the invasion, a Belgian law came into force that ordered the highest civil servants, the twelve Permanent Secretaries of the Ministries, to take over the civil administration and to cooperate with the occupier in order to safeguard Belgium. The government in exile wanted to prevent a repeat of the devastation and suffering of the previous war. It requested Alexandre Galopin, banker of the Société Générale, to form a committee and secure the payment of salaries, the food supply and the preservation of the industry.[7] This cooperation policy was officially called the 'policy of the lesser of two evils', the larger evil being that the Germans would take over the administration and industry. The military government pretended merely to exercise control. Its mission was to maintain order and to employ the economic and human resources for the German war effort. But it increasingly intervened in the civil administration, for instance with a succession of anti-Jewish measures as of October 1940. The Permanent Secretaries did not frustrate these measures, although they did have a degree of liberty to decide how cooperative they would be. In the autumn of 1942, when the Nazis ordered the deportation of the Belgian work force to Germany, they took a less docile stance. The line between cooperation and full-blown collaboration would often be blurred.[8]

Similar to World War I, the Germans immediately annexed the German-speaking region around Eupen, Malmédy and St. Vith. This meant that the population would be subjected to similar policies as in, for instance, Luxemburg or Elzas-Lorraine, such as forced conscription in the *Wehrmacht*. 8,700 young men would eventually fight at the Eastern Front.

7 Galopin would be assassinated by collaborators in 1944 (Dumoulin et al., *Nieuwe geschiedenis van België*, 1187).
8 Van Doorslaer, *Gewillig België*, 259-269 and 1113-1114.

Collaboration and resistance

As stated earlier, the national and local civil administration largely cooperated with the Nazis. But there were local differences. A sharp contrast has been revealed between Brussels and Antwerp with respect to the persecution of the Jewish population. In Brussels, the mayors collectively refused to distribute the Star of David in the summer of 1942; during that same period, the Antwerp police voluntarily started to round up over 1,200 Jews and handed them over to the Nazis.[9]

As described, many Flemish people rejoiced in the new order and the reintroduced *Flamenpolitik*. In 1940, the *Vlaams Nationaal Verbond* had seventeen seats in parliament and 30,000 members. It offered its cooperation to the military government in June 1940 and obtained high positions in the administration. It counted 41,000 members in 1941 and was the largest collaborating organization.

The francophone fascist movement *Rex*, led by Léon Degrelle, also collaborated, but its membership had already been declining on the eve of the war. The military government had little faith in *Rex* and awarded them fewer positions. When Degrelle enlisted in the *Wehrmacht* and assumed the German nationality, he alienated most of the remaining membership.[10]

Around 25,000 Belgian men are estimated to have joined the *Wehrmacht* voluntarily. Figures for the Flemish group diverge from 10,000 to 18,000. It is generally assumed the Flemish made up the majority of the volunteers. They were deployed at the Eastern Front, mainly in the repression of partisan groups. Research has established that some were involved in war crimes against civilians. Apparently there is no evidence to connect them to war crimes against Jews.[11]

Resistance

The earliest resistance organizations were formed in the francophone higher middle classes, mostly by pro-British former combatants of 1914-1918. The resistance expertise from World War I was put to good use. The successful espionage network *La Dame Blanche* was revived as *Clarence*. The famous illegal paper *La Libre Belgique* started to reappear in 1940, with the subtitle *ressuscité en 1940*. Its alleged circulation was impressive: 40,000 copies in 1942.

---

9 Saerens, 'Jodenvervolging in België in cijfers', 199-235; Van Doorslaer, *Gewillig België*, 1113-1114. The latter book is the result of a study commissioned by the federal government, in order to establish the degree of participation in and responsibility of the Belgian authorities in the persecution of the Jews. On the day the study was published, 8 May 2007, the prime minister of the federal government, Guy Verhofstadt, officially apologized to the Jewish community (Joris, 'Erkentelijkheidceremonie', 9).

10 Léon Degrelle managed to flee after the war and lived undisturbed in Spain until his death in 1994.

11 Seberechts, *Tussen Schelde en Wolchow*, 87-89 and 97-125.

The increasing repression stimulated the emergence of many resistance groups. They varied in size and activities, as well as in political and religious denomination. There were conservative, liberal, socialist and communist groups. Some were antiparliamentary and royalist, others democratic and republican. There were also Jewish resistance groups. The groups would be loyal to the Belgian state or not, and they would be francophone, Flemish or bilingual. They were armed and unarmed, they gathered intelligence, performed acts of sabotage, helped people in hiding, and set up escape lines for fugitives and allied pilots.[12]

After the German attack on the Soviet Union in June 1941, the communist resistance, which was predominantly francophone, became the most important pillar of the resistance. It initiated the cooperation of various groups in the 'Independent Front' *(Front Indépendent)*. It carried out both armed and unarmed activities, among which sabotage, illegal press, and organizing hiding places, for instance for those who evaded labor conscription and for Jews.

Compared to surrounding countries, the help given to the Jews is an impressive characteristic of the Belgian resistance. Several organizations provided such help but the most important was a Jewish organization, the *Comité de Défense des Juifs* (CDJ). It was associated with the Independent Front. The first anti-Jewish measure was announced in October 1940. It required the Jews to relocate to Brussels, Antwerp, Liege or Charleroi and to register. From May 1942, they were obliged to wear the Star of David. Soon, the raffles (raids) started. The CDJ started to organize hiding places and procure false papers. The help to Jewish children was delegated to a special *Commission Enfance*, led predominantly by women. The CDJ placed over 2,500 children with false identities in Catholic orphanages or families. It used an ingenious code system to keep track of the children. The Belgian government in exile and the American Jewish Joint Distribution Committee supported the CDJ financially.[13]

The clandestine press proved important in the mobilization of public awareness of the persecution of Jews. In July 1942, a special edition of *La Libre Belgique* wrote: 'Citoyens, par haine du nazisme, par fidélité à vous-mêmes, faites ce que vous ne faisiez pas: sur la simple vue de l'étoile jaune qui vous les signale, **saluez les Juifs**.'[14] There were several illegal papers in Yiddish and they admonished their readers that it was better to resist than to be rounded up.[15] The illegal paper of the Front Indépendent/CDJ, *Le Flambeau*, was well informed and as of March 1943 reported on rumors of the systematic killing of Jews in Polish con-

12 Dumoulin et al., *Nieuwe geschiedenis van België*, 1212-1223.

13 Caestecker, 'Reintegration of Jewish Survivors', 75; Steinberg, *Extermination*, 40. For the financial support, see Van Doorslaer, *Gewillig België*, 772-829.

14 Steinberg, *Extermination*, 14.

15 Steinberg, *Extermination*, 43-44.

centration camps. An unidentified pamphlet warned: 'DENONCER UN JUIF, C'EST L'ASSASSINER!'[16] Ultimately, about 60% of the 56,000 registered Jews survived.[17]

Belgium is unique in Europe in that the resistance once tried to stop a transport of Jewish deportees. From the summer of 1942, Jews were imprisoned in the former army barracks in Malines, the 'SS-Sammellager Mecheln'. The deportations to Auschwitz-Birkenau started on the 4th August that year. On 19 April 1943, three resistance fighters stopped a convoy near the station of Boortmeerbeek, 15 km southeast of Malines. From this 'convoy XX', consisting of more than 1,600 people, 230 people managed to escape, although 26 were eventually killed.[18]

It was the introduction of forced labor in October 1942, however, and the subsequent deportation of laborers to Germany, that caused the largest shock to the gentile Belgian population. Some 27,000 men managed to go into hiding with the help of the resistance. Almost 190,000 were deported to Germany. Prior to that date, 200,000 people had left more or less voluntarily. The 'voluntary' aspect was questionable in the circumstances. There had been 500,000 unemployed people and many may have felt compelled to leave.[19]

The francophone dominance in the organized resistance is generally acknowledged. Nevertheless, the figures indicate that Flemish resistance activity was not insignificant.

Table 1 *Resistance activity, in percentage of language group*[20]

	francophone	*Flemish*	*bilingual*
illegal papers	> 71	> 25	2
political prisoners	> 60	39	<1
Executed prisoners during the occupation	49	34	16

The victims

The eighteen days of battle in 1940 resulted in some 6,500 civilian casualties. Of the 600,000 to 700,000 servicemen, 5,000 were killed.[21] Belgian troops followed the British army when it retreated from Dunkirk and Ostend. Over 10,000 Belgians joined the British army, of whom 2,500 would be killed.

16 Steinberg, *Extermination*, 23 and 26.

17 The precise numbers mentioned in the literature vary due to technical matters of definition and the inclusion or exclusion of certain categories of people.

18 Steinberg, *Extermination*, 53-56.

19 Dumoulin et al., *Nieuwe geschiedenis van België*, 1165-1171.

20 Dumoulin et al., *Nieuwe geschiedenis van België*, 1213.

21 Dumoulin et al., *Nieuwe geschiedenis van België* and Lagrou, *Legacy of Nazi occupation* provide different numbers for servicemen.

The number of displaced people during the war totals over 300,000: Jews, forced laborers, voluntary laborers, enlisted *Wehrmacht* soldiers, prisoners of war (POW) and, at the end of the war, collaborators.[22] Over 200,000 Belgian POW's were relocated to camps in Germany in 1940. The *Flamenpolitik* meant that over 100,000 Flemish POW's were released within a couple of months, while some 65,000-80,000 francophone soldiers remained captive until the end of the war. A large part were required to work in the war industry in Germany. 1,700 would not survive.[23] Of the Belgians who voluntarily or involuntarily enlisted in the *Wehrmacht*, 2,000 would die at the Eastern Front.[24]

In 1940 between 55,000 and 70,000 Jews were living in Belgium, almost 1% of the total population of 7 million people. As mentioned, 55,670 Jews were registered. Almost 25,000 Jews were eventually deported, the majority from Belgium and a minority from France. This amounted to 45% of all registered Jews. Only 5% of the deported people, around 1,200-1,300, survived.[25]

The Sinti and Roma populations were much smaller and probably received no help to go into hiding. 351 were deported and only about 10 of them survived the war.[26]

Some 30,000 resistance fighters were apprehended and 16,000 were killed, either in action or in concentration camps. Fortress Breendonk became the most notorious Nazi prison and torture centre on Belgian soil and the main symbol of Belgian suffering and resistance. In this *Auffangslager* over 3,500 people were temporarily imprisoned (including Jews until the camp in Malines was set up in the summer of 1942). The majority were deported to German camps, but at least 185 people were executed in Breendonk as hostages.[27]

A small group of victims are the freemasons, who were accused of conspiring with the Jews to achieve world domination. In August 1941, their activities were prohibited and their possessions confiscated. Some high-ranking freemasons were assassinated, others taken hostage and a few were sent to concentration

22 Lagrou, *Legacy of Nazi occupation*, 157-159.

23 Lagrou, *Legacy of Nazi occupation*, 83.

24 Seberechts, *Tussen Schelde en Wolchow*, 87-89.

25 Van Doorslaer, *Gewillig België*, 619-620; Lagrou, 'Herdenken en vergeten', 121-122. There is uncertainty about the number of non-Belgian Jews residing in Belgium in 1940. Also, probably not everybody registered. The Belgian government in exile, by the way, twice considered helping Belgian Jewish refugees in France and Portugal leave for Belgian Congo. It finally rejected this possibility on the grounds of insufficient capacity to accommodate them. Only individual Belgian Jews received visa. Van Doorslaer, *Gewillig België*, 685-686 and 739-745.

26 A new study started in 2007 by the CEGESOMA. Of the few existing publications, see Gotovitch, 'Verfolgung und Vernichtung belgischer Sinti und Roma', 209-225.

27 Visitors guide of Het Fort van Breendonk, *De nazi-terreur*, 25.

camps.[28] There is no information about victims among homosexuals or Jehovah's Witnesses.[29]

The liberation

The allied troops liberated Belgium and Luxembourg between 2 and 12 September 1944. The resistance immediately started to round up suspected collaborators and sometimes executed them. The returning government's main concern was to restore its authority. In November 1944, it forced the armed resistance to hand in its weapons. A large protest demonstration by the resistance resulted in a shootout, wounding 45 people.[30] In December, the Germans launched the Von Rundstedt Offensive in the Ardennes and partly reoccupied Belgium and Luxembourg. After two months of devastating warfare, the allied troops won the battle at the end of January 1945.

The political situation at this time was volatile. All issues were riddled with the ancient rifts between the Walloons and the Flemish. The first three years after the liberation saw a quick succession of governments. The first were a combination of left-wing and liberal parties, but in 1947, the Catholic and socialist parties formed a coalition.[31] Apart from the material reconstruction, the purge of collaborators, the preparation for the repatriation of 300,000 deportees, the assistance of war victims and the demands from the former resistance, the governments were faced with the complicated question of the future role of king Leopold III.

The 'Royal Question'

King Leopold's behavior during the war had greatly reduced his popularity with the Walloons, while the Flemish population was more forgiving. After his liberation by the allied army, the king remained in Austria. He refused to accept the government's terms for his return. During the five-year long impasse, his brother, Prince Charles, acted as Regent. Elections returned to power the political parties that advocated Leopold's return, which made the Walloons threaten to secede from Belgium. The matter was finally resolved in 1950, when the organization of ex-political prisoners, the CNPPA, brokered a compromise: the King abdicated in favor of his son Baudouin.

---

28 Koppen, *Passer en Davidster*, 171, 197 and 209-214.
29 Interview Seberechts.
30 Lagrou, *Legacy of Nazi occupation*, 32 and 50.
31 Lagrou, *Legacy of Nazi occupation*, 93.

The purge (francophone) – the 'Repression' (Flemish)

After the war, over 200,000 people were accused of having collaborated with the Nazis.[32] 57,000 were sentenced, including 6,200 women. This is 0.8% of the pre-war population of 7,000,000. Approximately 2,900 people were sentenced to death, of whom 1,693 *in absentia*, and 242 were executed.[33]

The majority of the collaborators, and hence also the punished collaborators, were Flemish. A Flemish-nationalist subgroup among them has considered itself victimized ever since, seeking amnesty and compensation.[34]

Recognition and compensation: 'waffle iron politics'

The existence of the Belgian state after World War II was precarious. The successive governments were obliged to pacify the relations between the various population groups. Each group demanded recognition and compensation from the state and the governments tried to maintain a delicate balance in the distribution of benefits and costs. When a victim group of a particular denomination or political background gained recognition, groups of other denominations and backgrounds would lobby for recognition as well, and the government usually had to give in. In the vernacular, this policy is referred to as 'waffle iron politics': the different, not harmoniously related parts of Belgium are forged together by an external force.[35] Between 1944 and 1950, in a process of extensive political dealings, parliament adopted seven 'legal statutes' for different groups: two military and five civilian. Statutes are decrees that recognize a group as deserving public recognition for their wartime record or for their particular suffering. They also regulate the benefits (annuities), medical and social assistance and other services. Lagrou has described this extensively for the period until 1950.[36] Between 1970 and 2003, more victim groups were recognized. This resulted in some twenty separate categories – a kaleidoscope of victimhood.

The events unfolded roughly as follows. After the military had arranged its own statutes, the first post-war government started to draw up a statute for the civilian armed resistance. The unarmed civilian resistance felt neglected and claimed a statute as well. However, since francophone communists had dominated the armed and unarmed civilian resistance (in the *Front Indépendent*), the statutes and benefits for this group annoyed the Flemish-Catholic movement. They started to lobby vig-

32 Eeckhout, *Bronnen voor de studie van het hedendaagse België, 19e-20 e eeuw*, 555.
33 Aerts, 'De Kroon ontbloot', 15-47.
34 See several contributions in Gotovitch and Kesteloot, *Collaboration, répression*.
35 Interview Seberechts.
36 Lagrou, *Legacy of Nazi occupation*; see also Van Doorslaer, *Gewillig België*, 1040-1045.

orously to secure a statute for their members. Having fewer resistance fighters or resistance feats to boast, this involved some upgrading of their wartime record.[37]

The two statutes for political prisoners were among the most contested (one was for Belgians, the other for foreign members of the Belgian resistance). The term 'political prisoner' referred to anybody who had been imprisoned in Nazi prisons or concentration camps. This included not only resistance fighters, but also Jews persecuted on racial grounds, and political hostages. The first ministers for War Victims advocated an inclusive recognition of victims: the criterion should be the 'shared suffering' of the former prisoners, irrespective of the grounds for imprisonment.[38] This meant that Jews would be included. This intention failed, however, mainly due to obstruction by the Catholic party. They opposed it because there had been few Catholics among the political prisoners. Therefore, their supporters would not benefit from the statute in the same measure as communists and Jews. In the end, the resulting statutes were a compromise. They retained their inclusive character and some 40,000-42,000 were recognized as political prisoner, of whom 14,000 posthumously. However, the honorary title 'political prisoner' was only awarded to those imprisoned for resistance activities. This excluded most of the Jewish concentration camp survivors.[39]

The political prisoners, the illegal press and the civilian resistance fighters later succeeded in having their statutes equated with the military statutes, entitling them to military ranks and privileges. Much political struggle between 1945 and 1950 concerned the *refractaires*, the forced labor evaders. They wanted to be recognized as civilian resistance fighters although they generally had not been active in the resistance. In the end, they were included in the same statute, but the provisions gave more privileges to the resistance fighters. The deported laborers who did *not* evade later obtained their own statute as well.[40]

This chain of events demonstrates the process of 'waffle iron politics', but it also shows that in post-war Belgian society it was impossible to create an image of collective, national resistance. The resistance had many faces. There was a common characteristic to the legislation, however: it excluded Jewish victims unless they possessed the Belgian nationality or had demonstrably participated in the resistance. In fact, this excluded 95% of the Jews who had been living in Belgium in 1940. The discovery of the concentration camp system in May-June 1945 had caused a shock in Belgium, but as elsewhere in Europe, the media gave little attention to the particular fate of the Jews: their intended extermination.[41] This may

37 Lagrou, *Legacy of Nazi occupation*, 169-173.
38 Lagrou, *Legacy of Nazi occupation*, 221-223 and 242-244.
39 Lagrou, *Legacy of Nazi occupation*, 54-58.
40 Lagrou, *Legacy of Nazi occupation*, 169-173.
41 Smets, 'Herinnering aan de nazi-genocide', 99-112.

have been because the Belgian political prisoners and refugees outnumbered the returning Jewish survivors, as the following table shows.

Table 2 *Killed and returned Jews and political prisoners*[42]

	Jews	*Political prisoners*
killed	25,000	14,000
survived	1,300	27,000

Therefore, as elsewhere in Europe, for a long time the prime symbols of the Nazi atrocities were the camps for political prisoners, Dachau and Buchenwald. Yet, as early as January 1945, an official Belgian Committee for War Crimes had named the racial persecution of Jews on Belgian soil a war crime. This was before the full extent of the extermination of the Jews became known. While their report was accurate, it failed to reveal the Belgian participation in the war crime and made the Nazis totally responsible. In the end, it was used only in the prosecution of German criminals of war by the UN War Crimes Commission.[43]

Between 1950 and 1970, no new victim groups were recognized, but groups continued to lobby. In the 1970's, two statutes were adopted for people from the Eastern region around Eupen, Malmédy and St.Vith. One was for men forcibly enlisted in the *Wehrmacht*, who had been excluded from recognition and from compensation for physical damage. Of the 8,700 enlisted men, 1,600 had become disabled.[44] Statutes followed for sea fishermen (1984) and for the young men who in 1940 had responded to the government's summons to travel to the army recruitment centers in the south of France (1990).

Several new statutes have been adopted since the late 1990's. This is attributed to the fact that the Minister of Defense (who today has jurisdiction over war victims) was francophone. He also reopened some of the older statutes that had been closed.[45] In 1999, a separate statute was adopted for the victims of racial persecution. It is often called the 'Statute of the hidden child', but it actually pertains to orphans of deported Jewish, Sinti and Roma parents, and to children who were in hiding.[46] The majority are Jewish. In 2003, a separate law was adopted to grant annuities to the racially persecuted, independently of recognition under the statute.[47]

42 Lagrou, 'Herdenken en vergeten', 121-122.

43 Van Doorslaer, *Gewillig België*, 816-820 and 1040-1045.

44 Nonnenmacher, *La grande honte*, 157-8.

45 Interviews Kesteloot and Renkens.

46 Interviews Vanhoudt and Renkens; 'Loi instaurant de nouvelles mesures en faveur des victimes de la guerre (1)'. *Moniteur Belge* 26-02-1999, 5810-5811.

47 Interview Vanhoudt; 'Loi prévoyant de nouvelles mesures en faveur des victimes de la guerre', 11 april 2003. In this, Chapter IV, 'Mesures en faveur des victimes juives et des victimes tziganes', *Moniteur Belge* 22-05-2004, 28225-28228.

It has proved difficult to obtain recent statistics for all the different groups – those recognized under the statutes and those receiving annuities connected to or separate from the statutes. The historical development has resulted in such a complex situation as to baffle even the people employed at the various departments involved.[48] The following table provides an overview of the numbers of military and civilians of World War II who received annuities between 1950-1994. There is a remarkable increase in military victims in 1980. This is partly due to the adoption of the statute for the forced conscripts of the eastern regions, but is predominantly a generational effect: men who approached their retiring age realized that a disability entitlement would also increase their retirement pay, because several years would be added for its calculation.[49]

Table 3 *Numbers of military and civilians entitled to a disability pension, 1950-1994*[50]

	Military 1940-1945	*Civilian 1940-1945*
1950	47,034	25,651
1960	51,772	27,584
1970	48,328	23,426
1980	62,709	18,731
1990	38,233	8,782
1994	28,009	7,325

The number of civilian victims may have risen again after 1994 because of the new statutes. In 2006, 2,056 people were recognized under the racial statute, 126 of whom were orphans of deported parents.[51] Yet, the number of victims of World War II is obviously diminishing.

The Belgian war victims seem to value moral recognition of their victimhood, although this generally involves little more than a special card and a medal. Even groups who already receive financial compensation. The civilian war disabled, for instance, receive higher annuities than the groups recognized by means of a stat-

48 For the civilian statutes, this is the Direction générale Victimes de la Guerre. For the military and for the civilian statutes equaled with the military ones, this is the Ministry of Defense. In addition, the Ministry of Justice awards the military statute for intelligence agents and that of Transport the civilian statute for the merchant navy. See www.warvictims.fgov.be and www.mil.be.

49 Personal communication P. Lagrou.

50 Samoy, *Ongeschikt of ongewenst?* 156, 237, 326 and 471. In 1950, 95,000 victims of World War I were still receiving a pension. In 1980, this group had diminished to around 7,300: 4,898 military and 2,442 civilians (Samoy, *Idem*, 326).

51 Data supplied by Vanhoudt.

ute. Still, their organization worked ardently to obtain its own statute for the moral recognition of the Civilian Disabled ('Statuut van burgerlijk invalide'), which was in the process of being adopted by parliament in 2007.[52]

Compensation of physical damage: the IV-INIG

The statutes involve moral recognition of victimhood, not compensation for possible physical harm. The history of compensation legislation for physical disability due to war is an entirely different matter. After World War I, the Belgian state created provisions for such compensation, both for servicemen and civilians. Interestingly, the legislation was revised and elaborated *during* World War II. We will return to this shortly.

The service that is presently responsible for the medical and social assistance of all war victims is the *Institut des Vétérans – Institut National des Invalides de Guerre, Anciens Combattants et Victimes de Guerre* (IV-INIG). It also has a history dating back to the aftermath of World War I. In 1919, the state founded an institution for war orphans, the *l'Oeuvre nationale des Orphelins de la guerre / Nationaal Werk voor Oorlogswezen*, and another for the war disabled, the *l'Oeuvre nationale des Invalides de guerre / Nationaal Werk voor Oorlogsinvaliden.*[53] The surviving resistance fighters, in this war mostly intelligence agents for the British, were excluded from these provisions, except those who had been imprisoned or subjected to forced labor. However, those who had put their lives at risk, but had remained unharmed received neither recognition nor compensation. In 1919, the ex-intelligence agents founded the *Fédération nationale des Prisonniers politiques de la Guerre.* After lobbying for twenty years, the state in 1938 established the *l'Oeuvre Nationale des anciens Combattants, Déportés et Prisonniers politiques / Nationaal Werk voor Oud-Strijders, Weggevoerden en Politieke Gevangenen.*[54]

After World War II, when new victim groups emerged, the three institutes were restructured several times. In 1981, they merged into the *Institut National des Invalides de Guerre, Anciens Combattants et Victimes de Guerre* (INIG). In 2007, its cli-

52 Interview Vanhoudt.

53 During World War I, civilians had suffered heavily due to famine and destruction, the military from the trench warfare (poisonous gas). In addition, military psychiatry coined new syndromes such as 'shell shock' and 'trench syndrome'. Some 41,000 prisoners of war, additional hostages and political prisoners were deported to Germany. Apparently, many individuals developed what was alternately called 'Stacheldrahtpsychose', 'Stacheldrahtkrankheit' or 'psychose des barbelés'. Dumoulin et al. refer in this respect to A. Lurkin. *Les ronces de fer. Petits mémoires d'un prisonnier de guerre.* Brussel, 1920 (Dumoulin et al., *Nieuwe geschiedenis van België*, 836). I have not found any academic publications detailing these syndromes; nor have I been able to determine whether these were compensated.

54 Claisse, 'Reconnaissance et méconnaissance des espions après guerre', 87-98.

entele included over 10,000 individuals from 1940-1945 and 26 from 1914-1918. (In addition, it also served victim groups from, for instance, Korea and Congo.) The intention is to also include veterans from peace missions and the institute has therefore added *Institut des Vétérans* to its name, resulting in IV-INIG.[55] It is a federal and semi-independent institute, under the tutelage of the Minister of Defense, but with its own management. The victim groups participate through two committees. One with representatives from nine national military organizations, the other from seven national civilian organizations.[56] Coordinating the IV-INIG and the committees is the High Council, which is also the advisory council for the Minister of Defense. The High Council has to be consulted by the government on all matters concerning war victims, but can also proffer its advice unsolicited.[57]

The IV-INIG evaluates applications for compensation with the help of an official scale of physical damage: the 'Official Belgian Scale for the establishment of the degree of Invalidity', in short, the OBSI. The roots of this disability scale also reach back to World War I. Its history has not been well researched, but what little is known shows that the legislation process took a decisive turn during World War II.

The development of the OBSI[58]

World War I, with its sudden increase of victims and disabled, provided the stimulus to establish a system for the evaluation of physical war damage in particular and labor disability in general. Belgium took its lead from France, where the military constructed elaborate scales with categories of physical damage. Each category was equated with a certain percentage of disablement. The scales, called *barèmes* in French and *baremas* in Flemish, were not based on medical knowledge, but on conventions developed in jurisprudence. A Belgian *barème* was adopted in 1920.

In some countries, the percentage of disablement was perceived to reflect loss of income or labor capacity. Financial compensation aimed to supplement this loss. In Belgium, however, the percentage was used to calculate compensation for physical damage, irrespective of remaining employability or income. One could receive compensation even when fully employed.

In the 1930's, physicians apparently considered the Belgium system unsatisfactory and made appeals to develop a standardized 'Official Belgian Scale for the establishment of the degree of Invalidity'. The outbreak of World War II again resulted in sudden high numbers of victims. In addition, a surprising number of

55 Interview Renkens and www.inig.be.
56 See www.inig.be, of the Institute for War Victims. In addition, there are many Flemish and francophone organizations as well as *amicales,* friendship associations.
57 www.inig.be/PAGES/nlcs.html.
58 Mainly derived from Van Steenberge, *Schade aan de mens,* 187-202.

people with psychological complaints presented at hospitals; this happened for instance in Brussels.[59] These circumstances prompted a comprehensive review of the system.

It is unclear which person or office took the initiative. As described earlier, Belgium was under military rule, but the twelve Permanent Secretaries headed the civil administration. In any case, in September 1940 a Service for Disability Pensions was established, headed by the physician J. Julin. In addition, a committee started to prepare a proposal for the OBSI. The OBSI was now intended for war victims as well as for the disabled who were unfit for work. This 'Interdepartmental Committee for the structuring and approval of the OBSI' counted 26 members from the Ministries, the two railway companies and the Service for Disability Pensions. It seems they were all Belgian. The physician Julin probably also chaired the Interdepartmental Committee. He delegated the committee's work to ten sections of physicians, each responsible for a medical field. The sections drew up proposals for which disabilities and illnesses would merit mention in the OBSI and hence would be eligible for compensation.

The proposals were drafted in 1941-1943, approved by the Interdepartmental Committee and officially ratified by the Permanent Secretaries in a decree on 30 September 1943. The OBSI was separately published in 1944.[60]

According to a legal historian, it was only because of the absence of the official legislating power – parliament – that the OBSI could be adopted. A general guiding principle for all labor disability ran counter to the pre-war Belgium law and the Belgian parliament would never have approved it.[61] When the exiled government returned from London in September 1944, it declared all laws decreed during the occupation null and void. In 1946, however, the government restored the OBSI into force, with the restriction that it only pertained to war victims. The government apparently had two reasons to do so. First, the OBSI was the result of an extensive process in which a large number of medical experts had participated: it was a medical 'consensus document' *avant la lettre*. Second, the OBSI had already served to calculate annuities for war victims who had applied prior to 1945. A review would

59 An article of a certain professor Vermeylen, published in 1945, provided statistics of the numbers of patients that presented since 1932 at the *Institut de Psychiatrie* in Brussels (part of the academic hospital of the Free University). During May and June 1940, there had been an acute increase of patients, after which the numbers plummeted. Vermeylen. 'Evénements et psychoses', 129-148. A footnote mentions that Vermeylen had 'passed away' before the publication of the article, after having been detained in the prison of Huy. This was a Nazi prison, which means he was apprehended either as a political prisoner or as a resistance fighter. I have been unable to find more information about Vermeylen.

60 J. Julin, *Guide-Barème des invalidités*, mentioned in Van Steenberge, *Schade*, 234.

61 Van Steenberge, *Schade*, 235.

entail the revision of many dossiers.[62] Why these arguments did not apply to the dossiers of the disabled who were unfit for work remains unexplained.

The OBSI and psychological war trauma

As mentioned earlier, at the outbreak of the war people with psychological complaints presented at hospitals. One of the ten medical sections involved in preparing the OBSI consisted of the Belgian societies of psychiatrists and neurologists. This can be deduced from several reports published in their official journal, the *Journal Belge de Neurologie et de Psychiatrie* in 1941-1943.[63] Their official assignment by the Interdepartmental Committee is unknown, but the reports and discussions in the Journal focused on the question whether the category of traumatic neuroses (*névroses traumatiques*) was eligible to be included the OBSI; and in particular, whether war neurosis was.

Basis for the discussions was a paper written by a Dr. Marcel Moreau, who worked in the hospital of Ougrée, near Liege. The title of the paper was 'La question des névroses traumatiques et des névroses de guerre dans son état actuel'.[64] After an extensive review of the international literature, Moreau concluded that the traumatic neuroses should not be grounds for compensation. In his opinion, it had been demonstrated repeatedly that individuals with such a diagnosis quickly recovered when they were not compensated; in contrast, those who were compensated, recovered slowly or not at all. In short, they displayed what the Germans called 'Renteneurosen'. In addition, Moreau argued that the theory of an emotional shock causing a lasting trauma was unsound. Overall, it was in the interest of both individual and society not to compensate traumatic neuroses, including war neurosis.

Moreau's report was discussed on at least two occasions.[65] It met with approval, but also criticism. Yet nobody refuted his arguments. In hindsight, he at least founded his arguments on research evidence, which his opponents failed to do. The final proposal of the section of psychiatrists and neurologists for the OBSI is not known. The upshot was, however, that the *névroses traumatiques* were not included in the official OBSI that was adopted in 1943 and reinstated in 1946.

62 Van Steenberge, *Schade*, 235. He does not provide numbers.

63 I am indebted to Maria Teresa Brancaccio for having found the references, as well as for actually obtaining the publications.

64 Moreau, 'La question des névroses traumatiques et des névroses de guerre dans son état actuel', 97-124. The hospital of Ougrée catered to the large mine and steel plant of Ougrée Marihaye and Moreau refers to seeing many laborers who claimed disability on the ground of traumatic neurosis. I have been unable to find more information about Moreau.

65 On 25 July and 31 Oktober 1942. Société de Médicine Mentale et Société de Neurologie, 'Discussion du rapport du Dr. Moreau', 223-274; and 'Suite de la discussion du rapport du Dr. Moreau', 16-59.

This meant that those who presented only psychological complaints had no chance of being accepted at all. However, there was to be an exception. Political prisoners at some point after the war succeeded in having the OBSI amended to include a particular syndrome of physical and mental trauma: asthenia (article 904 of the OBSI).[66] This would exclusively benefit a subgroup of individuals who had been imprisoned in concentration camps for at least six months.

'The asthenia of political prisoners'

Ex-political prisoners were held in high regard in post-war Belgian society. More so than the resistance, the political prisoners represented war heroism in Belgium. The National Confederation of Political Prisoners of Belgium, (*Confédération Nationale des Prisonniers Politiques et Ayants-droit* or CNPPA) was well connected with political circles: the first Ministers of War Victims were ex-political prisoners.[67]

The criteria for recognition under the statute for political prisoners were imprisonment for at least 30 successive days; having suffered grievous bodily harm; or having died or been executed, in which case acceptance was posthumously. Prisoners of war, hostages and victims of retaliation measures by the Nazis could, under certain conditions, be equated with political prisoners.[68] In 1948, an additional decree was passed which detailed extra benefits for political prisoners who had been detained for at least 6 months.[69] Art. 8 of the decree stated: 'A fixed invalidity rate of 20 percent will be allowed to compensate the political prisoners' asthenia (...)'. The syndrome had not been mentioned in the statute for political prisoners and it was not defined in the decree. According to contemporary medical dictionaries, it meant weakness, lack or loss of strength. In the Belgian context, it referred to a combination of physical and mental loss of strength.[70] This is reinforced by a later interpretation which equated *asthenia* with 'concentration camp syndrome':

66 Interview Renkens. I have been unable to determine when this happened exactly.

67 The first Minister, Adrien Van den Branden de Reeth, played an important role in the preparation of the Statute. His successor was Jean Terfve, a communist who also stimulated the founding of the CNPPA. Van Doorslaer, *Gewillig België*, 1042.

68 Ministere des travaux publics et de la reconstruction. *Statut des prisonniers politiques et de leurs ayants droit.* Coordination par arrêté royal du 16 octobre 1954; Interview Renkens.

69 The article specifies: one of three circumstances: at least six months deported; at least six months imprisoned in Breendonk; of at least a total of one year imprisonment in other prisons or camps. 'Besluit van de Regent van 5 oktober 1948 houdende goedkeuring van de tekst van de samengeordende wetten op de vergoedingspensioenen', *Moniteur Belge*, originally 17 October 1948; Anonymous. 'Bijzondere voordelen aan de weggevoerden voor de verplichte tewerkstelling, die erkenning als politieke gevangene bekwamen of nog van begunstigde met het statuut van politieke gevangene', source unknown, 1.

70 Interview Renkens.

'The intention was to allow a fixed compensation to victims affected by the KZ syndrome, which was presumed present in everyone.'[71]

In normal procedures, one had to prove causality between the disability or illness and a war event. The political prisoners were exempt from this requirement.[72] Prisoners of war could also claim art. 904 for asthenia, on the condition that they had been detained for more than a year in specific camps.[73]

The fact that the Belgian political prisoners would use the concept of asthenia was no coincidence. It had a long history in Anglo-Saxon medical literature, where it was linked to war trauma in soldiers, i.e., combatants, and alternately called 'soldiers heart', 'effort syndrome' or 'neurocirculatory asthenia'. In the end, it was categorized as a neurosis, since no organic origin could be established.[74] After World War II, asthenia was revived by French physicians in the context of survivors of Nazi concentration camps rather than combatants. In the 1950's and 1960's, the international organizations of former resistance fighters and political prisoners organized several conferences on 'delayed medical consequences of the war'.[75] For instance, in 1954, in Copenhagen, the Danish Dr. Paul Thygesen and the French Dr. René Targowla addressed psychological symptoms. The latter reported on the syndrome of asthenia among deported prisoners. He described it as a well-known psychosomatic syndrome, which expressed itself in general weakness and exhaustion of the body, the mind and the vegetative system. It was accompanied by, for instance, heart complaints, depression, intellectual disorders and sleep disorders. According to Targowla, it was a chronic disorder, but with a latency period: often the victim would appear physically recovered and then succumb after several months or years. Asthenia influenced the individual's capacity for work and his relations with family and the larger social environment. Targowla explained the history of the syndrome and the name, saying it was in fact 'neurasthenia' but with a special aetiology. As to therapy he recommended extensive rest cures and 'trostgebende Psychotherapie', on the condition that it was accompanied by improvement of material conditions. He concluded 'In diesem Sinne stellt das französische Gesetz eine wirkliche Psychotherapie dar, die den Erkrankten seelisch zufriedenstellt und ihm sein Gefühl der Unfähigkeit abnimmt, indem es ihm eine substantielle Rente zuerkennt und ihm ermöglicht, einen angepassten Beruf auszuüben (...).'[76]

71 Van Steenberge, *Schade*, 409.

72 Art. 1 of 'Besluit van de Regent van 5 oktober 1948 houdende goedkeuring van de tekst van de samengeordende wetten op de vergoedingspensioenen'.

73 Anonymous. 'Bijzondere voordelen aan de weggevoerden voor de verplichte tewerkstelling, die erkenning als politieke gevangene bekwamen of nog van begunstigde met het statuut van politieke gevangene', source unknown, 2-3.

74 See for instance Shephard, *A War of Nerves*.

75 Such as the *Fédération Mondiale des Anciens Combattants* or the *Fédération Internationale des Résistants*.

76 Targowla, 'Syndrom der Asthenie der Deportierten', 30-47.

The definition given of asthenia at the end of the Proceedings of the conference in Copenhagen in 1954 is revealing: '... weiterer Begriff für die Folge der Einwirkung des gesamten Komplexes der Naziverfolgungsmethoden auf den Menschen.'[77] One can assume that the Belgian political prisoners, predominantly francophone, would have focused on the French contribution and would adopt its concept; even more so since Targowla was a member of the French *Commission d'Etude de la Pathologie spéciale des Déportés et Internés*. Obviously, the therapeutic recommendations, which included financial compensation, may have been a strong incentive as well.

The question of how asthenia became grounds for compensation in the OBSI remains unanswered. The archives of the CNPPA might provide an answer, for it is likely that the political prisoners lobbied for it. Another question is why the compensation only pertained to the particular group who had been imprisoned for more than six months. An explanation might be found in the post-war political struggles to obtain extra benefits while excluding another group. Perhaps the ex-political prisoners who conformed to the six-month clause were predominantly francophone. This was certainly true for the military prisoners of war who could also claim asthenia. As mentioned, the Flemish POW's had been released within a couple of months, whereas the majority of the francophone servicemen remained imprisoned the entire war.[78]

Help to Jewish survivors: a Jewish affair

The Jewish victims were almost entirely excluded from all legislation for heroes and war victims. Only the small group with the Belgian nationality were entitled to recognition, benefits and compensation for physical damage. Non-Belgians could not make use of the provisions the Belgian state had made or would make.[79]

Even before this became clear, the Jewish resistance organization *Comité de Défense des Juifs* (CDJ) had understood that its work would not end with the liberation of Belgium. The Belgian-Jewish community would need to be reconstructed, the fate of the deportees was still uncertain, and there were some 2,500 hidden children to be taken care of. The *Commission Enfance* of the CDJ had provided them with false identities and placed them with families and in Catholic institutions. They had to be retrieved and, when possible, reunited with their families. The CDJ decided to put its organizational expertise and network to use for the particular assistance of Jewish war victims. In October 1944, a month after the liberation, the

77 Michel, 'Gesundheitsschäden', 360.
78 Interview Renkens.
79 Van Doorslaer, *Gewillig België*, 1044-1045.

leadership of the CDJ officially founded *L'Aide aux Israélites Victimes de la Guerre*, in short AIVG. A private organization, it aimed to: '... venir en aide aux Juifs victimes de la guerre, notamment à ceux qui furent déportés ou dessaisis de leurs biens et d'assurer leur réadaptation dans la vie économique et sociale.'[80] The main financial sponsor was the American Jewish Joint Distribution Committee, mostly called 'Joint', the welfare organization that had already supported the CDJ during the war.[81] It would sponsor the reconstruction of Jewish communities throughout Europe. The AIVG became the most important support system for Jewish victims in Belgium. It served as the main contact for the government and was therefore the prime representative of the Jewish-Belgian community.[82]

The AIVG main office was in Brussels, but in 1944-1945, it opened offices in all towns with a substantial pre-war Jewish community: Brussels, Antwerp, Charleroi, Liege and Namur. They offered medical services, material assistance (clothing, furniture), an employment service, a service to supply loans, a juridical service to reclaim houses and possessions, and a service to locate family members. The Ministry of the Interior handed over the Jewish register compiled by the Nazis, which was used to check for deported individuals and to apply for damages.[83] The problems were enormous and became almost overwhelming when the concentration camp survivors returned after May 1945. That year, over 5,000 victims visited the offices of the AIVG, of whom 3,900 in Brussels alone. More than 200 people were employed by the AIVG to receive and help them. For elderly Jewish survivors, who suffered multiple problems, two homes were soon established.[84]

The main task the AIVG set itself was the assistance of the victimized children, 'l'avenir du judaïsme'. The retracing of the hidden children started immediately in November 1944, using the code system the CDJ had developed to keep track of them. In addition, there were children among the returning concentration camp survivors. Only 10% of the children could be reunited with both parents; 35% had lost one parent and 55% were full orphans.[85]

A main concern was to have the full orphans removed from the mostly Catholic institutions and foster families where they had been in hiding and to give them a Jewish upbringing. Obviously, Jewish adoption or foster families were not in abundance after the war and the AIVG soon started eleven orphanages. In some cases where the children had already been converted and the foster family or insti-

80 Massange, *Bâtir le lendemain*, 17. The term 'Israélites' rather than 'Juives' is telling of the times: Belgian politics wished to demonstrate that race was no longer an issue and banished the word Jewish. Caestecker, 'Reintegration of Jewish Survivors', 79-80.

81 Van Doorslaer, *Gewillig België*, 772-229.

82 Van Doorslaer, *Gewillig België*, 1036.

83 Massange, *Bâtir le lendemain*, 42.

84 Massange, *Bâtir le lendemain*, 23-25.

85 Caestecker, 'Reintegration of Jewish Survivors', 90-91.

tution refused to let them go, the AIVG would go to court.[86] In the course of 1945, the orphanages housed some 480 children, among whom a substantial number of camp survivors.[87] In addition, 229 lived with Jewish foster families, 64 with gentile families and four remained in a convent, all supervised by the AIVG.[88] The orphanages aimed to teach the children a profession so that they could live independently when they left the homes.[89]

The funding of these activities remained a constant struggle and the AIVG exerted itself to get support from the Belgian state.[90] A main problem was that almost 95% of the Jews who were deported from Belgium did not have the Belgian nationality. This applied to the hidden children as well: 75% had been born in Belgium but only 3% had the Belgian nationality. 66% were Polish and the rest were one of ten different nationalities or stateless (6%).[91] The Belgian state compensated on the grounds of nationality and in the aftermath of the war refused to create special facilities on racial grounds. However, through 'discrete lobbying' the AIVG sometimes got the state to make exceptions. It preferred such lobbying to public action, for fear of resurgent anti-Semitism.[92]

Until 1946, all Jewish camp survivors received an allowance upon their return to Belgium, irrespective of their nationality. The state also agreed to pay for the 2,000 to 3,000 Belgian-born children. It was a financial disaster for the AIVG when the state discontinued these policies in 1946: about 5,000 of their clients were not Belgian. In 1947, it could persuade the Belgian Ministry of Reconstruction to finance the orphanages retroactively from 1944.[93]

The last orphanage closed in 1959. The AIVG continued to track the children for a while in their independent life. Around this time, it had already started to notice psychological problems among the former pupils and in the Jewish survivors in general.

Psychological war trauma among Jewish survivors

In 1955, the AIVG became aware that a substantial number of children in the orphanages seemed to need psychotherapeutic assistance and that it was ill-equipped to provide this.[94] In the absence of psychiatrists or psychologists, the

86 Massange, *Bâtir le lendemain*, 26-28 and 68-71; Caestecker, 'Reintegration of Jewish survivors', 91-96.
87 Massange, *Bâtir le lendemain*, 31-35.
88 Massange, *Bâtir le lendemain*, 69.
89 Massange, *Bâtir le lendemain*, 71, 83-85
90 Massange, *Bâtir le lendemain*, 42.
91 Massange, *Bâtir le lendemain*, 26-31.
92 Caestecker, 'Reintegration of Jewish survivors', 78, 85, 89-90 and 97-99. Massange, *Bâtir le lendemain*, 59-60.
93 Caestecker, 'Reintegration of Jewish survivors', 89-90 and 97-99; Massange, *Bâtir le lendemain*, 59-60.
94 Massange, *Bâtir le lendemain*, 75-76.

8 social workers who acted as guardians would try to give some psychological guidance. Some individual staff members proved gifted lay psychologists, for example Siegi Hirsch, a director of one of the orphanages and himself a camp survivor. In the 1960's, Hirsch started training in the Netherlands as a social worker and psychotherapist. He became a family therapist, professor of psychology in Mons and eventually a specialist in traumas of the 'hidden children'.[95] However, despite good intentions, many orphans suffered bitter experiences, for instance due to changes in the staff or involuntary transfers to other homes when they started an advanced education. The children would often feel deprived of affection and assistance with important life events.[96]

After the pupils left the orphanages, a large part succeeded in building a more or less successful life, but some barely managed to support themselves financially and socially. The AIVG determined in the early 1960's that a great many suffered severe psychological or behavioural problems.[97] Also, its social workers regularly visited over fifty hospitalized psychiatric patients. When these patients were discharged from an institution, they often had nowhere to go.[98]

In 1961, the AIVG changed its name to Service Social Juif (SSJ). It supported a study which revealed that there were 298 mentally ill Jewish people in Belgium, of whom 138 were hospitalized. The ratio of hospitalized Belgian patients per 10,000 Belgian inhabitants was 26; in comparison, the ratio of Jewish patients per 10,000 Jewish inhabitants was definitely elevated: 46. Of the 298 surveyed patients, 87% had survived in a Nazi-occupied country and 12% had been detained in a concentration camp. In addition, 40% had lost close family through deportation. This raised the issue of the relation between war experiences and mental illness, but the question was apparently not studied in later research.[99]

De SSJ followed up on 193 of these 298 patients, while the *Centraal Beheer van Joodse Weldadigheid en Maatschappelijk Hulpbetoon* in Antwerp followed up on the other 105. The latter organization was founded in 1920 and catered to the Flemish-speaking Jewish community.[100] The SSJ also visited the Sinai clinic in Amersfoort, the Netherlands, where several Belgian-Jewish patients would be admitted.[101]

International developments at the time were to start outpatient clinics for formerly hospitalized patients. When the SSJ obtained extra funds, it opened two 'Centres Medico-Psychologiques' (CMP) in Brussels and Antwerp in 1962. The team consisted of two psychiatrists, a psychologist and two social psychiatric nurses,

95 Frydman, *Le traumatisme de l'enfant caché*, 124-127. Baumann. 'Siegi Hirsch'.
96 Frydman, *Le traumatisme de l'enfant caché*, 102-108.
97 Massange, *Bâtir le lendemain*, 110-112, 122, 157-159.
98 Massange, *Bâtir le lendemain*, 157-159.
99 Massange, *Bâtir le lendemain*, 157-159.
100 I have not obtained information about the Flemish organization.
101 Massange, *Bâtir le lendemain*, 157-159.

and was supervised by neurologist and psychiatrist Jean Dierkens. Between 1952 and 1958, Dierkens worked as a psychiatrist at the Brugman hospital of the Free University in Brussels, and the AIVG started to send many traumatized Jewish patients to him.[102] He later became professor of psychiatry at the University of Mons, but never published about his work with traumatized patients. The two CMP's operated independently as of 1967. That year, the Brussels CMP treated and surveyed 172 outpatient and 71 hospitalized patients. The CMP also worked in prevention: in 1963, it started weekly consultation hours in two Jewish schools, in order to assist parents with educational problems and to trace problems among the youth at an early stage.[103]

In the 1970's, the CMP was recognized as a 'Centre d'Hygiène Mentale' and the SSJ as a 'Centre de Service Social', which meant that the Belgian state took over funding. As a result the services had to be accessible to all citizens. The SSJ dropped the word 'Jewish' from its mission statement. It henceforth assisted with the 'réadaptation médicale, sociale, professionelle et économique des victimes de la guerre…' But it remained faithful to its origins: 'il tient particulièrement compte des besoins spécifiques de la population juive de la partie francophone du pays.'[104]

The SSJ and the CMP still exist in Brussels, as does the *Centraal Beheer van Joodse Weldadigheid en Maatschappelijk Hulpbetoon* in Antwerp.[105] However, while these organizations obviously developed expertise in the social assistance and psychological treatment of traumatized war victims, I have found no publications on their work. If they disseminated their knowledge, it was through other means. The CMP became renowned for its expertise. When in the 1970's Jewish fugitives arrived in Belgium, they were automatically sent to the SSJ-CMP.[106]

Research on and knowledge of trauma

The expertise of psychologically damaged war victims that was gained in the Jewish organizations does not seem to have spread beyond the community. In Belgium, the concept of psychological trauma is generally not linked to World War II. A search among Belgian institutions for mental health revealed several specialized treatment centers for psychotrauma, but none mentions treatment of victims of World War II. Similarly, a search of academic and professional literature on World War II and psychotrauma produced no results. The only source proved to

102 Personal communication P. Lagrou. Massange supplies no information about this psychiatrist.
103 Massange, *Bâtir le lendemain*, 157-159.
104 Massange, *Bâtir le lendemain*,182.
105 www.guidesocial.be/service_social_juif and www.centrale.be.
106 Massange, *Bâtir le lendemain*, 180.

be the *Bulletin Trimestriel* of the Belgian *Fondation Auschwitz*, and the Fondation's library.[107]

The *Fondation Auschwitz* was founded in 1980 and acts as the successor of the *Amicale des ex-prisonniers politiques d'Auschwitz-Birkenau, camps et prisons et forteresses de Silezie*.[108] Its aims are to keep the memory of the holocaust alive and to stimulate research on the topic. It does not present itself as exclusively Jewish but as an antifascist group. Therefore, its position is not uncontested within the Belgian-Jewish community. The *Bulletin Trimestriel* started to address psychological issues among holocaust survivors in the early 1990's. A.W. Szafran, psychoanalyst, professor of psychiatry and head of the Psychiatric Unit at the Free University of Brussels, was among the first to write about his work with survivors.[109]

Since 1988, the *Fondation* awards prizes for original and unpublished studies connected with the holocaust.[110] In this way it stimulated research that the Belgian academic communities seemed to ignore. Students submitted their MA or PhD-theses and the winners were encouraged to write a paper that was published in the *Bulletin*. After the first international conference on hidden Jewish children in New York, in 1991, papers in the Bulletin began to address this topic, some focusing on possible traumas. The first, in 1994, would result in a much-cited book – referred to earlier in this paper: *Le traumatisme de l'enfant caché. Répercussions psychologiques à court et à long termes*. The author, Frydman, had himself been a hidden child and lived in an orphanage of the AIVG after the war. He went on to become a psychologist and worked at the University of Mons-Hainaut. In the book he describes his personal experiences during the war, followed by the results of in-depth interviews with 35 formerly hidden children, to assess their psychological characteristics.

Orphanages were obviously not ideal environments for these children, who suffered not one but a series of accumulating traumatic experiences: being separated from parents, going to live with strangers, assuming another identity, living in constant fear, not being able to grieve, and for some, being found out, deported and surviving a concentration camp. According to Frydman, at the time many orphans had social adaptation problems, were distrustful of the staff and of their peers, and showed maladaptive behavior. It was 'every man for himself'. Frydman also remembers that no adult ever asked the children about their past sufferings

107 For instance, the library of CEGESOMA hardly contains literature on war trauma, and certainly no Belgian literature, except for an early thesis by a student of the Ecole Royale Militaire: J.M. Vermeulen. *La détention dans les camps de concentration allemands: conséquences psychiques d'une situation traumatisante*. Travail de fin d'études pour l'obtention du titre de licencié en sciences sociales et militaires, 1987.

108 The *Amicale* was founded in 1946 and open to Jewish and non-Jewish ex-concentration camp prisoners. When the number of survivors declined and the activities for recognition and compensation became superfluous, the Amicale founded the Fondation Auschwitz. Interview Thannasekos.

109 Szafran, 'Rouw zonder einde', 23-31.

110 *Bulletin Trimestriel*, 16 (december 1987-februari 1988), 140-142.

or present emotions. In the orphanage, they were again deprived of the possibility to grieve: they were always told how lucky they were to have survived.

The interviews, Frydman recounted, revealed many repressed feelings and traumatic memories. The long-term psychological consequences consisted of a disrupted, never-ending grieving process, fear of abandonment, distrust and anxiousness. Frydman later supervised self-help groups of formerly hidden children. In the absence of a 'psychotherapie systématique', he judged these groups to have had therapeutic effects for many participants.[111]

A nationally acknowledged war trauma

After the hidden children came on the scene internationally, several Belgian organizations were founded which started to campaign for moral recognition and compensation: *l'Association Belge de l'Enfant Caché* (housed in the main office of the SSJ in Brussels) and *l'Union des Déportés Juifs de Belgique, Filles et Fils de la Déportation*. It was in this context that the latest legislation for recognition and compensation was undertaken. For the first time, traumatic psychological experiences were an explicit argument in the debates about such legislation.[112] And it seems also to have been the first time that the discussion transcended the language barriers and became national. As described earlier, a moral Statute was adopted in 1999 for the recognition of the 'Hidden Children', followed by financial compensation legislation in 2003.

Contrary to the intention of the state, people who were recognized under the Statute subsequently filed applications for a disability pension, their argument being that recognition meant acknowledgement of mental war damage.[113] The application procedure had different outcomes in the Flemish and francophone regions. The committee in the latter granted the applications almost without exception on the grounds of Post-Traumatic Stress Disorder (PTSD). In contrast, the Flemish committee refused the applications almost without exception because no causal relation with the war could be proved. This again emphasizes the different experiences and memories of the war. It may also be related to the less prosperous economic situation in the Walloon region.[114]

111 Frydman, *Le traumatisme de l'enfant caché*, 181-200 and 233.
112 Kesteloot, 'La place de la guerre', 9.
113 Interview Renkens.
114 Interview Renkens.

In October 2007, a conference on Children of the Shoa organized sessions on trauma, with respect to the hidden children and their descendants.[115] It generally seems to be in this context that one hears the terms 'first' and 'second' generation applied.

Not acknowledged: traumas of other children

There were also people outside the Jewish community who suffered traumatic psychological experiences as children, during the war or because of the war. This was because their parents had chosen to become resistance fighters or collaborators. Interviews with children of killed or executed resistance fighters and children of collaborators revealed that both groups still lived with severe psychological consequences. After the war, the children of collaborators were condemned socially and had to live with the shame of the choices made by the parents they loved. The orphans of resistance fighters could be proud of their parents but developed aversion to the continuous celebration of their heroism. As one interviewee put it: 'We were sick of being seen as children of a hero rather than victims.'[116] The common denominator in these interviews seems to be precisely the notion of psychological trauma.

Conclusion

On a national Belgian level, the attention for psychological trauma of victims of World War II pertains to a particular group: surviving Jewish hidden children. That they suffered such trauma is generally accepted. Survivors of concentration camps, Jewish and non-Jewish, have never attracted such attention from researchers in psychology or psychiatry – nor, apparently, have they demanded it. It seems all victims were primarily concerned with moral recognition and financial compensation. Whether mental consequences of the war deserved treatment never seems to have become an issue, let alone what kind of treatment. A subgroup of the political prisoners and POW's were unique in obtaining recognition of a form of war trauma that included psychological complaints: 'asthenia'. However, they do not seem to have lobbied for specialized treatment.

115 Forum der Joodse Organisaties, 28 October 2007 in Antwerp. It was also the scene of a historic occasion. In a video message the mayor of the city, Patrick Janssens, apologized for the active role of the Antwerp authorities and police in the persecution of Jews during the war. This was done in response to the publication of the book *Gewillig België* by Van Doorslaer, earlier that year.

116 Ponteville and Kesteloot, 'Kinderen van verzetslui of collaborateurs', 30.

Among the Jewish survivors, it also took time before the psychological dimension received attention. The Jewish community had organized help in its own circles. Jewish professionals and scholars also studied the psychological problems of the victims and their descendants. Was their attitude determined by the war experiences, when they mostly had to organize their own survival? Had they accepted the general indifference of the Belgian state and public with respect to their exceptional fate? Alternatively, was it a result of the policy of 'discrete lobbying' and keeping a low profile? Perhaps all three were the case. In addition, there seems to have been a general tendency among Belgian authorities to 'delegate all topics with a typically "Jewish character" to Jewish representatives'.[117]

This may have been connected with the general situation in Belgium, where groups of different language and socio-political and religious backgrounds live in separate worlds that rarely interact. This separateness extends to the academic communities. For instance, in psychology and psychiatry, the francophone researchers and professionals have been mostly oriented on francophone countries, and the Flemish on the Anglo-Saxon countries and the Netherlands. They sometimes seem unaware of the work of colleagues in the other language communities, or at least they do not refer to it. In this context, the Jewish Belgian population is or was perhaps also a subgroup with a separate world. For an undetermined period after the war, Jewishness transcended the language barrier. As described, the AIVG founded socio-medical services in francophone cities and in Antwerp. It was the driving force of the reconstruction of the Jewish community and the prime representative of the entire Jewish-Belgian community.[118] In the 1960's, the language divide also seems to have begun to divide the Jewish community. In 1962, the successor of the AIVG, the SJJ, founded two Centres Medico-Psychologiques', one of which in Antwerp. They soon worked independently. Later on, the SSJ only catered to the francophone Jewish population.

Why psychological war trauma has never become an issue, socially or academically, remains an intriguing question. In the 1990's, the *Fondation Auschwitz* started a project to record testimonies of Belgian holocaust survivors, in collaboration with Yale University in the United States. The interviewers soon noticed that many interviewees evidenced a need to discuss their psychological condition. But the Belgian interview team did not include a trained psychotherapist, in contrast to their American and French counterparts. In the latter countries, the psychological repercussions after the war were part of the interviews. The Belgian team deemed it too risky to address the topic and decided to offer people a referral to a specialized psychotherapist. In the end, only a handful of interviewees made use of this

117 Van Doorslaer, *Gewillig België*, 818.
118 Van Doorslaer, *Gewillig België*, 1036.

offer.[119] Apparently, they did not insist that their psychological condition be part of the study by the *Fondation Auschwitz*. There may have been reluctance on the parts of the psychological researchers as well as the survivors. Both may have considered the psychological problems a private matter, perhaps to be treated privately but not to be addressed publicly.

Interviews

- C. Kesteloot, researcher at the Centre d'Etudes et de Documentation Guerre et Sociétés contemporaines / Studie- en Documentatiecentrum Oorlog en Hedendaagse Maatschappij (CEGESOMA), Brussels.
- F. Seberechts, researcher at the Archief en Documentatiecentrum voor het Vlaams Nationalisme (ADVN), Antwerp.
- H. Vanhoudt, Service Public Fédéral (SPF) Sécurité sociale, Direction générale Victimes de la Guerre / Federale Overheidsdienst (FOD) Sociale Zekerheid, Dienst voor de Oorlogsslachtoffers, Brussels.
- R. Renkens, head of the Social Department at the IV-INIG, Brussels.
- Y. Thannasekos, director of the Fondation Auschwitz, Brussels.

119 Interview Thanassekos.

3 From 'Deportation Pathology' to 'Traumatismes Psychiques de Guerre'

Trauma and reparation in post-war France (1940's-1990's)

» *Maria Teresa Brancaccio*

'Deportation Pathology' is a term coined by French doctors in the second half of the 1940's which refers to a variety of physical and psychological illnesses and disorders noticed among former deportees and internees since the close of World War II. The adoption of the term 'deportation' by the medical profession was significant as it reflected the currency that such term had acquired in France during the war. In the first place, 'deportation' referred to concentration camp survivors, i.e. members of the resistance, political prisoners and Jews. It was, however, a term that could be stretched to include other groups of people forcibly relocated to German territories such as the prisoners of war and labor conscripts.

This article looks at how the medical studies on deportee illness emerged and framed the experiences of war trauma of the groups of victims that were redefined as members of the 'deportee' community. The specific diagnostic definitions of psychic trauma introduced by the 'deportation pathology' are compared with the general definitions of psychological trauma of French war pension legislation (which were applied to all other groups of war victims). The theoretical and practical implications of this double diagnostic system are examined in relation to the war pension laws. Next, I address the developments that led to the decree of 10 January 1992 regarding the classification of war psychological disorders.1 The decree firmly established the diagnosis of 'psychological war trauma' in France and opened up the disturbing legacy of post-colonial war to reinterpretation in terms of post-traumatic syndrome.

After a brief introduction on the pre-war years – a period of crisis and conflicts that was to have a significant influence in the 1940's – I will deal with the war years in order to set the stage for the post-war discussion concerning reparations and war trauma. Next, the specific political and professional contingencies underlying

1 Décret du 10 janvier 1992 'déterminant les règles et barèmes pour la classification et l'évaluation des troubles psychiques de guerre'.

the emergence of medical studies on illness associated with deportation, and their influence on the reparative legislation are discussed. Finally, I will briefly discuss the transformations in the psychiatric definitions of psychological war trauma. Some recent developments in relation to the interpretation of the difficult and controversial memories of post-colonial conflicts in terms of psychological war trauma will be examined before some concluding remarks are made.

France in the 1930's

During the interwar period France increasingly became a destination for immigrants and political refugees. In 1927 the government passed a law that greatly simplified the process of naturalization. By the early 1930's, however, as the effects of the Great Depression spread in France, the presence of immigrants started to be resented, and intolerance and xenophobia were on the rise.[2] Both right-wing and left-wing parties came to the conclusion that the only way to deal with growing unemployment was to reduce the foreign workforce. The economic crisis, job competition and xenophobia fed into an animated debate on the 'Jewish invasion'. During the 1930's, with the exception of the period of the Popular Front, one government after another introduced measures aimed at limiting the number of immigrants, and controlling those already in the country. In the five years after 1931 half a million foreigners left France.[3]

In the same period, several financial scandals involving political representatives contributed to a sense of crisis and political instability. Anti-Semitism in the 1930's was not confined to immigrants. In 1933 a financial scandal broke out involving Serge Alexandre Stavisky, a second-rate Jewish financier, as well as politicians close to the prime minister, radical-socialist Camille Chautemps. This scandal soon became the pretext for a heated right-wing press campaign and political unrest. Massive demonstrations by right-wing veterans, patriotic and monarchist associations culminated in antiparliamentary riots. These attacks on the alleged corruption of the Radical Socialist Party involved attempts to discredit the parliamentary system, overlaid with vociferous xenophobia and anti-Semitism.

Nationalist right-wing movements, such as the monarchist *Action Française*, propounded anti-Semitism as a central tenet of their ideology. In 1935, the move-

2 As Shamir writes: the 'impact of the Great Depression on France was extensive and profound. It weakened the French industrial infrastructure by causing a substantial drop in production and investment... The policies adopted during the depression served to intensify the process of economic deterioration and ... steer[ed] France toward rigid ... maintenance of the gold standard and a high degree of trade protectionism.' Shamir, *Economic Crisis*, 227.

3 See Weber, *The hollow years*, 90.

ment had been outlawed after some of its members savagely assaulted the socialist deputy, soon to be prime minister, Léon Blum. The movement's ideology had supporters even among members of the National Assembly. When Blum became the first Jewish prime minister of France in 1936, 'anti-Semitism was an important focus for opposition to Blum's Popular Front government'.[4]

The rise of Nazism brought another 20,000 German refugees to France, and between 1933 and 1939 some 55,000 Germans passed through the country. Although these relatively well-off exiles did not face the same grassroots anti-Semitism that affected poorer eastern immigrants, during the 1930's their presence in the country was seen as a potential source of instability, likely to provoke diplomatic incidents and increase the risk of war with Germany. French politicians and the population alike were massively against the idea of taking part in another war. Memories of World War 1, with its 1,500,000 French victims, were still vivid in the 1930's. Towards the end of the 1930's, anti-Semitism intensified, which affected not only German but also French Jews. Public declarations by French Jews that their community was wholly against the war could not prevent anti-Jewish demonstrations.[5] In 1938, alarmed by the rise of anti-Jewish propaganda in the press and in public life, the government passed the Marchandeau law, which made attacks in the press against ethnic and religious groups a criminal offence. Such a measure, however, had almost no impact: by the end of the 1930's, political and economic crisis, job competition, and cultural differences had contributed to the widening gulf between French people and the foreign newcomers, and had revived an older strain of prejudice against the Jewish people who were born and raised in France.

The German occupation and the Vichy regime

When Hitler invaded Poland, war became inevitable. France and Britain declared war on Germany on 3 September 1939. Between May and June 1940, in less than six weeks, the French army was defeated and the German army reached Paris. Prime minister Reynaud resigned and old Marshall Pétain, named vice premier shortly after France fell to the Nazis, was asked to form a new government. Pétain called for the cessation of hostilities, and Parliament agreed by an overwhelming majority to grant him full powers to promulgate a new Constitution. Pétain

4 Marrus and Paxton. *Vichy France and the Jews*, 39.

5 By 1939 around 330,000 Jews lived in the country (i.e., they were 0.7 per cent of the total population). Between 190,000 and 200,000 were French Jews, (including the 55,000 who were naturalized citizens); while 140,000 were foreigners from Poland, Germany, Austria, the Soviet Union, Romania, Hungary, Czechoslovakia. See Weil, 'The return of Jews in the nationality or in the territory of France', 58.

immediately issued three constitutional decrees that made him head of the French state, with full powers. The Senate and the Chambers were adjourned indefinitely.

The armistice divided France into an occupied and a 'free' or unoccupied zone. The departments of Nord Pas de Calais were placed under German administration. The three department of the Alsace Lorraine were annexed to the Third Reich. A Southern zone was occupied by the Italian army in June 1940, when France was practically defeated by German army.[6] The armistice recognized the French government's sovereignty over the entire country 'respecting the rights of the occupying power' (in other words, insofar as the French government's policies were not in conflict with the wishes of the occupying power, at least in the occupied zone).[7] The French government had to pay exorbitant occupation costs; and if so requested by the German authority, had to hand over any refugees from the Third Reich. Pétain was unable to obtain any concessions regarding the approximately 1,800,000 French soldiers who were taken prisoner and then deported to German labor camps following the armistice.

Marshall Pétain was a hero of World War I who enjoyed great public popularity. Reynaud had turned to him in May 1940 at the start of the German attack on the Netherlands. In June 1940, given the strong and shared anti-war feelings described above, Pétain was seen by many as the savior of France, able to broker a peace and avoid fighting on national territory. His Vichy-based government was, in fact, an authoritarian regime supported by both the far right wing and more traditional right-wing politicians. In his first years, however, Petain's political base was much broader. It was the Parliament that was elected in 1936 (minus seventy Communist deputies who had been forced out by prime minister E. Daladier, plus others not able to attend the meeting) that had given Marshall Pétain full power.

The Vichy government's political program – the National Revolution – was an appeal to the nationalist right and to French Catholic conservatism. Communists, Jews, Roma[8] and freemasons were stigmatized as the enemies of the State, 'Travail, Famille, Patrie' replaced the motto 'Liberté, Egalité, Fraternité'.

The Vichy regime immediately adopted measures for the review of the naturalizations granted to immigrants since 1927. In July 1940 the French nationality of 15,000 people was revoked, 40 per cent of whom were Jewish. On 3 October 1940

6 In the Southern zone, which was controlled by the Italian army, no anti-Jewish legislation was applied and this made it into an area of protection for Jewish refugees. On 8 September 1943, with the announcement that the king and Marshall Badoglio had signed the armistice with Nazi Germany, however, the Italian army retreated from France and the Jews who had found refuge there were rounded up and deported.

7 Zuccotti, *The Holocaust*, 42.

8 Vichy authorities implemented restrictive measures against Roma even before the German occupation of the country. Deportations of Roma began from occupied France towards the end of December 1941. In the unoccupied zone, Vichy officials interned about 3,500 Roma, the majority of whom were later sent to Buchenwald, Dachau, and Ravensbrück. See 'Genocide of European Roma'.

anti-Jewish legislation was issued, the *Statut des Juifs*. It has been well established by historical research, that the *Statut des Juifs* was not adopted as a consequence of German pressure, but was an independent initiative of Vichy regime.[9]

The anti-Jewish legislation came 'from the government's desire to present a demoralized public with a visible scapegoat for the defeat, from a wish to preempt German regulation of the issue, and from the prejudices of Pétain himself.'[10] Besides, in 1940, Nazi Germany seemed the most likely winner of the war: to issue the *Statut des Juifs* was therefore also a way to secure a prominent role for France in the imagined 'new order' of the future.

The *Statut des Juifs* was to be applied immediately to foreign and French Jews throughout the country. Jewish people were to be excluded from high positions in the French civil service, in the officer corps of the army, and in professions that influence public opinion (teaching, the press, radio, film, and theatre). The statute also stated that a quota system would be devised to limit the presence of Jewish people in the liberal professions (law, medicine, etc). A second *Statut des Juifs* followed in June 1941 and this prohibited Jews from working in the liberal professions, commerce, and also industry. This second decree also stated that no exceptions would be made for Jewish prisoners of war. If returned from captivity, Jewish POW's would be subject to the anti-Jewish laws.

The anti-Jewish measures adopted between 1940 and 1942 had catastrophic consequences for the Jews of France.[11] Jews were deprived of the normal constitutional guarantees granted to citizens and visitors. Even if Pétain did not openly refer to Jews in his public statement, his popularity legitimated the defamation of Jewish people; the 'measures that linked national revival to anti-Semitism dulled the consciences of many French people toward a group officially blamed for everything from high prices to the defeat.'[12]

The Vichy Government's policy and the cooperation of French police with the occupying forces significantly contributed to Jews' subsequent victimization. The *Rafle du Vél d'Hiv*, the massive roundup in which 13,152 men, women, and children were captured in Paris on 16-17 July 1942, for instance, would have been impossible without the active collaboration of the French police forces across the city.

After the arrival of the Allies in Algeria (at the time Algeria was an integral part of French national territory), Nazi Germany occupied the so-called French 'zone libre' and there intensified arrests and deportations of Jewish civilians: a total of seventy four convoys left France between March 1942 and 17 August 1944. All but

---

9 See Paxton, *Vichy France*.
10 Zucotti, *The Holocaust*, 56.
11 Marrus, 'Vichy France and the Jews', 39.
12 Ibidem.

six of these trains arrived at Auschwitz, carrying 73,853 Jewish people in all. The vast majority were gassed upon arrival.[13]

Internal resistance

Pétain's announcement of an armistice with Germany was followed by the capture of more than one and a half million French soldiers by the German army. As a consequence, one of the priorities of the Vichy regime, in order to maintain popular consensus in France, was to provide all possible support to these military prisoners who were transferred to German labor camps, and to help their families. Pétain obtained an assurance from the Germans that the French POWs would be treated according to the terms of the Geneva Convention. He managed to secure the establishment of a charitable network, the 'Prisoner's Family', which operated as a branch of the French Red Cross. This organization worked to support the families of POWs both in the south and in the occupied zone.[14] To allow the return home of POWs, Vichy adopted a scheme called *Relève* (Relief). This consisted in promoting the voluntary departure of three civilian workers in exchange for each liberated POW.

After its initial popularity, however, the Vichy regime lost consensus. By the end of 1942 the brutal methods and wholesale deportation, which the police supported by arresting Jewish men, women and children, shocked popular sensitivities in France, and started to raise protests. In the same period, some prominent Protestant and Catholic clergymen raised their voices to condemn the government's racist policies. By 1943 'a majority of the French population thoroughly disapproved of the persecution of the Jews.'[15] More than the persecution and deportation of the Jews, however, the measure which undermined the regime's legitimacy was the introduction of the *Service de Travail Obligatoire* (STO), i.e. the compulsory work program which forced young French people into German labor camps. This was strongly resented by the entire population. Last but not least, by 1943 the rationing of food and fuel generated widespread popular discontent.

Between 1941 and 1942, a variety of organized resistance groups started to operate across France – both within the occupied and the unoccupied zones.[16] Forms of 'corporate' resistance also emerged in various social spheres including in art, literature and in medicine and the health services (we will address this

13 Zuccotti, *The Holocaust*, 206.
14 See Lagrou, *The legacy*, 106.
15 Poznanski, 'French apprehensions, Jewish expectations', 27.
16 Davies, *France and the Second World War*, 58-59.

subject in more detail below). These movements soon came to be known as the Resistance.

Internal resistance, however, differed across the German-imposed 'border' that divided France. The various key groups that operated in the occupied zone to the north were mostly anti-German. In the unoccupied zone resistance forces fought to undermine the Vichy regime and developed a left-wing program, aiming at radical political change in post-liberation France. In the south the majority of the resistance consisted of left-wing groups close to the Communist Party, the PCF, which from 1941 became the fulcrum of the Resistance.[17] Other groups were led by the Christian Democrats. By 1943 the Maquis, a loosely organized anarchic guerrilla-style movement, particularly strong in rural areas, and southern-based, was operating almost throughout the southern, unoccupied zone.

External resistance

The external Resistance movement was initiated in 1940 by general Charles de Gaulle from London. During the critical time of the Battle for France, then prime minister Reynaud had sent de Gaulle to London by as a Cabinet emissary. Like Reynaud, de Gaulle was implacably opposed to any armistice with Germany. Reynaud's Cabinet, however, collapsed while de Gaulle was still in London. When Pétain announced the armistice with Germany, de Gaulle appealed by broadcast from London to the French to resist the Nazi invasion and later to join in the fight against the Nazi occupiers.

Initially, de Gaulle's Free France group and the internal Resistance groups had very little in common. De Gaulle wanted an army-like resistance force to repulse the Germans, whereas internal Resistance groups tended to operate according to guerrilla tactics and left-wing, populist ideas. They were influenced by the experiences of the Spanish Civil war. The relationship between De Gaulle's supporters and the internal Resistance groups was initially one of mutual mistrust. Internal groups tended to regard those who had left France to join de Gaulle's Free France as deserters and cowards. The external Resistance forces, in their turn, were suspicious of the radicalism and left-wing political ideology of Resistance groups based in France. De Gaulle not only distrusted the left-wing groups, 'but tended to believe that he alone personified the anti-Vichy, anti-German crusade.'[18] By 1942 a sense of pragmatism in the face of a common enemy had served to overcome previous divisions. The military wings of the internal Resistance were united under the aegis of the Secret Army, and thereafter received support from

17 Ibidem, 60-62.
18 Ibidem, 64.

London. Given the predominance of Communists in the internal Resistance, winning Communist support was a vital part of de Gaulle's strategy. In May 1943, the creation of the *Conseil National de la Résistance* established the alliance of Gaullist and Communists in the national French Resistance, and it was immediately recognized by Moscow as the legitimate government of France. In June the de Gaulle-led CFLN (*Comité Français de Libération Nationale*) emerged as a government that would assume power once France was liberated.[19] By May 1944, the CFLN was transformed into the *Gouvernement Provisoire de la République Française* (GPRF) and on 26 August 1944, de Gaulle entered Paris triumphant. By the 23rd of October of that year, de Gaulle's GPRF had been recognized by the Allies. By the end of the wartime period, 'necessity and the force of circumstance had brought external and internal forces into an alliance of sorts; unity and shared purpose was never very strong, but it was just strong enough to enable France to emerge out of the trauma of the Occupation.'[20]

From 'exile' to 'deportation'

By 1942, Gaullist and Resistance propaganda focused mainly on the failure of Vichy's collaboration policies to tackle the question of the liberation of the French POWs. The regime's complicity in delivering French manpower to Nazi Germany was loudly denounced. With the introduction of the *Réleve* and the *Service de Travail Obligatoire,* Gaullist propaganda introduced a significant change in terminology and started to define expatriation to Germany as deportation. With the escalation of Jewish persecution and Jewish deportation, as well as arrests of resistance fighters, deportation became a universal concept, resisted by all in the broad alliance that made up the Resistance. 'In the resistance press and in the propaganda produced in London and Algiers, the distinction between deported Jews, arrested resisters, labour conscripts and workers leaving under the *Relève* or even under socio-economic constraints were deliberately blurred. Even the "exile" of POW's in captivity, the object of Vichy's mysticism, was assimilated into the universal category of "deportation".'[21] In 1943 the establishment of a Commission for Prisoners, Deportees and Refugees under de Gaulle's shadow cabinet further reinforced this blurring of boundaries, and reinforced shared opposition to the deportation policies.[22]

The creation of this Commission reflected de Gaulle's concern with repatriation and reintegration of all expatriates and refugees as a priority of the Resistance,

19 Jackson, *De Gaulle*, 21.
20 Davies, *France and the Second World War*, 64-65.
21 Lagrou, *The legacy*, 111.
22 Ibidem, 112.

and part of the liberation process. On the eve of the Normandy invasion, the Commission was transformed into a Ministry for Prisoners, Deportees and Refugees of the Provisional Government of the French Republic.[23] Repatriation operations were carefully planned by the Ministry and nothing was left to chance: '[e]ven the organization of repatriates into associations was taken care of by the Ministry, with its grand design for a unitary National Movement of Prisoners and Deportees, uniting three branches for POW's, labour conscripts, and political deportees' (a term that also encompassed the Jews).[24]

After the war, however, the idea of a unitary movement looked impracticable. As Rousso puts it: 'hundreds of associations were formed establishing what amounted to a veritable hierarchy of suffering: the volunteer resistance fighter did not wish to be confused with the "racial" deportee; the deportee did not wish to be mistaken for a prisoner of war; the prisoner of war was careful to distinguish himself from the "*deporté du travail*" [STO], the labourer "deported" to work in Germany for the Reich.'[25]

The associations, often in mutual competition, supported different definitions of resistance and deportation, returnee and refugee.

'Déportés et internés résistants' and 'déportés et internés politiques'

Immediately after the war, the definition of who was to be counted as part of the Resistance became a significant obstacle to the plans to form a unitary organization representing all deportees and internees. There were two conflicting definitions among deportee and internee associations. The first, mainly supported by Gaullists, was an exclusively 'combatant' definition of Resistance, i.e. the activity of the resistance fighters as recognized clandestine military formations. The second version, mostly advocated by the Communist party, supported an anti-fascist version of patriotism that regarded all non-combatant victims, as well as the so-called 'racial deportees', i.e. mainly Jews, as part of the Resistance forces.

In 1947, two draft laws were introduced to help define the legal status of a 'deportee'. They reflected the two very different definitions of Resistance mentioned above. When the laws were presented to the National Assembly during the parliamentary debate, the vice president of the Federation of (Resistance) Associations close to the Communist Party took an explicitly 'inclusive' position.[26] He

23 Ibidem, 113-114.

24 Ibidem, 128.

25 Rousso, *The Vichy syndrome*, 24.

26 *Fédération Nationale des Déportés et Internés Résistants et Patriotes* (FNDIRP). The Federation had a large number of Communist members but was did not consist exclusively of Communists.

argued that the law should recognize the equal suffering of different groups of deportees without considering the reasons motivating their arrest and deportation. Including victims of arbitrary arrests within the category of deportees, however, raised a major political problem, as it meant that communists arrested by the Daladier government in 1939 (at the time of the Soviet-German Pact) and subsequently deported to German concentration camps by the Vichy regime could also be accorded the official status of deportees. In August 1948, the Assembly finally adopted the draft law proposed by the Federation of Associations close to de Gaulle's forces.[27] This draft law only referred to 'internees and deportees of the Resistance'.[28] Protests by the groups of deportees and internees who had been left out by this definition soon prompted the National Assembly to pass a second law which also recognized 'political internees and deportees'.[29]

In nearly all respects the text of the second law was a duplicate of the first. The main difference was in terms of the rationale for deportation. Article 2 of the *Statut des déportés et internés résistants* specified that the reason for deportation or incarceration should be 'an act qualified as resistance to the enemy'. Article 2 of the *Statut de déporté et interné politique*, instead, did not require any motivation for arrest, deportation or internment, but just the fact that people were arrested, deported and interned (the only exception was in the case of initial arrest for common law offences). The *déportés et internés résistants* were entitled to recognition and the privileges of Resistance fighters.

For the rest, the same criteria applied in both laws, namely: i) deportation to a prison or a concentration camp in a territory under German control; ii) deportation to camps and prisons of the annexed departments of Alsace Lorraine; iii) internment irrespective of the place of detention for at least three months. (The duration corresponded to the minimum time of active service that entitled servicemen to a war pension. No minimum was required for those who had contracted an illness during internment or had managed to escape.) The title of *déporté* was assigned by the Ministry of *Anciens Combattants* and War Victims, assisted by a commission which included representatives of the Ministries of *Anciens Combattants*, the Interior and Finance and representatives of deportees and internees. The separate commissions (for the recognition of the status of deportee of the Resistance and political deportees) screened the deportees' requests and therefore had the power to penalize political adversaries. Lagrou, for example, reports that:

27 *Fédération Nationale des Déportés et Internés de la Résistance* (FNDIR).

28 Law no. 48-1251 (6 August 1948) '*Statut des déportés et internés résistants*'; and Decree no. 49-427, 25 March 1949.

29 Law no. 48-1404 (9 Septembre 1948) '*Statut des déportés et internés politiques*'; and Decree no. 50-325, 1 March 1950.

> '...Debeaumarchais, the machiavellian secretary-general of the FNDIR, boasted at its national congresses that he had personally obtained the rejection of 75 per cent of applications by members of the National Front, the resistance organization close to the Communist Party, and turned down the applications by arrested participants in the "housewife-demonstrations", organised by communist women's organisations to protest against distribution deficiencies under Vichy.'[30]

Labor conscripts of the STO also requested to be granted the status of deportees. Initially their claims were supported by the Federation of Deportees and Internees, which was close to the Communist Party. Eventually, however, the laborers of the STO were denied the status of Resistance deportees, as the National Commission of Deportees and Internees of Resistance argued that the title of *déporté* was reserved exclusively for those imprisoned in concentration camps. Such a position was reaffirmed more than once by the *Cour de Cassation*, which rejected all appeals presented to it by the association representing the STO's conscripts and formally forbade them to use the title of Resistance deportees.[31]

Deportation pathology

The Provisional Government's solicitous policy towards the repatriated also included paying attention to the condition of their health.[32] Many of the repatriated were in dreadful health after years spent in captivity. By the mid 1940's, the illness and disorders of concentration camp survivors and ex-prisoners were a major focus of French medical literature. Some of the earliest articles were written by doctors who had been interned in concentration camps, and dealt with a wide range of illnesses and disorders that were already observed among camp prisoners before their repatriation.

In May 1945, a group of French doctors who had themselves survived deportation to Buchenwald concentration camp reported their clinical observations to the *Académie de Médecine* (a consultative medical institution of the French government in the field of public health). Their observations centered on the illnesses and dysfunctions caused by prolonged malnutrition, heavy work, and poor sanitary conditions in concentration camps.[33] Among this group were the well-known internist Charles Richet, professor at the University of Paris and Robert Waitz, professor at the University of Strasbourg. By the end of 1945, more medical articles were

30 Lagrou, *The legacy*, 233.
31 See the verdicts of *Cour de cassation*, 23 Mai 1979 and 28 April 1987.
32 See Lagrou, *The legacy*, 120.
33 See Richet and Mans, *Pathologie de la déportation*, 33; Richet, 'Notes sur le typhus exanthématique'.

being devoted to health problems observed among concentration camps' inmates and the repatriates.

In France 'medical resistance' underwent a significant development between 1941 and 1943. In 1941 two Communist doctors, Jean-Claude Bauer and Maurice Ténine, created and edited a clandestine publication, *Le Médecin français,* to wage a campaign against the racist policies of the *Conseil de l'Ordre des Médecins,* as established by the Vichy government under the law of 7 October 1940. *Le Médecin Français* was closely associated with the medical association of the PCF and its circulation increased.[34] In 1943 the journal launched a campaign against the STO, and in December of the same year announced the establishment of the *Conseil Médical de la Résistance.* The journal prompted doctors to engage in the struggle and support the Résistance, to take care of wounded resistance fighters, to use any means to help French people avoid deportation to German territory, and to set up the Health service of the insurrectional army of the *Force Françaises de l'Intérieur.* In 1944 *Le Médecin français* became the organ of the *Comité médical de la résistance* and its publication continued until 1945. By the end of 1942 another clandestine journal, *Le Combat medical,* appeared. It was produced by the Parisian medical group within the *Mouvement National Contre le Racisme* (MNCR), a movement established in July 1942 by the Jewish section of *Main d'oeuvre immigrée* (part of the PCF). The journal denounced anti-Semitism, racism and Nazi medicine, and spread information on the appalling health and sanitary conditions of prisoners and deportees (providing evidence of promiscuity, lack of hygiene, and multiplication of epidemics).

By 1942 a number of doctors had joined the Resistance or were engaged in support activities within clandestine networks. One of the prominent figures was the academic pediatrician Robert Debré who, together with other medical colleagues and medical students, organized a clandestine health service within the Resistance.[35]

By October 1943 this *Service de Santé de la Résistanc*e and the medical wing of the National Front (PCF), were unified in a single organization, the *Conseil Médical de la Résistance* (CMR).

The CMR now regrouped a number of prominent medical professionals, notably among the Parisian academic elite. Because of its composition, the CMR was far more influential than its transitory, covert status might suggest. Robert Debré was

34 Twenty seven numbers were circulated between 1941-1945 and the number of copies went from 150 to 12,000 in 1945. See Poirier and Salaün, *Médecin ou malade?*, 187-196.

35 See 'Témoignage sur le Comité Médical de la Résistance'. Debré was one of only ten Jewish professors left in the country by 1942. As he obtained, in consideration of his professional achievements, a special exemption from the racial laws banning Jews from teaching, he was able to maintain his academic job until September 1943. By September 1943, 'as both a Jew and Resistant he was forced into hiding'. See Zuccotti, *The Holocaust*, 45.

by then one of the CMR's leading members. While he was in hiding, he developed the main lines of a model of comprehensive medical reform that was subsequently adopted nationally in France in 1958.[36] The CMR also effected the establishment in 1944 of the first French health ministry.

By 1946, a great deal of medical literature focused on the kinds of damage produced by starvation, cold, traumatic experiences, and lack of sanitation among deportees and internees. It is noteworthy that a number of medical dissertations were completed during the early post-war years by medical students who were themselves former deportees. Such medical studies emphasized the specific connections between concentration camp living conditions and a wide range of illnesses and disorders. These ranged from heart disease and osteopathy, gastric problems, a range of skin and internal organ conditions to gynecological and neuropsychiatric problems. In 1948, in a joint communication to the *Académie de Médecine*, Charles Richet, Louis-François Fichez,[37] Gilbert Dreyfus, and Henri Uzan called for more attention for the long-term effects of detention on the subsequent longer-term deterioration of survivors' health (which they termed their 'physiological misery'). On the basis of their clinical data, these doctors showed that even years after repatriation, the physiological condition of the survivors predisposed them to resurgences of physical and mental illness and drastically reduced their long-term resistance to a range of infections.[38] The collection of diseases that affected former deportees started to be referred to as *pathologie de la déportation* (deportation syndrome).[39]

Asthenia and traumatic memories

In the immediate post-war years, psychiatric disorders affecting former deportees and internees were dealt with as part of a wider, more general clinical picture dominated by the effects of starvation, infectious diseases, exhausting work, psychological and physical torture and dreadful living conditions.[40] Only a few articles focused

36 See 'Témoignage sur le Comité Médical de la Résistance'.

37 Fichez was interned in Compiègne. With Marcel Paul and Frédéric-Henri Manhès he established the *Fédération nationale des déportés et internés résistants et patriotes* (FNDIRP). See 'Témoignage sur le Comité Médical in Mauthausen'.

38 Quoted in Pross, *Paying for the past*, 83.

39 Initially the term was used informally. By 1956, with the publication of Richet and Mans' book *Pathologie de la déportation*, it became an official term. For bibliographic references on the medical studies conducted in France since the mid 1940's, See Richet and Mans, *Pathologie de la déportation*, 239-255.

40 One exception was the work by psychiatrist psychoanalyst Eugène Minkowski who published a study on psychological disorders in adults, young people, and children who had survived the concentration camps.

exclusively on neuropsychiatric diseases observed in former concentration camp populations.[41] One of the first to study the neuropsychiatric disorders of repatriated deportees was French psychiatrist René Targowla, who had already studied war-related psychiatric disorders after World War I.[42] He started his work in the second half of the 1940's.[43]

In 1950, Targowla described the *asthénie psychique des déportés* (deportees' asthenia syndrome) as a disorder whose main psycho-physical manifestations were asthenia, impairment of drive and vitality, inability to concentrate, and depression.[44] Thinking that psychic asthenia was caused by organic injury of the central nervous system, Targowla and others conducted examinations involving pneumo-electroencephalography, electroencephalography, cerebrospinal fluid diagnosis, and a range of neurological and psychiatric tests. In a random group of 300 former concentration camp prisoners, they found organic injuries of the central nervous system in more than three-quarters of those examined. These organic injuries were termed 'meningoencephalopathic'. Clinicians argued that the outcomes of these examinations supported the hypothesis that mental disorders observed among the sample had a cerebral organic origin. They also pointed out the correlation found between the degree of cerebral damage and the severity of the individual's mental disorder in their sample. They concluded that the neuropsychiatric consequences of deportation were mainly due to an accumulation of strains and trauma interacting with various organic factors (among the most relevant they indicated: long-lasting starvation, infectious diseases, fever, head injuries, low body resistance due to other illnesses, exhaustion from twelve to fourteen daily working hours, and, in particular for women, hormonal damage). They also pointed out that the severity of prisoners' disorders was directly related to the duration of imprisonment.[45]

The symptomatic patterns of deportees' and internees' disorders were, in many respects, similar to those of neurasthenia and traumatic neurosis, i.e. disorders that had become controversial during World War I when large numbers of ser-

41 See for instance Richet, 'Troubles neuro-psychiatriques observés à Buchenwald'.

42 His first publication on this subject (which is co-authored) is: Duhot and Targowla, 'Essay sur la psychose emotive des bombardements'.

43 Targowla, 'Pathological sequelae'. See also Pross, *Paying for the past*, 83.

44 The original meaning of the term 'asthenia' is lack of strength. 'Asthenia' was used since the end of the 19th century as a suffix in nervous and mental medicine as well as in other medical specializations to coin scientific terms. In psychiatry, by the second half of the 19th century, it indicated disorders caused by a diminution of psychic energy: in 1869 American neurologist George Miller Beard described a condition characterized by fatigue, anxiety, lack of concentration, worry and depression caused by the exhaustion of the nervous system energy reserve, which he termed 'neurasthenia'. French psychologist Pierre Janet used the term psychastenia as a kind of *weakness* in the ability to attend to, adjust to, and synthesize one's changing experience. See Janet, *Les obsessions*. In mental medicine, 'asthenia' indicated *mental fatigue*. See, for instance, Deschamps, *Les maladies*.

45 See Venzlaff, 'Mental disorders', 178.

vicemen were suspected of simulating them in order to escape active service and obtain a war pension or some economic compensation. Unlike soldiers, however, concentration camp survivors could hardly be suspected of exaggerating their symptoms of psychological distress. The diagnosis of asthenia emphasized the finding that survivors were more likely to be depressed and were therefore relatively unlikely to externalize their suffering.[46]

Targowla also described the problem of survivors' traumatic memories. In 1950, he published his study on the *syndrome d'hypermnésie emotionelle tardif*, a severe traumatic disorder characterized by haunting memories of the concentration camp. The syndrome, he argued, often appeared some time after repatriation and was frequently associated with amnesia and depression.[47] Several French medical studies based on observations of the illnesses and disorders of former deportees and internees were also presented to an international audience in 1954 at the International Meeting of Social Medicine – on the Pathology of Former Deportees and Internees – a meeting held in Copenhagen in June 1954. The meeting was organized by the International Federation of Resistance Fighters (FIR), a Soviet-supported international 'anti-fascist' organization based in Vienna. From 1954 on the FIR organized several international medical meetings on the illnesses and disorders affecting concentration camp survivors (see chapter 11).

The Decree of May 1953

In the early 1960's, looking back on the previous decade, Charles Richet underlined the crucial role of the FIR meetings in spreading research-based conceptualizations of the medical sequelae of deportation and detention, including a wider recognition of the range of various specific illnesses and even disorders that affected former deportees disproportionately, and continued to affect them many years after their return from the concentration camps.[48]

Richet's own clinical observations of concentration camp pathologies had started in Buchenwald, while he was still one of the prisoners there. His satisfaction with the emergence of this 'new branch of social medicine' was therefore understandable. Once he had returned to France, Richet was one of the first to call public attention to the health damages caused by deportation and internment. Clinical studies conducted by him and his colleagues on the health damage caused by deprivation, trauma, and violence, emphasized the multiple – and often delayed – pathogenic effects of concentration camp experiences. This research

46 Targowla, 'Pathological sequelae'.
47 Targowla, 'Les données de la narcose intraveineuse'.
48 Richet and Mans, *Pathologie de la déportation*, 33-34.

also shaped the legislative provisions of internee and deportee war pensions (the decree of May 1953, see below). The concept of 'medical sequelae' had considerably increased the possibility of establishing a casual link between a variety of illnesses affecting former deportees years after repatriation and their concentration camp experiences. Richet's medical treatise *La Pathologie de la Déportation* was first published in 1956, and soon became a reference book for professionals who conducted medical examinations of deportees and internees. The study appeared in two enlarged editions, in 1962 and in 1980. Richet was aware that all this had only been possible because of the government's support for such research. As he wrote:

> 'In France, deportees have been strongly supported and it is this that has made it possible to secure their rights and give them justice. It is because of the *understanding shown by the government and the National Assembly* that this has been able to happen. We French deportees have a sharp critical spirit and we are not inclined to systematically admire all that is official,[49] but we have to recognize the great honesty of this legislation and the integrity of those who apply it.'[50]

The legislation Richet was referring to here was the law on reparations, and in particular the integration of former deportees into the war pension law introduced by decree in May 1953. It was this law that firmly established guidelines for the classification and evaluation of invalidity due to illnesses contracted during internment or deportation.[51] The 'Introductory Remarks' (*Considérations Générales*) to the decree issued in May 1953 stated that the war had produced specific and severe pathologies among deportees and internees. It also stated that their medical-legal evaluation therefore had to be conducted according to new and specific criteria. Without making any distinctions between different categories of deportees and internees, the text enumerated the deprivations, abuses, and violence which they had suffered. The text also emphasized that, in most cases, former deportees and internees could not produce medical documentation as evidence that their illness was as a result of internment in a concentration camp or prison.[52] The medical-

49 Translation from French and emphasis in the quotation is mine.

50 Richet and Mans, *Pathologie de la déportation*, 35.

51 Decree 16 May 1953 no. 53-438 'déterminant les règles et barèmes pour la classification et l'évaluation des invalidités résultant des infirmités et maladies contractées pendant l'internement ou la déportation' (Journal Officiel 17 May 1953, 4467).

52 '... À l'action propre de armes de guerre se sont ajoutés la sous-alimentation scientifiquement organisée, les transferts de populations, la terreur policière avec les sévices, les compensateur, manque de sommeil, état d'affamement continu, action des intempéries et conditions de l'habitat joints à l'avilissement de la personne méthodiquement recherchée, à l'absurdité et la férocité du mode d'existence, la dégradation et la souffrance morale, la multiplicité et la diversité des chocs affectifs débilitants. Les exécutions sommaires les meurtres, les coups et sévices de tous ordres, les "expériences scientifiques", les accidents, les maladies et infections non soignées et ne dispensant pas du travail forcé ou soignées dans des conditions dérisoires, complétaient un

legal commissions were thus requested to assume that survivors' illnesses were a consequence of deportation and internment, also in the absence of medical documentation. This was not a minor point as it removed the main obstacle to obtaining a war pension. The onus was no longer on the deportee or internee to prove that their illnesses had originated in the concentration camp. Moreover, the decree of 1953 introduced the principle that all former deportees and internees had to be considered as affected by a global deterioration in their health, because of the *syndrome de la misère physiologique chronique progressive des camps*. In fact, the existence of such a generalized condition was considered the basis for their right to reparation. This indication was combined with the careful medical description of a wide range of illnesses and complications that could emerge even years after repatriation. The overall effect was to considerably expand and reshape the idea that there was a causal connection between illnesses and disorders that affected former deportees and internees at a later stage of their life and the hardships they had experienced during internment.

War psychological trauma after World War II

The decree of May 1953 thus established guidelines for the classification and evaluation of invalidity due to illnesses contracted during internment or deportation or as a consequence of that experience, that were different from the guidelines of the war pension legislation. As far as psychological war trauma was concerned, the war pension legislation maintained the diagnostic categories adopted during and after World War I ('psychoneurosis', 'neuropsychasthenia', 'male hysteria'). War trauma remained a disorder that rarely entitled those affected by it to compensation. Subsequent modifications to the war pension legislation issued in the 1950's and in the 1960's[53] did not introduce any relevant changes in relation to the diagnosis or the compensation of psychic war trauma.[54]

The decree of 1953 introduced the new diagnostic categories elaborated by Targowla, i.e. 'deportees' asthenia' and 'emotional hypermnesia' (literally: 'abnormally strong emotional memory of the past') as specific disorders related to the pathology of deportation. The decree's guidelines stressed that these two disorders were not

appareil de destruction de l'homme dont il ne semble pas qu'il y ait l'analogue dans l'histoire. Son application prolongée, massive et indiscriminée (enfants, femmes et hommes de tous âges, de toutes conditions et de toutes origines) a créé une morbidité particulière et nécessite au regard du code des pensions, des dispositions nouvelles sur lesquelles il convient d'attirer l'attention des médecins experts et surexperts et des commissions de réforme.' See decree 16 May 1953, 'Considérations générales'.

53 The 'code des pensions militaires d'invalidité' was passed on 26 April 1951 and a *guide-barème* was issued in 1956 and modified in 1961 and 1963.

54 See Crocq, *Les traumatismes psychiques de guerre*, 341-342.

to be confused with common diagnostic categories such as psychoneurosis and neurasthenia. The problem was that despite the decree's attempt to define these two disorders in an unequivocal way, their symptomatic manifestations strongly resembled those of older diagnoses. Emotional hypermnesia, for instance, was considered a discrete and severely debilitating condition that could last for years. Its symptoms were very similar to those of traumatic psychoneuroses.

The diagnosis of psychological asthenia was even more complex as its symptomatic pattern – physical and mental *fatigue,* emotional instability, inability to concentrate, diminished intellectual abilities, rumination, tendency to isolation – had strong similarities with symptoms of diagnostic categories such as emotional neurosis, neurasthenia, depression and neuropsychasthenia. The 1953 decree's text emphasized that the medical expert should be careful to avoid confusing psychic asthenia with common neurotic and neurasthenic disorders. But the possible diagnostic confusion remained, and this was no minor matter since diagnostic (mis)evaluation could result in a lower percentage of disablement and lower compensation.

It is noteworthy that the text indicated that the patients' attitude during medical evaluation was an important discriminatory criterion for a correct diagnosis. Asthenics were described as patients who had a tendency to minimize their disorders, adopt a self-effacing attitude, and show signs of physical asthenia. Neuropathics, on the other hand, were characterized by their histrionic tendencies, egocentrism, hypochondria, and obsessive thoughts.[55] Such indications were based on moral stereotypes of the genuine, depressive sufferer and the loud-mouthed malingerer, and revealed a deep-seated medical-legal scepticism concerning the medical status of war traumatic neurosis, neurasthenia and the like.

The medical-legal definition of 'deportation pathology' thus introduced a distinction between 'common' and 'exceptional' war-related pathogenic conditions and circumstances, creating a sort of double standard in terms of the medical-legal evaluation that took place.[56] The outcome of this double standard in relation to war trauma was that:

55 Despite these recommendations, the 1963 *circulaire* (administrative memo) addressed to the heads of the *réforme*-centers, medical experts, and presidents of the *réforme*-commissions indicated that the new diagnosis had not gained large currency among military doctors. The *circulaire* reminded administrators and medical specialists involved in the medicolegal evaluation that 'the decree of 1953 had introduced ... the notion that a certain number of illnesses were directly connected with the specific pathology of deportation' and that asthenia was the major and most frequent disorder among them. The *circulaire* added a revised description of asthenia as a psychosomatic syndrome caused by the combination of 'physiological misery', nervous exhaustion and psychological tension. Asthenia, the *circulaire* concluded, was directly related to the particular living conditions of the concentration camp. See Circulaire n. 591/B (16 July 1963) 'relative à la recherche de l'imputabilité de certaines infirmités se rapportant directement à la pathologie spéciale de l'internement et de la déportation'.

56 In 1973 the guidelines concerning the '*pathologie spéciale de l'internement et de la déportation*' were extended to also include to the French POW's who between 1940 and 1945 were imprisoned in Nazi 'punishment camps'

> 'the [reparatory] legislation was correctly applied to deportation victims, both for the diagnosis of the somatic and for the psychic sequaelae. To other groups of victims who suffered from war psychic sequaelae, on the other hand, the reparatory measures were only rarely and then often incorrectly applied.'[57]

In the following decades various developments at the national and international level converged to expand and articulate how the concept of psychological trauma was understood and operationalized in France. The first were related to the changes in theoretical approaches brought about by the increasing influence of psychoanalytic, phenomenological, and psychological approaches within psychiatry. The second was the increased public attention for the psychological conditions of victims of terrorist attacks that followed the appearance, at the end of 1985, of SOS *Attentats*, the first association for the protection of victims of terrorism.[58] Finally, the growing international medical attention for the (often delayed) and long-lasting disorder caused by traumatic events was stirred by the inclusion of the 'Post-Traumatic Stress Disorder' (PTSD) diagnosis in the third edition of the American Psychiatric Association's Diagnostic and Statistical Manual of Mental Disorders (DSMIII) in 1980.[59]

The majority of French psychiatrists were initially critical towards the neo-Kraepelinian approach of the American classification DSMIII, and consequently the PTSD diagnosis was not adopted in French classifications. Nevertheless, the category of PTSD placed psychological trauma at the centre of the psychiatric and medical-legal debate. And the idea that a traumatic event might have delayed psychological effects was not at all new – the same was said of the deportation syndrome after World War II. Many French psychiatrists who showed reservations regarding the DSM approach then readopted (and adapted) the old diagnosis of 'traumatic neurosis' (based on the psychoanalytic concept of neurosis),[60] or coined other terms such as '*traumatisme psychiques*' or '*stress traumatique*'.[61]

in which prisoners were subjected to particularly severe detention conditions. 'Décret n 73-74, 1973 déterminant les règles et barèmes pour la classification et l'évaluation des invalidités résultant des infirmités et malades contractées par des militaires au assimilés au cours de la captivité subie dans certains camps ou lieux de détention' (Journal Officiel, 20 January 1973, 815).

57 Crocq, *Les traumatismes psychiques de guerre*, 341.

58 In the same period the appearance of 'victimology' in French psychiatry and in criminology brought attention to the distressing psychological consequences suffered by victims of crime. See Fassin and Rechtman, *L'Empire du traumatisme*, 163-192.

59 A similar diagnostic category was later included in the International Classification of Diseases by the World Health Organization International (ICD-10, 1992).

60 See Barrois, *Les neuroses traumatiques*.

61 See Fassin and Rechtman, *L'Empire du traumatisme*, 182.

By the mid 1980's a few military psychiatrists were actively involved in the attempt to rehabilitate the concept of psychological war trauma.[62] In those years, a wider recognition of the long-term mental pathologies produced by war trauma was also advocated by associations representing veterans of the so-called 'North Africa operations', i.e. the Tunisian (1952-1954) and Algerian (1954-1962) wars of independence.

In 1983, a medical commission was established by the *Secrétariat d'État aux Anciens Combattants et Victimes de Guerre* in order to ascertain whether veterans of the North African wars were suffering from specific pathologies related to their involvement in the military during those conflicts. In 1985 the Medical Commission working group on mental health problems reported that many veterans suffered from *troubles psychiques de guerre* (equivalent to psychological war trauma); the delayed appearance of these problems and symptoms (*délai très variable de leur apparition*) was also emphasized. However, the working group's report concluded that: "contrary to what had been previously assumed, [such disorders] are not specifically connected with a given conflict" («*absence de lien spécifique avec un conflit donné, contrairement à ce qui avait pu apparaître à l'origine*»).[63] Such evasive conclusions were rejected by the veterans associations and by a number of military psychiatrists, who maintained that veterans of the Tunisian and Algerian wars showed a clear and specific range of mental problems and conditions that could be related to their involvement in these wars. The *Secrétariat d'État aux Anciens Combattants et Victimes de Guerre* promised the establishment of a broader medical commission for the purpose of conducting an in-depth study of the whole issue under dispute.[64] The veterans association requested changes similar to measures already adopted for Vietnam war veterans in the US. At that time, in fact, Post-Traumatic Stress Disorder diagnosis was reaching epidemic proportions among Vietnam veterans, and the US government was already providing many Vietnam veterans with both psychological support and economic compensation. The Algerian war in particular "was, in a sense, France's Vietnam."[65]

62 See, for instance, military psychiatrist Louis Crocq's lecture at the *Congrès de psychiatrie et neurologie de langue française* (1985) entitled 'Traumatic neuroses have to be recognized and compensated'. See Crocq, 'Les névroses traumatiques'.

63 *Journal Officiel du Sénat* (25/05/1989), 798.

64 Ibidem.

65 Gildea, *France since 1945*, 34.

The Algerian war: a traumatic legacy

Between 1954 and 1962 the French army and the Algerian nationalists fought one of the most violent wars of independence of the twentieth century. The experience left deep scars on all sides in the conflict: on the French side, and in Algerian communities affected by the war and divided by fighting. The war also created deep divisions within French society and a sense of guilt about committed atrocities, which served to undermine French national identity.

A French colony since 1830 and then incorporated as French departments from 1848, Algeria had a community of about one million people of French or European descent (*pieds noirs*). The country fell under the jurisdiction of the Ministry of the Interior since the Algerian *départements* were considered integral parts of the national territory of France. In November 1954, when the Algerian nationalists of the *Front de Libération National* (FLN) and the armed National Liberation Army launched an insurrection, there was wide consensus across the domestic French political spectrum that Algeria had to remain French. The FLN insurrection was considered a terrorist act on French territory by all parties in power. Initially the left-wing parties also considered intervention necessary to protect freedom and democracy in Algeria. Some even argued that military intervention in Algeria was a continuation of the French Resistance. Right-wing parties supported intervention with more patriotic arguments about national territorial integrity.

During the eight years that the fighting continued the French government continued to refer to the conflict as an internal 'public order' problem, and to impose censorship on coverage of the 'Algerian events', a term in a way reminiscent of the official use of the term 'Troubles' to describe the war in Northern Ireland or 'police operations' for the colonial war the Dutch fought against Indonesia. Besides the French professional army, the government also called upon those performing national service, the conscripted army, during the Algerian war. Guerrilla methods used by fighters of the *Armée de Libération Nationale* and the support they received from the local population made it almost impossible for the French army to gain control during the course of the Algerian war. By 1956, France had sent more than 400,000 troops to Algeria. Among them were 70,000 young men who, although they had already performed their military service, were drafted back into active military service. Resistance to the recruitment of soldiers for the Algerian war was not viewed sympathetically by any party or trade union.

However, the revelation in 1957 that the French army was systematically using torture and was kidnapping and murdering Algerian nationalists as well as French sympathizers of the FLN, served to undermine the political and moral legitimacy of the French mission in Algeria during the late 1950's. Intellectuals started to denounce the violent abuses of the government's military policy, and public opinion in France started to shift: it withdrew its consent to see this as a legitimate war, fought for defensive purposes.[66] The historically acquired image of the French army as a tool of liberation and civilization started to disintegrate during this period.

After a *coup d'état* by dissident French army officers with the support of the *pieds noirs,* and a French military putsch in Algiers in April 1961, president de Gaulle in May 1961 at Evian came to an agreement with the FLN, which was approved by the French electorate in a referendum held in June 1962.

The unfolding of the political plan, however, was accompanied by an organized campaign of resistance, in the form of a bloody terrorist campaign by the Secret Army Organization (OAS). The OAS consisted of dissident members of the French army – including veterans of Indochina who were determined to restore the French military position, already damaged by losses in Indochina – joined by extreme right-wing nationalists and *pieds noirs.* As independence approached the situation in Algeria in particular became very precarious. There were some 150,000 *harkis,* i.e. Algerians who had remained loyal to and fought alongside the French military forces. Many were killed by the FLN around the time of independence, as were up to 10,000 *pieds noirs.* By the summer of 1962, *pieds noirs,* Algeria's Jews and *harkis* were fleeing en masse to France: nearly two million people arrived from Algeria in just one year.

A conflict that had started as a 'police operation' thus ended up being one of the bloodiest and most unpopular post-colonial wars of the era. Some groups of new immigrants had more difficulties than others – the *harkis* and their families were the least recognized victims of the war. They were left to their own devices and were almost totally ignored by the French government, in spite of their evident and proven loyalty to the official French army. This neglect further discredited the professional army and generated new political and social tensions in metropolitan France.

The experiences of those who had been involved in the war were difficult to reconcile with official censorship and the description of the recent past as 'Algerian events'. The *Fédération National des Anciens Combattants d'Algérie* (FNACA), which was established in 1958, during the war, was unable to obtain veteran cards for its members until 1974. Furthermore, the different interpretations of the conflict by groups that had fought on opposite sides could not be combined in a single narrative. When the FNACA finally proposed 19 March (the date of the Evian Accords) as the official commemoration day for the Algerian war, other French veterans organizations argued that it was impossible to commemorate a sell-out and defeat

66 In a book entitled *La question* the editor of *Alger Républicain,* Henri Alleg, revealed his experience of arrest and torture by French paratroopers. The book was published in February 1958 with a preface by J.P. Sartre and sold 60,000 copies before it was banned six weeks later. Gildea, *France since 1945,* 28-29.

for France. The response of the *pieds noirs* was to establish their own 'Committee for the Respect of the Memory of Those Who Died for French Algeria'. Established in 1981, this organization was chaired by a National Front far-right deputy from 1986 to 1988. At the annual FNACA service on 19 March 1988, a protest was staged by demonstrators who wanted the commemoration to recognize the 10,000 *pieds noirs* and 150,000 pro-French *harkis* forces who had been massacred during the war for Algerian independence.[67] In June 1999 the French Parliament finally passed a law that redefined as 'war' what until then had been consistently referred to as "the operations in North Africa" or "*les événements d'Algérie*" (the Algerian events).[68] The veterans of the Algerian war (as well as those of the Tunisian and Moroccan conflicts) were thus included in the war pension code and obtained the same legal recognition as the veterans of previous wars.

The Decree of 1992: *troubles psychiques de guerre*[69]

In 1988, the *Secrétariat d'État aux anciens combattants et victimes de guerre* established a medical commission for the general revision of the classification of war-related mental disorders and the updating of the disability rates indicated in the national war pensions code. A study on the pathology of the North Africa conflicts was within this medical commission's remit.[70] The results of the commission's work appeared in the decree issued in January 1992, which established the guidelines for the classification and evaluation of the '*troubles psychiques de guerre*' (psychic war disorders).

The decree marks a notable rupture with the past: it proscribes all 'archaic' diagnostic terminologies referring to psychic trauma (such as neurasthenia, psychastenia and hysteria) and all terminology that carries offensive implications for the patient (such as '*pithiatisme*' and '*sinistrose*').

To distinguish itself from the theoretical approach of the North American psychiatric classification DSMIII (1980), the decree substitutes the term PTSD with 'war traumatic neurosis' or traumatic psycho-syndrome, and adopts the World

67 Gildea, *France since 1945*, 36.

68 Loi no. 99-882 du 18 octobre 1999, loi relative à la substitution, à l'expression 'aux opérations effectuées en Afrique du Nord', de l'expression 'à la guerre d'Algérie ou aux combats en Tunisie et au Maroc' parue au JO no. 244 du 20 octobre 1999.

69 Décret du 10 janvier 1992 déterminant les règles et barèmes pour la classification et l'évaluation des troubles psychiques de guerre (JO du 12 janvier1992).

70 *Journal Officiel du Sénat* (10/08/1989) Reply of the Ministry of *Anciens combattants* to the written question of Mr. Yves Le Cozannet (Réponse du ministère: Anciens combattants, Question écrite n° 04060 de M. Yves Le Cozannet publiée dans le JO Sénat du 23/03/1989 – page 469) p. 1230. On this point see also Crocq, *Les traumatismes psychiques de guerre*, 343.

Health Organization's diagnostic guidelines of the International Classification of Diseases (ICD-10, 1992).

Traumatic psycho-syndrome is here defined in the most general terms possible as a (subjective) reaction to a single traumatizing event or series of events; a reaction that has, in general, a delayed onset. In 2000, in a *circulaire* that further specified the decree's criteria of application, traumatic psycho-syndrome is defined as a 'psychic wound', "an unquestionable injury of the individual psychic personality caused by one or more external traumatic events."[71] In other words, the traumatic event is considered the main psycho-pathogenic factor. Such a reference reinforces the 1992 decree, which prohibits all theoretical reference to constitutional theories postulating an individual predisposition to the development of psychological problems in the diagnostic process. Furthermore, the assimilation of psychological integrity with physical integrity considerably raises the status of war-related mental disorder and improves the invalidity rate assigned to traumatic war disorders.[72]

Algerian war: divided memories and common suffering

By the 1990's, the difficult and controversial legacy of the Algerian war gradually resurfaced in the public debate.[73] Since then a number of books and articles have appeared on the memories of Algerian war. Archival documents and new revelations confirmed previous denunciations of violence, abuses, and illegal practices perpetrated by the French police in their repression of demonstrations against the conflict (in metropolitan France)[74] and by the French army in Algeria. After decades of denial and censorship, the systematic and massive use of torture by the French army was publicly confirmed by some of the same French generals who had used such methods during the Algerian war. In 2000, an article was published by the newspaper *Le Monde* based on the testimony of Louisette Ighilahriz, a former member of the Algerian *Armée de Libération Nationale* who had been captured by the French army and tortured for months.[75] Shortly after that, in an article pub-

71 Circulaire no. 75/DEF/SGA/DSPRS/DIR/XR/AL du 18 juillet 2000 'relative à l'application du décret du 10 janvier 1992 modifiant le chapitre des troubles psychiques de guerre du guide-barème des invalidités.'

72 See Lebigot and Colas Benayoun, 'Reconnaissance et réparation'.

73 See '17 octobre 1961: la longue liste de morts des archives de Paris', *L'Humanité*, 23 October, 1997.

74 In 1997, in an interview to the newspaper *Le Monde*, the director of the Paris Archive confirmed that documents still unavailable for public consultation confirmed the killing by the police of at least 90 people during the police attack to the peaceful demonstration of 17 October 1961,in which some 30,000 Algerians protested against the curfew imposed by the prefecture of police. The prefect of the Parisian police Maurice Papon who was responsible for the orders leading to the 'Paris massacre', in the 1980's was judged and convicted for ordering the arrest and deportation of 1,560 Jews between 1942 and 1944.

75 Beauge, 'Torturée par l'armee française'.

lished in the same newspaper, General Massu, who at the time was head of the paratrooper forces in Algeria, openly admitted (and regretted) the adoption of such methods by the army.[76] Further admissions by Massu's right-hand man, general Paul Aussaresses, brought new evidence for his direct involvement in twenty-four illegal executions of Algerians and two killings disguised as suicides, confirming the direct responsibility of the French government in the adoption of torture by the French army.[77]

The reopening of the debate on torture and on the extraordinary amount of violence that had characterized the 'dirty war' brought renewed psychiatric attention for the *troubles psychiques de guerre* in relation to the Algerian conflict. In December 2000, an article published by *Le Monde* suggested that 350,000 of the two million veterans of the Algerian war could still be suffering from (unreported) post-traumatic disorders caused by their war experiences. The article voiced the concerns of psychiatrists who maintained that veterans were reluctant to ask for psychotherapeutic help because of their feelings of guilt and shame for the actions they had performed (or witnessed) during the war. Following the arguments of traumatic psycho-syndrome, military psychiatrists like Bernard Sigg,[78] Claude Barrois, and Louis Crocq[79] called for more psychological attention for veterans' troubles and improved medical facilities.[80]

Two years later, with the establishment of the *Société franco-algérienne de psychiatrie* (SFAP) by French and Algerian psychiatrists, the discussion on the post-traumatic consequences of the Algerian war on veterans was extended to include the memories of other groups whose memories were linked, in different ways, to both the Algerian and the French societies such as the *harkis*, the *pieds noirs* and their children, and also the Algerian veterans, and the children of Algerians executed by the French army. The first meeting of the SFAP, significantly entitled 'Suffering and memory. The Algerian war, 1954-1962',[81] launched an appeal to conduct epidemiological studies in both French and Algerian society on the *troubles psychiques* caused by the war. Along with professional concerns for the

76 Beauge, 'Je me suis résolu à la torture'.

77 In 2001, General Paul Aussaresses indicated that the orders of torture and illegal executions of FNL members and sympathizers that he had carried out on Massu's orders, came from the French government. Aussaresses justified the use of torture in the Algerian conflict as necessary under the emergency circumstances. See Aussaresses, *Services spéciaux*.

78 Together with Claude Barrois and Serge Bornstein, two other psychoanalysis-oriented psychiatrists, Bernard Sigg is the author of one of the first French reports on war psychological troubles with delayed appearance. See C. Barrois, S. Bornstein, B. Sigg, 'Rapport sur les troubles psychiques de guerre d'apparition differées', AMIF, Numéro spécial 'Neuropsychiatrie', hors série no. 34 sous la direction de S. Bornstein, supplément au no. 348, 59-65, septembre 1986.

79 See Barrois, *Les névroses traumatiques*, and Crocq, *Les traumatismes psychiques de guerre*.

80 Beauge, '350,000 anciens d'Algérie'.

81 Congrès de la Société Franco-Algérienne de Psychiatrie, 'Souffrances et mémoires'.

still underdetected and untreated troubles of war veterans, the psychiatrists and psychoanalysts emphasized the common denominator of suffering that linked together war experiences of different groups. The different experiences (and different responsibilities) of military or social groups that had used, witnessed, or been victimized by the violence of the war were thus redefined as a common and generalized experience of psychological trauma. As psychoanalyst Alice Cherki put it, healing implied a "transformation of individual suffering into a memory that… [could] be shared by everybody".[82]

Conclusion

Deportation pathology and its categories of deportee asthenia and emotional hypermnesia closely reflect professional, political and social concerns of French society immediately after the war. The initiative and the engagement of doctors who themselves were former deportees, the influence of the medical resistance network, and the interests of the various emerging associations met with a combination of political and health concerns by the French government vis-à-vis the mass of returning deportees and internees. On the one hand, the May 1953 decree that introduced the deportation pathology was thus an indication of the particular attention that the government reserved for various groups of deportees and internees (former resistance fighters, Jews, political opponents). On the other, it was a way to avoid making distinctions between these groups. The guidelines for the medical-legal evaluation of survivors' rights to reparation emphasized the extraordinary amount of persecution, violence, deprivation and suffering that deportees went through, but carefully avoided specific reference to the different groups of victims. This enabled the government to apply a reparatory policy for the physical and mental disorders suffered by internees and deportees without having to acknowledge the dynamics that contributed to their victimization, and deal with the specific problems that affected the various groups of victims in post-war society. The medical research on deportation pathology also developed as a consequence of the Cold War and the international tensions it produced. The studies on the traumatic sequaelae of deportation and internment received the international support of the (pro-Communist) International Federation of Resistance Fighters. In the decades that followed the concept of psychological trauma was expanded and articulated as a consequence of the increasing influence of psychoanalytic, phenomenological, and psychological approaches within psychiatry, the emergence of associations for the protection of victims of terrorist attacks, and the

82 See Bernard, 'L'agonie psychique'.

increasing popularity (and scientific legitimacy) of the Post-Traumatic Disorder diagnosis. In 1992, the initiative of some military psychiatrists and the claims of veterans associations led to a reshaping and a full rehabilitation of the war trauma concept in French legislation.

Since the mid 1980's, these developments in psychiatry were paralleled by requests for reparation and public recognition of some of the associations that represented the veterans of the North African war, in particular the Algerian war. The veterans associations' requests coincided with the initiative of the military psychiatrists. The establishment in 1988 of a medical commission charged with the revision of the classification of war mental disorders led to the introduction, in 1992, of the PTSD concept in the French diagnostic system ('traumatic neurosis' or 'traumatic psycho-syndrome'). By the 1990's, the controversial legacy of the Algerian war – an unrecognized and most violent conflict that left unresolved political and social issues and deeply marked French and Algerian societies – re-emerged forcefully in French society. The first official acknowledgement by the French state that the "police operation in Algeria" was in fact a post-colonial war (1999) and the public admissions by high-ranking officers of the French army regarding systematic torture and illegal killing during the conflict were paralleled by a renewed psychiatric attention for the post-traumatic disorders of Algerian veterans. With the establishment of the French-Algerian psychiatric society, the psychiatric approach allowed a redefinition of different, and mutually contradictory war memories and experiences of different groups in the neutral and all-encompassing terms of post-traumatic disorder.

4 Negotiating Victimhood in East and West Germany 1945-2005

» *Svenja Goltermann*

When World War II ended in the European theatres of war in May 1945 the people in this 'destroyed continent' were confronted with the consequences of an escalation of violence and destruction which in this form had never existed before.[1] In September 1939 National Socialist Germany had unleashed a war whose effects were disastrous. According to estimates the total number of dead amounted to over 150 million, of whom more than half were civilians.[2]

Of course the death toll, gigantic as it is, only throws light on a part of the catastrophic effects of this war. It cannot measure at all what it meant to lose relatives or friends, to be injured or crippled, any more than the real suffering of those who had to bear dreadful hunger as a consequence of material destruction. The photographs of the destroyed cities can only serve here as 'a visual shorthand for the horrors of war',[3] permitting us to grasp at least approximately the immense extent of the destruction, misery and experience of loss, which was unquestionably greater in Eastern than in Western Europe. Nor were the Germans spared this suffering. This already became apparent as the war in the East intensified and the numbers of dead and wounded soldiers on the Eastern front increased substantially. Around 80% of the almost 5 million dead of the *Wehrmacht* fell in the last two years of the war.[4] And in the bitter and futile 'final battle' between January and May 1945 alone more than one and a half million soldiers and civilians lost their lives.[5] This 'total war' had, of course, already reached the civilian population long before as a result of the bombardment of the cities by the Western allies. The extent of the destruction in many German cities was inconceivably great. About 600,000 civilians died in the air attacks and millions of people lost

1 For a survey see Judt, *Geschichte Europas*, particularly 29-82, the quotation is on 82; see also Herbert and Schildt, *Kriegsende in Europa*, 7-34, and the other articles in this collection.

2 This figure includes the dead up to the capitulation of Japan on 2 September 1945. Cf. Mazower, *Der dunkle Kontinent*, 308.

3 Judt, *Geschichte Europas*, 32.

4 Herbert and Schildt, *Kriegsende in Europa*, 25.

5 Vgl. Geyer, *Endkampf*, 37-67, 37.

their homes.[6] A further external indicator for the social destruction and misery can be seen in the flight of around 14 million refugees and exiles to the West, which was triggered off by the advance of the Red Army in Winter 1944/1945. About 1.7 million of them died.[7] In addition it is certain that tens of thousands of women were the victims of mass rape by Soviet soldiers during their flight. For the Germans as well this war thus developed into a catastrophe which by no means ended with the capitulation. Millions of families were destroyed or torn apart and hunger was rampant, particularly in the big cities, so that fear concerning personal survival continued after the end of the war. Hundreds of thousands of prisoners-of-war also suffered under the after-effects of the war. Thousands died in the infamous 'Rhine Meadow Camps', which the Americans had set up along the Rhine for the internment of prisoners of war; the estimates lie between 6,000 and 40,000 dead.[8] However, the death rate in Russian prisoner of war camps exceeded this figure by far. It is estimated that about a third of the two to three million German soldiers captured by the Soviet forces died in the prisoner of war camps or on the way to them.[9] The stresses and strains of Soviet imprisonment were immense in comparison to the situation of the prisoners of war under the custody of the Western allies. In spite of the miserable living conditions and catastrophic undernourishment most of the prisoners were subjected to severe forced labor. The last of them would only return from Soviet imprisonment in 1956.

These measurable consequences of the war have long been known. In the now comprehensive historical literature on the recollection of the war and National Socialist persecution it is emphasized how personal suffering has been thematized by Germans since the end of the war. Numerous examples can in fact be found for both West and East Germany, which reveal the way in which the Germans emphasize their own status as victims, although the ideological form in which it presents itself differs in East and West and is profoundly influenced by the Cold War.[10] For example, in the official commemorations of the bombardment of Dresden and its civilian population in the GDR since 1950 the mourning for the victims is accompanied by the attribution of the responsibility for the suffering incurred to 'Western imperialists'.[11] Conversely, on the political stage of the Federal Republic there is no lack of statements placing the blame for the suffering of the

6 Henke, 'Deutschland', 339.

7 Figures taken from Hans-Ulrich Wehler, *Deutsche Gesellschaftsgeschichte*, 944.

8 On this point see Smith, *Die 'vermisste Million'*; also Overmans, 'Die Rheinwiesenlager 1945', 233-264.

9 See Hilger, *Deutsche Kriegsgefangene*, 71.

10 For a concise summary see Moeller, 'Germans as victims?', 147-194, 153ff.

11 See, among others, Niven, 'The GDR and the bombing of Dresden', 109-129; also Behrenbeck, 'Between pain and silence', 37-64, which examines the 'strategies of memory' in official commemorations in the early Federal Republic and the GDR.

refugees and exiles from the East and of the German prisoners of war in Soviet camps above all on 'Soviet terror'.[12] Finally, official statements on both sides of the border conceded that most of the Germans – including the soldiers – were essentially only the victims of Hitler and his 'criminal' elite. They had started this destructive war, which, however, 'was lost by everybody'.[13]

These findings illuminate the way in which Germans dealt with mass death and excesses of violence in the past and provide insights into the problem as to which kind of recollection of the National Socialist war and its dead were regarded as politically useful and socially necessary in the Federal Republic and the GDR. But this by no means clarifies the extent to which personal suffering and mental complaints resulting from this destructive war and National Socialist persecution were officially perceived, thematized and acknowledged. But the enduring immaterial damage resulting from the extreme violence of the war and from National Socialism in Germany and other countries, which continued beyond the post war reconstruction, has only attracted attention in recent years. More and more frequently we come across the assumption that the post-war societies which in part cleared away the material damage caused by the war at a breathtaking speed had been 'traumatized'. However, attributions of this kind present problems. Trauma research has indeed made its contribution to the questioning of the decades-long assumption that after this apocalypse of war and genocide many European societies had simply found their way back to 'normality'. It has for the first time drawn attention to the problem of a possible continued presence of violence in the private lives of all the survivors of this criminal war. Nevertheless the retrospective application of the concept of trauma is deceptive as it conceals more than it brings to light on the way the personal experience of the violence and the horrors of war as dealt with after 1945. In fact, it must rather be made clear that the assumption of a traumatization of the participants in the war is itself the product of an historical interpretative process which itself must first be clarified. It is, namely, a central assumption of the following account that the development of the scientific concept of trauma and its establishment in society must themselves be historicized.

In fact the perceptual horizon of society on the psychological consequences of these violent events changed fundamentally in the decades after World War II. This process evidently occurred in dependence on the state of psychiatric knowl-

12 The differences between the two states in regard to refugee policies and to the agitation of the relevant organizations are made clear in Ahonen, *After the expulsion,* and by Ther, *Deutsche und polnische Vertriebene.* On the returned prisoners of war, see Biess, *Homecomings,* with impressive examples for the constructions of the victim in both East and West Germany; see also Morina, 'Instructed silence', 323-343.

13 Moeller, 'War stories', 3.

edge dominant at the time.[14] In what follows, therefore, psychiatry will be examined as the source of interpretative patterns through which the public perception of human ways of coping with extreme experiences and the consequent suffering was considerably changed. The (self-)perception of people as victims of repression and terror did not remain unaffected either, as will be clearly shown later. In this regard the developments in both West and East Germany will be considered. Attention will be paid, in particular, to the international work on the state of knowledge, which played a role in both West and East Germany, and to the application of this knowledge in each of the countries under the given political circumstances. In both German states, namely, the established psychiatric school of thought stood not only within the shared tradition of German psychiatry since World War I. It also stood within the context of international science, which felt challenged by the large number of victims of the war and particularly by the new quality of the persecution perpetrated by the National Socialists. It can, therefore, be assumed that we are dealing with a case of the international 'scientific community', whose members in both German states were guided by their respective political and social givens and who strongly influenced the culture of memory in both countries with their rules on what is sayable. It was only after German reunification that the question arose as to how the West German discourse on the definition of a victim could provide a new regulation of the language to be used for the victims of persecution under the SED-regime.

Normalization

In view of the extreme strains to which both soldiers and civilians were subjected during the war and the post-war period it is not surprising that many doctors attempted to fathom the effects of these barbaric destructive forces on peoples' behavior. The approach of the psychiatric experts was indeed particularly pertinent, as the state had, during World War I, handed over to the psychiatric profession the competence for finding causal explanations for the mental sufferings of soldiers and for bringing the serious problem of 'war neuroses' under control. As the first medical periodicals reappeared in the territories occupied by the Western allies after World War II the claim to maintain this interpretative privilege was clearly expressed. Psychiatrists made it indubitably clear that they had a special responsibility in this question. From their point of view it was necessary to be on one's guard. Above all a close eye had to be kept on the situation in order to ensure that the war veterans did not once again assert the existence of mental complaints

14 For a detailed treatment see Goltermann, *Die Gesellschaft der Überlebenden.*

as a justification for the claim to a war victim's pension. Why should these 'existential wishes and security desires' – the true cause of this suffering, as the Nuremberg doctor Walter von Baeyer pointed out – not make their appearance in the post-war period as well, particularly in view of the prevailing economic distress?[15]

The medical periodicals were without doubt among the most important forums in which the psychiatrists could exchange their opinions on the psychopathological effects brought about by the devastation of this war. The reports of psychiatrists soon appeared, aiming to explain the evidently conspicuous behavior of many people in post-war Germany. Among them it was possible to observe a remarkable 'quietness'; some doctors spoke of an 'impression of torpidity'[16] or, like one doctor from Dresden, pointed to a particularly widespread 'apathy'.[17] Karl Bonhoeffer, in the meantime 74 years old and a recognized authority for psychiatrists in both East and West Germany, felt that the population of Berlin had changed in a striking fashion. 'The complaints about the deterioration of memory and retentiveness and of the ability to concentrate are fairly general' he pointed out, whereby 'exhaustion and affective disturbances' also occur in public. He explained: 'In the railway stations one can encounter at all times sleeping men and women, a general weariness of mood, a lack of the need to communicate, a tendency to explode easily for the slightest reason in the overfilled trains, glum, haggard, pale faces, disagreeable, peevish behavior' – there was virtually no end to Bonhoeffer's descriptions.[18] But like many of his other colleagues he was not astounded at this conspicuous behavior. It had been possible to observe such phenomena in World War I as well. But this time they were much more frequent than then, according to Bonhoeffer, for whom the explanation was all too obvious. In World War II the civilian population had been subjected to much greater stress as a result of the bombardment, the war within Germany and the flight from the East. On the basis of his own medical experience in 1946 a colleague from Dresden even formulated it as follows: 'The main victims of the war are the seriously disabled, the surviving dependants of the fallen, the displaced persons and those totally bombed out of their homes.'[19]

---

15 Walter von Baeyer, 'Zur Statistik und Form der abnormen Erlebnisreaktionen in der Gegenwart', in: *Der Nervenarzt 19* (1948), 402-408.

16 See, e.g. Jürg Zutt, 'Über den seelischen Gesundheitszustand der Berliner Bevölkerung in den vergangenen Jahren und heute', in: *Ärztliche Wochenschrift 1* (1946), 248-250, 250; Von Baeyer, 'Statistik', 408.

17 See Henßge, 'Reaktive psychische Erkrankungen in der Nachkriegszeit', in: *Psychiatrie, Neurologie und medizinische Psychologie 1* (1949), 133-137, 133.

18 Karl Bonhoeffer, 'Vergleichende psychopathologische Erfahrungen aus den beiden Weltkriegen', in: *Der Nervenarzt* 18 (1947), 1-4, 4. On the percecption of Bonhoeffer in East Germany, see, for example, Christel H. Roggenbau, 'Karl Bonhoeffer zum Gedächtnis', in: *Psychiatrie, Neurologie und medizinische Psychologie 1* (1949), 225-230.

19 Henßge, 'Reaktive psychische Erkrankungen', 134. In the Soviet Occupied Zone/GDR there was no official reference to refugees or exiles but only to 'resettlers' (*Umsiedlern*). On this point see Ther, *Deutsche und polnische Vertriebene*.

There could be no question therefore, either in West or East Germany, that psychiatrists were not aware of the mental stress prevailing during the war and the post-war period. In their eyes too stress, suffering and tension could still be found in post-war Germany. Nevertheless the psychiatric experts agreed that this conspicuous behavior did not amount to an 'illness'. They agreed, above all, that the changed forms of behavior of those affected would disappear again after some time. This opinion was at all events supported by the dominant psychiatric theories on the 'nature' of man and the normality of his capacity to cope with mental problems, theories which could apparently still be maintained after the war.[20] According to the theories the human organism possesses an amazing capacity to compensate for even the most severe mental strains. For this reason long persisting mental complaints and disturbances were not to be expected. It seemed equally out of the question that the war could trigger off serious mental illnesses such as, for example, schizophrenia.

Against a frequently held assumption it must be said that this way of seeing the issues was not a product of National Socialism.[21] It was not even restricted to German psychiatry. It can rather be traced back to the scientific conclusions drawn and established in German psychiatry in the course of World War i, which also gained a foothold in other European countries.[22] The assumption that this psychiatric point of view involved a purely instrumental understanding of the clinical picture in the interests of the requirements of war is clearly inadequate. It is rather the case that a series of empirical observations and therapeutic experiences during World War I hardened the assumption, long advocated by some psychiatrists, that mental disturbances could not be brought about by exogenous stress if indications of organic damage were lacking. For a psychiatry predominantly oriented on the natural sciences, which thus began to open itself up to the explanatory approaches of psychoanalysis, it became possible to explain in a scientifically convincing manner that the frequently occurring manifestations of trembling, shaking and paralysis during World War I were 'functional disturbances'. As the majority of the soldiers had not developed symptoms of this kind, even under severe strain, a mentally determined 'flight into the illness' could be assumed; in addition the existence of a genetically determined cause seemed plausible.

The psychiatric readings of the perceived conspicuous behavior in post-war Germany were determined to such a high degree by these established basic

20 See, among others, Bonhoeffer, 'Vergleichende psychopathologische Erfahrungen'; Hans-Werner Janz, 'Psychopathologische Reaktionen der Kriegs- und Nachkriegszeit', in: *Fortschritte der Neurologie, Psychiatrie und ihrer Grenzgebiete* 17 (1949), 264-293, and the 'Protokoll der zweiten Tagung der Gesellschaft für Psychiatrie und Neurologie, Jena', in: *Psychologie, Neurologie und medizinische Psychologie* 2 (1950), 347-348 (Haenisch, *Psychiatrische und neurologische Beobachtungen während der Flucht*, 1945).

21 See. e. g. Pross, *Paying for the past.*

22 See, among others, Lerner, *Hysterical men*; Micale and Lerner, *Traumatic pasts*; Shephard, *A war of nerves.*

assumptions that one can almost speak of a stubborn self-perpetuation of the psychiatric approach. 'Massive psychogenic manifestations' of long duration seemed in any case to be rare – that could evidently be asserted both for the soldiers of the *Wehrmacht* and for the civilian population affected by the bombing war. It was a case of 'simple startle reactions' which ought to have been treated after the bombardments. And in general these mental disturbances were 'overcome after hours or at most days'.[23] 'When life itself is at stake one does not have time to be ill', a psychiatrist practicing in West Germany explained, who, like most of his colleagues, was completely convinced of the functional character of disturbances of longer duration.[24] Bonhoeffer provides a similar formulation: 'In the case of the frightening effects of the exploding bombs on the civilian population the wish to flee into the illness makes no sense', he argues. Again, he suggests that for the homecoming soldiers 'hysterical reactions' had become meaningless for a completely different reason: the civilian population, which itself had experienced so much strain during the war 'had acquired a better yardstick for measuring the effects of harrowing experiences' and was quite simply 'more sparing in its willingness to show compassion'.[25]

From the point of view of the German psychiatrists the disappearance of 'war neuroses' in the shape of 'tremblers' was unquestionably decisive proof that the path followed since World War I of denying the causal relationship between the violence of war and mentally determined suffering was the right one. Nevertheless it was by no means the case that psychiatrists in West and East Germany concluded without exception in favor of functional disturbances. Another explanation for conspicuous behavior clearly existed, namely 'states of physical exhaustion' caused by extreme physical exertion and, above all, by hunger. 'The psycho-physical interplay makes it probable that hunger favored the pathological repercussions of mental commotion', an East German psychiatrist explained in 1949,[26] and he would have found the support of his West German colleagues. Immediately after the war many of them had already expressed opinions along these lines in the professional periodicals, which had resumed publication earlier in the West. In view of the catastrophic conditions of undernourishment and the rampant hunger above all in the towns – Bonhoeffer spoke of adults with a body weight of 35 to 40 kg – hunger provided an obvious explanation for the conspicuous behavior of many civilians.[27] In this regard too, the psychiatrists in all the occupied zones

23 Janz, 'Psychopathologische Reaktionen', 268.
24 Kurt Beringer, 'Über hysterische Reaktionen bei Fliegerangriffen', in: Heinrich Kranz (ed), *Arbeiten zur Psychiatrie, Neurologie und ihren Grenzgebieten*, 131-138, 136.
25 Bonhoeffer, 'Psychopathologische Erfahrungen', 4.
26 Henßge, 'Reaktive psychische Erkrankungen', 133.
27 See, among others, Jürg Zutt, 'Über den seelischen Gesundheitszustand', 248; Bonhoeffer, 'Psychopathologische Erfahrungen', 4, and Manfred in der Beeck, 'Psychische und charakterliche Veränderungen bei Hun-

thus followed the established state of psychiatric knowledge, as cases of this kind had after all been observed since World War 1. Nevertheless, in the professional public debates of East and West Germany a striking difference came to light: the question of how to interpret the psychological constitution of the soldiers returning from Soviet imprisonment was a problem which was discussed exclusively in the West and ultimately came to enjoy more and more attention. In contrast, not a single word was written on the subject in the leading professional journal of the East German psychiatrists throughout the whole period of publication, commencing in 1949.

Much can be said for the assumption that this silence was due to the official requirements of socialist friendship among the peoples. The formation of the ideological blocks thus had its effects on the scientific discourse, although it would be going too far to speak of an iron curtain between East and West German science.[28] As the periodical *Psychiatrie, Neurologie und medizinische Psychologie,* which was published in Leipzig, shows, the scientific findings of West German psychiatrists continued to be closely observed in Eastern Germany and were not seldom taken up.[29] It was even possible to find euphoric accounts of the modernity of psychiatric institutions in the West and of the therapeutic approaches adopted there.[30] But as far as the prisoners of war returning from Soviet camps were concerned there was silence. Other sources reveal, however, that doctors in the Soviet Occupied Zone were confronted directly after the war with the substantial health problems of prisoners returning from the Soviet camps. For example, a doctor in a camp for returning prisoners of war in the Soviet Occupied Zone not only explained to the East Berlin authorities that the former prisoners of war were suffering from a variety of physical and mental ailments such as undernourishment and depression. He also reported that those affected often even broke down 'without any recogniz-

gerzuständen (Beobachtungen in Gefangenschaft 1945/46 und Heimat 1947/48)', in: *Hippokrates 20* (1949), 44-47, 46f.

28 There are several examples supporting this thesis, see e.g. Bruno Lewin, 'Neurologisch-psychiatrische Untersuchungen und Beobachtungen an deutschen Kriegsgefangenen in Ägypten 1941-47', in: *Psychiatrie, Neurologie und medizinische Psychologie 1* (1949), 230-234. For a more general discussion of the argument, see Eghigian, 'The psychologization'; Eghigian, 'Was there a communist psychiatry?'.

29 See, among others, Herbert Zenk, 'Produktive Gestaltung der Fürsorge für Hirnverletzte', in: *Psychiatrie, Neurologie und medizinische Psychologie 2* (1950), 274-280; D. Müller-Hegemann, 'Betrachtungen zum Kongreß der Gesellschaft Deutscher Neurologen und Psychiater des Jahres 1953', in: *Psychiatrie, Neurologie und medizinische Psychologie 6* (1954), 203-209; 'Protokoll der Tagung der Medizinisch-wissenschaftlichen Gesellschaft für Psychiatrie und Neurologie an der Karl-Marx-Universität Leipzig (1955)', in: *Psychiatrie, Neurologie und medizinische Psychologie 8* (1956), 154-158 (contribution Dietrich).

30 See 'Eindrücke eines Besuchs in den westfälischen Anstalten Lengrich und Gütersloh', in: *Psychiatrie, Neurologie und medizinische Psychologie 9* (1957), 241-248; Ernst Kluge, 'Über psychotische Störungen bei Erschöpfung. Aus der Psychiatrischen und Nervenklinik Kiel', in: *Psychiatrie, Neurologie und medizinische Psychologie 3* (1951), 10-15.

able organic disorder'.[31] But there was no question of assuming that these mental ailments could be traced back to the experience of the prisoner of war camps.

For the psychiatric experts in the Western occupied zones this was at first also inconceivable, although, as Walter von Baeyer summarized the situation, the 'mental constitution' of many of the returned prisoners of war was characterized by striking 'contact deficits' and a general difficulty in 'taking up again old relationships in the family, the occupation and the entire social environment and in establishing new ones.'[32] However, the psychiatrists in 'the West' interpreted this state, which could evidently be observed in *all* of the returned prisoners of war, as a kind of avoidance reaction in the face of the reality of a 'collapsed society' and tended to attribute it essentially to personal 'disposition'. The serious physical emaciation which could be observed among countless returned prisoners of war alone suggested the assumption, as in the case of civilians as well, that the conspicuous behavior could be attributed to the in some cases severe malnutrition and undernourishment. Such a reading was also supported by the colleagues in internal medicine, who introduced the concept of 'hunger disease' or also of 'dystrophy' into the discussion among the medical experts.[33] From the point of view of the medical fraternity it could therefore be assumed that with the improvement of nutrition the mental condition of the returned prisoners of war and of the German population in general would necessarily be 'normalized'.[34]

In West Germany at least it was not long before both the psychiatrists and their internist colleagues admitted that this prognosis was all too optimistic, although it did seem to fit for the large majority of the population. After the currency reform the psychiatrists at any rate gained the impression that 'overcoming the lean years' had let to a leveling out of the 'psychological losses'.[35] The so-called 'late returnees' from Soviet imprisonment, who began to arrive in the Federal Republic at the beginning of 1949, made a 'fundamentally more favorable impression' than the returnees of the previous years, both with regard to their somatic capacities and to their mental constitution. When around 8,000 'returnees from Russia' arrived at a camp for returnees in the 'West' their nutritional condition was obviously such

31 See Biess, *Homecomings*, quotation on 92.

32 See Von Baeyer, 'Statistik', 407.

33 On this point see, e. g. Hans Malten, 'Heimkehrer', in: *Medizinische Klinik 41* (1946), 593-600. Von Baeyer, 'Statistik', 407, was one of the first to take up their interpretation in discussions among psychiatric experts. In the psychiatric patients' files of the von Bodelschwinghschen Anstalten in Bielefeld/Bethel the diagnosis 'dystrophy' is encountered from 1948 on, although it was only considered very tentatively as a possible cause of the mental disturbances. See, among others, the Hauptarchiv der von Bodelschwinghschen Anstalten (=HBAB), Bestand Morija, 4590.

34 This was predicted by Von Baeyer, 'Statistik', 407, among others; see Gerhard Schmidt, 'Gestaltwandel von Massenreaktionen auf Kriegs- und Nachkriegsüberlastung', in: *Fortschritte der Neurologie, Psychiatrie und ihrer Grenzgebiete 22* (1954), 125-129, 128.

35 Ibidem, 128.

that the head doctor surmised that these men had not 'undergone the strains and deprivation [...] suffered by the returnees of 1947 and 1948'.[36] But the doctors were not relieved about the health of these 'late returnees' for long. After some time complaints arose about mental troubles and physical ailments among them as well. Tachycardia, circulatory disturbances, insomnia and outbreaks of sweating, which were triggered off by the slightest stress, diminished their performance, in part substantially. And as with the returnees of the years immediately following the war clear shifts of mood, increased irritability, feelings of fear and inadequacy, resignation, a striking deterioration of the memory or a general lack of drive were part of the broad spectrum of the symptoms complained about.[37]

In view of these persistent ailments, which were hard to objectify, and of the longer lasting mental complaints, large sections of the medical profession in the Federal Republic felt challenged to re-examine the significance of exogenous and endogenous factors for the development of such health damage. In the sphere of internal medicine there were first signs of a readiness to assume long-term damage in the sense of a combined 'mind-body trauma', whereby it was also understood that severe mental strain could be a cause for lasting physical disorders. Psychiatrists did not go so far. They made increased use of the diagnosis of dystrophy derived from internal medicine, which allowed them to establish a causal connection between mental disorder and previous organic damage, in this case as a result of malnutrition and undernourishment during wartime imprisonment. In this way the psychiatrists remained, on the one hand, within the framework of the dominant psychiatric teaching, but, on the other, were provided with an opportunity to lend more weight to mental stress than had hitherto been the case. One could now hear from the psychiatrists that the period of re-convalescence was lengthened not only by the enormous physical strain; mental stress also contributed to the slowing down of the healing process.

In the background of these medical debates there was always the question of how decisions on the recognition of health problems in connection with pension applications could be more safely taken. This problem was not restricted to doctors in Western Germany. It also affected their colleagues in East Germany, although to a different degree, as the legal regulation of the care of the war-disabled differed in each of the occupied zones and later in the two German states. The war victims'

36 See Gert Sedlmayr, 'Wandlungen im Krankheitsbild der Ostheimkehrer', in: *Medizinische Klinik 44* (1949), 1223-1225, quotation on 1223. Similar information was received by the *Arbeitsgemeinschaft für die kulturelle Betreuung der Kriegsgefangenen und Heimkehrer beim Länderrat* (Working Community for the Care of prisoners of War and Returnees at the District Administration) as early as June 1948. Cf. 'Die Notstände der Heimkehrer. Bericht über die Tagung auf der Comburg bei Schwäb. Hall vom 9. bis. 12. Juni 1948', in: Bundesarchiv Koblenz, B 150, 339 (Heft 1).

37 Summarized in a pronounced fashion in: K. Franke, 'Katamnese der Heimkehrer', in: *Deutsche medizinische Rundschau 3* (1949), 1278; and Hans Kilian, *Zur Psychopathologie der Heimkehrer*, in: ibidem, 1278.

welfare service, which was taken up again in the Federal Republic in 1947 and was uniformly fixed when the Federal Welfare Law (*Bundesversorgungsgesetz*) of December 1950 came into effect, applied not only to persons who had done military service; it also included civilians whose health had been damaged as a result of war activities, resettlement, deportation or as a consequence of military occupation.[38] Thus those who had suffered under the bombardments, the expellees and the women who had been raped by members of the occupying forces all enjoyed in principle the right to claim welfare. In addition the surviving dependants of war disabled who had died could also apply for a war victim's pension in the Federal Republic. There was thus a wide range of possibilities for making an application, particularly as the conditions for the granting of a pension were already fulfilled if a doctor testified to a 25% reduction in earning capacity. As a result a large number of expert opinions and evaluation procedures became necessary. In 1953, for example, there were more than 4.2 million potential beneficiaries involved in more than one and a half million pending procedures. It was, moreover, the task of the doctors to carry out frequent re-examinations, in order to discover whether the reduction in earning capacity was still given to the same extent and whether the illness concerned could still be attributed causally to damage resulting from the events of war after a longer period of time.[39] According to the requirements of the welfare authorities of the Federal Republic it was clear that a purely temporal connection between the start of the health disorder and the war did not suffice for recognition as a 'war victim' and hence for a claim to welfare.[40]

Whereas in the Federal Republic the medical expert opinion required as a precondition for welfare claims was thus closely intertwined with the recognition of status as a war victim, the situation in the GDR was different in as much as there were no welfare arrangements specifically for war victims.[41] In contrast to the situation in the West the war disabled in the GDR did not have a special claim to welfare. For ideological reasons equal treatment of all the different groups of the disabled was aimed at, in order to avoid a particular emphasis on the status of the war victim. This approach was already expressed as early as 1946 in the periodical *Arbeit und Sozialfürsorge* (Work and Social Welfare), with the following – for the moment still programmatic – statement on the seriously disabled: 'The category of the seriously disabled must be understood today to include not only the *war* disabled, as was earlier the case, but all persons whose earning capacity [...]

38 See the Law on the Welfare of War Victims (Bundesversorgungsgesetz) of 20. December 1950, Göttingen (undated).

39 For a survey see Neumann, *Nicht der Rede wert*, 132-143; Diehl. *German veterans*.

40 On this point see *Anhaltspunkte für die Ärztliche Gutachtertätigkeit im Versorgungswesen*, and the subsequent issues.

41 See, among others, Manfred G. Schmidt, *Sozialpolitik der DDR*, 38.

is diminished as a result of damage to their health (deriving e.g. from accidents, maltreatment in concentration camps, injuries, illness, genetically determined disorders).' There is no longer any different treatment. Nowadays everybody who has suffered health damage is afforded the same care no matter where or as a result of what events he has suffered the damage.'[42]

For the doctors evaluating the claims of war victims in East Germany in the following years this meant that establishing the cause of the damage was of far less relevance than was the case with their colleagues in the West, who, on account of the special claim to a war victim's pension, had to treat the question of the role played by the war as a possible cause of the disablement differently. In comparison an East German writer presenting the principles for the medical evaluation of disablement in a manual in 1964 again stated that 'the temporal connection with military service alone is decisive for the recognition of war disablement'.[43] Put differently, this meant in regard to the evaluation procedure that in the case of all health disorders which occurred *after* the war classification by the doctors as war invalids or war disabled was out of the question. This was even true of prisoners of war in the GDR, who, like civilians, were excluded by definition from the category of the war disabled.[44] Consequently only some of the former members of the *Wehrmacht* were entitled to apply to the doctors for certification of the reduction in their earning capacity and their right to a pension as a result of damage to their health during the war. And of these only few received a pension, namely the seriously disabled who were medically certified as having lost more than two thirds of their earning capacity.[45]

Thus, although the doctors in East and West Germany alike had to certify the degree of reduction in earning capacity of the war disabled, a striking difference cannot be overlooked. Whereas in the Federal Republic a claim to a war victim's pension had to be examined even when the person concerned was capable of pursuing an occupation and earning an income, the task of the East German doctors was limited to deciding whether the applicant was incapable of working to such a degree that he would not be in a position to take up paid work 'corresponding to his strength and abilities' which would enable him to earn two thirds of what he needed to support himself.[46] In the GDR, therefore, the requirements for the medical certification of war disablement were closely tied to the demands of the labor

42 Foerster, 'Schwerbeschädigtenbetreuung', in: *Arbeit und Sozialfürsorge 1* (1946), 316-317; quotation on 316. H. Fischer, 'Über die Invalidenrente für Kriegsbeschädigte', in: *Arbeit und Sozialfürsorge* 7 (1952), 294-295, 294, also claims that war disabled have to be treated in the similar way like invalids or pensioners.

43 *Taschenbuch der ärztlichen Begutachtungen*, ed. G. Schiller and H. Weigel, 'Berlin (Ost) 1964', 218.

44 See ibidem, and H. Meyer, 'Aufnahme der Zahlung von Beamtenpensionen und Kriegsbeschädigtenrenten', in: *Arbeit und Sozialfürsorge 1* (1946), 163-165. Boldorf, 'Die Verdrängung', 237.

45 See *Taschenbuch der Ärztlichen Begutachtungen*, 218, and Boldorf, 'Eingliederung', 405f.

46 See *Taschenbuch der Ärztlichen Begutachtungen*, 217.

market, as can be generally observed in the social policies of the country.[47] This political guideline, which gave priority to the employment of all potential workers and was even legally regulated in 1956,[48] thoroughly corresponded, however, to the interests of many doctors. This is at least true of the psychiatrists, who for their part again saw the danger that a need for security alone might lie behind the health problems of their patients. Even in regard to persons suffering from brain damage as a result of the war an East German psychiatrist, for example, welcomed the fact that partial pensions would not be paid. He justified this as follows: 'The exclusion [of such payments], which was made necessary by the collapse of the single state system, has led to some fundamental changes in the behaviour of the severely disabled. Pension neuroses, aggravation, greed neuroses have become virtually unknown here in the meantime as the understandable wish to be a state pensioner is now pointless.'[49]

It would be too simple to interpret this attitude in a purely political fashion. The East German psychiatrists were doubtless guided in the question of recognition by the given political conditions. This was equally true of their West German colleagues, who, according to the renowned West German psychiatrist Kurt Schneider felt it to be 'inconceivable' in view of the countless numbers of civilian and military persons suffering from health damage 'if each of them [wanted to] present the State with the bill.' As Schneider curtly stated: 'A share in the common fate of a people cannot be rewarded with a pension'.[50] Nonetheless, in the actual psychiatric evaluation procedures in both states, convictions played a part which were owed to the current state of psychiatric knowledge and were by no means restricted to one country. Both in the East and the West it was taken for granted that the prospect of a pension could lead to a flight into the illness. Consequently, in the evaluation procedures of both East German and West German doctors there was a constitutive mistrust and fear that they might fall for 'pension neuroses' as was the case with the 'war tremblers' of World War I. In the GDR of course the damage to health had to be much more substantial if a pension were to be granted. But the question whether a 'silent flight' into illness lay behind a physical ailment was nonetheless of concern to the East German psychiatrists,

47 Boldorf, 'Eingliederung', 406. See as an example Zenk, 'Produktive Gestaltung der Fürsorge für Hirnverletzte', 274-280.

48 On this point see, among others, Bauerkämper, *Die Sozialgeschichte der DDR*, 7.

49 W. Lindenberg, 'Grundsätzliches zur Frage der Anerkennung von Hirnverletzungen', in: *Psychiatrie, Neurologie und medizinische Psychologie 1* (1949), 145-156, quotation on 147. With respect to long term inability to work see Werner Hollmann, 'Aktuelle Probleme der ärztlichen Begutachtung im Blickwinkel der Pawlowschen Lehre', in: *Psychiatrie, Neurologie und medizinische Psychologie 4* (1953), 392-397.

50 Kurt Schneider, 'Selbstmord als Dienstbeschädigung – Schizophrenie als Dienstbeschädigung', in: *Der Nervenarzt 21* (1950), 480-483, quotation on 480.

who referred to the experience of their West German colleagues, who were no less concerned about the problem.[51]

In spite of the different legal regulations, therefore, there was on the whole a remarkable degree of agreement among the psychiatric experts in both German states that extreme caution was necessary in the judgment of health complaints in the context of the evaluation of applications for pensions. Basic assumptions of the dominant psychiatric teaching since World War 1 thus had an impact on the psychiatric interpretation of mentally determined ailments in both East and West Germany, even though there was an observable tendency in both German states in the 1950's to admit a stronger influence of environmental factors on the rise and the course of health complaints. The argument that occasionally political reasons lay behind this rethinking cannot be readily dismissed. It is at least possible to come across sporadic calls for the abandonment of the concept of 'disposition' – a clear attempt to distance oneself politically from a supposedly National Socialist genetics. But the considerations of the East German psychiatrists as to whether man should not be understood more strongly 'as a somatic-biological and mental being'[52] were not dissimilar to the observable receptiveness of psychiatrists in the Federal Republic for psycho-somatic approaches. In both German states, however, this did nothing to alter the conviction that long-standing mental ailments that could no longer be traced back to organic damage were functional in nature and usually betrayed the existence of a 'psychopathic' personality.[53] This was noticeable in the psychiatric evaluations of former prisoners of war returning to West Germany from Soviet camps at the end of the 1950's, although the diagnosis of 'dystrophy' had for a time provided an interpretative option, which permitted psychiatrists to trace mental ailments back to the extreme physical and psychological strains of imprisonment. Nevertheless 'dystrophy' did not become a diagnostic *passepartout* which might have opened the door for the approval of pensions for those who had participated in the war. As soon as the permitted period of re-convalescence of two or at the most three years had been exceeded without the establishment of organic damage, West German psychiatrist again assumed

---

51 See, among others, W. Hollmann, 'Soziale Therapie und ärztliche Begutachtung der Arbeitsneurose', in: *Psychiatrie, Neurologie und medizinische Psychologie 8* (1956), 267-275, and Heinz Dietrich, 'Zum Hysterieproblem vom Standpunkt des Gutachters', in: ibidem, 10 (1958), 213-215, in both cases with explicit reference to the accounts of the Heidelberg psychiatrist Walter Ritter von Baeyer, who saw in many physical ailments merely a 'change in style' of the neuroses.

52 Hollmann, 'Aktuelle Probleme der ärztlichen Begutachtung', 392-397.

53 As can be read, e.g., in the *Taschenbuch der ärztlichen Begutachtungen* (Pocket Guide to Medical Certification) published in East Berlin in 1964 (626ff.) There we also find the definition of 'psychopathic personalities' as 'predominantly genetically determined abnormal characters'.

that the causes were genetic and suspected the existence of a 'tendency towards pension neurosis', as is evident from the medical opinions of the time.[54]

In the GDR this fear was also more strongly expressed from the middle of the 1950's on, as can be seen from the clearly growing number of professional contributions to the problem of medical certification. An example is provided by a report on a re-examination of patients with brain damage, whose ailments had been certified in an East German clinic between 1940 and 1945. The new findings of the year 1954 are revealing in many respects. It turned out that the reduction of earning capacity among soldiers had apparently been rated higher than that of other injured persons. As the author explains: 'This was probably due to the fact that in the course of the general tendency to recognize war damage many of those who had been wounded attempted to acquire, if not a direct pension, then at least other benefits such as tax allowances, handicap permits etc.' But above all it was necessary to criticize mistaken diagnostic decisions and in some cases it was even questionable whether the persons concerned had suffered from commotional disturbance at all.[55] In the professional scientific debates of the late 50's and early 60's the psychiatric experts agreed that a kind heart should not play a decisive part in decisions on pensions.[56] An overhasty decision in favor of disablement and the right to a pension on account of a mental ailment without organic damage was even contraindicated from a therapeutic standpoint as it would only lead to a chronification of the symptoms.[57] 'If the counseling doctor does not also dare to diagnose headaches and exhaustion as hysterical symptoms because other illness which are difficult to objectify might be concealed behind them then he is not fit to be a medical expert'. This is the harsh judgment of an East German psychiatrist. In his eyes nothing had changed in the last few decades in spite of a changed phenomenology of psychogenic manifestations. He explained: 'The similarity between the cause and the goal of a hysterical reaction at the front during World War I and the hysterical reaction to the internal conflict between individual wishes and the given conditions and requirements of a peaceful environment nowadays is all too evident. In both cases a person is called upon to set aside his own wishes and drives in the pursuit of the goals of a collective and to put up with frustration and deprivation; in both cases the hysterical reaction serves the purpose of gaining advantages of a vital, emotional and financial kind by means of flight into the "illness"'.[58]

54 For various examples see Goltermann, *Die Gesellschaft der Überlebenden.*

55 'Über statistische Erhebungen bei unseren alten offenen und gedeckten Hirnverletzungen', in: *Psychiatrie, Neurologie u. med. Psychologie* 6 (1954), 300-306, quotation on 305.

56 Hollmann, *Soziale Therapie*, 274.

57 'Protokoll der Tagung der Medizinisch-wissenschaftlichen Gesellschaft für Psychiatrie und Neurologie an der Karl-Marx-Universität Leipzig (1955)', in: *Psychiatrie, Neurologie u. med. Psychologie* 8 (1956), 154-158, 154.

58 Heinz Dietrich, 'Zum Hysterieproblem vom Standpunkt des Gutachters', in: *Psychiatrie, Neurologie u. med. Psychologie* 10 (1958), 213-215, quotation on 213.

In spite of the flexibility of the professional experts – as in the case of dystrophy – and of political considerations – as in the case of the East German silence on the ailments of the prisoners of war returning from the Soviet Union – psychological knowledge in East and West had in principle asserted itself in practice. In neither East- nor West-Germany had the central principles of a medical practice based on the natural sciences been abandoned, which took as its starting point the need to find objective causes for health damage. Accordingly a large majority of psychiatrists followed the then current concept of illness which only recognized the 'pathological' nature of mental disturbances if it was proved that 'pathological organic processes' were the cause.[59] In regard to ailments of a purely mental kind this meant that they were to a high degree regarded as the product of purely subjective feelings which probably expressed an unconscious weakness of the will and certainly indicated 'a mistaken attitude towards life with its demands and tasks.'[60] This was not to be encouraged by the provision of a pension. Consequently work was the therapeutic program, which was in fact spelled out in Eastern Germany as a measure of 'social therapy'. As it was accompanied in the GDR by a large number of political measures designed to promote the integration of the severely disabled into the working process, it was possible here, in view of the comparatively small number of pensioners, to trust that the lives of the great majority of the survivors of the last war life had returned to normal.[61]

Challenges

The dominant psychiatric teaching thus proved to be uncommonly stable in both German states during the first decade after World War II. In fact the assumption that mental ailments could not be traced back causally to the war at all was by no means met with incomprehension in post-war society. This can be demonstrated from the files of psychiatric patients in a West German clinic. They reveal that in

59 This understanding of illness was explicitly formulated in 1946 by the Heidelberg psychiatrist Kurt Schneider, 'Zum Krankheitsbegriff in der Psychiatrie', in: *Deutsche Medizinische Wochenschrift* 17 (1946), 306-307. His definition of illness remained virtually unchallenged in West German psychiatry until around 1960 and provided the basis for decisions on both questions of war victims' welfare and compensation for the victims of National Socialist persecution. This is also true of the insurance legislation in the GDR. The *Taschenbuch der ärztlichen Begutachtungen* of 1964 confirms that there a medical concept of illness was used according to which 'illness in a physical sense alone' existed. The book goes on to explain: Conditions which are only mentally determined are not regarded as causing health damage. Thus subjective factors brought up by applicants are excluded.' (628).

60 *Taschenbuch*, 626.

61 See Bohlmann, 'Die Eingliederung', 301-302; Albert Voß, 'Heimkehr der Kriegsgefangenen. Ihre Wiedereingliederung in den Wirtschaftsprozeß und berufliche Seßhaftmachung', in: *Arbeit und Sozialfürsorge 1* (1946), 73-74; Zenk, 'Produktive Gestaltung', 274-280.

their interpretation of the ailments a large number of returnees, wives of refugees and their families agreed without further ado with the judgment of the experts, when they did not trace the occurrence of the ailments back to the events of the war or imprisonment in the camps. Agreement of this kind can be observed above all in the years immediately following the war. But there were also objections, which, when compared with the quiet acquiescence of the years before, became clearly audible after the establishment of the war victims welfare in the Federal Republic, particularly as those concerned not seldom called upon the assistance of the war victims' associations and also took legal action. The former participants in the war on East Germany could not build upon the support of war victims' associations representing the interests of innumerable members of their organizations. There were no comparable pressure groups in the GDR and associations of the war disabled, who were even accused of pursuing 'warmongering aims', were forbidden for political reasons.[62]

This lack of symmetry was unquestionably significant in regard to the development of the different perceptions of the consequences of the war in the two German states. For in contrast to the situation in the GDR, there existed in the Federal Republic a forum for the former participants in the war, which intervened in the public and political debate on the kind of medical knowledge which should be regarded as valid on the issue of war disability. The ailments of the war returnees and, above all, of those returning from Soviet imprisonment, were at the centre of attention. They could be sure of the support of the *Verband der Heimkehrer, Kriegsgefangenen und Vermisstenangehörigen* (VdH) (Association of Returnees, Prisoners of War and Families of Missing Persons) which had been established in 1950 as the umbrella organization of the local returnee associations. One of the most important tasks of this body was to ensure the provision of medical care for the war returnees and to promote scientific research on dystrophy and post-dystrophic complaints. In 1955 the medical service of the VdH comprised around 2000 doctors working on an honorary basis, who were often also available to the returnees as voluntary providers of medical expert opinion. A scientific advisory board of doctors established in 1952 organized several conferences with the financial support of the VdH whose results were published by the VdH and thus made available to interested public opinion, although there was sometimes a delay of some years.[63] Although the majority of the contributions in the 50's dealt with the physi-

62 See Boldorf, 'Verdrängung', 243.

63 The results of the medical conferences of 1953, 1955 and 1957 were published together in: *Extreme Lebensverhältnisse und ihre Folgen* (Schriftenreihe des Ärztlich-wissenschaftlichen Beirates des Verbandes der Heimkehrer Deutschlands e. V., B. 7) ed. by the Verband der Heimkehrer, Kriegsgefangenen und Vermisstenangehörigen Deutschlands, Bad Godesberg 1959. The multivolume *Handbuch der ärztlichen Erfahrungen aus der Gefangenschaft* (ed. Ernst G. Schenck and Wolfgang von Nathusius, Bad Godesberg 1958ff.) was published

cal disabilities and complaints of the war returnees, the association and its 'war returnee doctors' were among the driving forces which vehemently opposed the widespread medical interpretation of many ailments as 'genetically determined'.

This debate, which can be characterized as a 'battle over heritability', gave an essential impulse to the opening up of the discourse on human ways of dealing with extreme stress in the Federal Republic after the middle of the 1950's. This was all the more the case as the war returnees from Soviet camps whose health had been damaged found the support of doctors of internal medicine, who showed that they were open to a psychosomatic approach, and this challenged the interpretative primacy of psychiatrists in regard to body-mind processes. This can be observed in the mid-50's in the expert committees set up by the *Ministerium für Arbeit und Sozialordnung* (Ministry of Labor and Social Affairs) in order to discuss and if need be to modify the medical regulations on the evaluation procedures in the context of war victims' welfare.[64] The protagonists of a psychosomatic approach presented their position with great self-confidence, and were capable of demonstrating convincingly to the committee members from science and politics that the former war participants were no longer willing to be characterized by psychiatrists as 'neurotics and dissemblers'. It was implied that general practitioners also distanced themselves from the viewpoint of the psychiatrists in such cases.[65] Although it is scarcely possible to test the truth of this assertion, the repeatedly expressed distrust of psychiatrists towards general practitioners indicates that it was not made up out of thin air.[66] At all events the psychiatrists – and this was evidently also the case in the GDR – had to face a changed situation and accept that a clear majority of people with mental complaints preferred to be treated by general practitioners or internists.[67]

Thus the West German psychiatrists of the mid-50's were confronted with growing professional competition, which was led by the advocates of psychosomatic forms of explanation. There is no indication in the relevant professional organs of psychiatry that this was a source of irritation for psychiatrists. But in the smaller circle of the expert committee it turned out that some of them were prob-

under the same title: 'Extreme Lebensverhältnisse und ihre Folgen'. The data on the medical service stem from Winkler, 'Männlichkeit und Gesundheit'.

64 See the discussion contributions and the lectures at the Tagung des Ärztlichen Sachverständigenbeirats für Fragen der Kriegsopferversorgung, 1956, in: Bundesarchiv Koblenz, B 149, 1955.

65 See, e.g. the lecture of the internist Max Hochrein, 'Kreislaufstörungen beim Spätheimkehrer', held at the Tagung des Ärztlichen Sachverständigenbeirats für Fragen der Kriegsopferversorgung, 1956. Bundesarchiv Koblenz, B 149, 1955.

66 On this point see, among others, Von Baeyer, 'Statistik', 404, and Ulrich Venzlaff, 'Die psychoreaktiven Störungen nach entschädigungspflichtigen Ereignissen', 42.

67 This is regretted e.g. by K. Höck, 'Zum Krankheitsbild der neurotischen Reaktionen in der heutigen Zeit', in: *Psychiatrie, Neurologie und medizinische Psychologie 12* (1960), 99-102, 101.

ably no longer really convinced that the established diagnostics and in particular the arguments in favor of 'genetic determination' provided a fitting explanation of the observable ailments of the former war participants. The Hamburg psychiatrist Hans Bürger-Prinz admitted at any rate that 'there is God knows no reason for refusing to see that a genuine case of depression in a case of dystrophy can last six years'. And he frankly added: 'There is no point here in speaking of neurotic fixations; in any case the concept of neurosis mostly kills the problem off without explaining it'. This, however, presented a challenge to all doctors who shared his discomfort.[68] They were challenged to find a convincing diagnosis for complaints of former war participants which always sounded the same and, according to the prevalent opinion, ought to have disappeared after a suitable period of re-convalescence.

In the second half of the 50's one could, therefore, get the impression that an etiological change was coming about in the Federal Republic in regard to a series of health disorders that could even possibly lead to a re-figuration of the diagnostic ascertainment of organically inexplicable ailments. But the introduction of a new diagnosis was a difficult undertaking for the medical profession. This is evidenced by the debates which arose on the diagnostic adequacy of 'vegetative dystonia'. Even internists who adopted a psychosomatic approach and spoke out in favor of this diagnosis nonetheless felt uncomfortable about the way it was used. The internist Max Hochrein, for example, complained that 'vegetative dystonia' has become 'nowadays a kind of last resort diagnosis, i.e. a receptacle for unclear ailments and unexplained pathogenetic relationships.'[69] Other colleagues, moreover, forbade the use of this diagnosis in their clinics, as the complaints involved did not amount to a new phenomenon and, in any case, there could be no doubt that they were genetically determined.[70] Overall it seems that the criticism of 'vegetative dystonia' as a diagnosis could not be easily refuted. Even the advocates of psychosomatics still found themselves faced with a general dilemma, which the internist Max Hochrein aptly put as follows in an appeal to his colleagues: 'What do want to call something that we all know but refuse to give a name to?'[71]

Such a cautious search for a different diagnostic toolbox was not unfamiliar to some doctors in the GDR. The East German psychiatrist Dietfried Müller-Hegemann complained in the year 1960 about the issue of a 'frighteningly high number of sick notes and even certifications of disability with the ominous diagnosis

68 Discussion contribution of Prof. Bürger-Prinz, Hamburg, in: Bundesarchiv Koblenz B 149, 1955.

69 Max Hochrein, 'Diagnostik und Therapie der vegetativen Dystonie', in: *Extreme Lebensverhältnisse und ihre Folgen*, vol. 7, 125-159, quotation on 125.

70 Discussion contribution Prof. Bodechtel, Munich, in: Bundesarchiv Koblenz, B 149, 1955; see also the discussion contribution of Prof. Hoff, Frankfurt, ibidem.

71 Concluding statement of Prof. Dr. Hochrein, in: Bundesarchiv Koblenz, B 149, 1955.

'vegetative dystonia', when some 'objective' signs of vegetative instability were accompanied by subjective complaints such as headaches, rapid fatigue or moodiness.[72] Thus there was evidently a professional debate going on in East Germany as well, which evidently led to conflicts in the practice of medical certification similar to those in the Federal Republic. They did not, however, indicate the awareness of a need in the GDR to pay a different kind of attention to the extreme stress resulting from the experience of war when looking for an etiological justification of the ailments. But there was one scientific and politico-moral challenge that the East German psychiatrists did take up. It concerned the problem of how the long-lasting mentally determined complaints of those who had been persecuted under the National Socialist regime could be adequately grasped.

In this field, however, the East German psychiatrists were by no means the pacemakers. They rather responded to a debate which had started several years before in the Federal Republic. It was brought about by the enactment of the Federal Indemnification Law for the victims of National Socialist persecution in 1956. Both the West German psychiatrists and the relevant federal authorities were then confronted to an increasing degree with the expectation of foreign doctors that the prevailing expert opinion on the judgment of compensation cases should be abandoned and the mental disturbances of those persecuted by the National Socialist regime should be recognized as late consequences of Nazi terror. The external pressure on West and East German psychiatrists differed widely on account of the different forms of compensation in the two states. In East Germany the right to compensation only applied to the persecuted who were currently resident in the GDR, whereas the Federal Law for the Compensation of the Victims of National Socialist Persecution of 1956 applied to Germany within the borders of 1937, but without making German citizenship or current residence in the Federal Republic a condition for the acceptance of claims.[73] For this reason doctors abroad had to be entrusted with the certification of the victims of National Socialist persecution. Although the judgment of the foreign colleagues by no means deviated fundamentally from that of the German doctors, the objections to the strict application of the psychiatric teaching prevalent in the Federal Republic did increase. For the New York psychiatrist Hans Strauss, for example, who expressed his annoyance over the practice of compensation in the Federal Republic in 1957, there was only one reason in many cases for the long duration of the mental ailments of the victims of National Socialism. It lay in the specific nature of the National Socialist perse-

72 Dietfried Müller-Hegemann, 'Bemerkungen zu aktuellen Fragen der medizinischen Begutachtung und zum Krankheitsbegriff', in: *Das Deutsche Gesundheitswesen* 15 (1960), 1368-1375, quotation on 1371.

73 One clause did however exclude persecuted persons currently resident in the GDR and Poland from the circle of those entitled to compensation. For details see the comprehensive survey of Goschler, *Schuld und Schulden*, especially 201 and 362.

cution itself which, according to Strauss, was founded on the 'total *lack of rights* of these people'. Strauss argued: 'They were the completely defenseless victims of any conceivable whim of their often sadistic overseers.'[74]

At the end of the 50's interventions of this kind in most cases unquestionably encountered great resistance both from the West German psychiatrists and from the compensation authorities. They followed the currently dominant teaching that mentally determined complaints without organic damage could not be rated as an illness and that a pension should therefore be refused. Accordingly they followed the valid guidelines of war victims' welfare in dealing with the new compensation matters. But some West German psychiatrists who were already concerned about the possible inadequacy of the dominant teaching proved to be wholly receptive for the arguments of their foreign colleagues and for the moral challenge presented by the claims to compensation of those who had been persecuted under the National Socialist regime. This was clear from the publications in the psychiatric journal *Der Nervenarzt*, in which deliberate efforts were undertaken to start up a debate on the possible mental effects of National Socialist persecution.[75] In the compensation authorities there were also examining doctors who not only referred to the newness and incomparability of the health damage but also saw legal possibilities for at least partially abandoning the restrictive compensation practice.[76] The decisive point was, namely, that the compensation of the victims of National Socialism fell under civil law and did not requires as strict a justification of the causes as war victims' welfare, which was organized in accordance with to the regulations of social law.[77]

Under these circumstances the compensation authorities of the Federal Republic were subjected to an enormous pressure to clarify the validity of the psychiatric knowledge presented to them, as they had to decide on the basis of psychiatric expert opinion from at home and abroad on the recognition of mental disturbance as damage to health due to an illness resulting from persecution. In the process

74 'Besonderheiten der nicht-psychotischen seelischen Störungen bei Opfern der nationalsozialistischen Verfolgung und ihre Bedeutung bei der Begutachtung von Dr. med. Hans Strauss (Abschrift), 5', in: Bundesarchiv Koblenz, B 126, 9903, vol 1. The text by Strauss was also published around the same time with identical wording in: *Der Nervenarzt 28* (1957), 344-350.

75 The start was made with a contribution by Walter von Baeyer, 'Die Freiheitsfrage in der forensischen Psychiatrie mit besonderer Berücksichtigung der Entschädigungsneurosen', in: *Der Nervenarzt 28* (1957), 337-343; this was followed, among others, by Strauss, 'Besonderheiten', in: ibidem 28 (1957), 344-350; Kurt Kolle, 'Die Opfer der nationalsozialistischen Verfolgung in psychiatrischer Sicht', in: ibidem 29 (1958), 148-158, and Ernst Kluge, 'Über die Folgen schwerer Haftzeiten', in: ibidem, 462-465.

76 See e.g. Der Innenminister des Landes Nordrhein-Westfalen, Abteilung V, an den Herrn Bundesminister der Finanzen, Bonn, 3. 9.1957, in: Bundesarchiv Koblenz B 126, 9838.

77 For details see Goltermann, *Die Gesellschaft der Überlebenden*, 279-292.

of clarification, for which medical conferences were especially held,[78] advice was taken from the head physicians of the compensation authorities, selected medical experts and skilled representatives of the legal profession. But the foreign medical experts could not be ignored for long, as the meetings were aimed at achieving a standardization of the practice of the evaluators. In view of the fact that diagnoses such as 'neurosis' or 'schizophrenia' were not used identically in different countries on account of the different national traditions of knowledge this was not an easy task. But on the German side as well doubts about the adequacy of the concept of neurosis as an explanation of health damage were so loudly expressed that in the minutes of the *Medizinische Hauptkonferenz* (Main Medical Conference) of 1958 it was recorded that all the participants regarded the concept of neurosis in the context of compensation claims as 'highly unsatisfactory' and felt that it should no longer be used.[79] Thus the need for the introduction of a new diagnosis could no longer be dismissed out of hand. But the circle of participants at first failed to find a solution. As the minutes of the meeting point out dryly but euphemistically, all of the experts 'found it difficult to introduce a new usable concept which fitted the facts of the case'.[80]

In this open situation the interpretation of an 'experientially determined personality change' developed by the Göttingen psychiatrist Ulrich Venzlaff found a hearing. In his study published in 1958 he by no means cast aside the dominant teaching completely. He protested, however, that 'mental illness' was possible, for example, when people were overwhelmed by suffering.[81] If this experience could not be coped with, if 'the personality suffered too deep a rupture, if contents and values on which life was built up were *irretrievably destroyed*, if a person was driven into isolation by his years-long suffering and affliction and no longer enjoyed any kind of communication, if a period of life was passed over in which the personality is shapeable and new sets of values and goals can be arrived at', then, according to Venzlaff, even incurable mental illness can sometimes occur. In precisely these cases the psychiatrist no longer wished to speak of a neurosis. He preferred the concept of an 'experientially determined personality change'.[82]

Even though the Federal German compensation authorities endeavored to assure foreign medical examiners, with explicit reference to Venzlaff, that they were also ready to assume the existence of 'particular mental damage' caused by

78 The so-called *Medizinische Hauptkonferenz*, which met yearly between 1958 and 1970, can be characterized as the coordinating point of this process of communication. For details see Goltermann, *Die Gesellschaft der Überlebenden*, 288ff.

79 Niederschrift über die medizinische Hauptkonferenz in München am 23. und 24. April 1958, 10, in: Bundesarchiv Koblenz, B 126, 9903, vol. 1.

80 Ibidem.

81 See Venzlaff, 'Die psychoreaktiven Störungen', 67ff; quotation on 69.

82 Ibidem, 74 (emphasis in the original).

persecution,[83] the fact could not be overlooked that in compensation practice the application of new psychiatric knowledge had to be asserted against the resistance of a broad front of doctors. If, however, one bears in mind that established medical interpretations always enjoy an extremely long life, it can be said that the new psychiatric reading was established in the Federal Republic within a remarkably short period of time. There are a number of reasons for this. One is the still precarious status of the Federal Republic within the Western alliance. This is shown by the fact that the Foreign Office even intervened several times in the compensation procedures in response to sharp criticism from organizations representing Jewish interests and urged the German medical officials to arrive at an agreement with their colleagues abroad.[84] Above all in the journeys they undertook in the USA to this end the German medical officials encountered severe criticism of their compensation policies. Both the reports in the American media and the behavior of the American psychiatrists made it unmistakably clear that the American side was not willing to tolerate the continuance of a restrictive recognition practice.

However it was, above all, the intervention of the courts which enabled the new psychiatric knowledge to win greater validity. In some regards the decisions of the courts even rendered the controversy among the psychiatric experts obsolete. In order to maintain their decision-taking ability in cases of conflict the legal authorities simply introduced a series of regulations on so-called 'reductions in the burden of proof', which in a number of cases made the disputes between the medical experts on the 'genetic determination' of an ailment superfluous. Among these was the so-called 'concentration camp assumption',[85] which became law in 1965. It established that in the case of all persecuted persons who had spent at least one year in a concentration camp a reduction of earning capacity of at least 25% could be attributed to the persecution. Proof was no longer needed, except in the cases of a higher reduction of earning capacity, for which a causal relationship with the persecution still had to be demonstrated.[86] The law nonetheless clearly took as its starting point the fact that psychiatric knowledge on the issue had changed. It permitted former prisoners in concentration camps whose applications for compensation had been turned down to apply for a reopening of the procedure.[87] Finally, in 1968, a decision of the Federal Constitutional Court provided that the

83 See the Entwurf des Protokolls der medizinischen Hauptkonferenz am 23. und 24.4.1958 für die ausländischen Vertrauensärzte (Anlage des Briefes vom Bayer. Staatsministerium der Finanzen an den Niedersächsischen Minister des Innern, 26.1.1959), in: Bundesarchiv Koblenz, B 126, 9903, vol. 2.

84 For details see Goltermann, *Die Gesellschaft der Überlebenden*, 299-318.

85 § 31, 2, BEG-Schlußgesetz (Final Law-Federal Indemnification Law) in: Bundesentschädigungsgesetz, Munich 1966[14], 23.

86 The BEG-Schlussgesetz (Final Law-Federal Indemnification Law) assumed imprisonment of at least one year in a concentration camp. See ibidem.

87 § 31 Abs. 2 gave retrospective validity to the regulation as of 1.10.1953.

recognition of health damage resulting from the experience of events must no longer necessarily be linked to the experience of measures of violence 'of particular severity and duration'. The controversial but hitherto unavoidable question as to when an 'extreme experiential constellation' was given thus clearly lost much of its weight.[88]

Of course these regulations in no way mean that applications for the recognition of mental damage were no longer rejected by psychiatrists. But the chances of those who had been persecuted in the past, particularly the survivors of the concentration camps, to achieve recognition of their mental ailments increasingly improved from the 1960's on. This was not, however, restricted to the Federal Republic. There were signs of such a development in the GDR as well. But the question of the possible mental consequences of persecution by the National Socialists was much less intensely discussed in the East German professional journals. However, the East German specialists did at least show that they were very well informed on the state of psychiatric knowledge on this issue in the neighboring country. Above all, Venzlaff's account of the 'experientially determined change in personality' and also other relevant writings of West German colleagues were well received.[89] The psychiatrist Dietfried Müller-Hegemann, whose publications reveal that he had a profound knowledge of psychiatric writings from the West, undertook a series of studies on people persecuted under the Nazi regime in the mid-60's, making observations in part similar to those of his Western colleagues. He pointed out that 'in a series of cases insufficient account had been taken of damage to the nervous system of persons persecuted by the NS regime, leading to a rejection of the pension applications'; these decisions ought to be revised after new medical examinations.[90] Furthermore, Müller-Hegemann was in the meantime convinced that 'the lack of pathological organic findings' in no way permitted the conclusion that the health damage concerned could not be rated as an illness.[91] In a teaching manual he published in 1966 he even states in a categorical and generalizing manner: 'On the consequences of imprisonment in fascist concentration camps and similar institutions there is an extensive literature which permits no doubt as to the severity of many manifestations of this kind. Apart from injuries caused by maltreatment, damage resulting from undernourishment and

88 Eberhard Schubert, 'Die derzeitige höchstrichterliche Rechtsprechung zum Neurosen-Problem im Wiedergutmachungsrecht, im Versorgungsrecht und in der gesetzlichen Unfallversicherung', in: RzW 19 (1968), 481-490, 485.

89 See also Dietfried Müller-Hegemann, 'Bemerkungen', 1373f., idem, 'Schädigungen'; id., 'Zum Problem der Neurose-Begutachtung', in: *Psychiatrie, Neurologie und medizinische Psychologie* 19 (1967), 10-14; Kaufer, *Die psychischen und neurologischen Spätschäden; Taschenbuch*, 628f.

90 Dietfried Müller-Hegemann, 'Über Schädigungen und Störungen des Nervensystems bei Verfolgten des Naziregimes (VdN) und deren Begutachtung', in: *Das deutsche Gesundheitswesen 21* (1966), 561-568, 562.

91 Müller-Hegemann, 'Schädigungen', 567.

inadequate hygienic conditions the mental after-effects must also be taken into account.'[92]

But it would be overhasty to assume that the perception of long-lasting mental disorders among the former victims of National Socialist persecution actually developed along similar lines in West and East Germany from the 1960's on. This is not the case, on the one hand, because there was a clear tendency in the Federal Republic to emphasize the mental suffering of the persecuted Jews more than that of other groups of the victims of National Socialist terror. In the GDR, on the other hand, more attention was paid to those persecuted for political reasons – in so far as they could be classified as being true to the system.[93] And there was a further important difference. In West and East Germany very different ideas were developed and established on the extent of the mental damage inflicted on the survivors of National Socialist terror. A number of West German psychiatrists, for example, already claimed in the 1960's that in the case of the victims of National Socialist persecution the claim to compensation was not the exception but the rule.[94] In the public memory discourse in the Federal Republic this assumption also soon won recognition; first indications of this can be found in the course of Adolf Eichmann's trial when, during an extensive debate on National Socialist crimes, the media adopted this pattern of perception with specific reference to expert psychiatric opinion.[95]

In this form, however, this trend towards a generalization of the assumption that the victims of National Socialists persecution had suffered mental damage was a Western phenomenon. The GDR did not follow suit – not even in regard to those it recognized as 'persons persecuted under the National Socialist regime'. East German psychiatric science even distanced itself explicitly from the assumption that mental damage to the persecuted was the rule. The psychiatrist Müller-Hegemann, for example, decidedly repudiated the tendency to over-psychologize and instead affirmed that the victims of National Socialist persecution were 'by no means all "mentally" ill'.[96] There was even a reason for this, which can be found in an East German dissertation of the year 1965. The author explains: 'A survey

---

92 Id., *Neurologie und Psychiatrie. Ein Lehrbuch für Studierende und Ärzte*, 653.

93 A comparison between the GDR and the FRG shows that this is especially revealing on the field of compensation for Nazi victims. On this topic, see, among others, Goschler. For the GDR see also Ottmar Geschke, 'Zur Sicherung der rechtlichen Stellung der VdN', in: *Arbeit und Sozialfürsorge* 5 (1950), 119-120, esp. 119, and Hanns Schwarz, 'Referate der Ärztekonferenzen in Kopenhagen (1954) und Moskau (1957)', Bd. I-III, in: *Psychiatrie, Neurologie und medizinische Psychologie* 15 (1963), 159-160.

94 See, among others, Ulrich Venzlaff, 'Gutachten zur Frage des Zusammenwirkens erlebnisreaktiver, vegetativer und hormonaler Faktoren bei Verfolgungsschäden', in: Helmut Paul and Hans Joachim Herberg (eds), *Psychische Spätschäden nach politischer Verfolgung*, 111-124, 111f. See also Walter von Baeyer, 'Erlebnisbedingte Verfolgungsschäden', in: Der Nervenarzt 32 (1961), 534-538, 535.

95 On this point see Goltermann, *Die Gesellschaft der Überlebenden*, Chap. III.2.

96 Müller-Hegemann, 'Problem', 13 (see n.72).

of the literature reveals that the greatest part of the publications on late damage after detention in concentration camps has been published in capitalist countries. This cannot be attributed to a keener scientific interest of Western psychiatrists and neurologists. The reason is, rather, that this problem has acquired significance almost exclusively in the Western states.'[97] As can be seen here, even the debate on the mental ailments of those previously persecuted thus became a part of the conflict of systems. For many years to come the East German perspective was at all events clear: the trauma of the persecuted could only be a problem for the West.

Pluralization

In the meantime, however, an as yet small group of former GDR citizens made itself heard in the Federal Republic, claiming to have suffered from mental stress and damage as political prisoners in East Germany and the Soviet Union which was comparable to that of the victims of National Socialism. Accordingly, this group, in the shape of the *Vereinigung der Opfer des Stalinismus* (Association of the Victims of Stalinism),[98] claimed that those concerned should not be treated any differently from a medical point of view than people persecuted by the National Socialists.[99] For political refugees from the GDR whose health damage had been assessed in accordance with the War Victims Law[100] the association demanded that legal regulations must be found which followed the 'softer' provisions of the Federal Law for the Compensation of the Victims of National Socialism.[101]

On this point the former prisoners from the GDR acted in concert with the *Verband der Heimkehrer* (Association of Former Prisoners of War), although in other respects the competition between the various victims' groups was all too evi-

97 Kaufer, *Die psychischen und neurologischen Spätschäden,* 59.

98 The *Vereinigung der Opfer des Stalinismus* (VOS) (Association of the Victims of Stalinism) was founded in West Berlin in 1950 on the initiative of a small group of former prisoners of the internment camps in the Soviet Occupied Zone. It is said to have had 3,000 members on federal territory by 1954. After fifty years of existence the number of membership cards issued to former political prisoners in this period was put at 35,000. According to the figures of the VOS the number of consultations with those who sought its help by far exceeded the number of its members (1952: 22 145 consultations in the head office alone). The figures are taken from Alexander Richter, *Vergesst uns nicht – wenn auch die Tage wandern und auch die Jahre. Eine Festschrift zum 50-jährigen Bestehen der Vereinigung der Opfer des Stalinismus e.V.*, Berlin 2000.

99 See, among others, 'Unsere sozialpolitischen Aufgaben', in: *Die Freiheitsglocke* 19 (1969), Nr. 221, 5-7, 5; 'Keine Angleichung an das BEG', in: *Die Freiheitsglocke* 17 (1967), Nr. 199, 10-11, 11; 'Vorschlag für eine Schlussnovelle zum Häftlingshilfegesetz (HHG)', in: *Die Freiheitsglocke* 16 (1966), Nr. 186, 3.

100 Claim to welfare in the case of health damage resulting from imprisonment had been accorded to political refugees since the enactment of the *Häftlingshilfegesetz* (Prisoners Assistance Act) in 1955, which was oriented on the *Bundesversorgungsgesetz* (Federal Welfare Act). See Bundesgesetzblatt I, 1955, 498.

101 See n. 100.

dent.[102] But as far as mentally determined ailments were concerned, both groups of victims were confronted with the fact that the recognition of mental ailments as it was beginning to be granted to the victims of National Socialism had by no means led to a general interpretation applicable to other groups.

In the early 60's, however, there had been indications that the highest instances of the Social Court were urging a greater weighting and acceptance of mentally determined ailments.[103] Among psychiatrists isolated voices could also be heard who, in view of the long-lasting mental complaints of the victims of National Socialism, pointed out that a more open psychiatric interpretation of mental disturbances might possibly be indicated in other cases as well. This was not a concession to 'war victims' in general. In this connection the Heidelberg psychiatrist Walter von Baeyer drew attention to those people who 'had to live for years without hope and under the most inhuman conditions in labor, penal and prisoner of war camps.'[104] Nevertheless, very little was heard of this group in the public debate of the 60's, in which Von Baeyer pleaded for a widening of psychiatric interpretations. Psychiatrists tended instead to present as convincingly as possible what they considered to be 'unique and incomparable' in the 'experiential situation' of persons persecuted by the National Socialists[105] and to answer skeptical critics in the psychiatric fraternity by elucidating on what was completely 'new' about the mental complaints they encountered.[106] And even those psychiatrists who fought for the acceptance of a new interpretation of mental disturbances continued to affirm that the strict medical and legal practice in dealing with claims in the context of war victims' welfare must be maintained.[107] In contrast to the heated debates of the early 60's on cases of compensation for the victims of Nazi persecution, the later discussions revealed that psychiatric opinions on the judgment of mental disturbances among war victims did not diverge so much. As the psychiatrist Friedrich Panse contentedly pointed out in 1965: 'In the Federal Republic, in which the long-proven guidelines for expert opinion on neuroses have up to now generally been recognized as valid, there are as yet less than 2% war disabled with pensions who owe the

102 It is sometimes asserted by former prisoners in the GDR that in spite of all the similarities the fate of prisoners of war in the Soviet Union differs substantially from that of the prisoners in the GDR, who were arrested by the Stasi (State Security Service). See, e.g. 'Für ein Gespräch mit dem VdH', in: *Die Freiheitsglocke 18* (1968), Nr. 207, 12-13.

103 See e.g. Bundessozialgericht, Urteil vom 11.11.1959, in: 'Sammlung von Entscheidungen der Sozialversicherung, Versorgung und Arbeitslosenversicherung, begründet von Hermann Breithaupt', 49 (1960), 148. Further evidence in Goltermann, *Die Gesellschaft der Überlebenden*, 326-334.

104 See Walter von Baeyer, 'Erlebnisreaktive Störungen und ihre Bedeutung für die Begutachtung', in: *Deutsche Medizinische Wochenschrift 83* (1958), 2317-2322, quotation on 2319.

105 Venzlaff, 'Erlebnishintergrund', 97.

106 Walter von Baeyer et al., *Psychiatrie der Verfolgten*, 111.

107 See, among others, Ulrich Venzlaff, 'Grundsätzliche Betrachtungen über die Begutachtung erlebnisbedingter seelischer Störungen nach rassischer und politischer Verfolgung', in: *RzW* 10 (1959), 289-292.

recognition of their disablement to psychiatric and, in particular, to psychogenic clinical pictures.'[108]

In order to improve the medical evaluation procedures of the 60's in the interest of both the war victims and the former political prisoners in the GDR, their respective associations attempted to secure the introduction of a 'reduction in the burden of proof' at the political level.[109] But here too the legislative authorities refused to yield. In particular, they were not willing to extend the application of the special regulations of the Federal Indemnification Law, which facilitated the recognition of the health damage suffered by the victims of National Social persecution, to war victims' welfare in general. This was especially true of the so-called 'concentration camp assumption', whose application to both the war victims and the former prisoners in the GDR was rejected. A new initiative started by the representatives of the former prisoners in the GDR at the end of the 60's, which again called for a harmonization of the regulations, was also unsuccessful. The initiative failed to find a majority in the committee of the German parliament which dealt with the matter. The Federal Minister for Expellees at the time conceded in a letter that the parliamentary committee was of the opinion that 'there was equality in terms of suffering and victimhood'. But the cases were nonetheless different. 'The Federal Republic – although it did not bear any blame for the illegal and criminal activities perpetrated under the tyranny of National Socialism – did after all have the duty [...] to accept the liability for these deeds.' For this reason it must compensate the victims in a law applying only to them. 'Such a liability, however,' he argued, does not exist 'in regard to the unjust deeds of those in power in the Soviet Occupied Zone'.[110] At first sight this sounds like a pragmatic argument. But the attitude of the federal politicians was also a political statement. For the former political prisoners of the GDR, at least, it was all too clear that they had failed to achieve acceptance of their central demand. In the words of the Association of the Victims of Stalinism this was to secure 'equal legal recognition for the victims of the concentration camps under both systems' in regard to the health damage and suffering they caused, but also to equate 'the two systems at least in regard to the use of political terror.'[111]

108 See Friedrich Panse, 'Der Krankheitswert der Neurose', in: *Der Medizinische Sachverständige* 61 (1965), 114-120, 119.

109 'Wir bleiben uns treu. Ergebnisbericht über den 8. ordentlichen Verbandstag des Verbandes der Heimkehrer, Kriegsgefangenen und Vermisstenangehörigen Deutschlands e. V. [1964]', 28-30, in: Archiv des Verbandes der Heimkehrer, Bonn; 'Gesundheitsschäden nach Haft und Gefangenschaft', in: *Die Freiheitsglocke* 14 (1964), Nr. 154, 8-9, 9.

110 Statement made by the Christian Democrat Kai-Uwe von Hassel, Federal Minister for Expellees Refugees and War Damaged' at the time in a letter reprinted in: *Die Freiheitsglocke* 17 (1967), Nr. 199, 11.

111 'Die Gleichstellung aller ehemaligen politischen Gefangenen als Verfassungsauftrag', in: *Die Freiheitsglocke* 17 (1967), Nr. 198, 2-3, quotation on 2.

After this rebuff by the federal government the organs of the associations calling for stronger recognition of the mental damage suffered by this group of victims as a consequence of their imprisonment were virtually silent for more than two decades. The situation changed, however, in the course of the *Wende* (the turning point) of 1989/90 which led to a new public debate on the crimes perpetrated by the GDR. With the accession of the new federal states to the Federal Republic a series of legal measures had to be enacted in order to regulate the rehabilitation and the compensation of victims both of National Socialism and of the government of the GDR. But it again soon became evident that former citizens of the GDR who made claims for health damage suffered in consequence of the repression of the SED (Socialist Unity Party of Germany) regime continued to be subjected, in regard to their material situation, to the restrictive practice governing compensation for war victims. Morally, however, they took their bearings from the more generous compensation accorded to the victims of National Socialist persecution. Even more than in the previous decades this brought about a literal race for recognition in which the victims of the SED regime competed for a share in the supposed privileges of the victims of the National Socialists. This competitive relationship was expressed in the long known but now much more loudly expressed demand that no difference should be made any more between the mental damage suffered by the victims of National Socialist persecution and that of the victims of the SED regime.[112]

In contrast, what did begin to change noticeably in the early 90's, however, was the attitude of a considerable number of psychiatrists who intervened much more aggressively than before in this debate. Other than might be expected, the psychiatric discourse on the mental strains of the SED regime was primarily determined by West German experts. This is at any rate the impression clearly given by the professional and popular scientific publications of the early years after the 'turning point'. The West German psychiatrists even asserted in part the existence of far-reaching mental disturbances among former citizens of the GDR, by no means restricting their accounts to the political prisoners of the early years of the GDR who in the past decades had demanded – often in vain – the recognition of their mental ailments. The psychiatrists now began to talk of a so-called 'Stasi Persecution Syndrome' as a way of characterizing the mental clinical picture. As early as 1991 the Cologne psychiatrist Uwe Peters summed up: 'The syndrome

112 See, among others, the Themenkatalog der VOS zum 1. SED-Unrechtbereinigungsgesetz (Catalogue of Topics Presented by the Victims of Stalinism on the Law for the Cleansing of SED-Sponsored Injustice), in: *Die Freiheitsglocke* 45 (1995), Nr. 524, 5-8, 6.; too late and disappointing for the victims came the Second Law, Das 2. SED-Unrechtsbereinigungsgesetz, in: ibidem, 45 (1995), Nr. 519, 7-8; 'Sind wir Opfer 2. Klasse?', in: ibidem, 44 (1994), Nr. 515, 9-10; 'Anerkennung von Gesundheitsschäden weiterhin unbefriedigend', in: ibidem, 44 (1994), Nr. 514, 3; 'Die schweren Folgen kommunistischer Haft. Vortrag vom 25. Juni 1994 beim V. Bautzenforum', in: ibidem, 44 (1994), Nr. 513, 12-13.

concerns an unknown number of the approx. 50.000 survivors. It is a sequel of a form of persecution now more generally named torture. The characteristics of the persecution include arrest, interrogations, degradation, humiliation, maltreatment, assault, mass detention in tiny rooms, hunger, cold, discrimination, defamation, disgrace, outlaw, social degradation, absence of rights, uncertainty of future, threatening life and stigmatising'.[113]

Although psychiatrists like Peters complained a few years later that the persecution syndrome caused by the reprisals of the State Security Service were too little taken into account, even among experts, it is nonetheless remarkable that this phenomenon had already found a place in the textbooks by the middle of the 90's.[114] In fact, the professional literature gives rise to the impression of a rapidly growing interest in this topic, which gave psychiatric science a new field for the application of the existing findings of trauma research. The field had already been prepared by psychiatric studies on the long-term mental damage suffered by the survivors of the holocaust. Above all, the findings of work which had already been published in the 60's in West Germany were seen to provide scientific proof of the long-term effects of persecution and imprisonment.[115] However, it still seemed to be necessary to emphasize the differences between the persecution under the National Socialists and that under the SED regime. 'They are at any rate so important', wrote Peters, 'that some people do not to wish to consider making a comparison at all.' But he did not share this opinion and explained: 'Such an attitude obviously works to the disadvantage of the victims of persecution by the Stasi, as the impression can easily arise that the experience of Stasi persecution is something which anyone can overcome. But it is precisely the experience with the survivors of the holocaust that speaks against this assumption. They have expanded our knowledge of the mental after-effects of persecution and of its treatment so greatly that it is imperative to extend the benefits of this knowledge to other, indeed to all survivors of persecution. For this reason the comparison should by no means be avoided, but required.'[116]

In order to explain this position it must of course be borne in mind that the official establishment of 'post-traumatic stress disorder' as a diagnostic category in 1980 had led to a general change in the perception and interpretation of mentally

113 U.H. Peters, 'Über das Stasi-Verfolgten-Syndrom', in: *Fortschritte der Neurologie Psychiatrie* 59 (1991), 251-265, quotation on 251.

114 U.H. Peters, 'Das Verfolgten-Syndrom', in: Volker Faust (ed), *Psychiatrie. Ein Lehrbuch für Klinik, Praxis, Beratung*, 519-524.

115 A pertinent study which was said to have provided proof of the traumatic after-effects of severe prison conditions has already been mentioned: Walter von Baeyer et al. *Psychiatrie der Verfolgten*. See, for example, M. Bauer and S. Priebe, 'Zur Begutachtung psychischer Störungen nach politischer Haft in der DDR', in: *Nervenarzt 66* (1995), 388-396, 388.

116 Peters, *Stasi-Verfolgten-Syndrom*, 252.

determined disorders.[117] But the willingness of psychiatrists to attribute a special quality to the mental strains caused by the SED regime unquestionably also presupposes their willingness to attribute a particularly unjust character to the regime and a potential victim status to its citizens. About a decade after the so-called reunification this perception was so firmly established among some psychiatrists that the number of potentially affected former citizens of the GDR seemed almost incalculable. As a scientist pointed out in a scientific journal in 2002: 'There were not only about 300,000 people imprisoned for political reasons in the German Democratic Republic between 1945 and 1989, partly exposed to physical and psychological torture, but also many more people subject to threshold traumatic experiences by harassment in public and private life. As a result, from a psychiatric perspective, there should be taken into account not only specific *post-traumatic stress disorders* (PTSD), characterized by reliving of the traumata in intrusive flashbacks, avoidance of circumstances associated with the traumatic experience, and increased psychological sensitivity and arousal.'[118]

It is not surprising, therefore, that in the slipstream of such changes in psychiatric science – or at least in some of its members – organizations such as the Association of the Victims of Stalinism have, until the most recent times, referred to the restrictive recognition practice in regard to the mental damage suffered by former citizens of the GDR and have not lose sight of the higher rate of recognition for the victims of National Socialism.[119] According to the accounts of the association this amounted to 80%,[120] whereas, following a statement of the Federal Government in 1999, 'the recognition of health damage resulting from imprisonment' had leveled off 'at merely 5%' for the former victims of the SED regime.[121] As the Association of the Victims of Stalinism suggested in an enquiry to the German parliament, as on many occasions before: Did this not amount to a breach of the principle of equality?[122]

It is too early to decide whether this assumption is widely shared by former citizens of the GDR. But there are indications that a considerable number of them saw themselves as being afflicted with mental disorders attributable to the SED regime.

117 On this point see, among others, Leys, *Trauma*.

118 J. Frommer, 'Psychische Störungen durch globale gesellschaftliche Veränderungen. Zur politischen Traumatisierung der Bevölkerung in den neuen Bundesländern', in: *Fortschritte der Neurologie Psychiatrie* 70 (2002), 418-428, quotation on 418.

119 See, among others, the Themenkatalog der VOS zum 1. SED-Unrechtbereinigungsgesetz, in: *Freiheitsglocke* 45 (1995), Nr. 524, 5-8, 6.

120 Themenkatalog der VOS zum 1. SED-Unrechtbereinigungsgesetz, in: *Freiheitsglocke* 45 (1995), Nr. 524, 5-8, 6.

121 The figures are from Freyberger, 4.

122 The question put by the association can be gathered from the official answer of the German Parliament, which was handed over to the association by a member of parliament in June 2007. Telefax to Herrn Alex Latotzky, VOS, 19. June 2007, in: Archiv der VOS, Berlin.

An activity report of the state parliament of Mecklenburg-Western Pomerania at all events states as early as 1999: 'Persons with serious psychological and mental disturbances are increasingly seeking advice from the state commissioner. The spectrum ranges from persons with a "Stasi Persecution Syndrome" to citizens with a pronounced psychiatric clinical picture'. These are, as the report explains, 'mental disturbances of various kinds directly or indirectly triggered off by political persecution, imprisonment, the perception of political despotism or the generally sensed climate of fear resulting from the activities of the Ministry for State Security'. But at the same time the report also issues a warning: 'The number of mentally ill is, however, also increasing who see the activities of State Security Service as the cause of their illness without having been subjected to observation and persecution.'[123]

The welfare offices, therefore, still tended to skepticism, asking whether the claims to recognition of mental disorders as a result of repression in the GDR were not often exaggerated. The politico-moral need to recognize victimhood seems in recent times to be making a more conciliatory approach necessary. The assumption that such a step is both politically and morally called for is evidently linked to a high degree to the fact that the scientific recognition of mental damage has also found official recognition. One can only suppose that federal and state politicians are also focusing their attention on electoral votes, even though the spread of the notion of trauma as an interpretative pattern is probably no less crucial. The Federal Ministry of Labor and Social Affairs at any rate issued a circular in May 2006, which decidedly suggested that in cases of 'mental illness' which only manifested themselves after a longer period of time, a causal relationship with the repression of the SED regime should be assumed, unless a 'definite alternative causality' could be established.[124] There was only one point on which the government to this day has not yielded: When it was a matter of legally establishing the equal status of the victims according to psychiatric criteria it insisted on the need for politico-moral differentiation. An official statement of the year 2007 ran as follows: 'It is doubtful whether the victim groups of SED injustice and NS injustice are "equal". These are victim groups of different forms of political persecution. The regulation of compensation for National Socialist injustice occurred in an historical and political context totally different from that of the compensation for victims of SED injustice. For this reason the legislator can regulate the preconditions for claims for compensation of the individual groups of victims differently, as the two victim

123 Landtag Mecklenburg-Vorpommern, Drucksache 3/637, 10.08.99, http://www.mvnet.de/landesbeauftragter/Bericht98.pdf.

124 Rundschreiben. Bundesministerium für Arbeit und Soziales, IVc2 – 47035/3 9. May 2006, in: Archiv der VOS, Berlin.

groups are not equal.'[125] The indications are that the conflict over the supposedly or actually justified lower evaluation of the suffering of the victims of SED injustice has long not come to an end.

Conclusion

There can be no question that this victim discourse in reunified Germany in some respects calls to mind the 'rhetoric of victimization' which many historians regard as being a typical and dominant characteristic of West German society in the 1950's. The opposite assertion, that the way of speaking about Germany's own victims in recent years represents a break with a taboo existing since the end of the war – at least as far as the Federal Republic is concerned – is in fact just as exaggerated.[126] It is only possible to speak of breaking a taboo in public discourse at best in regard to the subject of rape, not only in East but also in West Germany.[127] In other respects examples can be found in the public discourse of the Federal Republic which show that some people in the 50's even believed that the losses and sufferings of the Germans could be compared with those of the victims of National Socialism. The political debates in the German parliament in the early years on reparations for the victims of National Socialism, on the one hand, and the reintegration measures for returning prisoners of war, displaced persons and refugees on the other provide a series of examples.[128]

The question as to who was to be regarded as a victim of National Socialism was, therefore, always controversially debated. This quickly leaps to the eye precisely in the comparison of the two German states, which mourned the victims in public course in completely different ways. It turns out, furthermore, that the public discourse on the victims was not necessarily accompanied by the recognition of long-lasting mental ailments. The opposite was also thoroughly possible. In fact, it is clearly the case that throughout the decades from the end of World War II up to the present day both the perception and the recognition of mental ailments changed greatly. The decisive reason for this was that during this period the validity of the state of psychiatric knowledge on the mental resilience of human beings changed. This is equally true of East and West Germany, even though the formation of ideological blocks not only had an effect on the choice of the per-

125 Telefax an Herrn Alex Latotzky, VOS, 19. June 2007, in: Archiv der VOS, Berlin.

126 This debate was triggered off above all by Winfried G. Sebald, *Luftkrieg und Literatur*; Günter Grass, *Im Krebsgang*, and Jörg Friedrich, *Der Brand*. For a criticism see, among others, Moeller, 'Sinking ships'.

127 Grossmann shows, however, in 'A question of silence' that the issue of rape was indeed thematized in the years directly following the war.

128 See Moeller, 'Deutsche Opfer'.

sons whose ailments were publicly discussed but also influenced the choice of the psychiatric knowledge on the consequences of violence and terror which became officially established.

Nevertheless, remarkable agreements can also be observed. Psychiatrists in both East and West Germany were for a long time after the war convinced that the violence of the National Socialist war would not produce any long-term mental after-effects. A debate did indeed begin in West Germany after some years on whether this could also be assumed to the same degree for the prisoners of war returning from Soviet concentration camps. In East Germany there was silence on this question. But in the end it turned out that neither of the two countries abandoned the dominant state of psychiatric knowledge. It was also assumed on both sides of the internal German border that it was in principle necessary to proceed with extreme caution in the recognition of mental ailments in connection with applications for pensions. In both countries there was no question of abandoning the notion that long-lasting mental complaints are 'genetically' or 'functionally' determined. The fear of the 'pension neurotic' who only wanted to obtain financial assistance fraudulently was widespread among doctors and the authorities in both East and West Germany. It was a shared conviction that psychiatric complaints without organic damage could not be classified as an 'illness'. Accordingly, in the Federal Republic, a war victim's pension was not approved for mental ailments. Consequently those who made claims on the basis of such ailments were refused the official status of war victims. As far as it can be followed up, this could only be reckoned with under certain conditions and after a certain point in time. The way in which people interpreted their ailments proved at all events to be highly dependent on the interpretative possibilities available to them. In the Federal Republic, for example, it can be observed that the prisoners of war who returned in the course of the 50's took up psychosomatic forms of explanation which enabled them to link their ailments with the stresses and strains of their imprisonment. In the years directly after the war, on the other hand, it was seldom the case that those concerned traced their mental ailments back to their experience of violence. In the GDR this process of transformation was not set in motion to the same degree. It seems that the discourse on the recognition of mental disorders was to a great degree a Western discourse. It is this discourse which today provides the interpretative patterns which are the framework for the demands of many former citizens of the GDR for recognition as victims of the SED regime.

5 Where Have All the Traumatized People Gone?

World War II and its aftermath in Italy: trauma and oblivion

» *Maria Teresa Brancaccio*

In 1999, Donatella Levi wrote about her experiences as a Jewish child born in Verona in 1939, reflecting on the impact of Fascist racial laws, the war, and the Shoah on the lives and identity of children and adults alike.[1] After reading Anglo-American studies of 'survivor's syndrome', she puzzled over why so little attention had been paid to the traumatic effects of persecution and deportation in Italy. Why had it taken until the 1990's for the Italian public to recognize the suffering of Jewish people under Fascism and during World War II?[2] Bearing in mind that persecution, detention, and deportation had different rationales, characteristics and implications for different groups under Fascism and during World War II, Levi's questions could also be extended to political and military deportees.

World War II was a shattering and complex experience in Italy. Fascist Italy entered the war allied with Nazi Germany in June 1940. After catastrophic defeats, internal crises (e.g. food and fuel shortages and repeated aerial bombardment of major Italian cities), and the Allied invasion of Sicily, the Fascist regime came to an end in 1943. Marshall Badoglio (the new prime minister appointed by the king in early September 1943) signed a secret armistice with the Allies while the country was still formally a German ally and its untimely proclamation threw the country into chaos: the army was left without orders and many were taken prisoner by the *Wehrmacht*. The king and Badoglio fled south and established a government under Allied protection while the German army quickly occupied the north and the centre down to Rome.

1 Levi, 'La psicoanalisi italiana'. In: Maida (ed.), *1938. I bambini e le leggi razziali in Italia*, which is based on the proceedings of a meeting on the consequences of the fascist anti-Jewish laws for children held in Turin in 1998 to commemorate the sixtieth anniversary of the introduction of the first anti-Jewish laws in Italy in 1938.

2 The first Italian publication presenting an overview of the international literature on the psychological effects of deportation was published in 1991. See Verri Melo, *La Sindrome del sopravvissuto*.

With German support, Mussolini established a new Fascist government (*Repubblica Sociale Italiana*, or *Repubblica di Salò*) in the occupied territories: Jews, political opponents, and civilians were deported to extermination and concentration camps in the Third Reich. The Allies and the Italian resistance movement that emerged after the armistice fought against the Germans and the Republic of Salo and Italy plunged into civil war. Eventually, the Allies and the Resistance liberated the country, ending the war in early May 1945.

In the post-war period, few psychiatric articles dealt with the traumatic effects of war and deportation. Still, even limited interest soon faded and official definitions of psychic trauma included in post-war reparations legislation remained predominantly based on organicist constitutionalism. Memories of persecutions and deportations too faded in the decades after the war, only to resurface in Italy quite recently.

This article seeks to identify the social, professional and political contingencies that shaped prevailing attitudes toward persecution, deportation, and wartime violence in Italy. The starting point is the discussion of the concept of 'traumatic psychoneurosis', first adopted by Italian psychiatry during World War I, which remained the main diagnostic category to refer to neurological and psychological disorders associated with wartime trauma after World War II. Next, after a short overview of Fascism and World War II, the article deals with the trajectories of different groups of war victims and the reparatory legislation.

The emergence of traumatic psychoneurosis in Italy

Influenced by on-going debate over 'traumatic neuroses' in German and French psychiatry, medical interest in post-traumatic nervous and mental disorders also emerged in Italy during the early twentieth century. Already since the second half of the nineteenth century, a growing body of international medical literature addressed the nervous and mental impact of railway and factory accidents on workers. With the introduction of the first workers' accident insurance legislations, debates over post-traumatic disorders among victims of workplace accidents transcended the clinical sphere, giving rise to medical-legal controversies over workers' eligibility for compensation.[3]

During World War I, 'traumatic psychoneurosis' became Italian psychiatry's main frame of reference for dealing with nervous and mental disorders among servicemen.[4] As with the English and French, increasing numbers of soldiers were

3 For the reception of this topic in Italy, see Morselli, *Le neurosi traumatiche*.

4 The first medical reports in Italy appeared during the Italian-Turkish war of 1911-1912. For the first reports in World War I on this subject see Consiglio, 'Le anomalie nel carattere dei militari'.

referred to the medical services exhibiting deafness, muteness, amnesia, paralysis, and mental exhaustion with no apparent organic cause. A flurry of medical publications on traumatic psychoneurosis (a term that included traumatic hysteria and neurasthenia, as well as *isteronevrastenia nervosa, psiconeurosi da spavento*, and *psicastenia melancoliforme*) resulted. More and more servicemen reported puzzling symptoms such as sudden paralysis, confusion, deafness etc., and the issue became a serious problem in Italy and elsewhere. As with work-related accidents, some medical professionals voiced concerns about possible malingering. For military doctors, identifying fraudulent cases became part of the standard assessment routine.[5] Nevertheless, the wartime experience of physicians and psychiatrists refocused medical interest on the role played by emotions in the appearance of psychic disturbances.

Italian psychiatry after World War I

Dominant medical theory in Italy maintained that war-related nervous and mental disorders affected predisposed individuals; combat circumstances simply triggered a latent constitutional weakness (*fragilità*) or inherent mental illness already present just below the surface. In general, psychiatrists viewed traumatic psychoneuroses – that is, hysteria-like symptoms and neurasthenia – as transitory states treatable with brief therapy and a period of rest and recuperation. As a consequence, traumatic psychoneurosis was considered neither a disorder attributable to combat, nor a condition that resulted in long-term disability.

At the end of 1918, at the first National Convention For the Assistance of War Invalids (*Convegno nazionale per l'assistenza agli invalidi di guerra*), prevailing medical theories on traumatic psychoneurosis were incorporated in the criteria for determining eligibility for a disability pension. Common psychoneurosis was thus legally defined as only a temporary condition not caused by war directly. As a consequence, a diagnosis of psychoneurosis did not qualify one for a war pension.[6]

In Italy, as elsewhere, medical debates over organic versus psychic or emotional etiology in the formation of psychoneurosis continued into the early 1920's. By the first decade of the twentieth century, Freud's theories made limited headway among Italian psychiatrists. After the war, psychological approaches to war neurosis (such as those devised by Rivers or Simmel) met with interest among certain psychiatric circles. Widespread belief in organic predisposition notwithstand-

5 For a discussion of the role played by Italian psychiatrists in World War I see Bianchi, 'Psychiatrists, soldiers and officers'.

6 Ibidem, 251-252.

ing, certain psychiatrists emphasized the 'pathogenic' influence of combat along with the role of emotions and psychological dynamics in the genesis of nervous and mental disorders.[7] Most authoritative psychiatrists, however, remained firmly anchored in the biological approach. In his opening speech on the occasion of the 26th Meeting of the Italian Psychiatric Society held in Rome in 1923, the Society's president Enrico Morselli resolutely rejected 'new theories that were not based on experimental research'.[8] Discussion about the uncertain etiology and controversial medical status of psychoneuroses clearly demonstrated the professional apprehensions of an older generation of psychiatrists toward the growing popularity and the theoretical appeal of psychological medicine. Even the distinguished psychiatrist Gustavo Modena – among the first Italian psychiatrists interested in Freud's theories in the 1910's – argued that 'psychogenesis' was simply jargon used to conceal the empirical deficits of psychoanalysis and that psychological explanations could only complement naturalistic and biological study. Arguments by Marco Levi-Bianchini in favor of psychoanalysis[9] were firmly rejected by Modena and others. Clearly, there was little room for discussion of theories deemed incompatible with the tenets of the Positivist school. In the subsequent years, psychoanalysis continued to occupy a marginal position within the Italian Society of Psychiatry. However, contacts between those interested in Freud's theories and the Vienna Psychoanalytical Society strengthened with the foundation, in 1925, of the Società Psicoanalitica Italiana by Marco Levi-Bianchini and Edoardo Weiss. The latter (a psychiatrist and a psychoanalyst who studied in Vienna) was a member of the International Psychoanalytical Association.[10] The first Italian psychoanalytic journal, the *Rivista italiana di psicoanalisi*, appeared between 1932 and 1934. However, interest in psychoanalytic theories and a therapy was largely limited to intellectual circles. In 1938, as a consequence of anti-Jewish laws, the Italian Psychoanalytical Society was dissolved, since most Italian psychoanalysts were also Jewish. Most emigrated in order to avoid persecution. The 'racial legislation' also damaged distinguished representatives of the Positive School, like Jewish psychiatrist Gustavo Modena who, at the time, was vice-president of the Italian Psychiatric Society. Like other Jewish medical professionals, he was expelled from the society and dismissed from his post.[11]

In July of the same year, Arturo Donaggio, director of the neuropsychiatric clinic at the University of Bologna and Morselli's successor as SIP president, signed the Manifest of Racial Scientists. Although Donaggio's support for Fascist

---

7 Pellacani, 'Le neuropatie emotive', 62.
8 See 'Atti del XXVI Congresso'.
9 See Levi-Bianchini in 'Atti del XXVI Congresso', 55-57.
10 The Italian Psychoanalytical Society was recognized by the International Psychoanalytical Association in 1932.
11 Peloso, 'Psychiatry and psychiatric patients', 70.

racial theories was not widely shared by his colleagues, nonetheless the SIP now became associated with Fascism in a fashion it had avoided until then.[12]

Fascism and Italian Jews

During the second half of the 1920's, Fascist government became a regime. The institutional asset of the old Liberal state was left in place, but devoided of its democratic substance. Between 1925 and 1929 the 'Fascist revolution' in Italy aimed at a comprehensive transformation of political, economic and social institutions. The regime established new institutions that would enhance support for Fascism, and incorporate the masses into the state in a way Liberals had failed to do.

The role of the Italian prime minister was transformed from *primus inter pares* into the source of all executive power, accountable, not to parliament, but directly to the king alone. Mussolini appointed and dismissed his own ministers, who served as his dependent subordinates.[13] He also exercised direct control over government agents in the provinces, the prefects, and through them, the security forces. Furthermore, as a result of the reforms of 1926 and 1928, the elective element in local government was abolished. Through the top-down appointment of local councilors and mayors (renamed *podestà*), the power of the provincial prefects, and through them the power of the central government, was notably enhanced.

A succession of 'exceptional' laws and decrees issued in 1926 and 1927 suppressed freedom of expression, association and assembly. A separate system of justice and policing was set up for political crimes. Liberty could now be limited by official decree without recourse to regular courts, and a Special Tribunal (*Tribunale Speciale*) was established for political trials. The death penalty for serious 'crimes against the state' was also reinstated. Punishments for anti-fascist intellectuals and other 'undesirables', including homosexuals, included imprisonment and banishment to remote areas of the south and the islands (*confino*). In 1926, the leadership of the Communist Party was arrested. Subsequently tried by the *Tribunale Speciale*, they were sentenced to more than twenty years imprisonment.

In the same years, the OVRA, the Italian secret police, was established and headed by bureaucrats from the Interior ministry. Through its vast and pervasive network of agents, the OVRA successfully infiltrated anti-fascist groups in Italy and abroad. The Fascist regime equipped itself with powerful instruments to coerce dissidents and extract obedience to its dictatorship, but it also employed more subtle methods. The regime encouraged collaboration and a network of informants,

---

12 Ibidem, 69.

13 Pollard, *The fascist experience*. See also Lyttelton, *The seizure of power* and Payne, *A history of fascism*.

who helped the police eliminate opposition through anonymous denunciations. In the 1930's, following its consolidation of power, the regime continued to control and intimidate opponents, both actual and potential. Detailed files were kept on dissidents, mail was regularly censored and political opponents were subjected to physical and psychological terror.[14]

The Racial Laws of 1938

Italian Jews were arguably the most integrated in Europe. In the *Risorgimento* their struggle for emancipation and the struggle for the creation of a unitary state 'were virtually synonymous'. At the time of the Dreyfus case in France, the Jewish general Giuseppe Ottolenghi was the Italian Minister of War and the tutor of the royal family. By 1910, Italy had its second Jewish President of the Council.[15] As Sarfatti's well-documented study shows, Italian Jews were slightly less fascist than the rest of the Italian population, but many of them had adhered to Fascism.[16]

Anti-Jewish persecution starting in September 1938 was therefore a 'breach of the pact of equal citizenship' established in the Risorgimento.[17] The laws passed between 1938 and 1943 excluded Italian Jews from education, academia, various sectors of employment, the armed forces, the National Fascist Party, in short from every aspect of Italian society. The legislation represented a major 'rupture in Italian history'.[18] As Sarfatti writes, the aim of Fascist regime was to eliminate all Jews – foreign as well as Italian – from the country.[19]

When Italy entered World War II, all foreign Jews still living in the country were interned. Individual entries of foreign Jews in the country (that were already declared illegal in 1938) were strictly banned. in 1940-1941. The government revoked Italian citizenship to Jews who had acquired it after 1918. '[I]n 1940-1 the government started to work on a law that would expel Italian Jews once and for all and officially communicated this intention to the Union of the Italian Jewish Community'.[20] As the war spread, however, such a plan became difficult to realize. Between 1940 and 1943, the government adopted measures for extending internment and forced labor also to Italian Jews.

---

14 See Franzinelli, *I tentacoli dell'Ovra*.
15 See Stille, 'The double bind of Italian Jews', 25.
16 See Sarfatti, *Gli ebrei nell'Italia fascista*. As Stille points out, 'Italy was a virtually unique case in Europe, a country where Jews were often Fascists.' Stille, 'The double bind of Italian Jews', 22.
17 See Sarfatti, 'Characteristics and objectives', 75.
18 Ibidem.
19 Ibidem, 76.
20 Ibidem.

Italy in World War II

In Italy, the war years were characterized by a crescendo of violence culminating in the German occupation of 1943. In June 1940, military authorities warned that Mussolini's decision to enter the conflict on Nazi Germany's side was untimely – they were acutely aware of the country's insufficient military preparation – and some senior Fascist politicians considered the move unwise. Indeed, Mussolini's aspirations for a war of territorial conquest that would enhance Italian power in the Mediterranean soon proved illusory. The badly equipped Italian army and its inept military strategy ended in a series of humiliating defeats in the Balkans and North Africa. Italy relied increasingly on German military support as the alliance devolved into a frustrating relationship of military dependency on the Nazis.

In July 1943, shortly after the Anglo-American troops landed in Sicily, Mussolini's leadership was challenged by the Grand Council of Fascism, a consultative body consisting of senior Fascist politicians. Mussolini was dismissed and subsequently imprisoned and the Grand Council voted in favor of re-establishing a liberal regime, declaring an end to Fascism. King Vittorio Emanuele III appointed Marshall Badoglio as the new Italian prime minister. The hope for an end to the war was shattered by Badoglio's initial public announcement that Italy would continue to fight as an Axis ally. On 8 September 1943, the announcement of a secret armistice signed between Marshall Badoglio's government and the Allied forces threw the army and the country into total chaos. Many Italian soldiers were taken prisoner and deported or executed by their former German allies and the Nazi army occupied the Peninsula down to Rome. The country was divided in two. In the occupied territory, Mussolini became head of the newly formed *Repubblica Sociale Italiana*, a puppet state controlled by Nazi Germany. In the south, liberated by the Anglo-American forces, Marshall Badoglio and the king established the Kingdom of the South. In October 1943, they declared war on Germany. Between 1943 and 1945, the country was the theatre of exacting battles between the German forces entrenched in the occupied zone and Allied strategies relying on massive aerial carpet bombing to crush German resistance.

In autumn 1943, Jewish deportation also commenced in the German occupied territories. The census of the Jewish population of 1938 and the existence of concentration camps already established by the Fascist government by 1940 greatly facilitated the capture and deportation of Jews, as well as citizens who refused to serve in the army or cooperate with the newly established *Repubblica Sociale*.

Jewish persecution

Late September 1943, Nazi extermination policy extended to Italy and, in November, the RSI government issued its own anti-Jewish proclamation. The 32,307 Italian Jews and foreign refugees who lived in the occupied territory were now trapped in a double police system. The first stage of organized persecution started in October 1943, with the arrival of a German flying unit in Italy.[21] Their first raid took place in Rome on October 16, directed at the Jewish quarter: a thousand Jews were rounded up and put on a train for Auschwitz. The Germans then moved to the North and carried out surprise raids in all major cities with the collaboration of the local Italian police. Between October and December all captured Jews were transported to Auschwitz.

The policy of the *Repubblica di Salò* was outlined in November during a general assembly of the *Partito Fascista Repubblicano*. Point 7 of an eighteen-point program stated that Jews were effectively considered 'as having an enemy nationality'. On 30 November, the Interior Minister issued police order no.5 which ruled that all Jews, of Italian or foreign origin, were subject to arrest and internment, with their assets forfeit. From the beginning of December 1943, *Questori* (provincial police detachments of the RSI) carried out the arrests. This marked the start of a period far worse than the previous one, because Italian police officers were in possession of all the addresses of Jews from the previous census carried out by previous Fascist government. From February 1944, Fossoli camp, a large transit camp near Carpi chosen for its proximity to a railway junction, fell under German authority. A permanent office was established within the Gestapo to keep an eye on the arrest of the Jews and to organize their efficient deportation.[22]

In Italian territories under German administration, the German police carried out the arrests directly. Prior to deportation, the Jews arrested in Fiume, Trieste and Padua, as well as part of those arrested in Venice, were detained in a camp at Risiera di San Sabba, also a place of torture and death for many anti-fascists and partisans. The total number of victims of the Shoah is estimated at 8,529, that is '26.24 percent of the entire Jewish population' living in Italy 'just before the German occupation in September 1943'.[23] As Liliana Picciotto argues, such a percentage is by no means small when compared, for instance, to Shoah victims in France (estimated at 21-22 percent of the total).[24]

21 See Picciotto, 'The Shoah in Italy', 212.
22 Ibidem, 214-219.
23 Ibidem, 220-221.
24 Ibidem, 221.

Resistenza

By 1942 anti-fascism was on the rise. Communists and socialists began clandestine operations and started an underground press. Republicans, radicals and liberals joined together to form the Action Party (*Partito d'Azione*). A new Christian Democratic Party (DC) was formed with the support of the Vatican. After Mussolini's fall (25 July 1943) the parties formed anti-fascist committees, but they were still numerically weak. It was only after the armistice (8 September 1943) that they 'emerged into the limelight'. In September, they formed the *Comitato di Liberazione Nazionale* (National Liberation Committee) and called upon the Italian people to join them in the Resistance against Nazi-Fascism.

The partisan movement consisted of members and sympathizers of political parties that were outlawed by the Fascist regime, recruits escaping military service in the RSI, and potential 'guest' workers who wished to avoid deportation to Germany. Most of the 'bands' were associated with political parties. In the beginning of the Resistance, Communists made up about 70 percent of the total partisan mobilization ('Garibaldi brigades'). The second largest partisan groups were the 'Justice and Liberty brigades' – radical and democratic anti-fascists from the *Partito d'Azione* and the Justice and Liberty (*Giustizia Libertà*) movement, an anti-fascist group founded in Paris in 1929 by Italian refugees. The Justice and Liberty brigades were committed to establishing a republican democracy and to introduce political measures aimed at correcting economic distortions and injustices of the capitalist system. The Socialist Party, that in 1943 incorporated the *Movimento d'Unità Proletaria* and was renamed *Partito Socialista Italiano di Unità Proletaria* (PSIUP), formed the 'Matteotti bands'. The Socialist Party was considerably smaller than before the war and, unlike the Communists, had not maintained contact with the working class during the war. Although, in August 1943, the party program 'talked the language of revolution of the workers' socialist republic (...) in reality it contained a great number of ideological positions, ranging from the cautious reformism (...) to the young revolutionaries.'[25]

The Christian Democratic brigade, the 'Green Flames', emerged from Catholic Action, particularly the youth sections, and was supported by members of the clergy sympathetic to the Resistance. The participation of the Catholic movement in the struggle against Fascism underlined the fact that it was a popular struggle, not a revolutionary socialist or communist movement. As time passed, an increasing number of workers fleeing from persecution and arrest in the factories, military conscripts fleeing from the *Repubblica di Salò*, escaped prisoners of war, and Italian Jews (about 2,000) joined the Resistance.

---

25 Ginsborg, *A history of contemporary Italy*, 13-14.

In the regions under German occupation, the various political parties cooperated in the clandestine Committees of National Liberation (CLN). Actionists and Socialists hoped that CLN's would form the basis of a new democratic organization after the war. They organized the fifteen partisan republics and had their own tribunals. In January 1944, the central CLN in Rome invested the committee in Milan with extraordinary powers of government in the North, naming it the National Committee for the Liberation of Upper Italy (CLNAI). The CLNAI was virtually a provisional government and the Allies felt obliged to recognize it as the official representative body of the Resistance. However, they took some measures in order to keep the partisan units in line and to make sure that they were disarmed as soon as their area of operations was liberated. Since the Soviets instructed the Communists to cooperate fully with the Allies and to abandon all thought of a social revolution, the CLNAI worked closely with the Allies, providing temporary administration for the liberated areas, purging fascists from local government and the police, and handing over Milan with a workable administration. About 100,000 armed fighters (among them a number of women) took part in the Resistance and 'many thousands of others helped in some way.' Casualty figures among partisans were far higher than those incurred in regular warfare.[26]

In 1944, the *Associazione Nazionale Partigiani Italiani* (ANPI) was formed with the aim of establishing a census of the Resistance movement members. An organization dominated by Communists, the ANPI played a prominent role as a major Resistance organization immediately after the war. By 1947, however, it had lost its central position. Political tensions at national and international level led the non-communist members to leave the ANPI and to establish two other partisans' associations.

The laws for the reintegration of Jewish rights

The racial laws were not repealed with the fall of Fascism (25 July 1943), allegedly in order not to alarm the German ally.[27] As Mario Toscano noted, the abrogation of the Anti-Jewish legislation was not a priority 'either for the Badoglio government or the bureaucracy in Rome, or for the media or some distinguished representatives of the Holy See.'[28] On the 22nd of September, i.e. after the armistice, Badoglio informed the prefects of the provinces liberated by the Allies (Bari, Brindisi, Lecce, and Taranto) of the imminent abrogation of the legislation limiting the civil and political rights of 'citizens of Jewish race'. Such a measure was indeed requested by

26 Ibidem, 70.
27 See Toscano, 'The abrogation of racial laws', 149.
28 Ibidem, 149-150.

article 31 of the text of the 'long armistice' that was signed in Malta with the Allies on September 29. The abrogation of the legislation was a slow process. In its initial stage, it was hampered by an administration still permeated by a racist mentality. Finally, two royal decrees were issued, one concerning the re-establishment of civil and political rights for Italian and foreign citizens 'declared or considered of Jewish race', the other concerning the re-establishment of their patrimonial rights. The publication of the latter decree was postponed with the argument that its publication might provoke a worsening of the conditions for the Jews in the *Repubblica di Salò*. In June 1944, the liberation of Rome, the gradual reorganization of the administration, and the presence of a reorganized *Unione delle comunità israelitiche italiane* accelerated the process. In October 1945, the decree on the restoration of patrimonial rights came into force. Between the autumn of 1944 and 1947, a corpus of laws was issued to annul the anti-Jewish legislation issued by Fascism since 1938, and from 1943 by the RSI. Restitution of assets did not proceed without problems: returning assets confiscated during the Republic of Salò and the German occupation in particular proved quite difficult.[29]

The post-war policy towards veterans and deportees

At the end of the war, the terms 'veterans' and 'deportees' covered a large variety of groups with distinct experiences. The largest group consisted of the more than 600,000 former *Internati Militari Italiani* who had refused to continue the fight on the German side and had paid for their refusal with internment and forced labor. Then there were between 42,000 and 45,000 deportees – about 8,000 of them were Jews and the others were anti-fascists, members of the Resistance, individuals who had supported resistance activities in various ways, as well as people who were arrested during roundups.[30] Of this group, only about 4,000 survived. Within the group, however, the Jewish deportees had by far the highest mortality rate. The category of veterans also included the prisoners of war – approximately one million individuals coming back from Australia, India, North Africa, England, the Middle-East, United States, Yugoslavia, and the USSR.[31]

The measures adopted for the repatriation of veterans and deportees proved severely inadequate. Many of them had to face long and difficult journeys home

29 Ibidem, 150-154. See also Pavan, 'Gli incerti percorsi della reintegrazione'.

30 On 17 April 1944, for instance, 1,500 men between the ages of 16 and 60 were taken prisoner by the German army in an isolated Roma neighborhood and transported to Germany. See Isastia (ed.), *Il ritorno dei prigionieri italini*, 14.

31 Ibidem.

and on their return were met with indifference or even hostility.[32] The government did not adopt any measures to secure comprehensive documentation concerning deportation and carry out a census of the deportees and internees. Moreover, the veterans and deportees' associations were looked upon with mistrust by the government. When, in 1945 in Turin, the newly established association of military deportees ANEI (*Associazione Nazionale Ex Internati*) demanded from the authorities to be recognized as a national association, the Ministry of the Interior sent a circular letter to the prefects asking them to discourage such initiatives. In addition, the prefect of Turin was requested to urgently gather information on the ANEI promoters, on the Association members, its political program, and on their relationship with other associations. Concerns regarding the emergence of veterans' movements similar to those which appeared after World War I, however, were not counterbalanced by the adoption of appropriate relief measures.

Italian government established an institute exclusively for the history of the Resistance, and showed remarkably little interest in other victims of war and deportation. The void was filled by two organizations: the National Association of Deportees (*Associazione Nazionale Deportati* or ANED – mainly representing political deportees) and, in 1955, by the Centre for Contemporary Jewish Documentation (CDEC). The local sections of the ANED became the major point of reference for political deportees. Both the local and the national organizations soon acquired a major role in promoting educational events, conferences, research on the theme of deportation. The CDEC realized a major and detailed study on the history of Jewish deportation from Italy and established itself as a high-profile research and documentary institution.

Post-war Italian psychiatry

The war deeply affected the Italian public health system. Aerial bombardments, the lack of medicines, drastic reductions in food and fuel supplies, and the requisitioning of resources and institutions for the military took their toll on the entire health system. Mental hospitals in particular were heavily hit by the war, suffering casualties among patients, nurses and doctors alike. In October 1946, the Italian Psychiatric Society (SIP) sent a questionnaire to some 200 psychiatric hospitals and clinics for nervous and mental illness across the country.[33] The aim was to assess conditions in psychiatric facilities after the destruction and deprivation caused by the war. The report, based on returns of questionnaires from 120 institutions (among them 66 of the 69 psychiatric hospitals in Italy), made for

32 See Rossi Doria, *Memoria e storia*.

33 In total two hundred institutions, including 69 mental hospitals.

grim reading, depicting a scenario far worse than the SIP anticipated. Forty-five of sixty-six psychiatric hospitals in question were located near significant military targets such as railways and factories. Only thirty hospitals reported no great damage, while the rest had suffered from either direct hits from aerial bombings targeting nearby military objectives, or simply because they were close to the front line. Fifty hospitals reported that the military – mainly the German army – had requisitioned or stolen everything that could be removed. This included beds, medication, and medical equipment.[34] All institutions reported enormous difficulties, scarcity of food, medicines, and clothes for the patients, as well as the absence of water and electricity. It was estimated that aerial bombardments and close proximity to fighting on the ground caused three hundred casualties among patients and staff.[35] The number of patient deaths attributable to the deprivations of war in psychiatric hospitals, however, was far greater: according to different reports, it ranged from 24,000 to 30,000.[36] Under such extreme circumstances, it is hardly surprising that research activity was very limited and that many neuropsychiatric journals did not appear regularly during the war years.[37]

Trauma after World War II

At the end of the war, due to the circumstances discussed above, only a limited number of medical articles appeared on nervous and mental disorders among military personnel, civilians, and deportees. One was a review of the international literature on the relation between 'affective psychosis' (mania, melancholy anxiety) and wartime among the general population. In this study, the director of the provincial psychiatric hospital of Imola, Andrea Mari, discussed the surprisingly limited psychic effects that repeated traumatic events such as aerial bombings, closeness to the fighting zone, and prolonged safety concerns had on the local civilian population of the area. His review of the international literature on this subject confirmed his direct observation. With the exception of a slight increase in anxiety disorders observed among the population in the year preceding the war, the international literature consistently reported a net diminution of such disorders together with a marked diminution of the total number of patients admitted annually into psychiatric hospitals during the entire duration of the war.[38] The drastic reduction of patient populations in psychiatric hospitals during the war was a phe-

34 Padovani and Bonfiglioli, 'Le vicende storiche'.
35 Ibidem, 381.
36 Peloso, 'Psychiatry and psychiatric patients', 70.
37 Padovani and Bonfiglioli, 'Le vicende storiche', 384.
38 Mari, 'Guerra e psicosi'; Padovani, 'Esperienze e considerazioni'.

nomenon that puzzled psychiatrists in Italy as well as in France and Belgium. Statistical data for the pre-war years showed relatively stable intakes, with slight but gradual annual increases in hospitalizations for severe mental illness. To account for the reduced intakes during the war years, some psychiatrists pointed to war-related problems such as logistical difficulties or population displacement from cities to safer country areas. Others argued that wartime conditions might positively affect individuals suffering from severe mental illness. Even a few reported that the bombings and chaos of war caused unexpected improvements in the condition of some chronically ill hospitalized psychiatric patients.

As far as the general populace, medical reports indicated that the traumatic experience of the war had little psychiatric effect on most. In his review of the international medical literature, Mari explained such phenomenon in psychological terms. He argued that it was an indication of 'the efficacy of the individual's defense mechanisms, resilience [and] ability to maintain equilibrium [when confronted by] war's noxious factors'.[39] In facts, however, the limited number of wartime mental and nervous disorders could hardly be explained by organic theories. If distressing and traumatic conditions that involved the whole population for an extended period of time did not result in increased waves of neurosis and mental breakdowns, then the theory of constitutional predisposition clearly had to be revised or at least revisited, since circumstances should have unleashed latent mental disorders at an unprecedented rate.

Italian psychiatric literature on mental disorders in the army indicated that an epidemic of traumatic paralysis and hysterical syndromes similar to the ones that had characterized World War 1 did not resurface. Psychosomatic troubles – stomach and heart problems – however, increased.[40] A similar phenomenon was noted in the German army and might be interpreted as the outcome of militaristic values – discipline, obedience, courage, sacrifice – inculcated in an entire culture through education and youth organizations under both dictatorships. Still, psychoneurosis remained a fairly common diagnosis among servicemen. Data reported by military neurologist Giorgio Padovani on 3,023 patients examined between June 1945 and December 1946 at the Military Hospital in Turin showed that psychoneurosis was most common among higher ranks: 356 of the 708 officers (i.e. 50%) and 111 of the 282 non-commissioned officers (i.e. 40%) received such a diagnosis. Among the 1,240 soldiers observed, only 339 (i.e. 27%) were diagnosed as psychoneurotics. In keeping with a class-related diagnostic tradition from World War 1, the author traced a distinction between the psychoneurotic disorders affecting the officers (mostly showing symptoms of psycho-asthenia and neurasthenia, i.e. depression, psychic exhaustion) and enlisted men (hysteria, often associated with

39 Mari, 'Guerra e psicosi', 29.
40 Ibidem.

'emotional epilepsy', i.e. convulsive crisis not caused by organic factors). Such distinctions emphasized a distinct etiology for each group. Officers suffered conditions caused by the loss of 'nervous energy':[41] their command functions drained their cerebral energy as dual responsibilities to their men and superiors required constant, exhausting mental alertness. Ordinary soldiers, on the other hand, suffered from hysterical disorders in which, as Padovani put it 'the traumatic factor acts as a catalyst for the constitutional predisposition.'[42] Other categories in Padovani's sample were (in decreasing order): 384 invalids, 112 partisans, 93 young military conscripts, 40 women, 27 police officers, 27 civilians, and 20 former military internees. Apart from the obvious numerical discrepancy between other groups and the military, it is interesting to note that psychoneurosis accounted for at least half of all diagnoses of women and police officers, i.e. men responsible for public order in the months following Liberation. Padovani explained the frequency of psychoneurotic disorders in the latter group as a product of their difficult task in the tumultuous post-war period.

In the second section of his article, devoted to 'clinically interesting cases', Padovani deals with three episodes of traumatic neuroses among military deportees. Like the doctor Furio Martini, who published on this subject in 1946, Padovani was an army captain in the medical corps captured and deported to German territory during the war. Both he and Martini explained traumatic neurosis and psychosis within the somatic paradigm of constitutional predisposition. Yet, especially Martini, who served as a doctor in the concentration camp of Fullen Ems (Westfalia) during his detention, vividly described inhuman conditions for Italian military deportees. Living in 'poorly kept...and overcrowded barracks', they were obliged to 'perform heavy and uninterrupted work, in all weather, and under the constant surveillance of bestial guards', so badly malnourished that '...the bone structure becomes clearly visible under the skin'.[43] In his article 'Polyneuritis in war prisoners', Martini alternated descriptions of camp inmates with accurate medical information on the infirmities and infections that ravaged their bodies, giving a detailed account of a reality still unknown to many of his Italian colleagues in 1946.

In 1947, psychiatrist Ottorino Balduzzi, who had been deported to Mauthausen for his resistance activities, challenged the widespread belief that war experiences, even the most difficult and painful ones, would not affect essentially sane individuals. During a presentation at the 23rd Meeting of the Italian Society of Psychiatry, he explained how, before the war, he held the same view as his colleagues, but his

41 According to the neurological theory of the time that the nervous system only had a limited amount of available energy.
42 Padovani, 'Esperienze e considerazioni', 189.
43 Martini, 'Polinevriti', 476-477.

detention in Mauthausen concentration camp changed his mind. There he witnessed individuals who 'did not seem affected by any pre-disposition [to mental illness]' develop schizophrenia and 'paranoid syndromes'.[44] Balduzzi's contribution, however, was largely ignored and medical interest in the psychopathologies arising among concentration camp inmates and prisoners of war was fairly limited and short-lived.

In 1950, the psychiatrist Gherarducci complained that he could find nothing in the Italian medical literature on psychic disorders affecting prisoners of war after their repatriation. He reported on twenty-two former prisoners of war hospitalized in his clinic since the end of the war to 1948. Most of these patients, he stated, had not suffered any psychical disorder during their time in captivity. Yet after their repatriation, they had manifested symptoms of severe depression and apathy that became increasingly severe and 'culminated in psychotic illness'.[45] Five of them already displayed symptoms of illness while prisoners of war. The rest – mostly young men aged twenty-five to thirty – suffered no psychical disorders during their captivity. Gherarducci hypothesized that 'exogenous factors' – e.g. the sudden transition from captivity to freedom, prolonged nervous tension, the different climatic conditions, anxieties about their relatives – could have evoked the disorders. Although he stressed the role played by 'strong emotions' in the evolution of psychoses, he nevertheless concluded that detention in the camps had [only] 'accelerated the appearance of the illness' in predisposed individuals.[46] Gherarducci reported the locations of camps where the patients had been kept prisoner and the duration of captivity, but made no distinction between the different regimes inmates were subjected to in German work camps and in camps for prisoners of war located in Africa, Great Britain or the United States and did not try to establish any relationship between the patients' living conditions during captivity and their subsequent illness.

War pension legislation

In the post-war period, the National Association of Mutilated and Disabled Veterans (ANMIG) made repeated appeals to the Parliament to quickly pass a war disability compensation. At the 12th National Congress in 1949 (31 October-5 November), the Association's President emphasized the government's moral and legal obligation to grant war pensions to all who had served their country. He stressed the Association's non-partisan stance and its respect for the differing political

44 Balduzzi, 'Interlocuzione al XXIII Congresso', 207.
45 Gherarducci, 'Alcune considerazioni', 20.
46 Ibidem, 36.

and religious beliefs of its members, maintaining its goal was to preserve justice and freedom. This formulation, coupled with previous declarations, indicated the ANMIG's intention to represent all servicemen, even those who fought for the RSI. Furthermore, the Association's Central Committee threatened that if the government failed to enact a pension reform bill by the end of 1949, they would mobilize nationally. The ANMIG's request was effective and soon after the Ministry of Treasury recommended reforms to the Italian Parliament. One amendment of the ANMIG to the government's pension bill was the inclusion of 'mutilated and invalids belonging to the armed forces of the RSI and, consequently, their widows and orphans'. The ANMIG also argued that 'in the vast majority of cases, RSI's mutilated and invalids had to obey the "de facto" government'. The Association insisted the Italian state should recognize all sacrifices for the country in a spirit of pacification and human solidarity. In June 1950, however, 'on the basis of juridical and moral principles', the Senate refused to extend the provisions to include the disabled veterans of RSI, pointing to the law on war pensions, which concerned only those who had fought for the legitimate government. Still, the senators recognized an obligation on humanitarian grounds to meet the needs and allay the suffering of the RSI combatants who were disabled or had been killed during the war, stressing the need to provide for their families. The Senate invited the government to first provide war pensions for the disabled and the families of those who died serving the legitimate government, and subsequently to present measures to support mutilated and disabled RSI veterans, as well as the families of those who had perished.[47] In the early post-war years, however, the treatment of RSI veterans was a highly sensitive and controversial issue. In order to avoid political struggles and delaying the war pension reform, the ANMIG dropped the issue temporarily. The first law was passed in June 1950. It addressed work reintegration of the war disabled, i.e. the first measure requested by the ANMIG at the 1949 meeting.[48] Shortly afterward, a law on war pensions was passed. This was the law of 10 August 1950, n. 648, on war pensions, primarily concerned with veterans and partisans, who held the same status as active duty servicemen in 1945,[49] but also included victims of deportations and accidents caused directly by the war.

Disorders such as common neurosis and neurasthenic syndromes (except in their more severe forms) were considered transitory conditions for which a once-off indemnity was established, with a major exception for the most severe cases. Severe psychiatric conditions, i.e. those indicated by the law as 'compromising (nearly) all mental abilities' – such as traumatic dementia (i.e. caused by commotion, blows, etc), schizophrenia, paralytic dementia, epileptic dementia, and severe

47 Senato della Repubblica, *Atti Parlamentari*, 17703.
48 Law of 3 June 1950, published in J.O. 28 June 1950.
49 Decree of 4 August 1945, art. 4, n.467, 'Estensione benefici in favore dei combattenti'.

depression – entitled individuals and their families to a war pension. For those diagnosed with a severe neurosis or a similar disorder, however, the pension was largely limited to a temporary entitlement.

On the basis of Article 98 of the law, all recipients of war pensions suffering from conditions open to potential improvement, such as severe neurosis, traumatic psychoneurosis and psycho-asthenia (depression), tuberculosis, and certain heart disorders, were subject to mandatory, periodic re-evaluations by the medical commission. Those who did not comply were sanctioned with the loss of their pension. And although granted the right of appeal, their pensions would be discontinued until the appeal had been heard and accepted. Such strict controls offended many veterans, who felt they were being treated as possible malingerers. Indeed, the discretionary powers of the administration contrasted with the serviceman's right to a war pension as a right confirmed by the same law. A group of members of Parliament (Christian Democrats) therefore presented a proposal to revise the law. The Parliamentary discussion that followed was dominated by arguments for the State's moral obligation toward veterans. Everybody agreed that article 98 was judicially tenuous and offensive on ethical grounds. The Christian Democrat MP and physician, Mario Ceravolo, raised an analogous issue, namely the uncertainty surrounding the clinical severity of such disorders as traumatic psychoneurosis and psychoneurasthenia. Fervently, he argued that the impact of suspending or withdrawing pensions could be extremely detrimental to sufferers of traumatic psychoneurosis and similar disorders. Ceravolo inverted previous arguments used by psychiatrists to deny war pensions to psychoneurotics (i.e. that to assign such war pensions hindered their recovery). He maintained that the emotional security of a pension actually ameliorated the conditions. Subsequent decisions to end pension allowances, he argued, could presumably produce a sudden relapse.[50] Despite the Minister of the Treasury's defense of the existing war pension allocation system, the legal modification was approved by a large majority from across the political spectrum.

On the basis of Article 10, the law of 10 August 1950 also covered Italian civilians who had suffered health damage for reasons directly connected to the war, or had been subjected to torture and other forms of ill-treatment during internment in a foreign country or under enemy forces. In principle, therefore, the law seemed to entitle a wide variety of civilian war victims, including political and Jewish deportees (or in case of death, their families), to a war pension. The law's provisions gave the impression that the onus of proof was reversed under Articles 3 and 10, which specified that death or invalidity caused by wounds, lesions or illness suffered during detention were presumed to arise from the war, unless

50 See Camera dei Deputati, Legislatura II, *Atti Parlamentari*. (Discussioni, Seduta 4 dicembre 1956), 29545-29549.

there was proof to the contrary. In practice, however, it was impossible for relatives of deportees (be they military, civil, political or Jewish) who disappeared in unknown circumstances, to prove the causal link with war. Restrictive application of the law and insistence upon detailed documentation made it very difficult for some to successfully apply for a war pension or indemnity, even though they were formally entitled to it.

Jurisprudence demonstrates how the bureaucracy often processed pension requests sluggishly and not infrequently took an indifferent and unsympathetic attitude toward the tragic circumstances of the persecuted and deported who sought to claim the financial recompense to which they were formally entitled. In addition, military medical commissions which had to 'assess the causes and amount of the damage to the physical integrity of the serviceman or civilian' ignored studies from international conferences, which demonstrated a significant statistical correlation between former experiences of detention in a concentration camp and various physical and psychological illnesses.

A good illustration of indifference and denial was the case of Dosolina Sforni, a Jewish partisan arrested by the SS in Turin in March 1944 and subsequently deported to Auschwitz. Shortly after her return to Italy in 1945, Dosolina Sforni, who already suffered ill-health during detention, lapsed again and had to be hospitalized several times. A few years later, her unstable condition made it impossible for her to work. She was diagnosed as suffering from psychoneurotic syndrome, valvular cardiopathy, and arthrosis. Her medical certificate stated her pathological condition resulted from suffering and ill-treatment she experienced in the concentration camp. Accordingly, she applied for a war pension. The military medical commission assessing her request confirmed the medical diagnosis, but denied any causal link between her illness and her detention in the concentration camp. As a result, her pension request was rejected. In 1966, her lawyer appealed against the decision and petitioned anew. The court complained about a lack of medical documentation concerning the state of her health during her internment in Auschwitz, leaving her lawyer to retort that such documentation simply could not be produced. He reminded the court that the law was clear, that illness contracted during internment or as result of torture and ill-treatment entitled an individual to a war pension. As late as 1970, the Ministry of the Treasury reaffirmed that specific medical documentation was required to demonstrate that Mrs. Sforni's health condition had originated in Auschwitz before they could re-examine Mrs. Sforni's pension request. At this point, Mrs. Sforni's lawyer, seeing that the Ministry persisted with its unreasonable request, brought the case to the attention of Communist Senator Umberto Terracini. Shortly afterward, Terracini, in a Senate inquiry, pointed out the absurdity of the Ministry of Treasury's request. He deplored the general ignorance of the administration about the circumstances of deportation to concentration camps. Terracini's vigorous speech proved highly effective, and the Ministry of Treasury soon informed Mrs. Sforni's lawyer that her request for a pension had finally been accepted.

Mrs. Sforni's lawyer was not the only person to approach Senator Umberto Terracini with problems about war pensions. The Senator, by that time seventy-five years old, personally experienced the hardships of political persecution and imprisonment under Fascism. In 1952, he, together with eleven other mostly left-wing Senators, had proposed a law in favor of political (anti-fascist) and victims of racial persecution from the rise of Fascism to 1943. In order to contextualize the discussion of traumatic neurosis within Italian legislation, however, we should need to consider the broader implications of the international debate.

Deportation and trauma from an international perspective

In the immediate post-war years, doctors from various countries realized that the living conditions in the camps deeply affected the health and resilience of camp survivors. Initially, only a few authors addressed the psychological effects of deportation, but studies on survivors' psychological problems multiplied by the 1960's. At the initiative of the International Federation of Resistance Fighters (Vienna), several international medical meetings were organized in the 1950's and early 1960's to discuss the physical and psychological conditions of former deportees.[51]

The first international reparation from the German Federal Republic for camp survivors turned out to be a 'political turning point'[52] with ample international resonance. 'After the belated beginning of individual indemnification payments in 1953, the survivors faced an unsympathetic, recalcitrant German bureaucracy... [and the tendency of] the courts and their experts to assume a direct causal link between physical and psychological damages.'[53] In other words, psychological damage tended to be recognized only in connection with demonstrable physical injury. Like Italian psychiatry, German psychiatry was still predominantly biological and was based on the rather narrow definition of psychological trauma elaborated since World War I. From this point of view, 'the conditions in the camps caused long-term psychological problems only for the relatively few survivors who had suffered serious neurological damage or had already been prone to psychological complications before their imprisonment. Consequently, in the eyes of the courts, the majority of the survivors could not suffer from long-term psychological

51 The International Federation of Resistance Fighters (FIR) promoted the following international meetings: Copenhagen (1954), Paris (1954), Moscow (1957), Brussels (1958), Liège (1961), Bucarest (1964). See Verri Melo, *La Sindrome del sopravvissuto*.

52 The expression and the line of the argument are borrowed from Kansteiner, 'Testing the limits of trauma', 99.

53 Ibidem.

impairment, which would entitle them to continued support from German taxpayers'.[54] This was a fundamentally unsympathetic position towards people who had undergone the ordeals of deportation and life in concentration camps. This caused outrage, especially among foreign medical professionals with direct or indirect knowledge of camp experiences of survivors. In the United States, the German-born psychiatrist Niederland had been seeing former deportees in his practice since 1947. Like many of his colleagues in the United States, he was a trained psychoanalyst at a time when there was a strong focus on the psychotherapeutic treatment of war neurosis. Niederland was engaged as an independent psychiatric expert in camp survivor indemnification cases, and became an outspoken advocate of survivors' claims. What he identified as 'survivor syndrome' was a specific cluster of symptoms affecting camp survivors.[55] During the 1960's, Niederland and others continued to work on the psychological disturbances of the survivors – symptoms including anxiety, depression, psychosomatic illnesses, psychotic behavior, intense feelings of guilt, and disturbances of cognition and memory.[56] By framing the psychological suffering of camp survivors in a specific diagnostic category, they successfully established a firm connection between traumatic camp experiences and troubles affecting former deportees at a later stage. As Kansteiner points out, the advocates of survivor syndrome departed from conventional psychoanalytic wisdom. In their opinion, the extreme brutalization in the camps was the sole explanation needed for the whole complex of post-war survivor symptoms. The causes of trauma were thus squarely located in the camp system and the psychic injuries it inflicted on survivors.

The 'Terracini Law'[57]

The 1950 law on war pensions favored reparations to military personnel,[58] the partisans, and – albeit with the limitations indicated – of those civilians and military, who (for a variety of reasons) had been victims of deportation, war-related violence in Italy and abroad. For those who had actively opposed Fascism since 1919 and paid a high price for it – persecution, imprisonment, and death – no reparative measures had yet been established. Likewise, there were no reparative measures for

54 Ibidem.
55 Niederland, 'The problem of the survivor'.
56 See, for instance, Niederland, 'Clinical observations'.
57 Law 10 March 1955, no. 96 'Provvidenze a favore dei perseguitati politici antifascisti e razziali e dei loro familiari superstiti'.
58 With the exception of volunteers and military conscripts of the *Repubblica di Salò*.

the Italian Jews who, since 1938, had seen their lives suddenly shattered and had suffered the severe exclusion and restrictions imposed by the Fascist racial laws.

Since 1947, with the onset of the Cold War, the national and international political situation had changed considerably. In 1945, with the election of Ferruccio Parri – member of the Action Party and deputy commander of the combined Resistance forces – as prime minister of the Italian Republic '[t]he Resistance had come to power.'[59] The following years witnessed the development of 'two vast opposing fronts: one having its focal point in the employing classes, the Christian Democrats and the United States; the other centred on the working class, the Communists and Russia.'[60] The ideological clash of interests between the two fronts deepened the political cleavages between leftist and centrist parties which had previously cooperated as anti-fascists. Both sides fought a bitter political campaign for the general election of 1948, heavily influenced by the international events. Socialists and Communists presented a united platform (Democratic Popular Front) against Christian Democrats. The latter benefited from a massive injection of material aid for Italy from the United States ('Interim Aid'), and from the Vatican support.[61] In addition, as Ginsborg argues, '[t]he Communist *coup d' État* in Prague did a great deal to damage the chances of left-wing victory in the Italian [1948] elections.'[62] The overwhelming victory of the Christian Democrats' (48.5 per cent of the votes and an absolute majority in the Chambers of Deputies) was achieved at the expense of both left- and right-wing parties, and influenced the political scenario for the next decade.

In 1952, thirty years after Fascism rose to power and years after the liberation, a law in favor of the victims of the Fascists regime's violence was, in Terracini's words, a necessary measure to rectify a serious injustice.[63] The National Association of Italian Antifascist Political Persecutees (ANPPIA), established in 1948, had obtained little support from the government, apart from the reintegration of those who lost their livelihood for anti-fascist ideas or activity. In the first draft of the bill, however, the Jewish persecution was not mentioned at all. Later, Italian Jews were mentioned as beneficiaries under the law, but, even after the inclusion, Jewish persecution hardly received mention in the parliamentary debates concerning the text of the law.

In March 1955, after a long and tortuous journey – in the right-wing dominated political scenario brought about by the general elections of 1953[64] – Parliament

59 See Ginsborg, *A History of contemporary Italy*, 72.
60 Ibidem.
61 Ibidem, 115.
62 Ibidem, 113-117, quotation on 116.
63 Corradini, *Il reinserimento*.
64 In the 1953 elections the neo-fascist party *Movimento sociale italiano* went from 526,670 votes to 1,580,395 votes and the *Partito Nazionale Monarchico* (National Monarchic Party) from 729,174 to 1,856,661 votes.

passed the law 'Compensations in favor of victims of political or racial persecution and of their surviving relatives' (also known as 'Terracini Law').[65] The law was aimed at Italian citizens who were persecuted for anti-fascist political activities before 8 September 1943, and who had lost at least 30% of their ability to work as a consequence of:

- imprisonment for political crimes; measures such as *confino*, or preventative incarceration;
- violence and torture suffered in Italy or abroad by military and paramilitary fascist organizations (or by emissary of the Fascist Party);
- criminal conviction for crimes related to riots during anti-Fascist manifestations;
- continuation abroad of anti-fascist activity with participation in the Spanish War;
- *confino*, imprisonment in a concentration camp[66] or imprisonment in consequence of anti-fascist activity pursued abroad.

The law established that a pension of the same amount would have been awarded 'in identical circumstances to Italian citizens who, after July 7, 1938 suffered persecution on racial grounds'. It also established a commission nominated by the President of the Council in agreement with the Ministries of the Interior, Justice, Treasury, and Welfare. The commission consisted of one member representing the Presidency of the Council of Ministries; three members representing the ministries mentioned above, and three representatives of the ANPPIA (Association of Italian Antifascist Political Persecutees). The Union of Jewish Communities was not represented. (This was rectified only in 1998, after a ruling of the Constitutional Court.)

The application of the law and its interpretation

The circumstances listed by the law referred exclusively to Fascist persecution of anti-fascist activities. The law, however, did mention reparative measure should also take into consideration 'Italian citizens who, after 7 July 1938 (and before 8 September 1943) suffered persecution on racial grounds'. Although the rationale for and methods of persecuting the Jews were substantially different (i.e., they were not persecuted for their deeds, but simply for being Jews), it seemed reasonable to assume that the law only required one to document suffering as a consequence of

65 It is noteworthy that the law was passed shortly after the law that introduced measures to support mutilated and disabled RSI veterans, and widows and orphans of those who had perished in combat.

66 Shortly before the war, the fascist regime had established concentration camps for political opponents, foreign Jews and Roma people.

the racial laws. Nonetheless, applications from Jewish citizens were turned down en masse with the argument that the anti-fascist political activity was not documented in their requests. In the first decades, the prevailing legal interpretation was that active anti-fascism remained an indispensable requirement for the pension application. This restrictive interpretation resulted in a lack of recognition for the violence and discrimination suffered by Italian Jews as a consequence of the racial laws. Those who appealed were told by the *Corte dei Conti* that their appeal was 'unfounded'. In 1980, a modification to the law was passed.[67] Yet, even after the introduction of the new law, the decisions of the various local branches of the *Corte dei Conti* proved fairly contradictory and often still guided by a restrictive interpretation. In January 2003, for instance, the *Corte dei Conti*'s first judicial section rejected the appeal of an Italian Jewish citizen with the argument that restrictions imposed by Fascist racial laws on the whole Jewish community – exclusion from public schools, from teaching, from public of employment, and so forth – would not be considered acts of moral violence perpetrated against individual Jewish citizens according to the law of 1955 and its subsequent modifications.[68] Shortly after, however, another appeal presented by a Jewish woman expelled from a state school in 1939, gave the impetus to reach a solution for an authoritative and unambiguous interpretation of the law. After an extensive debate on the case, a ruling by the *Sezioni Riunite della Corte dei Conti* in March 2003[69] finally clarified that the implications of anti-Jewish legislation (such as the expulsion of Jewish students from state schools) were a form of moral violence by the state which violated fundamental rights. The recognition that the effects of anti-Jewish legislation were to be considered as acts of moral violence by the state did not introduced the notion that such legislation, along with material damages, had also caused psychological damage. The ruling of 2003 maintained that exclusions and restrictions imposed by the anti-Jewish laws were acts of moral violence in so far as such laws violated fundamental human rights. Any notion of the psychologically traumatizing effects of persecution and deportation remained alien to Italian reparative legislation.

Conclusion

As Donatella Levi correctly pointed out in 1999, Italy demonstrates a remarkable lack of empathy for the psychological effects of persecution, war and deportation. In this article, I have considered the reasons for this scarce attention to war psycho-

67 Law no. 932, 1980 'Integrazioni e modifiche alla legislazione recante provvidenze a favore dei perseguitati politici antifascisti e razziali'.

68 Corte dei Conti, Sezione prima giurisdizionale centrale di appello, Sentence no. 29-2003, 27 January 2003.

69 Sezioni Riunite della Corte dei Conti, Sentence no. 8-2003, 25 March 2003.

logical trauma, which can be partly understood as a consequence of the dominant psychiatric approach of the 1940's and 1950's, and partly explained as the result of the marginalization of Fascism and the wartime experiences and memories of various groups: Jews, military internees, and political deportees.

The Fascist *ventennio* and World War II produced profound political and social divisions in Italy. In the early 1920's, governments proved increasingly unable to deal with widespread social and political unrest. The virulent struggle between left-wing and right-wing political groups, the systematic use of brutal methods by the Fascist squads to intimidate and suppress political opponents, and the subsequent establishment of the Fascist dictatorship led to the justification of violence and repression as legitimate political tools. The 'rupture' in the national community caused by the anti-Jewish legislation, the chaotic situation resulting from the armistice (with the social, geographical and military division that followed), and the contribution of the Salò Republic to the extermination of the Jews, produced deep divides in the national community. In the post-war years, the political decision to build national unity around the memory of the Resistance masked the difficulty of coming to terms with the legacy of Fascism and the war years. The post-war governments' lack of initiative to integrate the memories of political and 'racial' deportees and military internees in the national history resulted in the development of separate memories which, for decades, were barely acknowledged outside the groups involved.

This is exemplified by the unsuitability of the reparative legislation for certain groups of victims, the restrictive interpretations in the application of the legislation, the lack of concern for the victims'(objective) difficulties in producing the documentation required by the reparative laws, and by the sluggish and petty attitude of the bureaucracy. It can be argued this is all the outcome of what the Italian historian Paolo Pezzino has defined as 'strategies of oblivion' when he discusses the transformation of the Resistance into a founding myth of the 'new' republican Italy.[70] He argues that the memory of a controversial past that is still a potential source of conflict which 'gave rise to the widespread tendency to create strategies of oblivion. [...] [I]n post-war Italy multiple, non-communicating, and potentially conflicting memories were made to merge by the dominant political authorities into a "public memory", so as to lay the foundation for a new collective identity. [...]. In this construction of memory, oblivion, or the manipulation of events in order to construct an image that caters to necessity, becomes as essential as the transmission of events.'[71]

70 Pezzino, 'The Italian resistance', 397.
71 Ibidem.

6 Collective Suffering

Consequences of World War II in Luxembourg[1]

» *Sonja van 't Hof*

The memory of World War II is very much alive in Luxembourg, perhaps even more than elsewhere in Europe. In 2005, 60 years after the liberation, five separate days were devoted to commemorate and honor various groups involved in the war. This may surprise foreigners, who often know little about the war period in Luxembourg other than the battle of the Ardennes in 1944-1945. One of the smallest of the European countries – around 290,000 inhabitants in 1940, of whom some 4,000 Jews – Luxembourg tends to be overlooked in comparative historical research.

In many respects, Luxembourg was probably of minor importance to the Nazis. The country was invaded because the German army needed passage to France and because they wanted control over the mining and steel industry in the south of Luxembourg. In addition, the Nazis considered Luxembourg as racially and culturally belonging to Germany. In the context of this book, Luxembourg presents an interesting case. The occupation policy affected the entire population and one might expect ample psychological consequences. Did these emerge, and if so, were they acknowledged by the general public and the state?

Introduction: the emergence of national identity

The occupation policy also influenced the post-war experience of the population as 'Luxembourgers'. Their sense of a national identity had only begun to emerge since the beginning of the twentieth century. Nationalistic sentiments gained strength during the Interbellum and took definite root during World War II.[2] This was a relatively new phenomenon, since for centuries the Luxembourg territory had been disputed and traded between European kingdoms. After Napoleon's defeat in 1815, the European nations formed Luxembourg as a Grand Duchy in personal

1 I am indebted to Benoît Majerus for comments and suggestions on an earlier version of this paper.
2 Interview Dostert; Majerus, *Lieux de mémoire au Luxembourg*.

union with the Netherlands: the King of the Netherlands was also Grand Duke of Luxembourg. Belgium seceded from the Netherlands in 1830 and the First Treaty of London, in 1839, granted two thirds of Luxembourg's territory to Belgium. The remaining Luxembourg state was guaranteed independence and neutrality. Luxembourg therefore celebrates 1839 as its official independence date, although the relation with the Netherlands ended only with the death of the king in 1890. The title of Grand Duke passed on to a male relative of the German Nassau family.

Because of the continuous changes in formal nationality, there was little conception of a national identity until the twentieth century. In addition, the mining industry attracted large groups of labor migrants from Germany, Italy, Belgium, France and Poland. Vice versa, Luxembourg residents would live, work and study for periods in surrounding countries. The official language was French, but almost everybody also spoke German and the local language: Letzeburgs. Until well into the nineteenth century, the latter was only a spoken language.[3] Luxembourg is still multilingual. Some newspapers and journals feature articles in three languages.

The experiences of two wars, and especially World War II, dramatically changed the population's experience of their independence. In World War II, most resistance organizations were based on patriotic motives. People acted and died for *la patrie*.[4] The exiled Grand Duchess Charlotte became the population's moral beacon. The collective post-war memory focused on the patriotic resistance and its alleged collectiveness. It highlighted the country's shared suffering and heroism. Since no historical research on the war started until the 1970's, the description of the resistance prior to that period consisted of ego documents and was mainly 'self description'.[5]

The war, the occupation and the resistance all play a prominent role in the collective memory because they were experienced as justifying the existence of Luxembourg as an independent state.[6] They first consolidated, and now maintain, feelings of a distinct national identity. The state has deliberately conducted a policy of national memory. The presence of the state in both the commemorations and the monuments seems to support this contention.[7]

The collective memory of the war in Luxembourg is fraught with myths.[8] This can be said of any country, but the discrepancies between research findings and public memory indicate sensitivities to a measure that seems to have been over-

3 Interview Dostert.
4 Dostert, 'Vive Letzebuerg', 366 and 381.
5 Schoentgen, 'Resistenzorganisationen nach dem 2.Weltkrieg', 521; interview Dostert.
6 Dostert, 'Résistance et reprise politique', 25-50; Schoentgen, 'Resistenzorganisationen nach dem 2. Weltkrieg', 519-551; Scuto, 'Mémoire et histoire', 499-513.
7 Scuto, 'Mémoire et histoire', 501-2.
8 Interview Dostert. See also Dostert, 'Reserve-Polizei-Bataillon 101', 81-99; Schoentgen, 'Resistenzorganisationen nach dem 2. Weltkrieg', 519-551; Scuto, 'Mémoire et histoire', 499-513; Majerus, 'Leidensgeschichte' 48-9.

come in most European countries. For instance, a publication in 2006 addressed the difficult cohabitation of collective memory and factual history, mentioning several persistent myths. It was preceded by a note from the publishing house, stating it did not share the author's conclusions 'sur un sujet particulièrement délicat de notre histoire nationale'.[9]

To understand the situation at the beginning of World War II, we present a brief overview since 1914.

World War I and the Interbellum[10]

The nineteenth century powers had guaranteed eternal neutrality to the Grand Duchy of Luxembourg. Germany violated this guarantee in 1914 by invading Luxembourg and Belgium. The Grand Duchess at the time, Marie-Adelaide, and the government protested, but remained in Luxembourg, trying to continue the policy of neutrality. The Germans did not interfere too much with the political processes, but the country suffered increasing food shortages.

After the German defeat in 1918, however, the Grand Duchess and the government were perceived as collaborators. Liberals and socialists advocated the republic; parts of the population were in favor of association with France or Belgium. Luxembourg's independence was at stake. The solution was to have the Grand Duchess abdicate in favor of her sister Charlotte in 1919. A referendum was to determine not only the political fate of Luxembourg but also its economic structure, since its economy was not viable on its own. In September 1919, 80% voted to remain a Grand Duchy; in addition, 75% voted for a customs union with France. France declined and in 1921 an economic union was concluded with Belgium.[11]

Despite attempts to disentangle the mining and steel industry from the German economy, German enterprises, capital and laborers returned in the late 1920's and early 1930's. The Luxembourg political elite during the Interbellum were predominantly Catholic, corporatist and anticommunist. After 1933, the government hardly acted against the growing Nazi influence among the German organizations in Luxembourg. This was mainly out of a growing fear of a new war.[12] The Nazi policies resulted in several waves of refugees in Luxembourg, notably of German Jews and political opponents.

On the eve of the war, in 1939, Luxembourg celebrated its centenary with public festivities. For the first time, the population publicly showed some sense of

9 'Remarque' preceding Scuto, 'Mémoire et histoire', 499.
10 Mostly derived from Wallerang, *Besatzung*, 20-43, and interview Dostert.
11 Wallerang, *Besatzung*, 22; Maas, 'L'identité nationale', 16-36; interview Dostert.
12 Wallerang, *Besatzung*, 22.

national feeling and in large numbers wore pins with the Luxembourg emblem, a red lion.[13]

The occupation 1940-1944: Heim ins Reich

Although it strived to remain neutral, the Luxembourg government did not wish to repeat the humiliation of World War I and had prepared for the evacuation of the Grand Ducal family and the government. Directly after the invasion on 10 May 1940, they were moved to safety. They ended up as a government in exile in London, where they kept in close contact with the allied powers, notably the British and the Americans.[14]

The German army staff and ministry of Foreign Affairs opted to treat Luxembourg as it did Denmark: occupied but neutral. Hitler, however, decided differently. The Nazis considered Luxembourg and its population as racially, historically and culturally belonging to Germany, as they did with other German-speaking countries or territories, such as Sudetenland, the Baltic states, Alsace-Lorraine, and the Belgian eastern districts of Eupen, Malmédy and St.-Vith. These were to be annexed and re-Germanized ('zum deutschen Volkstum zurückgewonnen') and, of course, Nazified. The phrase *Heim ins Reich* ('Home into the Reich') was coined to refer to this general policy.[15]

Late July 1940, Hitler appointed Gustav Simon as head of the civil government. Simon, an old companion from the National Socialist Labor Party (NSDAP), was a *Gauleiter* in the neighboring district of Koblenz-Trier.[16] He was placed directly under Hitler, hence outside the state hierarchy. Simon took orders only from Hitler and was accountable only to him. Apparently, Hitler hoped this would ensure a speedy Nazification. As a result, Simon had great autonomy in conducting the annexation and re-Germanization.[17]

Apart from the usual measures taken in all countries – 'Gleichschaltung' of the media, censorship, abolishment of political parties and parliament, rounding up of political opponents – the Nazis started a complete administrative turnover and intensive economic plundering.[18] Simon initially seems to have considered the Nazification of the population a matter of social and cultural policy, but he increasingly had to resort to terror. He banished all supposedly non-German influences

13 Wallerang, *Besatzung*, 20-43; documentary *Heim ins Reich, 2004*; interview Dostert.
14 Dupong, 'Le gouvernement en exil', 34-6; interview Dostert.
15 Wallerang, *Besatzung*, 51-52; Dostert 'Vive Letzebuerg', 368-371.
16 The NSDAP had divided Germany in districts or *Gau*.
17 Wallerang, *Besatzung*, 51-55.
18 Wallerang, *Besatzung*, 90-94.

from public and cultural life. German became the official language in the administration, schools, the media and in public life. The use of French was officially prohibited on 1 June 1941, Letzeburgs a year later. The French names of towns, streets and even persons were Germanized. Employees in all sectors were first encouraged, and later obliged to join the collaborating *Volksdeutsche Bewegung* (VdB), founded directly after the occupation. Refusal meant dismissal. As in Germany, education became the means to indoctrinate the youth and to force them into compliance. Attendance of extracurricular political activities became compulsory and pupils were obliged, on pain of expulsion from school, to join the *Hitlerjugend* or the *Bund Deutscher Mädel*. The Nazi party hierarchical structure – in descending order *Ortsgruppenleiter*, and *Zellen-* and *Blockleiter* who figured as spies – was installed in order to secure complete social control over the population.[19]

All remnants of French influences were to be removed, and this extended to the church. The Catholic monasteries and convents were abolished in 1941 and their possessions confiscated, with the exception of female orders working in hospitals. In fact, the persecution was fiercer than in Germany, where the clergy were protected through an agreement with the Vatican.[20] Of course, the Jewish population was also targeted, as will be discussed later.

Resistance: 'Deutschfeindlichkeit'

Since Luxembourg only had a small voluntary army (*Fräiwellegekompanie)* of 460 men at its disposal, the male population generally lacked military training and mentality. Armed resistance, sabotage and espionage were therefore hard to organize and occurred only sporadically. The largest share of risky, clandestine activities were non-armed and pertained to producing and distributing clandestine papers or pamphlets, helping persons in hiding, and guiding Luxembourg fugitives and French and British soldiers across the borders (as *passeurs*, which proved a very risky occupation indeed).[21]

The international literature usually limits the definition of resistance to voluntary, deliberate, risky and clandestine opposition. For two reasons resistance took on a broader meaning in the Luxembourg context. First, one of the greatest resistance feats concerned a non-violent disruption of a census, in 1941, in which the population refused to give the demanded answers (see below). Second, the Germanization and Nazification policy penetrated almost all areas of public and private life. Historians are still debating whether the resistance was pre-

19 Wallerang, *Besatzung*, 55-82.

20 Some 58 clergymen were arrested in the course of the war for resistance activities, of whom at least 16 ended up in Dachau. Wallerang, *Besatzung*, 82-6.

21 Dostert, 'Vive Letzebuerg', 371-379.

dominantly of a patriotic or also of an antifascist nature.[22] For whatever reason, many people resisted membership of the collaborating *Volksdeutsche Bewegung* and similar organizations for as long as they could. For instance, in four years 700 pupils were dismissed because of their opposition to Nazification. Students in secondary schools were also among the first to organize resistance groups in 1940.[23] (Luxembourg did not have a university at the time.) The population in general showed their anti-German attitude by boycotting German exhibitions, theatre performances and films, and by increasingly attending church, to the annoyance of the Nazi authorities.[24] Their attitude also showed in small, sometimes symbolic acts of dissidence, disobedience and recalcitrance. For instance, people would wear the centenary pins with the red lion, issued in 1939; openly at first and later on the inside of one's coat.[25]

Therefore, in order to define 'resistance' in Luxembourg, it has been suggested to adopt the description used by the occupier, which was '*deutschfeindlichkeit*' in attitude or behavior.[26] This may have had an effect on the public judgment of acts of cooperation or collaboration. The grey area of daily life often necessitated some form of cooperation from all European citizens under German occupation. However, in the Luxembourg context the boundaries between resistance, cooperation and collaboration may have become even more blurred.

Pivotal national war memories

One event that stands out in national memory is the census (*Personenstandaufnahme*) that Simon had scheduled for 10 October 1941. He intended to establish that the Luxembourgers were in fact German by origin. To secure the desired result, the population was instructed to answer 'German' on three questions concerning their nationality, extraction and mother tongue. Resistance groups, however, feared that the results would be used to justify annexation and started a campaign through pamphlets and word of mouth to answer 'Drei mal Letzeburgesch'. To the surprise of the Nazis and the resistance alike, a large proportion seemed to do so. Often figures of 90-95% are mentioned in the literature. This, however, has never been established, since the Germans abandoned the count when the first soundings were unfavorable. Be that as it may, the annulment of the census was presented by the resistance as a capitulation of the Germans before the patriotism

22 Majerus, 'Le débat existe', 60-63.
23 Wallerang, *Besatzung*, 79-80; Dostert, 'Résistance et reprise politique', 29 and 34-37.
24 Dopfeld, 'Auszüge aus S.D.-Berichten', 49-52; Wallerang, *Besatzung*, 133.
25 Dostert, 'Vive Letzebuerg', 366-367; Wallerang, *Besatzung*, 169; documentary Heim ins Reich, 2004.
26 Dostert, 'Résistance et reprise politique', 26.

demonstrated by the Luxembourg people.[27] The event served both the post-war myth that the whole nation resisted the occupier and the growing feelings of a national identity. This is buttressed by the fact that the yearly remembrance day of the war, la *Journée commémorative nationale*, takes places on 10 October.

Only a few days earlier an upsetting event had taken place which may have contributed to the disruption of the census. On 6 October 1941, a first group of young men and women were forcibly transported to Germany. Voluntary recruiting for the *Reichsarbeitsdienst* (RAD) had had little success and Simon had ordered a 6 month labor conscription. Apparently, the train left while family members sang a tune called 'Lëtzeburg for the Lëtzeburger'. It is estimated that ultimately some 14,800 men and unmarried women worked in Germany.[28]

A year later an even more dramatic decree was issued: for young men, the RAD was followed by conscription in the *Wehrmacht*. Some 1,500-2,000 men had already voluntarily enlisted, but the *Wehrmacht's* losses were substantial. Although the annexation of Luxembourg was never formally ratified, Simon declared the Luxembourgers German citizens and therefore obliged to serve in the German army. On 18 October 1942 the first convoy of 2,000 men left for Germany. They were mostly transferred to army units at the Eastern front, where some, though not all, engaged in combat. Eventually all Luxembourg men born between 1920 and 1927 were drafted, more than 11,000 in total.[29]

The national memory of the forced conscription is highly emotionally charged and has both a collective and a fragmented part. Collectively shared is the heroic side of the population's reaction. Following the announcement of the conscription on 30 August 1942, brief strikes broke out throughout the country. Although the strikes remained local, they became nationwide in the national memory. This distortion may be due to the violent reaction of the Nazis. Many strikers were apprehended and 21 of them were eventually executed in SS-camp Hinzert, near Trier. It was this gruesome effect, according to a recent analysis, that magnified its cause.[30]

Hinzert, by the way, was the concentration camp for over 1,600 Luxembourg resistance fighters and political prisoners. It has become the national symbol of suffering. The camp is derelict, but beams from the site were used to erect a cross at the cemetery of Notre Dame in Luxembourg City, where the exhumed remains of 78 executed resistance fighters are buried. In 1974 it was officially decreed a national monument and it now bears the name *Monument national de la Résistance*

27 Dostert, 'Résistance et reprise politique', 37; Scuto, 'Mémoire et histoire', 506.
28 Hohengarten, *Zwangsrekrutierung Luxemburger Staatsbürger*, 13-15; Wallerang, *Besatzung*, 89-90.
29 Wallerang, *Besatzung*, 110-116.
30 Scuto, 'Mémoire et histoire', 506-507.

et de la déportation. It is arguably the most important site for national commemorations of the war.[31]

Other consequences of the conscription were experienced in far more diverse ways, resulting in fragmented memories. Of the more than 11,000 men conscripted, some 8,000 complied. 2,850 of them would die in combat or after being taken prisoner by the Red Army. But an unknown number of soldiers saw little or no combat action at all.[32] Another unknown number deserted. An estimated 3,500 men evaded conscription (the *réfractaires*). A minority was able to flee the country and some 2,500 went into hiding in Luxembourg, often in mineshafts and forests. They could only survive with the help of the entire population. Despite intensive search efforts, few were caught by the German police. This happened mostly if they tried to flee the country with the help of *passeurs*. It was a logistical feat of the resistance to organize the money, the necessary sustenance and the distribution network, but apparently the population as a whole managed to keep silent.[33]

The penalties for evasion and desertion, however, were severe. 250 caught evaders and deserters were killed in camps and prisons.[34] On the basis of the German concept of '*Sippenhaft*', the families of the executed strike leaders, *réfractaires* and deserters were forcibly relocated to camps in Eastern Germany, Silesia and Sudetenland. Until August 1944, this totaled 1,138 families, almost 4,200 people.[35]

Hence, almost the entire population was affected by the conscription in one way or another. Although the various experiences could hardly be unified in a collective memory, the conscription is generally considered the worst measure the population endured.[36] It is understandable that with all its ramifications, the conscription had long-term political and social consequences after the war, which divided the country. In that sense, it became a national trauma, as will be described later.

Lesser experiences: the Holocaust

The fate of the Jewish population made far less of an impression on the Luxembourg citizens, both during the war and for a long time afterwards. For instance,

---

31 Wallerang, *Besatzung*, 108-109.

32 Wallerang, *Besatzung*, 110-116; interview Dostert.

33 Wallerang, *Besatzung*, 110-116; Dostert, 'Résistance et reprise politique', 33-4; Dostert, 'Vive Letzebuerg', 375-376.

34 Among the victims of the massacre of 800 prisoners in Sonnenberg/Slonsk (January 1945), there were 91 Luxembourgers who were mostly detained for desertion. A month later, in Sachsenhausen, 19 men from the former Freiwëlligekompanie were executed for persistently refusing to enter the Wehrmacht. Wallerang, *Besatzung*, 115-116; documentary *Heim ins Reich*, 2004.

35 Wallerang, *Besatzung*, 86-90.

36 Wallerang, *Besatzung*, 196. See also documentary *Heim ins Reich*, 2004.

only 2 cases are documented of Luxembourgers taking in and hiding Jews.[37] Figures of deported and killed Jewish people are hard to establish and different estimates are circulating. The size of the Jewish population in 1940 is uncertain. Based on a recent and thorough study, it has been estimated at almost 4,000. Some 1,000 possessed the Luxembourg nationality.[38]

It is assumed that directly after the invasion, over 3,100 Jewish persons fled or were expelled. (A convoy of 1,200 people with visa for Cuba left for Portugal under the protection of the Gestapo.[39]) The Luxembourg government in exile asked several non-European countries for visa in vain.[40] Of the 3,100 Jewish refugees, almost 700 reached safety and 550 survived in France or Belgium. The majority, however, were eventually deported from France or Belgium to German camps.[41]

In September 1940, just a couple of months after he was installed as head of the civil administration, Gustav Simon introduced the first of many measures to remove Jews from all public spheres, expropriate their enterprises, possessions, homes and livelihood, and put extreme restrictions on their daily activities. As of July 1941 the Jews had to wear a yellow armband, replaced in October that year by the Star of David. This was earlier than in Belgium, where it came into effect in May 1942.

That same October month, almost all the remaining 700 Jewish inhabitants were assembled in the monastery of Fünfbrunnen (or Cinqfontaines) in the north of the country. From here, the first transport left for Lodz in Poland on 16 October 1941 – in fact the first deportation of Jews in Europe. It took place completely undisturbed, even though it happened only ten days after the first transport of labor conscripts. The transports were completed in 1943. Of the 700 Jews transported from Luxembourg only 54 survived, which corresponds to a death rate of 92.[42]

As to possible Sinti or Roma victims, the U.S. Memorial Holocaust Museum in Washington estimates that around 200 Sinti or Roma were deported from Luxembourg. This number is sufficiently large to have left traces in German administration records and in the memory of the Luxembourgers. None exist, however. There is no evidence that these groups resided in the country during the war.[43]

37 Schoentgen, 'Juden in Luxemburg', 17-19; Wallerang, *Besatzung*, 101, note 391.
38 Commission spoliation, *Rapport Intermediaire*, 9-10.
39 Marx, 'Calvaire des Israélites', 569-572.
40 Doorslaer, *Gewillig België*, 685-686 and 739-745.
41 Commission spoliation, *Rapport Intermediaire*, 9-10.
42 Wallerang, *Besatzung*, 99; Commission spoliation, *Rapport Intermediaire*, 9-10.
43 Interview Dostert. For the map of the U.S. Memorial Holocaust Museum see http://www.ushmm.org/wlc/media_nm.php?lang=en&ModuleId=10005395&MediaId=359.

After the War: the State and the Resistance

During the occupation, the resistance organizations operated mainly locally and separately. They only united into a front in March 1944, 6 months before the liberation. The UNION *vun de Lëtzebuerger Fräiheetsorganizatiounen* therefore had little wartime action to boast, but it would nonetheless deploy its numerical and moral force after the war. In the first weeks after the liberation on 9 September 1944, it acted as a police force, maintaining order and rounding up suspected collaborators. Convinced of having proved to be the nation's moral elite, UNION also had political ambitions.[44] While still in London, the government-in-exile had started the reconstruction of the pre-war political and economic order, issuing a series of decrees. UNION contested the legitimacy of the government, because of its having abandoned the country and its alleged pre-war sympathy towards the Nazis. The largest organizations within UNION had been disappointed with pre-war parliamentary democracy and now favored a monarchist, catholic and corporatist state.[45] On the return of the government to Luxembourg at the end of September, UNION demanded an important role: to act as advisory committee of the government, to be consulted on all appointments for high-ranking positions, and to be represented in all committees that dealt with the reconstruction and the purge of the country, and with the repatriation of deported citizens. Prime-minister Pierre Dupong refused: the demands were unconstitutional, bypassing and surpassing those of parliament.[46]

UNION represented the resistance – but it did not represent all the victims of the war and the occupation. In December 1944, former political prisoners and political deportees founded the *Ligue Luxembourgeoise des Prisonniers Politiques et Deportés*, or LPPD. It made a point of stating its political neutrality.[47] The LPPD became very influential, acting as a pressure group for the moral and material compensation of their members. From July 1946, it published a bimonthly journal entitled *Rappel*, the volumes of which testify to the numerous letters and memoranda with demands written to politicians.[48] In addition, the LPPD wanted to keep the memory of the war and its atrocities alive. The LPPD published several *Livres d'Or*, for instance in 1952 the *Livre d'Or de la résistance*, and in 1990 the *Livre d'Or*

44 Schoentgen, 'Resistenzorganisationen nach dem 2. Weltkrieg', 523-526; Dostert, 'Résistance et reprise politique', 44-48.

45 UNION wanted to limit the number of foreigners to 5% of the population and bar the return of Jews, except those with the Luxembourg nationality. Dostert, 'Résistance et reprise politique', 43-44; Wallerang, *Besatzung*, 126-7.

46 Dostert, 'Résistance et reprise politique', 47-48.

47 For a brief history of the LPPD, see Schoentgen, 'Resistenzorganisationen nach dem 2. Weltkrieg', 533-536.

48 For an example see LPPD. 'Mémoire concernant les dommages corporels', 375-382.

des camps. They contain lists of victims, deceased and surviving, and historical accounts.

The conscripted soldiers also organized themselves. In November 1944, the *réfractaires* founded the *Ligue, Ons Jongen*, but the organization was open to all conscripted soldiers. Parents founded an *Association des parents des enrôlés de force*. Considering their numbers, the conscripts and their families could not be ignored by politicians. Their efforts for recognition as victims soon received support from the communist and socialist parties.[49] The former resistance was indignant. It pointed out that there had been a choice: many conscripts evaded and went into hiding. In the opinion of the resistance, a considerable number of conscripts had been voluntary members of the *Hitlerjugend* or the SA.[50] The conscripts claimed force majeure: family situations did not always allow individuals to go into hiding. The allegations of both camps contained a degree of truth.

Much later, in 1960, the *Fédération des Victimes du Nazisme, Enrôlés de Force*, or EdF, was founded. Both the name *Victimes du Nazisme* and the name of its journal, *Les Sacrifiés*, expressed the intention to be recognized and compensated as victims. (As will be described later, the conscripts revived their struggle in 1960.[51])

Remarkably, the conscripts tried to manoeuvre themselves into the resistance as well. They often claimed to have sabotaged the *Wehrmacht* or German police forces, or to have committed acts of resistance. The recurrent theme is that a Luxembourg soldier at one point, at the spur of the moment, saved a civilian from being killed by a German.[52] The contrary, participation in war crimes committed by the Germans, was never recounted. Yet research has uncovered that several Luxembourgers were indeed involved in war crimes against Jews in Poland, in a reserve police battalion and most probably in the *Wehrmacht* as well. The publication of this study in 2000 has to this day not evoked a single public response.[53]

In total more than thirty associations of persons affected by the war sprang up, including a dozen *Amicales*, friendships circles of former resistance fighters or concentration camp prisoners.[54] A *Conseil de l'Ordre de la Résistance* (COR) acted as coordinating body for the resistance and political prisoners. It was involved in awarding different titles and medals for (deceased) resistance fighters.

49 Bonifas, *Dédommagement des enrôlés de force*, 51-2. The socialist party had immediately after the war called for amnesty of collaborators as well. Schoentgen, 'Resistenzorganisationen nach dem 2. Weltkrieg', 541-546.

50 Schoentgen, 'Resistenzorganisationen nach dem 2. Weltkrieg', 543.

51 Bonifas, *Dédommagement des enrôlés de force*, 8-9, 49-52 and from 73.

52 Scuto, 'Mémoire et histoire', 510-11; for examples see the documentary Heim ins Reich, 2004.

53 Dostert, 'Reserve-Polizei-Bataillon 101'; interview Dostert.

54 For a list see LPPD, 'xxxe anniversaire de la libération des camps', 125.

Reconciliation policy: uniting yet dividing

In December 1944, the Germans started a desperate offensive in the north of Luxembourg. The two-month Von Rundstedt offensive, or battle of the Ardennes, was responsible for a third of all material war damage in the country and some 2,500 civilian casualties. At the end of February 1945, the Allies defeated the Germans.

The government finally succeeded in regaining control of the police – which had been taken over by UNION – and the judiciary, and in restoring the pre-war political institutions. This extended even to persons: wartime prime minister Pierre Dupong and minister Joseph Bech, both *Parti Crétien-Social* (PCS), had occupied posts in successive cabinets since 1926 and 1921 respectively, alternating as minister and prime-minister. Dupong remained prime-minister until 1953, after which Bech again took over until 1958. Hence, together they were largely responsible for the reconstruction and purge of the country, and for the foundation of compensation legislation.[55]

UNION accused the government of inadequately purging its own ranks.[56] The resistance, however, was no longer united. As early as June 1945, sections had formed a new political party: the *Groupement Patriotique et Démocratique* ('Patriotique' was later abandoned, hence: GD). The GD presented itself as liberal-democratic and its main points were to bring war criminals and collaborators to justice, to repatriate deportees and conscripted soldiers, and to fully compensate all damages for the population. In the election in the autumn of 1945, the GD secured 9 of the 51 seats in de *Chambre des Députés*. Two GD-ministers were appointed to crucial cabinet posts: Charles Marx to *Assistance Sociale et Santé Publique*, which included repatriation, and Eugène Schaus to the Interior, which included a department for War Damages (*Dommages de Guerre*).[57]

The government was not only concerned about the financial and social devastation, but also about Luxembourg's independence. The country needed to secure its place among the European nations by claiming to have been on the side of the Allied countries from the start. This required a unified national memory, with collective resistance and martyrdom at its core, rather than a memory divided by resistance and collaboration. This in turn required a policy of reconciliation and a 'politique de mémoire'. In this respect, the national authorities were successful. The portrayal of a collective anti-Nazi attitude of Luxembourg remained uncontested by the Allied states and the independence was secured.[58]

---

55 For succeeding governments see http://www.gouvernement.lu/gouvernement/gouvernements_precedents.
56 Dostert, 'Résistance et reprise politique', 47-48; Wallerang, *Besatzung*, 138-142.
57 Schoentgen, 'Resistenzorganisationen nach dem 2. Weltkrieg', 527-530.
58 Scuto, 'Mémoire et histoire', 501.

But while the reconciliation policy was successful externally, it met with large problems internally. The resistance shunned the former conscripted soldiers. The rift between the resistance and the collaborators was also not easily overcome. Judicial enquiries were started against 9,000 suspected collaborators, but the final number of convictions was around 2,300 (0.8% of the post-war population). Politicians did not help matters by starting to advocate amnesty as early as 1948. Although their pleas were made in the context of a national reconciliation policy, parts of the population grew convinced that the purge was not taken seriously. Despite fierce protest from the resistance, collaborators were amnestied in 1953.[59]

In the meantime, it had become clear that the country's financial situation did not allow compensating for all war damages. This added to the disillusionment of the resistance and the general population. The unity and solidarity that the government tried to maintain soon vanished. If anything, the rifts seemed to widen. From the early 1950's, UNION and the LPPD constantly attempted to secure a privileged treatment in the compensation of war damages; the government, though publicly assenting to their demands, nevertheless considered the interests of other groups as well. It tried to smooth out the differences and to establish more or less equal compensation for all. This was deeply frustrating to the members of UNION and the LPPD. The tensions led to the creation of several persistent myths, with the purport that collaborators and traitors were in fact given priority over the patriotic victims.

Defining war victims

Luxembourg had no experience with victims from the Great War and had to invent organizations and procedures. The history of the legislation for compensation has been described in various publications.[60] A history of the medical care for war victims is lacking. Attention for Jewish survivors is scant and no separate Jewish organization or *Amicale* seems to have emerged. The following descrip-

59 Wallerang, *Besatzung*, 137; Schoentgen, 'Resistenzorganisationen nach dem 2. Weltkrieg', 535. The few German war criminals, such as the former head of the Gestapo in Luxembourg, were released in 1959. Contrary to popular belief, the purge was conducted adequately according to Dostert. Directly following the liberation, a considerable number of people tried to settle quarrels by denouncing neighbors and acquaintances. The majority of the accused had to be released quickly because of lack of evidence or evidence of mistaken identity. However, this caused lasting suspicions of corruption of the judiciary and politics among the population (interview Dostert).

60 See for instance Bonifas, *Dédommagement des enrôlés de force;* Schoentgen, 'Resistenzorganisationen nach dem 2. Weltkrieg'; Dostert, 'Résistance et reprise politique'. The journal *Rappel* served to shed light on various aspects of the legislation process.

tion is therefore inevitably incomplete, based on scattered information and two interviews.[61]

Les Pupilles de la Nation[62]

One of the first groups to be recognized as victims were orphaned children. They were seen as innocent victims and also as the future of the nation, deserving special attention and support. In July 1945, on the instigation of UNION, the state decreed the establishment of an *Oeuvre des Pupilles de la Nation*. It was to support children who had lost one or both parents during the war or afterwards as a consequence of the war. The state emphasized that it did not support the children out of charity, but out of national duty, as a repayment of a national debt.[63]

The children would enjoy material support, which took into account the standard of living the family had been used to before the war and the financial support it already received. In addition, they could request moral, social and medical assistance, support with education until the age of 21 or until their studies were completed, and with employment. The Oeuvre made a distinction between orphans of civilians and orphans of 'patriotic victims', the deceased resistance fighters, political prisoners and soldiers of the allied armies. The first group was officially called *Orphelins de Guerre*; the second group received the honorary title *Pupilles de la Nation*. The Pupilles with the honorary title were more privileged. The decree stated: 'Ils ont également droit à une aide adéquate. Mais les Pupilles de la Nation bénéficient d'un droit de priorité.' This was also elaborated in various articles of the bylaw of the Oeuvre.[64] It is not entirely clear how they received priority, since generally the groups were jointly referred to as 'Pupilles'. It seems to have entailed a kind of affirmative action: with equal qualifications, jobs in public administration went to the honorary Pupilles.[65]

Recognition as a Pupille had to be applied for with the Oeuvre's board, but it appears that the organization actively stimulated such applications. Only the Luxembourg nationality was a precondition and orphans of Jewish Luxembourgers were included. The first children were recognized in 1947: 362 Pupilles and 337

61 The interviews were conducted with the aforementioned P. Dostert, assistant professor of history at the Université de Luxembourg and director of the Centre de Documentation et de Recherche sur la Résistance (CDRR), and with M.J. Elcherot, 'inspecteur principale' of the Service des Dommages de Guerre Corporels, Ministère de la Santé Publique.

62 Mostly derived from: Amicale des Pupilles, *D'Pupilles*.

63 Arreté grand-ducal du 27 juillet 1945 portant création de l'Oeuvre des Pupilles de la Nation. In: Amicale des Pupilles, *D'Pupilles*, 357; Loesch, 'Les Pupilles', 673-5.

64 Arreté grand-ducal du 27 juillet 1945 and 'Statut de l'Oeuvre'. In: Amicale des Pupilles, *D'Pupilles*, 357 and 363-375.

65 Amicale des Pupilles, *D'Pupilles*, 370.

Orphelins.[66] Full orphans would be placed with foster families; the others would live with their remaining parent. This was usually their mother, who would retain full parental rights. The protection of the Oeuvre was additional.

The Pupilles were presented as a special group in society: 'Parmi les victimes de la guerre les Pupilles (...) occupent le rang privilégié qui est dû au respect et à la vénération que la nation porte à la mémoire de ses héros et de ses martyrs'.[67] The first president of the Oeuvre, Alfred Loesch, occupied a high post at the Grand Ducal court. This ensured a lasting connection between the Pupilles and the Grand Ducal family. The yearly *Journée nationale des Pupilles* was celebrated on 24 June. It was probably no coincidence that this was also the name day of the heir to the throne, later Grand Duke, Jean. Members of the Grand Ducal family would receive a party of 11-year old Pupilles, while other school children paid homage to the fallen martyrs at the Hinzert Cross.[68]

It is obvious that the Pupilles served a role in the state's policy to construct a collective national memory. This may explain why in writings often no distinction between the two groups of orphans was made. They were jointly portrayed as inheritors of the resistance, the bearers of the moral values and the solidarity that their parents had shown: 'ils affirment l'honneur contre l'opportunisme, l'abnégation contre le compromis (...).' They demonstrated 'que les sacrifices subis et les souffrances endurées en commun sont un des éléments constitutifs de la Nation, et que celle-ci doit être défendue autant par l'esprit de résistance de la population que par l'effort des armées.'[69]

The emphasis on the collective resistance, suffering and solidarity as the foundation of the Oeuvre is a salient and recurrent feature to this day.[70] The 'resistance' part seems slightly odd to outsiders. First, as said, a third to half of the children were orphans of civilians. Second, in 1967, to the horror of the former resistance, a new law for war victims came into effect and as a result the children of deceased conscripted soldiers could be admitted as well. (This law will be returned to later on.)

In total around 960 children were adopted by the Oeuvre. Children could also be adopted if one of their parents died after the war, as long as a causal relation to the war could be argued. This, and the later inclusion of children of *Wehrmacht* soldiers, explains why the last children were adopted as late as 1972.[71]

In 1997, the former Pupilles founded an *Amicale des Pupilles de la Nation*. It is both a friendship organization and an interest group vis-à-vis the state. An impor-

66 Amicale des Pupilles, *D'Pupilles,* 386.
67 Loesch, 'Les Pupilles', 673.
68 Amicale des Pupilles, *D'Pupilles,* 377; Loesch, 'Les Pupilles', 673-5.
69 Loesch, 'Les Pupilles', 675.
70 'Préface' in Amicale des Pupilles, *D'Pupilles,* 15.
71 Amicale des Pupilles, *D'Pupilles,* 425.

tant aim is to stay in contact with national and international resistance organizations – a clear indication of how the memory of collective resistance is maintained.[72]

Distinctions

Directly after the war, several military and civilian distinctions were created. The first was a posthumous military distinction *Mort pour la Patrie*. Both the distinction and the words 'Mort' and 'Patrie' were novelties. The former resistance expected it to be a privilege to be bestowed only on patriotic victims, but it was also awarded to deceased forced conscripts.[73] Until 1972, a total of 4,400 individuals received this posthumous title.[74]

The distinctions for civilians were proposed by the *Conseil de l'Ordre de la Résistance* (COR). The *Croix de la Résistance* was awarded posthumously, the *Médaille de la Résistance* to survivors. The latter was eventually awarded to over 1,100 people. In 1967, the government created another distinction, the *Titre de Résistant*. This was awarded to over 1,350 people. Remarkably, research has shown that the two groups overlap only partly.[75]

When the *Amicale des Pupilles de la Nation* was founded in 1997, one of its first actions was to request the *Titre de Résistant* for their members. Obviously the former Pupilles did not qualify as resistance fighters and the request was denied. It was probably made with an eye to a higher annuity.[76]

Compensation policy: The laws of 1950 and 1967

The 1950 law for war damages

In November 1945, a bureau of *Dommages de Guerre* was installed at the ministry of the Interior. Its minister, Eugène Schaus, immediately started to work on compensation legislation and introduced the first important law for war victims. It was adopted in 1950: the *Loi du 25 février 1950 concernant l'indemnisation des dommages de Guerre*. The law explicitly did not entail moral recognition of victims, but only pertained to the compensation of material, political and physical damage. Political damage referred to losing one's job and income, for instance after refusing to join

72 Amicale des Pupilles, *D'Pupilles*, 429.
73 Bonifas, *Dédommagement des enrôlés de force*, 51.
74 Schoentgen, 'Resistenzorganisationen nach dem 2. Weltkrieg', 542; *Livre d'Or des victimes*, 1972.
75 Dostert, 'Résistance et reprise politique', 38.
76 Interview Dostert.

the VdB or after deportation. These were the 'destitués politiques'. In the context of this study, we will limit ourselves to the compensation of physical damage.

Physical damage was only acknowledged when it was demonstrably and directly caused by circumstances of war. But also eligible for compensation of 'physical damage' were legal inheritors of deceased victims *(les ayants-droit)*: widows and orphans, parents and sometimes even siblings, if they had depended on the income of the deceased. The law included foreigners and stateless people who resided in the country during the war, those who lost the Luxembourg nationality through Nazi measures and those who gave it up in order to join an Allied army. It explicitly excluded only those who had demonstrated a 'non-patriotic attitude'. This did not necessarily imply the labor conscripts and the *Wehrmacht* soldiers. Both were explicitly mentioned in the law as entitled to compensation for physical damage (art. 45).

The definitions excluded Jewish survivors when not of Luxembourg nationality, which meant almost all survivors. Similar to France and Belgium, deportation on racial grounds was not acknowledged in the legislation. Since citizenship had never been required to live in Luxembourg, most of the Jews residing in Luxembourg in 1940 either had the German nationality or no nationality at all. But since the Luxembourg government had decreed in 1941 that all measures taken by the occupier were null and void, they remained German or stateless according to the Luxembourg law and were excluded from all compensation legislation.[77]

The evaluation of applications for physical damage was assigned to a new Service for Physical War Damages, the *Service des Dommages de Guerre Corporels*, placed under the direction of the Minister of the Interior and War Damages.

1950: The 'Service des Dommages de Guerre Corporels'

Individuals who applied for annuity for disability or illness caused by war and occupation, and for reimbursement of medical costs, had to prove their Luxembourg nationality and a war record. The validity of these claims was verified by the staff of the Service. In addition, a medical attestation would have to argue a direct causal relation between the complaints and particular war circumstances. This was checked by physicians designated by the Service (*médecins-conseil*). Staff and physicians would present their evaluations to the *Commission de rentes*, which submitted proposals for compensation to the minister of the Interior.

The law of 1950 founded the system of evaluation of physical damage on the existing social security provisions for industrial injuries and labor disability (art.

77 Arrêté grand-ducal du 22 avril 1941, déterminant l'effet des mesures prises par l'occupant; Arrêté grand-ducal du 13 juillet 1944, modifiant l'arrêté grand-ducal du 22 avril 1941 déterminant l'effet des mesures prises par l'ennemi.

49 of the law: *Code des Assurances Sociales traitant des prestations en cas d'accident de travail et de maladie professionnelle*). This meant that, firstly, only physical damage, not psychological damage was recognized. Secondly, applicants were evaluated on the degree of *incapacity to work* and not on the disablement itself. The awarded annuity was calculated as a percentage of loss of income, using the mean of the actual income of 1937-1939 as a basis. As a result, victims with a low income in those years received a lower annuity than victims with a high income, even if the injury sustained or the incapacity to work was exactly the same. This was one of many objections raised in later years.[78]

Considering the content of LPPD's bimonthly *Rappel* in the 1950's, the political prisoners were dissatisfied with the law as well as with the responsible politicians and the work of the Service. A greatly contested issue was that the years of imprisonment in camps were not double-counted for the annuities of political prisoners, whereas those of former military combatants were. The LPPD also perceived various breaches of political promises. The widows of patriotic victims, for instance, eventually received less compensation than they had been promised. Furthermore, the LPPD judged the Service wanting in many respects. To their extreme frustration, it took the Service more than 5 years to set up a system to evaluate applications and calculate annuities, and even longer to start actual payments. In 1953, over 14,000 applications had been filed and no official payment made, only advances.[79] Payments finally started in 1955, retroactively to 1944, but to parents of deceased victims. The numbers show that the majority were parents of military victims, i.e. mostly conscripts.[80] The other two groups, the widows-orphans and the injured-ill victims, had to wait until 1959.

The Service also failed to formulate instructions for physicians for a systematic medical examination and this introduced arbitrariness in the evaluations. The LPPD wanted the Service transferred from the ministry of the Interior to Public Health. This was to be effected much later. The Service was not just suspected of incompetence. One of the main themes of the LPPD in the 1950's and 1960's was the supposed preferential treatment of collaborators by the Service (and by politicians and the state in general). One author in *Rappel* reminded his readers as late as 1966: 'Die Luxemburger Ärzteschaft, mit drei Ausnahmen, trat schon frühzeitig und ohne Druck der Besatzungsmächte geschlossen der VdB bei.'[81] The government had not helped matters by proclaiming amnesty in 1953, thereby fully

78 Interview Elcherot.

79 LPPD. 'Mémoire concernant rentes', 286-289; LPPD. 'Mémoire concernant dommages corporels', 375-382.

80 Bonifas, *Dédommagement des enrôlés de force*; See the table of payments since 1944 in 'Service des dommages de guerre corporels 2005'.

81 Anonymous, 'Das muss auch einmal gesagt werden', 317.

restoring the collaborators' civil rights. They could apply for compensation as well. The LPPD protested in vain.[82]

The LPPD now became convinced that the purge had been deliberately superficial. It suspected that the state thwarted the patriotic victims because of their political potential and moral influence. Both allegations are tenacious myths.[83] In the perception of the patriotic victims, they did not receive the preferential treatment they were entitled to, which they interpreted as being discriminated against. The procedures of the *Service des Dommages Corporels* exacerbated matters. Concentration camp survivors felt treated discourteously when having to prove the causality between their inflictions and war circumstances. In the small society of Luxembourg where everybody knew each other, tensions rose over who were or were not recognized as victims.[84]

The former resistance did not stand alone in its dissatisfaction. The forced conscripts criticized the law as well. They had revived their fight since 1959, after they had been excluded from the indemnity treaty concluded with the German Federal Republic. The treaty compensated victims persecuted because of the racial, ideological or religious policies of the Nazis. But it only compensated victims who were excluded from national compensation policies. The conscripts were not excluded from the 1950 law.[85] The protests from both the resistance and the conscripts culminated in a final legislation effort for war victims, taking place between 1964 and 1966.

The 1967 law for victims of Nazism

The *Conseil de l'Ordre de la Résistance* (COR) in 1964 again insisted on the moral recognition of the resistance through a legal statute. The minister of the Interior at the time, Pierre Grégoire, invited the COR to submit a law proposal. Grégoire was a former resistance fighter who had spent almost 4 years in concentration camps, and was obviously sympathetic to the COR's request.[86] Within a year the COR presented a proposal with a long list of demands. Apart from moral recognition, the main points were a new and official representative body for the resistance, a *Conseil National de la Résistance* (CNR); a new medical-social service for the systematic examination and the assistance of victims; double-counting of years of imprisonment in camps or in hiding for annuities; and the presumption of cause of physical damage ('présomption d'origine des dommages corporels'). This was

82 Comité Exécutif, 'Amnestie', 129-130.
83 Interview Dostert.
84 Interview Elcherot; interview Dostert.
85 Bonifas, *Dédommagement des enrôlés de force*, 8-9, 49-52 and from 73.
86 Schoentgen, 'Resistenzorganisationen nach dem 2. Weltkrieg', 519.

adopted from the French law, which specified that medical complaints in political prisoners were presumed to have been caused by imprisonment unless proven differently. Once recognized as a political prisoner, one was guaranteed an annuity.[87]

The close collaboration with Grégoire's ministry did not prepare the COR for what followed: the final proposal by the government in 1966 did not address the resistance but *all* victims, including the forced conscripts. It was the government's avid desire to close the chapter on the war consequences and the continuing demands by the various victimized groups. It proposed a comprehensive law that would resolve, once and for all, all consequences for all groups. It was therefore a compromise.

In the proposed law entitled '...ayant pour objet diverses mesures en faveur de personnes devenues victimes d´actes illégaux de l´occupant', the government created the long-desired title for the moral recognition of resistance fighters: the *Titre de Résistant*. It gave a broad definition of resistance, which included disobedience and recalcitrance (corresponding to the concept of *deutschfeindlichkeit*). It created a *Conseil National de la Résistance*, which would also advise on the bestowing of the *Titre de Résistant*. Finally, it adopted the double-counting of years of imprisonment for financial compensation. Despite this outcome, the resistance was horrified. These previously coveted points suddenly seemed a poor result now that other groups benefited from the law as well. The COR wrote that 'Finalement, quelques dispositions *de moindre importance* de ce projet de statut furent reprises par le Gouvernement (...)' (italics mine).[88] Despite repeated protests from the resistance, it took the *Chambre des Députés* in 1967 only two days to adopt the law, by a large majority. The headline in the communist newspaper read: 'Nazi-Opfer wieder geopfert'.[89]

The former conscripts were disappointed as well. They received lower pensions and felt they were deprived of moral recognition and an official body to represent them. They certainly were not represented by the new CNR, which combined being the moral conscience of the nation with advocating the interests of the former resistance. These interests included thwarting the conscripts, for instance when they attempted to erect their own monuments.[90] Allegations that former conscripts demonstrated higher mortality at a younger age in 1974 led to an additional law supplying higher pensions. The allegations were later disproved, the law was maintained.[91]

87 Schoentgen, 'Resistenzorganisationen nach dem 2. Weltkrieg', 542-546; COR, 'Exposé des Motifs', 534-539.

88 COR. 'Statut légal de la Résistance', 255-260; COR. 'Exposé des motifs', 534.

89 'Loi du 25 février 1967'; Schoentgen, 'Resistenzorganisationen nach dem 2. Weltkrieg', 542-545.

90 Schoentgen, 'Resistenzorganisationen nach dem 2. Weltkrieg', 542-545. Bonifas, *Dédommagement des enrôlés de force*, 87.

91 Bonifas, *Dédommagement des enrôlés de force*, 90.

Between 1944 and 1989, 7 billion Luxembourg francs were spent on compensation for physical war damages. 44% consisted of pensions for civilian victims, 49% of pensions for military victims and 7% of treatments and medical appliances for both groups.[92]

Two more laws were adopted to ensure equal compensation for the forced conscripts, pertaining to moral and material damages.[93] Since the early 1990's, some rapprochement between the resistance and conscripts has taken place, but the divide is still apparent. In 2002, a *Centre de Documentation et de Recherche sur la Résistance* was established. A year later, the *Conseil National de la Résistance* was replaced by a *Comité directeur pour le Souvenir de la Résistance.* In 2005, the *Fédération des Victimes du Nazisme, Enrôlés de Force* was granted its own *Centre de Documentation et de Recherche sur les Enrôlés de Force,* and also a *Comité directeur pour le Souvenir.*[94]

Psychological war damage

In all the legislation, was there any attention for possible psychological consequences of the war? As stated earlier, the 1950 law for physical war damages did not acknowledge psychological complaints. The *Code d'Assurances Sociales* it was based on only allowed for schizophrenia, which agreed with the organic rather than psychological status of the disease. How often this diagnosis was made over time is not clear. In 2005, three military and two civil victims received annuities because of schizophrenia.[95] However, several individuals with psychological complaints were recognized on humanitarian grounds, even if a causal relation with the war could not always be established.[96]

In the 1950's, asking for psychological help was tantamount to admitting to madness. Also, the victims were mostly still young and mainly wanted to resume their life.[97] Yet, early on former political prisoners drew attention to possible psychological consequences of imprisonment in concentration camps. They were clearly informed by the international conferences that took place in the 1950's, which reported on the specific concentration camp pathology observed by French

92 Bonifas, *Dédommagement des enrôlés de force,* 98.

93 Bonifas, *Dédommagement des enrôlés de force,* 93-7.

94 'Loi du 4 avril 2005', *Mémorial* 20 avril 2005.

95 Service des Dommages de Guerre Corporels 2005, 6.

96 Interview Elcherot. An interesting detail: the Service twice refused a concentration camp survivor reimbursement of LSD-treatment in the Netherlands, at the psychiatric clinic of professor Jan Bastiaans. The refusal pertained to the use of LSD as a therapeutic drug. The Service's final decision in 1998 stated: 'La prise en charge du traitement LSD n'est pas prévu par les dispositions réglementairs et statuairs de la sécurite sociale.'

97 Interview Dostert; interview Elcherot.

physicians, the *asthénie chronique* (chronic asthenia).[98] This was allegedly a syndrome of physical, intellectual and psychological exhaustion. The least physical exertion was impossible, and concentration and memory were afflicted. On the psychological level (called 'morale' in French), they showed 'émotivité accrue, sautes d'humeur, irritabilité (...)'. They would have 'crises d'inconscience presque délirante où le sujet revit les drames du camp'.[99] In a special edition of *Rappel*, commemorating the tenth anniversary of the liberation, the LPPD addressed a memorandum to the politicians, in which it demanded: 'Que fait-on chez nous pour les asthéniques – ces gens vieillis avant l'age, souffrant par moments d'une fatigabilité très pénible? (...) Ils finiront par figurer sur la liste noire de l'Office, dit "des simulateurs", si souvent rectifiée à cause de plusieurs décès inattendus et regrettables.'[100]

During the preparations for the 1967 law, the COR tried to include the concentration camp pathology, pointing out that both the French and Belgian governments had recognized 'la présomption d'origine et d'intégrité physique au moment de l'arrestation pour toute la pathologie de la déportation, y compris l'asthenie chronique progressive et sénescence prématurée'.[101] But the Luxembourg government, as described, disregarded this demand. It does not seem to have denied the existence of a concentration camp syndrome. Rather, it displayed several evasive strategies to avoid acknowledging it. One was to deny the demand with reference to the 1950 law; another was arguing that the syndrome had already been acknowledged by the *Service des Dommages de Guerre Corporels*. In 1968, parliament met with the *secrétaire d'Etat à la Santé Publique* at the time, M. Vouel. They discussed the law adopted in 1967 and particularly the concentration camp pathology. Vouel declared that the Service had for some time known and used a report on the delayed consequences of imprisonment in camps. (It is unclear which report he referred to.) Vouel also declared to have expanded the *Commission de Rentes* to include representatives from the LPPD, the Ligue des Mutilés et Invalides de Guerre, and with a physician specialized in the 'pathologie postconcentrationnaire'. This guaranteed, said Vouel, that such cases would be treated according to the medical state of the art.[102] The physician, however, remained unnamed and unknown.[103] Apparently, his public role was very limited and he did not publish in medical journals.

98 See *Rappel* 8 (1953), 281-283 and 559; *Rappel* 9 (1954), 59-63; *Rappel* 10 (1955), 528-529.
99 Anonymous, 'Conséquences de la déportation', 59-63.
100 LPPD, 'Mémoire concernant dommages corporels', 380.
101 COR, Exposé des motifs, 539.
102 Anonymous, 'Statut de la Résistance (suite)', 57-8.
103 It may have been dr. Eugène Ost. In his opening speech at the XXXe Anniversaire de la Libération des Camps, Edouard Barbel names Ost as having attended the international conferences on the consequences of deportation and camp imprisonment. In: 'XXXe anniversaire de la libération', 381-383.

It has not been possible to study the validity of Vouels claims, or their results. Clearly, the 'pathologie postconcentrationnaire' never became a formal ground for recognition by the Service. The interviewees, Dostert and Elcherot, emphasized they had never heard of any specialized physicians or psychiatrists, or of special treatment for concentration camp survivors in Luxembourg.

There was one other public event where the topic was raised. In May 1975, the LPPD organized the 30th commemoration of the liberation of the concentration camps. This special occasion was devoted to the concentration camp syndrome. In his opening speech to the conference the president of the LPPD, Edouard Barbel, stated: 'Le problème du syndrome concentrationnaire n'est pas une question médicale récente. (...) On aura dû considerer, à priori, tout concentrationnaire comme un grand malade et le traiter, dès le début, comme tel.' According to Barbel, the majority of camp survivors would sooner or later suffer from the syndrome, which he alternately called 'concentrationnaire' and 'asthénie psychique.' According to Barbel, the symposium had been organized in order to help these diseased comrades, 'objectif principal qui reste à nos organizations et qui devrait être aussi celui de l'État (...).'[104]

The keynote speaker at the symposium was the Dutch professor of psychiatry Jan Bastiaans, known in the Netherlands for his treatment of concentration camp survivors. He was introduced by a Dutch documentary on his work, announced as *Verstehst du jetzt, warum ich weine?*[105] This film shows a session in which a camp survivor, under the influence of LSD, recounts his camp experiences and achieves emotional catharsis. Shown with German subtitles, it was followed by a discussion with Bastiaans and film director Louis van Gasteren. In the afternoon, the film and the discussion were repeated in the presence of his Royal Highness the Grand Duke Jean.

According to a report of the day, it was a 'succès éclatant', attended by 350 people, among whom cabinet ministers, members of parliament, former ministers, physicians, psychologists and teachers. Unfortunately, the discussion after the film, in which apparently Luxembourg physicians participated, was not reported.[106] There is therefore no means to establish the level of knowledge or acceptance of the syndrome at the symposium.

104 LPPD, 'xxxe anniversaire de la libération', 381-383.
105 In Dutch *Begrijp je nu, waarom ik huil?* Director Louis van Gasteren, 1969.
106 LPPD, 'xxxe anniversaire de la libération', 381-383 and 396-397.

Conclusion

From the scattered material it would seem that from the end of the 1960's, there was some public attention for and recognition of psychological war trauma, in the sense of the French definition of concentration camp syndrome. The French definition contains both medical and psychological components, but in the Luxembourg context the latter were not addressed separately. The syndrome was apparently acknowledged in medical circles and at a governmental level. Yet, authorities and physicians ignored the repeated requests for special recognition and for special medical attention.

When considering Luxembourg's experiences during the war, one could imagine that more groups suffered psychological trauma. Two recent publications indeed point this out. In the book on the *Pupilles de la Nation* several former Pupilles testify to having suffered from psychological difficulties all their lives. Some sought psychological assistance.[107] However, the topic of psychological trauma is not addressed separately in the book. The study of the forced conscripts' struggle for compensation emphasizes that in addition to severe physical problems, many of the surviving conscripts suffered psychological trauma. It devotes a specific section to psychological trauma, referring to the conferences organized in the 1960's by the international organizations for political prisoners on the delayed consequences of war and deportation. It also mentions a study conducted by the French physician M.-A. Crocq, revealing post-traumatic stress syndrome among 1,400 forcibly conscripted French soldiers from the Alsace-Lorraine region.[108]

Therefore, attention for psychological war trauma seems to have been both present and absent in Luxembourg. It seems to have been acknowledged as a fact of life rather than something needing health care arrangements. The question may be: why? Clearly, only tentative explanations can be suggested.

The first is that the government did not wish to single out groups in legislation. Giving priority to patriotic victims in terms of moral recognition was as far as it wanted to go. The second explanation is that society at large did not favor singling out a group either. It has become commonly accepted – and is true to a degree – that almost all Luxembourg citizens suffered physical and psychological hardship during the war, either in Luxembourg or abroad. There were the members of the resistance, the concentration camps survivors, the forced laborers, the people in hiding, the deported families and the conscripted *Wehrmacht* soldiers, some of whom also became prisoners of war. Residents in Luxembourg had to endure the intrusive Nazification policy. It should also be remembered that large parts of the population experienced actual war action at the start of the war and in 1944-45,

107 Amicale des Pupilles, *D'Pupilles.*
108 Bonifas, *Dédommagement des enrôlés de force*, 40-46.

during the final battle of the Ardennes.[109] All these people felt victimized, which is demonstrated by their high degree of post-war organization, including the many *Amicales*.

The third explanation is related to the second: if everybody suffered psychological hardship, psychological complaints may in fact have been so widespread as to have little value for the recognition of a special group of victims. A fourth explanation may be the orientation on the French concept of the concentration camp syndrome and on the French and Belgian situations in general. This shaped the demands, which were highly politicized and made in a context which remained highly politicized as well. Medical and psychological complaints may have been viewed as components of a political, strategic negotiation process rather than as an actual social and medical problem needing special health care arrangements.

Interviews and other sources

- P. Dostert, assistant professor of history at the Université de Luxembourg and director of the Centre de Documentation et de Recherche sur la Résistance (CDRR), 10 December 2007.
- M.J. Elcherot, 'Inspecteur principale' of the Service des Dommages de Guerre Corporels, Ministère de la Santé Publique, 11 December 2007.
- *Heim ins Reich. L'échec d'une annexation*. Documentary by Claude Lahr, Luxembourg 2004.

109 Interviews in Wallerang, *Besatzung*, 249-254; documentary *Heim ins Reich*, 2004.

7 From Totalitarianism to Trauma

A paradigm change in the Netherlands

» *Jolande Withuis and Annet Mooij*

In this chapter we will try to connect aspects of the Dutch aftermath of World War II that at first sight may seem unrelated and are not usually analyzed together, belonging as they do to different fields and disciplines.

Changes in medical and psychological thinking about the consequences of the war, the prevalence of war-related health problems, the development of a 'war welfare system' and the success of the concept of trauma, will be analyzed in the context of the post-war political history, especially the rise and decline of the Cold War, and in the context of the – no less conflict-ridden – history of remembrance and the organizations of victims and veterans. In short we will show how memory developed from 'totalitarianism' as the key concept in interpreting the war, to 'trauma' as the primary term in which to think about it – a shift from politics to psychology.

This also means that mental health developments will not be described from the perspectives of patients or therapists, but from a historical sociological viewpoint. Medical science does not develop in a laboratory or social vacuum. A long-term sociological analysis should demonstrate dynamics and processes that those personally and directly involved in the process cannot see, in the case of medical developments: patients and therapists. Such a sociological analysis may appear overly critical, cold and detached. However, analyzing the rise of 'trauma' as a social and historical process does not deny the existence of war trauma, nor does it intend to trivialize suffering.

Occupation and deportation

Though its aftermath now takes up more than sixty years, World War II in the Netherlands only lasted for five days. That is, if we look at the 'war' in the literal sense of the term only. In the early morning of May 10, 1940 the German army invaded the Netherlands – a country that had not been involved in any war in its territory for a hundred years. Five days of fighting followed, in which 2,300 Dutch soldiers died. On May 14 the German *Luftwaffe* bombed the city of Rotterdam and killed about 800 citizens; thousands became homeless. Under the threat of other cities being bombed the Dutch surrendered. The Queen and her ministers left the country for London where a Government in Exile was installed. The Netherlands was occupied.

During the German occupation, which lasted until May 5, 1945, approximately 225,000 citizens lost their lives (of a population of almost nine million). Among the dead were about 7,000 members of the Dutch resistance, executed or died in concentration camps, and about 102,000 Jews. This number means that 75% of the Dutch Jewish population was killed, which is a high percentage as compared to other countries. Occupation forces started rounding up and deporting Jews in February 1941; deportations were completed in September 1944. About 25,000 Jews went into hiding; in the end one third of them were still arrested. Hiding was dangerous for those who went into hiding as well as for the people who helped them.

In the spring of 1942 the Germans introduced the so-called *Arbeitseinsatz,* a law that obliged Dutch men between the ages of eighteen and forty to go to work in Germany. To escape this forced collaboration some 325,000 men went into hiding. More than 600,000 men did work in Germany for some time, sometimes after being caught in street *razzias*. Their death toll is estimated at about 8,500.

Southern parts of the Netherlands were freed by allied forces in the autumn of 1944; the northern parts, including the big cities, still had to endure the extremely hard winter of 1944-1945, in which 20,000 lives were lost due to cold and hunger.

After the liberation in May 1945, approximately 4,500 surviving Dutch Jews, 8,500 Dutch political prisoners and about 380,000 *Arbeitseinsatz* workers who were still in Germany returned to their country where the Jews found their families, friends and social world largely annihilated.

Dutch World War II not only took place in The Netherlands but also in the Dutch colony of the Netherlands East Indies, now Indonesia. From March 1942 on, the Netherlands East Indies were occupied by the Japanese. All servicemen and mobilized soldiers were made prisoners of war while a large section of the Dutch civilian population was confined in internment camps, the men separated from women and children. About 15,000 people died in these internment camps, and more than 8,000 Dutch men died as military prisoners of war.[1] When the independent Republic of Indonesia was proclaimed after the Japanese defeat of August 15 1945, the Netherlands started a colonial war in which about 200,000 soldiers fought. They fought a lost cause; in 1949 the Netherlands formally recognized the independence of Indonesia. These developments caused the start of a huge migration. Approximately 300,000 Dutch Indonesians returned to the Netherlands after the war, or set foot ashore there for the very first time.

1 Van der Ploeg and Weerts, *Veteranen in Nederland,* 13; Van Goor, *De Nederlandse koloniën,* 317-320.

The laws: 1945-1972[2]

Which then were the laws, statutes or regulations to which various groups of victims could appeal in the first post-war decades?

The regular soldiers as well as conscripts who were killed or became disabled in the first five days of the war in May 1940 came under the 1922 military pension scheme. The population of Rotterdam were the first recipients of a new type of war aid. After the bombardment of the city private individuals and government came into action to help the victims. Subsequently, in April 1945 in London a basic benefit was announced for citizens who as a result of the bombardment were no longer able to make a living or who had lost everything. Until 1984 this minimum relief scheme at the lowest level was the basis for the provision of aid to this group.

More generous, and also the subject of nationwide collections, attention and debate, was the *Wet Buitengewoon Pensioen* (WBP, Extraordinary Pensions Act), enacted in the summer of 1947 as a result of the cooperation of the government and the former resistance organized within the *Stichting 1940-1945* (Foundation 1940-1945).

The WBP awarded pensions to widows and children of resistance fighters who had been killed and to resistance fighters who could not earn a living at pre-war standards because of war-related health problems. Jewish victims deported 'solely' because of their 'race' and not because of resistance activities, did not qualify. They had to turn to the municipal authorities, where they could apply for some dole-like group schemes at the minimum level.

Heartless as it may seem that in 1947 the former resistance achieved a pension only for 'their own' (it took another 25 years before Jewish survivors 'got' a comparable law), history offers some explanation for this outcome.

During the occupation years one major concern was the fate of the children and widows if resistance men were killed. Most of these men were no soldiers. They received no wages for their activities against the German occupation and in peacetime earned their living with normal jobs. To make it possible to participate in the resistance, others would have to take care of their wives and children, even more so if they died, were arrested or went underground.

To this end a clever support structure was set up to provide for the families of resistance fighters during the war. At the same time, the Dutch government operating from London exile promised that no family should worry about the future. Post-war Dutch society would gratefully take responsibility for the next of kin of all those who fell fighting for their country.

2 Based on Van der Leeuw, 'De ontwikkeling van de overheidszorg'.

And so it happened. In the autumn of 1944 foremen of the Dutch resistance founded the above-mentioned *Stichting 1940-1945*, that would take care of disabled comrades and the next of kin of those who had died. Immediately after the liberation money was raised through public collections, legates, voluntary extra work, profits from published autobiographies of ex-political prisoners, and a gift from the Queen. The Stichting also brought heavy political pressure on the first post-war governments in order to achieve the WBP and played a large role in the grounding of the law's juridical philosophy. The WBP was based on the philosophy of 'fictional state employment.' The resistance fighter or his next of kin got a pension *as if* he had been employed as a civil servant during the war; he was supposed to have been under contract with the state. Following this philosophy, most of the funds necessary to pay WBP pensions came from the state; the implementation of the law remained largely in the hands of the Stichting, which also offered social work and holidays for the resistance widows.

Victim organizations: 1945-1972

Immediately after the liberation, ex-resistance fighters established associations to organize reunions and to protect their interests, for example the pensions. Jewish survivors lacked this kind of politically influential organization and strong pressure groups. Their interests were not represented by the most important of these post-war organizations, which excluded Jewish members who had not been active in the resistance movement. For instance, a condition for membership of the strong Association of Ex-Political Prisoners (*Expogé*), founded in September 1945, was imprisonment. But not imprisonment as such. *Expogé* was no association of *déportés*. Imprisonment had to have been punishment for resistance activities; Jews who had been deported 'solely' because of their being Jewish could not become members. The same went for the workers for the *Arbeitseinsatz*. They could not apply for membership. An attempt in the late 1940's to organize their own association failed.

Besides this gap between Jewish victims and resistance, the fast developing Cold War produced intense hostility among the former resistance members themselves. The optimistic feeling of 1945 that the pre-war religious, political and class distinctions would disappear in the new Netherlands thanks to the togetherness of the war years, rapidly melted away. Around 1948 the communists, who had met with goodwill after the liberation because of their courageous resistance to the Germans and their big losses, became the new enemy. For *Expogé* the fight against world communism became an important goal; an initial step in this endeavor – following the 1948 coup in Prague – was the expelling of the many communists from the organization. From 1949 onwards, former concentration camp inmates belonging to the Dutch communist party or any of its front organizations could no longer be members of this association of political prisoners. Also, communists were no longer appointed on the Board of *Stichting 1940-1945*.

On the list of suspected front organizations the so-called 'camp committees' figured highly. Contrary to their image, these *amicales* (as they are known internationally) were in no way simply supportive clubs of fellow sufferers. They often had more or less hidden political goals. Former prisoners fought bitterly about the camp remembrance. Some committees became bulwarks of communist political manoeuvring; the communist victims linked the remembrance of the camps directly to their actual political struggle against the Dutch government and 'capitalism'. *Expogé* on the other hand reasoned: better no monuments or reunions of former camp inmates at all, than running the risk of supporting a front organization. In the fifties this even went so far that *Expogé*, despite its strong objections against the government policy to pardon German war criminals, did not protest against such policy for fear of supporting a communist campaign.

Especially distrusted by government and non-communist ex-resistance was the Netherlands' Auschwitz Committee (NAC), that was founded in 1956 after an international initiative of the Polish government. The NAC board indeed consisted mainly of communist party members, even party members who had never been deported at all.

During the Cold War the Jews fell between two stools as it were. On the one hand *Expogé* fought communism (and considered the NAC to be communist) and fostered its 'active' resistance identity (as opposed to 'passive' Jewish victimization). On the other, communist ideology saw capitalism as the enemy and included Jewish victims as victims of Nazism just like the resistance, denying that there was anything special about this group. The NAC in those Cold War years emphatically did not consider itself a *Jewish* committee. The committee stressed the common antifascist cause of Jews and left-wing resistance.

While communists during the Cold War saw capitalism as a first stage of fascism, their counterparts (and former camp-mates) in *Expogé* saw communism as a new form of totalitarianism. Both sides of the former resistance defined the Cold War within the frame of reference of World War II. World War II had been a war against totalitarianism for *Expogé* as it defined itself during the fifties, and now a new totalitarian threat had to be confronted, a threat that Dutch communists were part of. The communists in their turn stated more and more that World War II had essentially been a war against communism. The two contradicting views of the former resistance thus mirrored each other. Both groups emotionally and cognitively continued World War II.

To formulate it in another way: during the coldest Cold War years World War II was defined within a narrow political paradigm. In this political paradigm victims could be enemies. They certainly did not see each other as fellow-victims, nor did they define themselves as victims. 'Victim' was too passive a name to put on the proud activity of resistance. The perspective on the violence of 1940-1945 was not psychological but political.

Mental war damage and remembrance 1945-2005

At the same time – and this is a finding worth some reflection – almost nobody in those years appeared to be suffering from war trauma. Looking at the WBP, between 1947 and 1970 about 90% of the pensions went to the relatives of dead resistance fighters. (There are no statistics on the health of the Jewish survivors in these first post-war years as there was no law to which they could appeal.) The remaining 10% were resistance fighters who had become disabled or had returned ill from a concentration camp. Although the original closing date for application, 1948, was dropped because even three years after the end of the war new cases came forward, the number of new applications declined so sharply in the early fifties that termination of the Act was again considered.

The graphics on the numbers of applicants for a resistance pension follow the same pattern as the number of mental and public health publications on war-related health problems. Contrary to what one would expect, the attention paid to the war damage does not show a decline from fierce beginnings towards zero later on.

For our research into psychiatric thinking on World War II consequences we studied a broad base of medical literature. Among other things we analyzed sixty volumes of the *Maandblad Geestelijke volksgezondheid* (MGV, Monthly on Public Mental Health). The journal is written and read by professionals such as psychiatrists, psychiatric nurses, social workers and policy makers, and it presents contemporary insights into the broad field of social psychiatry and mental health. Just counting pages regarding World War II is revealing, as is evident in the table below. In the first years MGV spent almost one-third of its pages on war-related problems. This was followed by an almost complete absence of the subject during the fifties and sixties. Attention revived again between 1970 and 1980, where after 'trauma' remained a major topic but was no longer associated primarily with World War II.

The sharp decrease during the fifties is not only similar to the developments in the number of WBP-applicants but also to developments in the amount of World War II books published and monuments built. In the initial post-war years a considerable number of books, brochures and autobiographies about the concentration camps were published and read. As to monuments, so many ideas were submitted to the municipal and national committees running this department that government put a stop to it.

% Editorial pages on WWII in MGV	
1945-1946:	32%
1947-1949:	6
1950-1960:	0.3
1960-1970:	0.3
1970-1980:	3
1980-1990:	1.5
1990-2000:	0.8

By 1948, however, the public had had enough. The feeling grew that the subject of 'war' should be brought to a conclusion. In the mid-sixties interest rose again. Between 1960 and 1965 a long television series on the war years, 'De bezetting' (*Occupation*), was broadcast, and some years later repeated, which kept Dutch families glued to their more and more prevalent television sets (the proportion of households with televisions grew in those years from 25% to 68%). From then on, interest grew. In 1995, half a century after the liberation, the fifth of May, 'Liberation Day,' officially become a National Holiday – a decision many victims experienced as a late victory over the governmental neglect from 1945 on.

Remembrance also changed qualitatively. In the early post-war years monuments, rituals and publications emphasized national resistance, not the annihilation of the Jews. Dachau, not Auschwitz symbolized the evils of Nazism. Genocide became the central focus in war remembrance after about 1980, an important early impetus being the study on the persecution and destruction of the Dutch Jews by historian J. Presser, published in 1965.

Back to psychiatry. Four periods can be distinguished in the development of medical theory and in the prevalence of war-related health complaints between 1945 and 2005.

1945-1948: Early understanding

The existence of MGV in itself proves that even during the occupation years mental health professionals were concerned about the post-war state of public health and the health of the most victimized groups. The monthly was conceived by doctors and social workers, who before the war had been involved in the emerging mental health movement, and was based on the conviction that when the war was over, extra care would be needed. The first issue was published in the autumn of 1945 and contained articles in which psychiatrists warned the public about psychic war damage.

In 1946 the Jewish psychoanalyst Jaap Tas, who had survived Bergen-Belsen, published a perceptive article on the effects of concentration camp imprisonment and on what might be the (possibly long-term) psychical consequences of such an experience. Fundamental in his view was the inability of sufferers to express emotions like fear of death, and anger about humiliation, and the fact that this necessary repression lasted for a relatively very long time. Contrary to the 'normal' war experience, this repression was not alternated with periods of relaxation and pleasure.

World War I had shown that a short intensive experience of fear or shock, such as being shot down as a pilot, was less harmful in the long run than the seemingly endless, powerless, fearful waiting in the trenches. The experience of intense powerlessness, as it turned out, was one of the major factors that caused psychic damage. Tas' plea illustrates that before 1945 there was no such thing as an accepted medical or psychological theory to understand the impact of the concentration camp experience. Comparing these new war experiences with the medical knowledge of World War I, Tas felt obliged to convince his readers that having been imprisoned in a concentration camp, despite being a situation without armed conflict, might be a serious threat to one's mental state.

Tas also predicted that the atmosphere to which the survivors returned would be decisive for their later wellbeing. In this regard he shared the disappointment of the surviving Jews. Though their homes were robbed or taken by others, their jobs were gone, and their culture and social environment was destroyed, survivors often had to find out for themselves if their families were dead or missing, and had to rebuild their lives while they received almost no care and were not made to feel welcome. One of the measures Tas suggested was large-scale availability of psychotherapy. This was not realized. Psychotherapy was an unusual, unknown and scarce treatment in 1945. Soldiers who had fought in the May days of 1940, however, or who returned from the Netherlands East Indies with nervous complaints, could be treated in the *Militair Neurose Hospitaal*. Tas presented this as an example of how camp survivors should be treated.

A second important author was Eddy de Wind, a physician and psychoanalyst like Tas, and a survivor of Auschwitz. During his career De Wind would write many articles on psychic war damage. In his first article in 1949, 'Confrontation with death,' De Wind thoroughly examined the differences in terms of inner experience and lasting psychic damage between concentration camps designed as punishment and camps designed for genocidal extermination. In the first category, the chance that prisoners would die was considerable and they certainly were aware of it – all around them their friends were dying. However, one could try to behave sensibly and to make the most of any opportunity, such as avoiding the quarry and trying to get a job with a roof over your head or with some extra food.

In contrast, the death camps were intended solely for the destruction of those who arrived there. According to De Wind the human mind cannot cope with such knowledge. Realizing this reality, De Wind explained, meant insanity or regression to mental childhood. This regression – 'going back' to an early phase in psychic development – meant living in a state of being in which one no longer calculates any future, but just survives by the minute and by the day. At the same time, however, to have any chance to survive, one should not give up hope or stop caring, as this meant certain death. Trying to survive required a two-way mental habitus: regression on one side, and constant alertness on the other.

After their liberation, those who had escaped the gas chambers faced the mental task of recovering from this regression. Such a recovery demanded immense personal care, attention, and professional therapists who were capable and willing to descend into an imaginary hell that their patients had actually lived in. None of these were available. De Winds early emphasis on the distinctive experiences of surviving death or concentration camp was unique and is still not fully recognized.

Not writing in any post-war Dutch periodical but nevertheless remarkable in his sharp prevision of possible health damage was military psychiatrist Joost A.M. Meerloo. In the early war years Meerloo, who worked for the psychology department of the war ministry, published a book and several articles on the psychiatry of war and peace. In 1942 he fled to England, where he was one of the authors of the UNRRA (United Nations Relief and Rehabilitation Administration) report of June 1945 on the expected 'Psychological problems of displaced persons.' He also wrote a military report in Dutch in which he warned that the 'lost psychic balance' would prove a larger problem than the physical war damage. Regression, vulgarization, feelings of inferiority and distrust, feelings of superiority, cynicism and nihilism were among the possible psychological outcomes of the war years. Meerloo particularly pointed out the burden that the lack of privacy in the camps put on psychic well-being.

If authors like De Wind, Meerloo and Tas had insights like this, why was psychological care for war victims almost non-existent and why did public and medical interest disappear in the late forties?

It is important to realize that the victims, and most of all the Jewish victims, often kept silent, not only because their stories frequently were not welcome, but also because their stories were too gruesome to tell. Many victims tried not to remember, and to resume or rebuild their lives: family, children, and work – an attitude stimulated by the rebuilt Jewish social work institutions.

At that time the mental climate was totally different from what it is now. Dutch society was not yet permissive and affluent, but ascetic and austere. Although the liberation had caused joy and spontaneous festivities, individual happiness was no common goal as it is today. Unhappiness was no mood to indulge in. The reconstruction of the fatherland required work, not reflection. Silence was golden. It was considered brave to declare the past a closed chapter. Complaining was certainly not considered proper conduct. Psychoanalysis was an avant-garde treatment, known only to a small elite sector of the population. Popular thought was that one was either sane or insane and the insane belonged in asylums. 'Treatment' belonged to that stigmatized world of insanity.

Society was not yet secularized. Priests and clergymen still deeply influenced personal life, just like Christianity was still a powerful influence on government. After the war it was widely feared in these milieus that moral decline and social chaos loomed. But liberals and social-democrats were also touched by this moral panic. Would it be possible to discipline the wild unkempt hordes returning from the camps and from the resistance where men and women had had to make their own decisions? Even some of the most law-abiding parts of pre-war Dutch society had acted against the German occupiers and had lived in a state of lawlessness.

There was special concern about the supposed threat of the supposed natural male authority. During the years that men had been in hiding or deported by the Germans, women had acted as heads of their families. In the eyes of the rising profession of social workers, family relations had become abnormal and pathological. Society had to be disciplined and normalized.

This 'back to normal' attitude dominated the resistance elite too. 'We didn't do it for the honour or for money; nor does the former resistance claim privileges or special positions,' they said in every possible way. To avoid stimulating the rise of a sectarian resistance culture, the Stichting closed the clinics it had started in 1945 to help former resistance fighters regain their health. Their illnesses were mostly due to camp life, for instance tuberculosis and hunger edema. In cases where no clear somatic disorder was established, the ailments were nevertheless assumed to be physical. Psychic disorders in this rather masculine milieu were not considered – not by the patients themselves, but even less by the resistance elite, afraid as they were of spoiling people into lasting maladjustment. The prescription was: get back to normal.

Last but not least, Dutch 'reconstruction moralism' was also no stranger to psychiatry. In these first post-war years one could roughly distinguish two perspectives. Doctors like Tas and De Wind, who had themselves survived a camp or been in hiding, tended to be more concerned about psychic damage and personal unhappiness than about moral decline and social chaos. On the other side, professionals and spiritual leaders were afraid that society would be unable to return people to normality. The first medical approach focused on damaged individuals, the second on society as a whole. The latter won. Analyzing contemporary publications one notices how fear of social unrest gained priority over concern about damaged individuals.

1948-1968: Low prevalence

Although this shift to social normalization certainly was stimulated by non-medical factors like reconstruction moralism and the beginning of the Cold War, it was also an outcome of former psychiatric opinions.

Unlike Germany and Great Britain the Netherlands did not participate in World War I, so *Kriegsneurose* and *shell-shock* were no Dutch diseases. In connection with insurance pensions, however, the Dutch medical world during the thirties was aware of the debates about the psychogenesis of these disorders and had discussions about 'traumatic neurosis' – the phenomenon that people after, for instance, work accidents do not recover even when their physical health is restored. Could fright, shock, powerlessness or confrontation with death by themselves cause illness and inability to work? Two central issues from this pre-war debate returned in the post-war medical thinking on war trauma: *ziektewinst* (secondary gain) and *premorbide persoonlijkheid* (pre-morbid personality).

The first dilemma, secondary gain, concerns the question as to whether immaterial and material attention (such as pensions and treatment) might keep patients ill. The psychodynamics of secondary gain differ from malingering, but the two are often mentioned in the same breath. (A malingerer *is* not ill, but pretends to be; secondary gain is illness caused by social arrangements that make it more comfortable to stay ill than to take up daily tasks again.) In combination with the above-mentioned moral panic, the concept of secondary gain led to the conclusion that 'spoiling' people would confirm their neuroticism and maladjustment.

The second pre-war concept to be continued after 1945 was so-called pre-morbidity; this concerns predisposition and is a classic issue indeed. The central question here was: is it possible that dramatic events or stressful periods would cause damage in a person who had been a healthy, non-neurotic, stable adult personality before this event?

This possibility was a problem for organicistic psychiatry as well as for psychoanalysts. The first category fostered the basic assumption that no outside force could chronically harm a healthy mind in a healthy body. The second group still acted according to the classic theory that neurosis is rooted in childhood. How does one relate camp experiences to oedipal conflict? In those years the concept still was war *neurosis*, not yet trauma or post-concentration camp syndrome.

During the fifties and early sixties dominant medical opinion held that those who did not recover from their wartime experiences had been vulnerable before the war. Their symptoms were not caused by the war but expressed pre-existing neuroticism or constitutional defects. In daily medical practice the concepts 'secondary gain' and 'predisposition' were often tainted with arrogance, paternalism and distrust. Many medical practitioners lacked knowledge about what some of their patients had gone through. However, their opinion that most war victims would recover without special attention was confirmed by the fact that there were few patients who still seemed to suffer from war illnesses. Even the *Militair Neurose Hospitaal* was closed in 1963.[3] A relative outsider could believe in good faith that war victims had recovered.

But had they? We don't know. The assumption that war was over and everybody was well again certainly neglects complaints like sleeplessness, nightmares and mild or severe obsessive behavior, but in those days complaints like that were privately borne, suffered in silence and more often than not accepted as peculiarities one lived with. Victims were seldom aware that others suffered similar complaints, or that one could ask one's doctor for help. Nevertheless, recent detailed study of the monthly of the ex-political prisoners shows that already during the fifties it was acknowledged between the lines (and from the early sixties on more and more also in the lines themselves), that many of the comrades were not well at all.[4]

1968-1980: Rise in psychological complaints, development of a war welfare policy

As statistics show, the calm silence 'on the war' radically came to an end in the late sixties. Quite suddenly large numbers of new applicants knocked on the WBP's door. Whereas in the twenty years between 1950 and 1970 approximately 6,000 new clients requested a pension, in the following ten years some 8,000 members of the former resistance applied. With a rapidly decreasing population, the number of applicants almost *tripled*. The increase in the number of applications started in 1968 and reached a peak in 1977.[5]

A WBP pension is not supposed to be compensation for hardships; it compensates for loss of earning capacity due to invalidity as a consequence of resistance activities. To be entitled, one must be ill and the illness must be caused by the war. Our data show that a quarter of a century after the war many people became – or thought of themselves as – ill as a consequence of their wartime activities, or came to express complaints they had thus far borne in silence.

Which then were their ailments? Contrary to the situation around 1950, almost all problems were now psychological. Some doctors tried to distinguish different forms of psychic consequences, such as 'psychosomatic' and 'psychogenic'. However, it proved impossible to use this precise classification in medical practice. Most of the complaints were vaguely somatic without discernible physical substrate. Eddy de Wind, one of the first to observe the mysterious wave of new patients, in 1966 introduced the generic title 'late consequences' to stress that the new patients seemed to have been functioning well for some twenty years.

3 Van der Ploeg and Weerts, 15, 16, *Veteranen in Nederland.*
4 Floris de Heus, trainee report ; De Ridder, *De geest van het verzet.*
5 Van der Leeuw, 'De ontwikkeling van de overheidszorg', 95.

The fact that no clear physical cause could be established in most of the new cases caused problems in the medical examination procedure prior to the granting of a WBP allowance. Conflicts arose about the question as to whether or not these psychic handicaps were caused by the war. After all, if the patient had always been weak, his illness was not caused by his wartime experiences, so he was not eligible for a pension.

This suspicious approach, however, and the accompanying concepts of pre-morbidity and secondary gain, were fast becoming socially unacceptable. Times were changing. Patients not only grew in numbers but also in assertiveness. They wanted to be taken seriously by doctors. New applicants for a WBP pension started protesting against the often very long and bureaucratic admittance procedure and against what they considered the arrogant, ignorant and insensitive attitude of the medical examiners who decided on 'their' entitlement. The protesters had the wind of democratization in their sails. More than before, authorities felt obliged to listen. Victims were increasingly considered worthy participants in the debate about their treatment. Organizations were set up as well as pressure groups demanding faster procedures, higher pensions and broad admittance criteria. Furthermore, their protests won support from some doctors who were willing to stand behind their patients when they appealed negative WBP decisions. These doctors confirmed that more former camp prisoners and former members of the resistance had breakdowns, and – an important additional note – that these were patients who had successfully rebuilt their lives after the war. They blamed their colleagues for their lack of understanding of the 'post-concentration camp syndrome'. They presented as new medical insight that their patients' breakdowns were the late consequences of their war experiences followed by hard work and deep silence after the war (a deep silence that, as we showed before, certainly did not exist between 1945 and 1948), and also because their strength was diminishing as a result of ageing.

Quite a fundamental result of this development was that it became taboo to look into the medical history of patients or to consider the possibility that a pension might prevent recovery. In the light of the growing number of new patients, the lack of evidence-based medical theory on their ailments and the general feeling that these victims had been neglected too long, the most humane medical practice then seemed to be to throw the concepts of pre-morbidity and secondary gain on the social and scientific rubbish dump. Though it was rarely possible to prove any hard causal relationship between health complaints and war past, it was considered inappropriate to burden the victims with the task of proving their case or going through lengthy and demanding appeal procedures. More often than not this first generation of patients felt ashamed about their symptoms, and furthermore, hadn't they suffered enough during the war?

In 1971 the law was adapted to the new practice that the burden of proof that one's ailments were caused by the war no longer rested on the plaintiff. The burden of proof was reversed: from now on, when a person who could prove that s/he had been a member of the resistance developed health problems, these problems, whatever their nature, were almost always assumed to be caused by the war.

1972: The case of the Breda Three

Illustrative for the change in social and cultural climate (and in itself also a cause for a deepening of this change) was a political event in 1972.

We might call 1972 the year in which the Netherlands was publicly confronted with the large scale existence of the KZ or 'post-concentration camp syndrome'. Early that year the Roman-Catholic Minister of Justice decided to release from prison the last three German war criminals: Kotälla, Fischer, and Aus der Fünten. His determination to set these so-called *Drie van Breda* free – the 'Breda Three', after the city in which their prison stood – caused a storm of anger, especially among members of the former resistance and among surviving Jews.

Their protest began mostly as a political protest. The minister was accused of being insufficiently aware of the political dangers of his policy with regard to the growing neo-Nazi movement in the German Federal Republic. Soon, however, the damage his decision might do to the wellbeing and mental health of the former victims of the sinister trio became the central topic. Release would harm the survivors' health.

As a result of the fast-growing indignation about the possible release, a special parliamentary hearing was organized. At this hearing a long line of spokespersons from Jewish and resistance organizations evoked the gruesome images this subject brought to the survivors' minds, the nightmares still haunting them, and the suicides attempted by comrades. They had no doubt whatsoever that releasing the Breda Three would aggravate this suffering.

Parliament was also addressed by several psychiatrists. Just like the victims' organizations, they warned Parliament that setting these criminals free might be too heavy a burden for their patients and for war victims in general to bear. This opinion was new: only three years earlier, when the imprisoned war criminals had also been an issue, mental health professionals had argued in favor of release, saying that hate hurts those who hate and that victims' resentment would create more unhappiness among victims than the possible shock of deporting the three to Germany.

The only speakers now in favor of release were lawyers and probation officers. They underlined from a humanitarian perspective how bad the prisoners' situation was and argued that keeping them imprisoned no longer served any reasonable purpose.

The hearing was the first ever parliamentary session to be broadcast live on national television. Added to this, the gripping documentary drama *Begrijpt u nu waarom ik huil* was aired on television in the same week, under the pressure of the anti-release lobby. 'Do you now understand why I cry?' was never meant to be shown to a lay audience. It was made in 1969 to inform health workers about the symptoms and treatment of the until then mostly unknown 'late consequences' of the war. The documentary shows a therapeutic session of a former inmate of the German concentration camp Sachsenhausen and professor Jan Bastiaans, a psychiatrist who in those days was fast becoming famous for his treatment of war victims. Bastiaans used LSD as a therapeutic medium. Under the influence of this drug the patient is expected to remember his camp experiences and achieve emotional catharsis. And that is exactly what we witness.

In between the hearing and the documentary the yearly procession in remembrance of the 'February Strike' (the Dutch strike of 1941 against the rounding up of Jews, one of the rare anti-German demonstrations in an occupied country) grew into a mass demonstration against the release of the Three.

All these manifestations of intense grief caused a dramatic reversal in public opinion; political opinion soon followed. In her dissertation on the infamous 'Breda Three,' historian Hinke Piersma shows that in 1972 the Dutch Lower House decision *not* to release them after all, was the outcome of feelings of guilt following the realization that the Dutch resistance had not saved the nation's Jewish citizens, a new responsiveness to victims and the recently discovered KZ syndrome. Nobody wanted to be accused of repeating earlier wrongs. Nobody wanted to be accused of a prolonged lack of attention for wartime suffering. The minister was forced to abandon his plan.

The case of the 'Breda Three' illustrates in still another way how tied up medical developments were with the post-war social and political history of the war victims, for it was not just the heartbreaking stories of the victims that caused the minister's defeat. A second and no less important reason that the opposition against release won was that the minister found himself confronted by a *united* front of resistance fighters and Jewish survivors. Until then no such united front had existed.

In the seventies the landscape of the Dutch survivors' organizations radically changed. After years of bitter hostilities and indifference, communist and non-communist, Jewish and non-Jewish survivors found common goals from the seventies onward. The fierce anti-communism was softening. The Communist party was allowed broadcasting time and for the first time since 1948 its members were allowed to become aldermen. These new political relations expressed themselves in the world of the war organizations. The clash between the war victims and the minister of Justice around the 'Breda Three' was in fact the first occasion when *Expogé*, NAC and the communist resistance acted together. Their united performance resulted in new forms of cooperation that in later years strongly influenced government policy on issues concerning World War II, especially regarding war criminals and government provisions such as pensions and mental health care for war trauma victims.

The new psychological (instead of political) approach of the past brought about a new unity among the former resistance and among resistance organizations and Jewish organizations. Seeing each other as victims suffering from trauma transcended former disagreements. 'Aren't they victims as well?,' asked the president of the formerly anti-communist Buchenwald *amicale* rhetorically about the communist ex-*Buchenwalders* when the two hostile Buchenwald committees that had existed since the liberation, joined forces in 1977.

1973: The case of the WUV

All of these changes are even more visible in the developments concerning the law that would at last provide a war benefit for holocaust survivors. During the sixties the NAC had demanded that disabled or ill Jewish survivors should be entitled to a WBP-pension. This claim was denied as late as 1968 on formal grounds but in actual fact because the committee did not represent all Jewish survivors and, still suspected of being a front organization, was seen as acting only for goals of political agitation. However, when the interior Cold War ebbed away, the concept of 'post-concentration camp syndrome' was accepted and the holocaust more and more became the central focus of war remembrance, the NAC quickly developed into a respected committee. Now their claim for a pension was supported by the former resistance and all political parties. In 1973 a law was passed that – at last – entitled Jewish war victims in case of illness to a state benefit.

The *Wet Uitkeringen Vervolgden* (WUV) (The Benefit Act for Victims of Persecution), also grants financial support to people who had been interned in the camps in the Netherlands East Indies during the Japanese occupation and who had returned to the Netherlands during or after the Indonesian struggle for independence. The noun *vervolgden* ('persecuted') indicates that all those who were persecuted, i.e. not for their actions (such as resistance) but for their mere existence, were entitled to a benefit. The supplements and privileges that since 1968 had decked out the *Rijksgroepsregeling*, a dole-like arrangement executed by the municipalities, were not enough to quench the need for societal recognition for the endured suffering. The 'special obligation of solidarity' which is the legal foundation for the WUV, did meet this need. Even more than in the WBP the causal link between health complaints and war experiences in the WUV was 'assumed', so did not have to be proven.

The number of WUV applications exceeded all expectations. The prognosis had been 4,500. Ten years after the WUV took effect more than 75,000 applications had been made, a number that would later rise to well over 100,000. Only 30,000, less than one third, were actually entitled to WUV benefits. The fact that there were so many applications was not caused by the applications of Jewish survivors, but by the massive flood of Dutch Indonesians entitled to a pension, many of whom had been locked up in internment camps as children.

In the same year that the WUV was introduced, a special war trauma clinic opened its doors. The construction of this clinic was also accelerated by the parliamentary debate on the Three. During the debate the minister could not help but notice the change in atmosphere. He realized that this unwelcome development was brought about by the sudden massive realization of how many people still suffered from their wartime experiences. One of his attempts to hold on to his plan to release the Three was the strategic offer to provide the money to start a specialized clinic. This proposal was rejected as a cheap exchange. The victims wanted the clinic, and they wanted the minister's plan abandoned, and supported by public opinion achieved both. Within months after the debate, while the prisoners stayed in prison, construction of the specialized war trauma clinic started. The reversal of power relations in favor of the victims also became visible in the governmental promise that no war criminal would be released without the consent of the victims. This promise rested on the now generally accepted assumption that release would aggravate their traumatic pain.

And more was to come. From the seventies on psychological war damage became a national issue and an important target of governmental policy. The Ministry of Health came to include a special war welfare department, responsible for national war remembrance and the care for war victims. An Advisory College was installed; an amply staffed help-desk was set up to help clients secure benefits or inform them about possible treatment; mental health professionals were informed about war trauma; brochures and books were published; victim groups were initiated and received financial support; pilgrimages to the camps by victims and their families were funded, etcetera. This war welfare policy is still continuing (this research project is also one of its results).

Also from 1973 (almost ten years before the famous *Generations of the Holocaust* by Bergmann and Jucovy) the first Dutch publications appeared on 'the second generation': the children of Jewish and resistance victims who as adults were experiencing the psychic consequences of the fact that their upbringing had been colored by the war. Their request for recognition and attention was soon rewarded. For twenty years post-war children of Jewish parents and parents who had been active in the resistance, could claim an autonomous WUV or WBP pension if they suffered from a second generation war trauma. In 1994 however an end was put to this arrangement. From then on government financial support for the second generation war victims consisted in the possibility of receiving longer psychotherapeutic treatment than any other person could get at almost no cost.

This, to be sure, was also the sole economy measure taken in this field. For the rest the war victims department was the only governmental department that was spared budgetary cutbacks through the years.

1980-2005: Culture of trauma

The year 1972 witnessed the public discovery of the phenomenon that a victim can suffer from the psychic consequences of experiences as much as a quarter of a century after they occurred. Now widely known as Post-Traumatic Stress Disorder (PTSD), this newly recognized phenomenon was then simply named 'late psychic consequences'. Until that time terms such as 'post-concentration camp syndrome' or 'war trauma' were simply not part of Dutch social vocabulary. In the mid-fifties edition of the commonly used Dutch dictionary 'Van Dale', the term 'concentration camp syndrome' did not exist and the lemma 'trauma' consisted of just one line, referring only to a *physical* wound. A traumatologist in those days was a surgeon specialized in traffic accidents. Today 'trauma' first of all means *psychic* trauma. The lemma is extended and the dictionary also contains the verb 'to traumatize', the word 'stress' and new adjectives like 'traumatic' and 'post-traumatic'.

In the following years the post-concentration camp syndrome became common knowledge. It became clear that more people were suffering from the symptoms of this syndrome than anybody realized. Victims, professionals, the public and the media became convinced that long-term war damage was widespread and propagated this new knowledge. Soon also an explanatory theory emerged: the disorder was the outcome of the lack of state care in the immediate post-war years and of the 'conspiracy of silence' between 1945 and 1970. The myth was created that until the seventies nobody had ever known that the fear, the hardships, the threats and the loneliness of the long stay in a concentration camp or persecution and the loss of beloved ones by genocide, could take their toll even after a quarter of a century. This myth lives on to this day.[6]

During the eighties ever more categories of people defined themselves as victims of war and claimed eligibility for support or at least 'recognition'. For instance, ever increasing numbers of civilian war victims came forward, claiming permanent physical damage from bombardments, acts of war or confinement. The largest group amongst them were the workers for the *Arbeitseinsatz*, who in the late forties, often being considered semi-collaborators, had been excluded from the resistance organizations. Contrary to then they now succeeded in building their own strong lobby. They saw their previously started emancipation legally sealed with the arrival in 1984 of the Wet Uitkeringen Burger-Oorlogsslachtoffers 1940-1945 (WUBO) (Benefit Act for Civilian War Victims 1940-1945). In order to bring the new law to the attention of those who were entitled, the ministry even

6 Medical thinking here contains an inner contradiction, because the concept of PTSD tends to put all causal emphasis on the 'shocking experience' itself, neglecting factors like context and aftercare. On this subject we will return in part II.

put into action a special apparatus to approach possible clients nationwide, even if they had no need for a pension and did not consider themselves victims of war.

In addition to the children of the resistance and former 'hidden children', in these years the children of parents who had collaborated with the Germans also fixed attention on their specific psychological problems. A delicate matter, but after some hesitation, and supported by psychiatrists and several resistance women, they were admitted; their problems have been 'recognized' by the aid and service agencies.

All of these groups either had or started their own organizations and pressure groups. The seventies and eighties show an explosion of new associations of and for victims of war. Fellow-sufferers sought each other out, organized themselves in committees and got more attention than ever before.

Especially on the part of the former inhabitants of the Netherlands' Indies the increase was impressive. The forced migrants, who before often had no relation to the 'motherland' at all, insisted that the *bersiap*, the period of the colonial war, be classified as part of 'World War II'. In actual fact the Dutch and 'Indo' population during the bersiap years had to be protected against the violence of the Indonesian freedom fighters by their former Japanese persecutors.

When the American Psychiatric Association in 1980 recognized PTSD as a disorder, this decision was warmly welcomed by Dutch war professionals, who had long wrestled with the question how the new illness should be named. Before 'PTSD' came to the rescue different proposals had been rejected. 'War neurosis' was taboo because it was not a neurosis, that is to say: the cause of the disorder was not to be situated in childhood experiences and emotional conflicts. 'Post-concentration camp syndrome' failed, as did KZ syndrome, because war victims who had never seen a concentration camp suffered from comparable symptoms. One psychiatrist suggested 'existential-emotional stress syndrome', because the KZ symptoms also struck those who had lost their jobs or their partners.

It can be enlightening in the case of illnesses like these – with their vague symptoms – to analyze the *functions* a denominator fulfills. One of the uses of PTSD certainly was that it made it possible to recognize very different kinds of war experiences as possible causes of illness and that it standardized the diagnosis for purposes of insurance and research. Another was that by stating that an *external* stressor was the one and only cause of the symptoms, the new official disorder seemed to end the old debates on predisposition and secondary gain once and for all. It also accommodated some sensitivities of the resistance. For these men (for they were mostly men), grounded as they were in the years of heroic austerity, giving in to psychic complaints was a difficult task. These men needed a 'real' illness to visit a doctor, and they did not want to hear about possible marital or work-related problems and even less about youth traumas. In order to be acceptable to themselves, their illness had to be caused without any doubt by the war and it had to be medically justified. Surviving Jews had the same kind of reasons not to indulge in vague illness. 'In Auschwitz to be ill meant: dead, and after the war we needed all our energy to rebuild our lives.'

And then there were the perpetrators: the *Indië-veteranen*, the former soldiers who after the war in the West had ended went to Indonesia to keep 'Indië' Dutch. Between 1945 en 1949 they fought and lost a dishonorable battle, and from the eighties on they wanted to be recognized as victims instead of being silenced or shamed as war criminals or colonizers. PTSD does not differentiate between victims or perpetrators, or to put it sharply: PTSD allows perpetrators to become victims (as we saw happen with the Vietnam veterans).

Since the rise of PTSD Dutch soldiers have become the objects of psychological care. In 1990 the Defense Ministry published a policy paper on the 'care for veterans', in which the necessity of psychological care is recognized; PTSD in this paper is described as a considerable occupational risk. Since this memorandum was accepted by parliament all Dutch soldiers who are sent out on peace missions or, for example, to former Yugoslavia and Afghanistan receive psychological relief and aftercare. Also, to prevent psychological complaints the soldiers' efforts are given due attention and honor in the annual *Veteranendag* (Veterans' Day) that from 2005 has been organized on the birthday of the late prince Bernhard. On Veterans Day the Prince of Orange takes the salute of the soldiers marching by.

Notwithstanding some critical voices, PTSD became the unitary concept by which the former war neuroses became recognized. Among the early critics was Eddy de Wind, who considered classifying the late consequences of Auschwitz under the same title as the consequences of traffic accidents a new form of denial. Later studies confirmed De Wind's fear that the rapid recognition of all kind of victim groups under the common denominator PTSD would diminish the understanding of the extremity of Jewish suffering.[7]

After about 1990 war trauma and trauma in general in the Netherlands became basic social knowledge; psychotraumatology developed into an accepted medical discipline; together with the USA, UK and Israel, the Netherlands belong to the most active and large membership groups in the International Society for Traumatic Stress Studies (ISTSS). All these developments were stimulated by the fact that the Dutch government founded a sizeable apparatus to propagate the new medical insights.

7 De Haan, *Na de ondergang.*

Summary

In this chapter on the Netherlands we distinguished four periods in medical-psychological thinking on mental war damage and in the prevalence of such complaints. If we now try to relate these periods to the social and political history of the victims and to the cultural and mental changes in the Netherlands since 1945, we find some striking correlations.

1945-1948

National reconstruction. No Jewish organizations; strong, rather masculine resistance organizations taking the initiative to care for their disabled companions and for the widows and children of the dead. Stigma on psychic disorders; fear of maladjustment, spoiling and social disorder among mental health professionals and among the resistance elite; the early understanding of possible psychic consequences disappears; no visible or expressed psychic complaints.

1948-1968

Cold War, relative public silence on World War II. Totalitarianism seen as the former and the future danger for our free society. Fierce conflicts between the communist and the non-communist members of the former resistance; large gap between resistance and Jewish survivors. Low prevalence of psychic war disorders.

1968-1980

End of interior Cold War; increasing prosperity; growing interest in World War II; mental and cultural changes towards democratization, emancipation, expression of emotions. Diminishing of conflicts among the resistance and of gap between resistance and Jewish survivors. Discovery and public knowledge of post-concentration camp syndrome; exploding number of patients; new laws, new provisions.

1980-2005

Culture of trauma: DSM recognition of PTSD; lots of new organizations of all kinds of categories of (war) victims; ever more people identify themselves as being 'traumatized.' Transformation of trauma as a source of shame into a source of 'recognition'.

The early post-war concern about individual psychic damage disappeared during the Cold War, when the victim organizations split. Recognition of possible psychic trauma reappeared as the interior Cold War ended and victim organizations were again on speaking terms. In other words: seeing war survivors as victims of psychological damage reinforced the lessening of hostilities that came with the decline of the Cold War.

Both developments together brought about a new unity among victims, and this unity – though never free of tensions and always fragile – in turn strengthened the tendency to define survivors primarily as victims of trauma. The results of our research show that the former hostilities softened not only because of the decline of the Cold War but also as a result of the rapid development of a trauma culture in the Netherlands. As much as politics had divided ex-prisoners, psychology united them and offered opportunities and common goals in demanding provisions for their welfare.

The fragile unity of the survivors that was shattered soon after the war was revived thanks to the psychological outlook on the past. World War II was transformed from a political issue concerning totalitarianism (in which former communist prisoners were seen as future enemies), into a psychological issue in which all political prisoners, resistance fighters and Jewish survivors (and other, new, victim groups), and also the former inhabitants of Indonesia, were the possible or even probable victims of traumatic stress. This brought material as well as immaterial profits: victims could feel progressive and liberal in overcoming their distance towards the former communist resistance and the surviving Jews, and they were collectively rewarded with ample provisions.

The concept of PTSD stimulates this mutual 'recognition': aren't we all suffering from the same disorder? This reinforced the Dutch model of war welfare policy that stimulates victim unity and neglects or even denies real differences. The concept of PTSD swept away meaningful differences in war experience, background, world view and degree of suffering. It also swept away the ambition to search for causal relations between patient, experience and symptom. Whereas in the first years that the 'late consequences' were noticed conscientious attempts were made to link the symptom a person suffered from (being afraid to board a train) to his experiences (escaped from a train), as more groups were recognized as war trauma sufferers, the connection between general malaise and war experiences was increasingly taken for granted.

Distinctions between victim groups were lost in a compelling atmosphere of mutual recognition. Uniting all survivors under the label 'victims of war trauma' and tabooing differences as an unwanted 'hierarchy of suffering' blends historically different experiences. At the same time, however, this propagated sameness puts into motion a victim rivalry, that became visible for instance in publications by Dutch Indonesians who claimed that the Japanese internment camps had 'really' been termination camps like Auschwitz. The late discovery of war trauma in the Netherlands was an ambivalent process of simultaneous recognition and denial.

This transformation was stimulated by the cultural revolution of the sixties. Contrary to usual assumptions and pretensions, we do not consider the change in psychiatric paradigm from about 1970 on (the move away from pre-morbid personality, secondary gain and causality that needs to be proven), the pure result of medical 'progress'. The social, political, cultural and mental revolution of the sixties steered medical opinion about the possible consequences of war.

The medical turnabout also expressed itself in the conviction that the late consequences were due to decades of lack of 'recognition.' Whereas around 1950 doctors, the resistance elite and the public at large assumed that *attention* would result in psychic weakness, after about 1972 a *lack* of attention was assumed to be the cause of psychic weakness, which was no longer labeled 'weakness' but was transformed into 'syndrome' and later into 'disorder'.

This theory of trauma caught on – the victims, the public, the medical and psychological professions, and last but not least politicians, all took to it. Mental weaknesses that had once been private, shameful and disrespected, now became public and even respectable – on one condition, the suffering should be caused by a respectable traumatic experience like 'the war.' The key to recovery changed from 'adaptation' (in the austere morality of reconstruction) to 'recognition' in the more easygoing atmosphere after the seventies. Speaking about war-related mental problems in the late forties and fifties always centered around the necessary 'adaptation' of the survivors to the new normality. In the eighties and thereafter the debate was always about 'recognition'. Recognition surely was the responsibility of the government, the therapist etcetera, whereas the responsibility for adaptation had been that of the victims. The world was turned upside down.

8 A Psychiatric Study of World War II Survivors

The case of Poland

» *Jacek Bomba and Maria Orwid*

History

Poland entered World War II in September 1939 on two fronts. On 1 September Nazi Germany invaded the country from the West, and on 17 September the Soviet Union invaded from the East. The result was the partitioning of the Polish state. The western part of the country, which had been seized by Germany, was divided up: the Nazis annexed some areas to the Third Reich and appointed a variety of occupying authorities to govern others. None of the occupied regions was ruled by Polish authorities collaborating with the Nazis. The mass persecution of civilians, ranging from deportations to the systematic extermination of entire sections of the population, lasted till 1944/1945. The Nazis started by ridding themselves of intellectual groups (notably university lecturers and the clergy), exterminating groups seen as constituting a burden on society (such as mental patients), followed by the wholesale extermination of the Jewish and Romani population. Help offered to those designated for extermination was severely punished, often leading to the death of the helpers and their families, often of whole villages.

The eastern part of the country was incorporated into the republics of the Soviet Union. Officers and civil servants captured by the Red Army were later murdered, a war crime known as Katyń, from the name of the village in which the Germans discovered mass graves in 1943. (The Katyń massacre was acknowledged half a century after the event by Soviet president Boris Yeltsin, however not as a war-crime.) Polish nationals who escaped from the Nazi onslaught and found themselves in eastern Poland, having no permanent address there, were deported to the Asian part of the Soviet Union, often to the prisons and gulags generally referred to as 'Siberia'. Some later joined the Polish Army, which left the Soviet Union to fight on the Western front. Poles from these territories later joined the Polish military units that were fighting alongside the Red Army on the Eastern front.

Various armed forces formed in Nazi-occupied Polish territory from October 1939 onwards waged a guerrilla war with the Nazis. The majority were integrated into *Armia Krajowa* (AK), which was accountable to the government-in-exile in London. The most important of the military actions against the Nazis were the Warsaw Ghetto Uprising in April 1943 (ZOB – Jewish Combat Organization), the Vilnius Uprising of July 1944, and the Warsaw Uprising of August 1944 (AK). The Ghetto Uprising was initiated when ŻOB learned of Nazi plans to annihilate the Jews who had been herded together in Warsaw Ghetto; they were to be transported to Treblinka extermination camp. Only a few fighters survived the Nazis' brutal crushing of the insurrection.[1] The action in Vilnius liberated the city from the Nazis, as the Red Army was approaching. But many fighters were arrested and sent to prisons and gulags by the Soviets.[2] The Warsaw Uprising ended with the total demolition of the city, in spite of some help from Western allies, with the Red Army staying on the far bank of the river Vistula.[3]

There were other acts of resistance against the Nazis, such as illegal forms of education, including university courses, illegal cultural events, information in the form of newsletters, humanitarian aid and so on. The underground organization (operating under the auspices of the Polish government in exile) Council to Aid Jews (Żegota) was involved in issuing false Aryan documents and in providing other means of support, especially by finding hiding-places.

Following the end of World War II in May 1945, part of the pre-war territory of Poland was incorporated into the Soviet Union and part of the pre-war territory of Germany was incorporated into the new Polish state. The new Poland was free of the Nazis, but the Soviet army that had liberated Polish soil from the Nazis would remain in the country until early 1990.

Between 1944 and 1947, underground groups engaged the pro-Soviet administration in guerrilla warfare, and they were consequently declared enemies by the Soviets and the Polish government established under Soviet protection.

Between the Nazi invasion of the Soviet Union in 1941 and the Red Army's push to the west in 1944, groups of Ukrainian nationalists who had inhabited the southeast territories of Poland before 1939 sided with the Third Reich's revolt against the previous dominant powers in the region, first Polish and then Soviet. Both official military units and more informal groups were involved in the mass murder of Jews and Roman Catholics living in this area. After 1944 the Ukrainian Insurgent Army (UPA) in southeast Poland continued to conduct a guerrilla war with the Polish Army. This war ended in the mass relocation of Ukrainians/ Rusyns ('Ruthenians') to the northwest region of Poland.

---

1 Tanay, *Passport to life.*

2 Skarga, *Innego końca świata.*

3 Dynowska, *All for freedom*; Steiner, *Varsovie 44*; Śreniawa-Szypiowski, *Powstanie Warszawskie.*

Large numbers of people who had held the Polish nationality before the war were repatriated from territories annexed to the Soviet Union in 1945-1947 and resettled in the west of the country, in areas annexed to the Polish state in 1945. Many Jews who had survived the Holocaust and the war in Soviet territory left Poland between 1945 and 1947, hoping to reach Palestine. It should be noted that when Holocaust survivors returned to their pre-war dwellings they were given a cold reception and sometimes faced open anti-Semitism. Pogroms took place in several towns. The number of people who were killed trying to recover property that had been entrusted to neighbors is difficult to determine.

Between 1949 and 1956 the pro-Soviet authorities introduced a dictatorial (often referred to as Stalinist) regime, significantly curtailing liberties and stepping up the persecution of political opponents. In 1956, following Stalin's death in 1953, workers staged riots against the regime, and militiamen killed about a hundred people in June that year. A few months later the system was liberalized somewhat, with changes in the senior ranks of the ruling party. These changes are known as the 'Polish October' of 1956. At the same time, certain changes took place in relations with the Soviet Union. One was a fresh wave of repatriation, this time largely of Polish citizens who had been deported to the Asian part of Russia and to other Asian Soviet republics. But 1956 was also a time of rebellion against the Soviet Union in Hungary; there was strong support for the uprising among Poles, who manifested their solidarity with the Hungarian rebels. It was also a time of significant change in public debate, freedom of expression in the arts and freedom of opinion. The ruling Workers' Party adopted a more liberal attitude to the Catholic Church. Yet each of these freedoms was slowly curtailed again over the following decade, although the restrictions never equaled those of the Stalinist period.

The social and political unrest of 1968 – this time initiated by university students – led to an internal power struggle within the ruling party. This time, politicians used anti-Semitism to resolve both social unrest and conflicts among party activists. The Communist Party's policy was not merely anti-Semitic, it was directed against the intelligentsia as well. Still, the next exodus of Polish Jews, probably the largest one, ensued at this point.

Workers' riots in 1976 and the repressive measures taken against them led to organized opposition among the intelligentsia, who offered help to the oppressed workers and their families. The subsequent workers' strikes in 1980, which were supported by the intelligentsia, were crushed by military force, but by the end of the decade the protests had resulted in free trade unions (Solidarity), and democratic elections were held in 1989. This was a beginning of an ongoing process of transformation.

For a half of a century (1939-1989) Poland lived through a series of turbulent events, including the loss of its independence and dramatic changes to its sociopolitical system. The latter introduced new divisions and generated new definitions of patriotism and the rationale underlying the state, as well as leading to a new understanding of independence itself. The definitions of terms such as 'war victims' and 'combatants' also changed. And with these altered definitions came significant changes to formal decisions about financial support and social privileges.

Historical research has shown that the traditional concept of a 'war victim' in no way covers all those who suffered during World War II. Even the period demarcated as 'wartime' is open to question. The beginning of the war is easy to pinpoint, but its end is difficult to determine. The Nazis' policy of mass extermination, the mass repression practized by the Soviets, and bloody conflicts between Poles and Ukranians/Rusyns and between Poles and Germans, accompanied by the cruelty of the occupying forces all caused enormous suffering.

One of the most significant consequences of Poland's domination by the Soviet Union was that it focused attention on a single perpetrator of aggression, namely Nazi Germany. The Soviet Union was to be perceived as a mighty and friendly supporter, the most important power that overcame the Poles' biggest enemy – the Nazis. This meant that large groups of war victims were overlooked for decades. Only certain groups of victims were officially recognized, paralleling the selective recognition of heroism and the meritorious conduct of soldiers and participants in the resistance movement. This was reflected in changing legal regulations on war victims and the state's support for them.

Legal aspects

Polish legislation never used the term 'war victim' until the most recent acts of parliament. Even so, preambles to acts of parliament, and details or interpretations of law, provide clear definitions of the groups of people who were regarded as the 'victims' of war. The trauma of World War II, and the suffering it caused, influenced almost the whole of Polish society, including – about this there can be no doubt – later generations. It is obvious that it is impossible to compensate an entire nation for the suffering it endured. So the legislative effort seeks to identify those who experienced extreme torment and those who acted with outstanding merit.[4]

The first piece of legislation enacted by the parliament-like KRN (State National Council, the first legislative assembly created in 1944, which supported the pro-Soviet administration), on 23 July 1945, determined that financial support would be provided for the surviving relatives of people who had lost their lives as resistance and guerrilla fighters, 'fighting for the liberation of Poland from Hitler's aggression'. So in post-war Poland, the first definition of war victims was confined

4 Kochański, 'Polska 1944-1991'.

to families whose loved ones had been killed as soldiers or partisans fighting the Nazis.

Four years later, however, on 26 October 1949, a new law confined the definition to the relatives of those whose lives had been lost in the 'democratic' fight for 'the safety of the people's authorities'. 'The people's authorities' refers here to authorities established under the protection of the Soviet Union.

New legislation introduced in 1956 declared that financial benefits were conditional on the existence of a health disorder attributable to time spent in service. Instead of 'military disability', this act referred to 'war disability', a wider definition that embraced health problems arising from underground wartime operations. This meant that large groups of war victims who had been stripped of their status as 'combatants' were now rehabilitated as a result of political changes.

The law on pensions for 'war and military invalids' was reviewed by parliament on 1968. The new act emphasized that health disorders arising from combat and resulting in an incapacity to work were a precondition for eligibility for financial benefits. In 1974, parliament decided that the decision as to whether a health disorder was related to the war must be taken by a military medical committee, while the degree of incapacity to work should be assessed by a different medical committee appointed by the state's social security agency.

In 1982, parliament adopted an act on 'the specific rights of combatants', which defined as combatants, *inter alia*, 'persons who were imprisoned in Hitler's concentration camps and prisons on political, ethnic or racial grounds'. But it still excluded those regarded as enemies of the Soviet Union and of communism.

The parliament elected in the first democratic elections held in 1989 changed this law in 1991, passing a new act on 'combatants and some victims of the war and the post-war period' that accorded combatant status to 'all Polish citizens who [had] fought for their country's sovereignty and independence, risking their lives and health on battlefields – in the Polish Army, allied armies, underground independence organizations, and in civil activity involving a risk of reprisals'. The act stated that 'The governments of the Third German Reich, the Soviet Union and the apparatus of communist repression are responsible for the suffering of many Polish citizens on the grounds of nationality, politics or religion. They caused the deaths of millions and the disability of many'. People serving in the Soviet Union's NKVD and other groups involved in action 'against the Polish nation' were excluded from the definition of combatants. The act included a list of 'activities equal to those of combatants': the active participation in bodies encouraging national insurgence; the administration of the underground state during the 1939-1945 war and of underground organizations between 1945 and 1956; fighting for the sovereignty and independence of the Polish State in military units until 31 December 1945; the organization of professional illegal teaching between 1939 and 1945; fighting to retain the Polish character of territories taken during partitioning between 1914 and 1945; participation in the Posnan uprising of 1956 or the Coast rebellion in 1970. But the list also included: captivity and imprisonment in Soviet camps, Hitler's prisons, concentration camps, extermination centers and other places of isolation. In 1999 another item was added to the list: namely, furnishing Jews and other people with shelter between 1939-1945, and thus risking the death penalty. The 1991 law also widened the definition of 'repression in the war and post-war period' to include the placement, on political, national, religious or racial grounds, in Hitler's prisons, concentration camps and extermination centers, other places of isolation (ghettoes), places of isolation and extermination for children, as well as Soviet prisons and camps, places of Soviet deportation, and Polish prisons between 1944 and 1956. This law significantly extended the timeframe, embracing World War I and almost the entire period of the Soviet domination of Poland.

In 2002 the Polish Parliament, once more reviewing the law on those incapacitated by war and military action, differentiated between those 'incapacitated by war and military action' and 'victims of the war and the post-war period'. This significantly increased the number of persons granted combatant status; at the same time, however, financial support was allocated only to those incapacitated as a result of repression.

The Allies' decision concerning Poland and its classification as belonging to the Soviet Union's area of influence was to a large extent responsible for the arbitrary recognition of specific groups of war victims as such. Even soldiers who served either in official or underground armies were recognized as combatants or excluded from this group arbitrarily. The victims of the war with the Soviet Union had to wait for such recognition for decades, as did those who suffered persecution on racial and ethnic grounds.

For the entire period of the dictatorship of the Soviet-dependent communist party in Poland, changes in the legal regulations covering war victims were perceived as a deliberate injustice. However, as is customary under a dictatorial regime, there was no open public debate. 'War heroes' and 'war victims' had been proclaimed by the ruling communist party, with the use of its propaganda apparatus and in the manner of propaganda. It was even impossible to mourn, officially, the loss of those who had been killed by parties other than 'the enemy'. It is entirely possible that the absence of public debate may have contributed to the growing role of the medical approach to the consequences of war. Medicine may be harder to exploit for political reasons than other branches of science and other domains of social life. At least, such is Polish experience.[5] The universal trend towards

5 Szymusik et al., 'Psychiatry in Eastern Europe'.

the medicalization of social problems in the second half of the twentieth century should also be taken into account here, however.

Polish medical studies on war victims

Medicine was brought into the problem of war-caused victimization at a relatively late stage in history. Combat-related health disorders were first described on a large scale during and after World War I. The theory of traumatic stress disorder is rooted in observations on the deterioration of health connected with war. World War II is seen as the beginning of the repression of large groups of civilians and of the industrialization of extermination. The amount of suffering that was experienced during World War II seems enormous, and, even several decades on, is still impossible to comprehend.

It is our objective here to trace the contribution of medicine, especially psychiatry, to the study and conceptualization of the victimization caused by World War II. A focus on medical studies performed in Poland will exemplify the development of an approach from a traditional one towards the integration of the social, psychological and biological aspects of human life.

The first results of medical studies on victims of World War II appeared in Polish medical journals as early as in 1945 and related in part to the general health of concentration camp survivors, but also, more specifically, to the medical consequences of prolonged starvation, both in concentration camps and in ghettoes.[6] In 1946 the first report was published on the criminal medical experiments that had been conducted in Ravensbrück concentration camp.[7] But as early as 1947, the results of studies on the impact of war on the mental life of children, youngsters and adults were published in journals of psychology.[8] By the end of 1940, an article on the health of prisoners-of-war had been published in a journal of military medicine.[9] This development of medical and psychological research was suspended during the years that followed, of the Stalinist regime.

In 1961, Józef Bogusz, professor of surgery at Kraków medical school, edited the first issue of the medical monthly *Przegląd Lekarski* ('Medical Review') subtitled *Oświęcim* (Auschwitz), dealing entirely with problems arising from Nazi concentration camps. Besides the problems studied immediately after the war, such as malnutrition, the first issue of *Przegląd Lekarski – Oświęcim* presented the results

6 Sluzar, 'Wyniki badań klinicznych'; Tomaszewski, 'Następstwa przewlekłego głodzenia'; Fejkiel, *Choroba głodowa*; Apfelbaum, *Choroba głodowa*.

7 Mączka, 'Operacje doświadczalne'.

8 Baley, 'Wpływ wojny na psychikę', 'Psychiczne wpływ'; Putkiewicz, 'Próba badania wpływu wojny na'.

9 Stein, 'Psychonerwice jeńców'.

of medical studies initiated only a few years earlier.[10] The former represents the contribution of physicians – who were themselves Auschwitz survivors. The latter is an example of studies suggested by survivors.

It is difficult to answer the fundamental question: why then? Why had Bogusz, himself a Holocaust survivor, started to edit *Przegląd Lekarski – Oświęcim* in 1961? Why had it taken until 1961 for psychiatrists to turn their attention to the problems of concentration camp survivors? Did it have something to do with the political changes that took place in Poland in the mid-1950's? Were the closer exchanges with the West of any importance? There is another factor that should be taken into account. Immediately after the war, there was a shortage of many kinds of trained specialists. Polish intellectuals had been one of the target groups that Nazis and Soviets alike had sought to destroy. The next generation of students had to reach maturity, and only then could they touch the pain of loss.

The first few issues of *Przegląd Lekarski – Oświęcim* were published in Polish and in conference languages: English, French, Russian and Spanish. But resources were soon cut off and for the next years the journal appeared only in Polish. Still, excerpts were translated into Japanese (1982), German (1994) and English (2005)[11]. *Przegląd Lekarski – Oświęcim* published the results of medical studies on concentration camp survivors, medico-historical studies on medicine in Nazi camps, memoirs of former prisoners, biographical essays, psychological studies on concentration camps, philosophical essays on totalitarianism, and reviews of the literature. Later issues tackled broader problems of war and medicine, as well as specific problems relating to concentration camps. The majority of published studies were written by Polish authors, but the journal also included articles submitted by authors from Austria, Czechoslovakia, France, Great Britain, the Federal Republic of Germany, Israel, the Netherlands, Romania, Sweden, the United States and Yugoslavia. *Przegląd Lekarski – Oświęcim* came to an end in 1991, after the death of Professor Bogusz and the permanent withdrawal of financial support.

The Kraków Auschwitz study was conducted under the supervision of Antoni Kępiński, who was inspired by his friend and brother-in-law, the physician Stanisław Kłodziński, an active member of the Auschwitz Society, an organization of Auschwitz concentration camp survivors. The research project was launched in 1959. Its specific task was to describe the experience of concentration camp imprisonment and the consequences of this experience.[12] The team, consisting of Roman Leśniak, Jan Mitarski, Maria Orwid, Adam Szymusik and Aleksander Teutsch,

10 Kowalczykowa, 'Starvation disease'; Leśniak et al., 'Some psychiatric problems'.
11 Ryn, *Auschwitz survivors.*
12 Leśniak et al., 'Zagadnienia psychiatryczne', 'Some psychiatric problems'; Kępiński, 'Some psychosociologic problems'.

interviewed and examined a hundred former Auschwitz prisoners, members of the Society, who volunteered to take part in the study. They adopted a methodological approach that was qualitative rather than quantitative in nature. The data collected in the Kraków project were initially analyzed using several parameters. Teutsch, who studied adaptation to the extreme conditions in the camp, found that the reason for imprisonment was crucial to the development of a survival strategy.[13] Those who had been imprisoned for political reasons had been more highly motivated to fight for their lives, since their ideology reinforced their strategies. Adjustment to concentration camp conditions required a specific sort of emotional anesthesia and a particular kind of relationship with other prisoners. Survivors frequently emphasized the crucial importance to them of these two factors. Their age at imprisonment appeared to be less important.

Orwid studied the post-war problems experienced by former prisoners of Auschwitz concentration camp.[14] She stressed that they formed the main reference group of their co-prisoners, more important than that of relatives or other friends. Her observations showed that the post-war adjustment of former prisoners seemed to be more difficult for them than their adjustment to the camp.

Szymusik identified the main symptoms of a deterioration in mental health after imprisonment in Auschwitz concentration camp.[15] He found that the former prisoners suffered from progressive asthenia, neurasthenic neurosis, encephalopathy, premature involution, depressive-apathetic states, anxiety neurosis and epilepsy. The term 'KZ Syndrome' was later proposed to cover the entire spectrum of post-camp health consequences.[16]

Leśniak, studying personality changes arising from the concentration camp experience, described general characteristics in this connection as: 1. depression; 2. suspiciousness; 3. explosiveness; 4. depression-suspiciousness.[17]

The Kraków team was aware that the language and terminology developed within the fields of psychopathology and clinical psychiatry were inadequate to describe either the concentration camp experience or the post-war problems of former prisoners. To interpret their observations, Kępiński's team employed the concept of 'terminal experience'. The Kraków Auschwitz Study concluded that to survive the extreme stress of imprisonment in a concentration camp required specific adaptation mechanisms, and that these resulted in a chronic disorder of adaptation mechanisms to life after liberation accompanied by a severe deterioration in health. It was postulated that the specific syndrome consisting of symp-

13 Teutsch, 'An analysis of adaptation', 'Psychological reactions'.
14 Orwid, 'Remarks on adaptation', 'Socio-psychiatric after-effects'.
15 Szymusik, 'Psychological disorders', 'Progressive asthenia'.
16 Kępiński, 'The so-called "KZ-syndrome"'.
17 Leśniak, 'Personality changes', 'Post-camp personality alterations'.

toms of depression and anxiety should be included in the classification of health disorders as 'KZ Syndrome'.

The Auschwitz essays of Antoni Kępiński

In initiating the Kraków Auschwitz Study, Antoni Kępiński had set out to answer a personal question that was of immense importance to him: 'How could the horror of extermination have happened?' Rejecting the assumptions of classical and analytical psychology, that is, of a basic drive towards aggression, and of traditional psychopathology, such as psychopathy, sociopathy or moral insanity, he looked instead for mechanisms underlying the unprecedented evil of genocide. The results of his quest were published in a series of essays in *Przegląd Lekarski – Oświęcim* between 1962 and 1972 (see Bibliography).

Analyzing the memoirs of the first Auschwitz commandant, Rudolf Höss, he reached the conclusion that the atrocities of Auschwitz were performed by 'Everyman'.[18] Unimaginable evil can be perpetrated by anybody. He presented a hypothesis that total submission to an ideology makes someone into a robot that is dedicated to achieving the goals set within that ideology. Such submission requires a person to relinquish his inner freedom, the precondition for individual moral self-examination. The idea was developed and discussed in his next paper, along with a concept of the importance of a sense of responsibility.[19]

In his analysis of data relating to Auschwitz he developed the concept of a 'mechanical' society as a metaphor for a totalitarian system. Although this was written in the context of Auschwitz, it refers to any socio-political system that sets aside human values. He tried to show that the origins of 'good' and 'evil' are essentially the same. Human beings are eager to accept explanations that offer a less painful picture of the surrounding world. But:

> 'The ability to transform the surrounding world, which one may regard as a specifically human quality, embraces the widest possible span of contradictions in terms of human nature. This ability leads to heroism, dedication, the arts, the sciences, but also to cruelty, abuse and murder. It is to change the shape of the world that wars are waged, that people are victimized in camps and prisons. Whatever does not fit in the structure that is to be enforced is seen as alien and hostile, and as such must be destroyed.'

18 Kępiński and Orwid, 'From psychopathology of Übermenschen'.

19 Kępiński, 'Anus Mundi'.

> 'Similarly, on an incomparably higher level, one can encounter in human life a situation in which one is dominated by an idea, one that seems strange at the beginning, but in time becomes one's own. One no longer sees anything besides [this idea], one becomes ready to sacrifice life – one's own and those of other people (usually the lives of others are easier to sacrifice). (...) One loses one's identity; thoughts, feelings, actions are no longer expressions of one's own personality, but reflections of the structure accepted from outside. (...) People possessed by the same idea become as identical as twins; there is a reduction in social differentiation, but an increase in effectiveness (understood as seeking to fulfill the same tasks, setting aside everything else). Consequently, human beings who are not imprinted with the same idea become obstructions to its realisation, they become the enemy, impediments, and must be eliminated.'[20]

Of particular interest here is the process in which people lose their individual characteristics, their identity, and identify instead with something external rather than basing responses on their individual experience and an inner continuous sameness.

> 'People who were [defined as] obstructions, objects designated for extermination, eliminated from the path to a new world, accepted their fate in different ways. Some had no time to recover from the shock of suddenly finding themselves in the hell of concentration camp before their lives came to end. Others welcomed death with the fatalistic conviction of the inevitable. Still others wanted to survive at any price. And since convenient arrangements were accessible in an extermination camp, as a rule, for only for those who killed, and those who were the masters, some tended to take on the behaviour of their oppressors. (...) Nevertheless, (...) survival required, to some extent, overcoming the tyrannical law to stay alive at all costs. Those who stayed totally within this law lost their humanity, and with it, often any chance of survival. Among the human characteristics important for survival were an inner ability to oppose the external reality, the creation of an alternative world, dreams about future, memories of the past, or more realistically through friendship, helping others, organizing an 'alternative life' as opposed to the camp life.'[21]

Seeking to explain survival in concentration camp, Kępiński approached the difficult problem of the relationship between the desire to live and ethics, between guilt and responsibility. He insisted that survival requires the resistance to the overwhelming demands of biological needs and finding support in an 'alterna-

20 Kępiński, 'Anus Mundi'.
21 Kępiński, 'Genocide crimes'.

tive world'. In his opinion, 'the standards of normal life could not be followed' in conditions such as one may imagine existed in concentration camps. Kępiński often compares the situation of a concentration camp prisoner to that of a person suffering from schizophrenia. The emotional anesthesia crucial to the effective adjustment to camp's inhuman conditions reminds him of an autistic component in this disorder. This helps him to develop his concept of 'so-called KZ Syndrome', in which – he insists – symptoms may vary significantly, although the underlying dynamics is the same. Moreover, he uses the findings of the Auschwitz Study to develop his own humanistic, anthropological concept of psychiatry. In his view, the experience of mental illness, especially of schizophrenia, may be compared to the terminal situation that exists in a concentration camp.

The Endlösung

It is well known that Poland, or rather the 'General Government', the central area of the country under Nazi occupation, was the place where ghettoes were located and where the extermination of most European Jews took place. Hundreds of thousands of people sent there from various parts of Europe, or expelled from their homes, were crammed into small areas in Polish cities such as Łódź and Warsaw. Many were imprisoned in concentration camps and millions were transported to extermination camps, the largest of which was Auschwitz. A small proportion of Polish Jews survived the Shoah. Those who survived had lost their families and friends and many of them emigrated. Their situation in Poland was difficult. The Nazis had made it a crime punishable by death to help Jews in their struggle to survive in Poland. But even in those tough times, many did survive thanks to the help of Poles. On the other hand, in many places Poles provided no help, silently accepting the extermination of the Jews or actively participating in it. Even after the war, Jews were killed in organized pogroms in several places.

For decades, there was a failure to understand the horror of the Holocaust. Survivors were treated not only with indifference but often with suspicion. Many saw it as incomprehensible that someone who had been sent off to be killed had evaded the fate of her/his brothers, and often assumed that the person concerned must have collaborated with the occupying forces.

In addition, internationalism was the ideology officially declared by the Communist party that ruled Poland after 1944/45. In this situation, many Jewish survivors who stayed in post-war Poland continued to live in disguise. They used the names they had adopted during the war and continued to pretend they were non-Jews. For decades, no research was done on the problems they faced. The problems arising from the Holocaust and faced by survivors can be traced in the arts.

It appears that for many years after the war, the Polish community lived in a kind of divided consciousness. A significant proportion had witnessed the Holocaust and had lost friends and neighbors. Their loss was channeled into the official anti-German attitude promoted by official propaganda.

Psychiatric studies of Holocaust survivors living in Poland and their children

No studies of the specific consequences of the Holocaust trauma – in either a medical or a socio-psychological sense – were conducted in Poland until 1989. Yet one publication back in 1946 contained observations on starvation that had been recorded in the Warsaw ghetto in 1942.[22] The unique characteristics of the Nazi persecution of the Jews, including the 'final solution' strategy and technology, as a part of the common memory of war, were approached by artists rather than scientists. Studying the consequences of the war trauma, for instance in concentration camp survivors – mainly political prisoners – psychiatrists had adopted an existential approach to human life in an attempt to understand the Auschwitz phenomenon. Maria Orwid writes:

> 'We believed at the time that it was honest to approach the impact of Nazi ideology on human beings from an existential, universal human position. There was also a specific need among those who had survived the Holocaust, as well as among those who were interested in it, to remain silent. One may surmise that the pain was overwhelming. There were some writers in Poland, notably Adolf Rudnicki, who did broach the problem. Even so, people did not talk about it, even privately, and psychiatrists did not comprehend its significance. Meanwhile, the communist regime, while officially espousing internationalism, used anti-Semitism in forms of socio-political manipulation. Anti-Semitism was used as a tool in conflicts with opponents, independently of their origins, at various points in post-war Poland, a trend that peaked in March 1968. These factors made it difficult to talk about the past, even for survivors. At the same time this did not encourage other people to become involved in discussing the Jewish problem. Quite the opposite, it prompted the emigration of many survivors and instilled fear in those who decided not to leave the country. To sum up, what we were dealing with at that time was "the Polish memory". The "Jewish pain" was still too great.'[23]

Inspired by Kisker's Symposium on the Holocaust in Hannover, 1989, Maria Orwid launched a research program aimed at gaining an understanding of the problems of Polish Jews stemming from their experience of the Holocaust. Her team of co-workers consisted of Ewa Domagalska-Kurdziel, Kazimierz Pietruszew-

22 Apfelbaum, *Choroba głodowa*.
23 Orwid et al., 'Psychosoziale Folgen des Holocausts'.

ski, Ewa Czaplak, Ryszard Izdebski and Martia Kamińska. Their study was a part of the Judaica Program of the Research Centre for Jewish History and Culture at the Jagiellonian University, founded and led at that time by Professor Józef Gierowski. Orwid and her team were well aware of the difficulties posed by this subject, and knew that any clinical, scientific approach to it could prove inadequate. They also felt that nothing new could be discovered by studying a problem that had already been explored in depth by artists and philosophers. Earlier studies of Auschwitz survivors had convinced them that psychological and psychiatric theories and the language they use cannot describe or explain the experience of those have survived traumatic events, or indeed the syndromes that are manifested in these survivors. Sociologists have reached a similar conclusion.[24] Nevertheless, over thirty years of studying 'KZ syndrome' problems and her own personal experience during the Holocaust prompted Maria Orwid to set up a research program aimed at producing a better understanding of the problems of Polish Jews stemming from their experience of the Holocaust. An additional motivation was her conviction that personal contact with people who had survived an extreme situation (in this case resulting from Nazi ideology) was a necessary part of training in psychiatry and clinical psychology.

As Poland had no register of Holocaust survivors, the only way of reaching out to people appeared to be through the 'grapevine'. The criterion for classification as a survivor was that the person had been living within the territory of Poland during the Holocaust; there was also a 'second generation' category, the criterion for which was that at least one of the person's parents was a survivor.

In the early stages of the study, the people invited to participate more often refused than consented to be interviewed. Some denied their Jewish origins, some feared repercussions, and others flatly refused to revisit a painful chapter that they wished to consider closed. This changed in 1991, with the founding of the Association of Children of the Holocaust in Poland, a group that provided a framework of reference for many of these Holocaust survivors.

The interviews followed a clearly-defined structure based on the Kraków Auschwitz Study questionnaire, which was developed to cover specific problems of the Holocaust and – for the second generation – problems of identity. In the latter case, a genogram technique was employed to explore the intergenerational transmission of values and trauma, as well as the person's life history.

The work involved in this program generated severe emotional problems for the team members. The burden of the Holocaust appeared to be almost impossible to bear, even by professionals experienced in psychotherapy. Some of them refrained from doing any interviews for varying periods of time, using explana-

24 Bauman, *Nowoczesność i zagłada.*

tions or rationalizations such as a lack of free time or situational exhaustion. Counter-transference emotions underlying such decisions had been described earlier.[25]

Survivors had been selected for interview on the basis of the following criteria: 1) they belonged to a well-assimilated Jewish minority in pre-war Poland, being fluent in Polish and familiar with local customs, which enabled them to survive; 2) they did not leave for the West or for Israel amid successive waves of Jewish emigration from Poland. The study set out to identify differences, if any, between Holocaust survivors and the Polish survivors of concentration camps interned there for political reasons; as well as differences between Jewish survivors living in Poland and in the West. The aim was to analyze the feelings of national identity of the second-generation group, especially the offspring of mixed marriages, and to clarify the impact of the family on the development of identity.

The findings revealed that in general, Holocaust survivors living in Poland present symptoms of PTSD similar to those exhibited by other concentration camp survivors and Holocaust survivors who have been studied.[26] Their suspiciousness and their protracted silence concerning their Holocaust experience do not differentiate them from other survivors. Like others, they were eager to marry, create a home and to have children, to build up a family environment and a feeling of safety. They were also over-anxious in their parental attitudes. However, their average educational level was higher in comparison to the Holocaust survivors studied in other countries. Yet another difference identified was that their silence did not relate only to their Holocaust experience, but extended to their Jewish origins. In the main, they tended to marry non-Jewish spouses in an attempt to blend into the social environment and forget the past. Their family structure was characterized by a close, possessive attitude on the part of Jewish fathers towards their children (especially daughters). Nevertheless it was typical of the whole group that their main goal – complete assimilation into Polish society and the negation of their hereditary tradition – remained unrealized. Fears connected with origins, feelings of alienation and endangerment, appeared at various moments in their lives.

The psychiatric perspective allows for the interpretation of this specific failure as a healing process. Opening up these two key topics within the family, that is, the Holocaust and the question of origins, can facilitate the family's internal communication, while at the same time the sense of alienation can be diminished through new reference groups such as the Association of Children of the Holocaust.

Publications on the Holocaust and on concentration camp survivors often emphasize the atmosphere of silence and blocks impeding interfamilial and inter-

25 Dasberg, 'Psychiatrische und psychosoziale Folgen'; Gampel, *Some reflections on counter-transference*; Nathan, 'Children of Holocaust survivors'.

26 For example by Kuch and Cox, 'Symptoms of PTSD', or Stoffels, *Schicksale der Verfolgten*.

generational communication,[27] but in the group studied in Poland there was a double taboo: one on discussing personal experience as well as a fundamental taboo concerning Jewish origins.

For many years the scientific literature addressed the problem of survivors' children as a separate issue.[28] It has been agreed that the past and present mental state of parents exerts a fundamental influence on children's development, not only within the problem studied. Yosii Hadar, using a psychoanalytical paradigm, has written that the mental life of survivors' children starts with the Holocaust, since their first experience is the horror experienced by their parents. It has also been established that over-protective parenting (often connected with anxiety) increases the difficulties experienced by their children (i.e. the second generation) in the process of separation/individuation. Yet another problem emphasized is that of silence extending over important areas of life, stemming from the taboo on the Holocaust experience. The 'tabooization' of the Holocaust experience is not easy to explain. The study we refer to, and eleven years of a group-therapy process make it possible to suggest a hypothesis, that this permanent concealment stems from the pain arising from the Holocaust, the trauma, enormous losses and a generalized distrust of the world. One Polish-Jewish writer, Bogdan Wojdowski, writes of what he calls a 'Jewish fate'. Many survivors did not want to continue this 'fate'; they decided to repudiate their heritage and to erase the horrible past. They did not want to remember; the memory was too painful. They cherished a deep desire to blend into Polish society, to marry Polish spouses and bring up their children as gentiles.

Of course, neither the official anti-Semitism nor the kind of prejudice that is not expressed consciously but shows itself in 'small talk', helped the survivors to come to terms with their past. It has been a long, difficult and painful process, which continues to this day, to make them feel more secure. For the past twenty years, they have become freer in their choices in the country's more liberal, democratic atmosphere.

The breaking of the Jewish taboo, the numerous books, papers and meetings – most notably the creation of the Association of Children of the Holocaust in 1991 – as well as the growing interest in Jewish culture and today's easy modes of communication with the outside world (especially Israel) – all these things have helped survivors to open up to some extent, though not yet entirely. Another factor is the growing number of people who are eager to listen with empathy.

One may hesitate as to the contribution of the concept of trauma, which has become familiar throughout the world over the past few decades. It is possible that this concept provides a framework within which it is easier to comprehend

27 Hadar, 'Existentielle Erfahrung oder Krankheitssyndrom?'; Haesler and Hofheim, 'Die Unmöglichkeit zu trauern'.

28 Nathan, 'Children of Holocaust survivors'.

the individual fates of survivors. This may possibly be one of the effects of the medicalization of the problems experienced by victims, including Holocaust survivors. If this is the case, we would be speaking here of medicalization in the contemporary sense, which embraces the social, psychological and spiritual aspects of human existence.

The research revealed certain specific characteristics in the upbringing of the children of Poland's Holocaust survivors. They were the offspring of mixed marriages, in which the Jewish partner desperately tried to achieve complete assimilation into his or her Polish surroundings; this significantly influenced the children's upbringing. Besides the taboo on the parent's Holocaust experience they were also raised in ignorance of their Jewish origins (with the exception of children whose parents were both Jewish).

This secrecy surrounding origins, initially subconscious and later conscious, generated a kind of family and social vacuum and a break in trans-generational continuity. As one would expect, a relatively large proportion (about 30%) of second-generation interviewees reported anxiety states in early childhood. At examination times many displayed an overanxious attitude (especially towards their own children), difficulties in anxiety control, and feelings of guilt towards their own parents.

Their emotional bonds within their generational families were very strong, especially with the mother. But in families of male survivors, the child-parent bond with the father was stronger. The declared life goals of the second-generation interviewees concerning the task of upbringing and their family life appeared similar to those of their parents. Nevertheless, many had serious problems in their professional careers, in spite of achieving a high level of education (all but two were university graduates). They were also less effective in founding families and having children: only half were married, and even some who had married were childless. All these points may bear some relationship to separation-individuation problems arising from their background as second-generation Holocaust survivors.

The second-generation Holocaust survivors living in Poland differ from those living elsewhere in terms of solving problems of identity. Only one in twenty was untroubled by doubt concerning his/her identity. Jewish culture and tradition mattered to all, and all were interested in exploring their roots. Meanwhile they had been assimilated into the Polish community and shared Polish problems. At the time they were interviewed they did not have a sense of belonging anywhere. However, it was discovered that their identity with Jewish tradition was based on loyalties with those who had perished and those who had suffered more. It would be difficult to find more convincing proof of Ivan Boszormenyi-Nagy's theory of invisible loyalties within the family.[29]

29 Boszormenyi-Nagy and Spark, *Invisible loyalties.*

Medical studies of Romani victims of World War II

The Roma Gypsies too were the object of Nazi persecution and efforts at extermination. But only quite recently has any research has been done on the consequences of the war for this ethnic group. The number of Romani victims is unknown, as this population was nomadic until 1960, and as such they were not included into pre-war Polish population registers. Itinerant Romani earned their living as artisans, artists or fortune-tellers. They did not have any representatives recognized by the state.

The Nazis labeled the Romani an inferior race; they deprived them of all rights and set out to exterminate them along with the Jews. The Romani were placed in ghettoes together with Jews. Special military units killed thousands of them. Documents from Birkenau concentration camp alone reveal that 20,000 Romani – men, women and children – were gassed and incinerated there. Romani frequently ran from places of extermination to seek shelter in the woods. Some managed to survive with a little help from local villagers, generally in the form of food.

After World War II, the government of the Polish People's Republic took no interest in the Romani people who were living in poverty, continuing their nomadic style of life. But in the 1960's the authorities forced them to settle in fixed homes. They were given flats, often flying in the face of their customs and needs. Many were punished as destructive vagabonds. This policy amounted to a traumatic and violent assault on the Romani people's need for freedom and translocation.

Some few Romani welcomed their new homes as an improvement in their living conditions. Nevertheless, even these settled Romani groups have not adapted well to their new social conditions. The children are poorly educated and there is a high level of illiteracy. Still, the situation of the Romani has gradually changed. The third generation of Romani Holocaust survivors values education, and they have given rise to a Romani group of professionals and intellectuals.

Still, the traditional Romani community has remained isolated and hermetically sealed off from the outside world. Studying Romani culture requires a specific kind of internal observation, since traditional communities are unapproachable even for those Romani who are interested in studying their own cultural roots and traditions.

Even after 1989, the problems experienced by the Romani population group as war victims failed to be recognized. Still, Romani intellectuals called successfully for the founding of non-governmental organizations to address certain specific problems faced by the Romani. These organizations opened up questions relating to the problems and rights of this ethnic group.[30]

---

30 http://www.stowarzyszenieromow.hg.pl/ogolne/OsrInf/OsrInfor.html

Of all the groups persecuted by the Nazis, the Romani were the last to achieve recognition. Only after 1991 were they finally accorded the status of combatants, enabling them to apply for financial support to offset the health problems deriving from persecution, like others who had been persecuted on the grounds of race.

In 2004 The Union of Polish Roma approached the professor of psychiatry at the medical college of the Jagiellonian University, seeking a psychiatric assessment of Roma Holocaust survivors identified by the Association. The research team (Dr Maria Kamińska, Professor Maria Orwid, Dr Krzysztof Szwajca and Dr Kinga Widelska) examined a total of 55 Romani survivors. Opinions were issued in respect of each individual. The group studied consisted of elderly people, but younger than the Jewish Holocaust survivors. They had survived in hiding, usually in the forests or in villages in extremely difficult conditions: freezing temperatures, near-starvation and an unrelenting danger of capture and death.

The psychiatrists found it very difficult to establish any rapport with these Roma survivors. The subjects did not understand the tasks they were asked to perform, and appeared anxious and distrustful. Few had graduated from secondary school. It proved almost impossible to elicit any information from them concerning their early childhood experience, including the events relating to the persecution.

The dominant symptom was anxiety, often in the form of pathological fear of objects such as uniforms, dogs, noise or strangers, or fears concerning their children's futures. Another symptom was a disruption of the power of memory. Survivors repeated their only memories almost uniformly in the same terms: 'Fear, running away, hunger, blood, and people being killed all around'.

The majority of these survivors suffered from very poor physical health. They had a long history of treatment for cardiovascular or other somatic disorders. A process of involution had started early in life, similar to the syndrome described in other survivor studies as *involutio praecox*.

Serious forms of PTSD were diagnosed. Nevertheless, the government was rather reluctant to accept the existence of a causal relationship between the Romani's experience with attempts to exterminate them as a group and their disability. As a result, more Romani were refused war benefit in comparison to members of other groups.

The Polish victims of the war in the East

Polish citizens who survived Soviet repression were not recognized as war victims either in legislation or by the medical establishment until 1990. Their status as victims was not addressed or even brought up until the process of political transformation was launched. The problem of Katyń illustrates this. Between 1945 and 1991, the Polish authorities classified the Soviet mass murder of Polish Army officers and Polish government officials at Katyń (and other places of their imprisonment) as a Nazi war crime. However, this did not result in any provision for bereaved families as war victims. It was impossible to assess the consequences of Soviet persecution for Polish citizens, since it was officially denied that any such persecution had taken place. It should be noted that the Jewish Polish nationals who survived deportation to Siberia in World War II were in the same position. Since the official definition of the Holocaust imposed clear limits in terms of time and space they were not recognized as Holocaust survivors.[31]

The political changes of 1989 included a clear anti-Soviet reorientation. This included a sympathetic attitude for those persecuted in the East, as well as for those who had suffered from the political repression carried out by the Polish secret service.

Besides the political context, we must bear in mind that both the government and society at large came to recognize and accept the scientific and social importance of extreme war trauma far more clearly in the 1990's. Growing numbers of books, papers, and articles in journals and newspapers appeared on the effects of trauma, creating a higher level of understanding and more readiness to deal with these problems. The general discourse of trauma, as developed in worldwide research, prepared the ground for greater understanding.

We should also stress the passage of time, which, contrary to popular belief, reinforces memories rather than weakening them. Secrets have gradually been deconstructed. The victims have become more willing to talk, especially those who had kept their resentment bottled up in silence longer than others.

All victims now have a more empathic and accepting audience. The knowledge that the whole world has lost its innocence has made itself felt. Summarizing, the concept of trauma has been addressed openly and incorporated into political and economic policies.

Problems relating to the trauma of deportation were first studied in the 1990's, over forty years after the traumatic events took place. From the beginning, the experience of deportation and its consequences was compared to that suffered by other Nazi concentration camp survivors and Holocaust survivors studied in the past.[32] By 1980, the vast majority of 'Syberians' (the term used for the deportees to the Asian part of the Soviet Union, Siberia, Kazakhstan, and Uzbekistan), were advanced in years or had experienced deportation in early childhood. They had been deported for periods ranging from a few months to fifteen years. Even so, all the published findings are similar. The degree of PTSD diagnosed in Siberians

31 Tanay, 'Powstanie w getcie Warszawskim'.

32 Gierowski, 'Ferne Nachwirkungen einer Stressbelastung', 'Zaburzenia posttraumatyczne'; Prot, 'Późne skutki wczesnej traumy'.

ranged from 65% to 100%.[33] Besides PTSD, serious somatic health disorders were also diagnosed in Sybiracs.[34] Further analyses of the data relating to 204 deportees revealed post-traumatic personality disorders in those who had been deported at under five years of age.[35] Yet even in spite of such evidence, the social security agency very rarely recognizes any causal relationship between the Sybiracs' health problems and the trauma of deportation.

Martyrdom as part of identity

It seems that everyone, in Poland, is a victim of World War II. It is appropriate to add a few observations on the mythology underlying Polish identity at this point, to clarify the difficulties that long impeded the proper recognition of the medical, psychological and social consequences of the war.

It is true that the Nazi occupation of Polish territory was highly repressive. It included the 'Final Solution' of the 'Jewish Problem', which the Nazis implemented in this country. It is also true that the Soviet Union invaded Poland on 17 September 1939 and occupied the eastern part of the country, later joining the Allies, with Polish military groups and Red Army units fighting the Germans side by side. So at the end of the war, the Allies' view was that Poland was now under the influence of an ally. But this was an ally that had entered the war with an act of aggression against Poland. The majority of those who participated in the anti-Nazi underground, including the military resistance, did not accept the international decision to leave Poland under the influence of the Soviet Union. Polish soldiers who had joined the armed forces of other countries (such as the British Air Force) or the Polish forces that had fought on the Western fronts (in Italy and the Netherlands, for instance) decided to emigrate, and some never returned home.

But Poland has a myth of suffering dating back to the nineteenth century, after the loss of independence in the 'Partitions of Poland' in the eighteenth century. Romantic writers created a messianic myth of the nation that suffered for all others. This myth, together with entrenched Catholic tradition, formed the background of Polish identity and of efforts to regain independence. Polish Catholicism was a major factor, since two of the three empires that had divided Poland up between them were of different Christian denominations. But this messianic myth was based on a mix of the Judaic tradition of the chosen nation and the Christian evangelical tradition.

33 Jackowska, 'Psychiczne następstwa deportacji'; Monieta and Anczurowski, 'Nasilenie objawów zespołu stresu pourazowego'.

34 Walczewska et al., 'Ocena aktualnego stanu zdrowia'.

35 Rutkowski, *Następstwa urazów psychicznych*.

After World War II it became clear that Polish Christians and Polish Jews were caught up in a contest to see who had suffered most. The rather strong tendency towards anti-Semitism in Poland does not suffice to explain this rivalry after the Holocaust. It cannot be understood without reference to the myth of the Polish nation's messianic role, as developed in nineteenth-century Romantic thought. This notion had been borrowed, in a sense, from the deeply-held Jewish belief in being the chosen nation. Combatant status had been granted to various sections of the population, in response to political changes. But the legal position of combatants' organizations was decided in a non-democratic way. In consequence, several groups were deprived of their rights and any means of representation. Leaving these factors aside, the messianic myth may have been responsible for the competition that ensued among different groups of victims. The Romani, Sybiracs, Poles who had experienced Ukrainian nationalist persecution during the war, Ukrainians who happened to live within territories annexed to the Polish state, Germans in a similar position, Silesians, underground fighters after 1945, political prisoners in the Stalinist period and even those who suffered while continuing to fight against Soviet totalitarianism up until 1989, all were caught up in a form of rivalry for victim status.

The process described above has attracted comment before, and efforts to deconstruct the myth of messianic suffering were first launched in the late 1980's. The most important of these, perhaps, was the debate on the Holocaust and the position that Polish Christians had adopted at that time.

In 1986 Józef Bogusz organized the conference 'War, Occupation and Medicine' in Kraków.[36] It focused entirely on concentration camp survivors and Polish-German relations. That same year, a historian, Józef Gierowski, then rector of the Jagiellonian University, held a symposium on the position of Jews in pre-Enlightenment Poland, with the participation of Israeli researchers. This conference looked for the sociological and legal – rather than religious – roots of anti-Semitism in Poland. In 1987, Jan Błoński published in the Catholic weekly *Tygodnik Powszechny* a seminal text on the attitudes adopted by the Poles during the Nazi extermination of Jews, looking specifically at the uprising in the Warsaw Ghetto.[37] This text provoked a debate that is still going on today. Czesław Miłosz, winner of the Nobel Prize for poetry, had published a poem on the same topic back in 1946 (Campo dei Fiori), that had gone almost unnoticed at the time. One of the consequences of trauma is to freeze the emotions of those who witness it. Defrosting takes time.

The past twenty years have seen many detailed studies of Jewish problems, and these, together with the reconstruction of the missing Jewish culture, constitute an

---

36 Bogusz, 'Wojna i okupacja a medycyna'.
37 Błoński, 'Biedni Polacy patrzą na getto'.

important 'stream of culture'. But the Holocaust survivors have now also received attention, along with, finally, the other survivors of wartime persecution.

Two significant publications on these problems have appeared just recently. They are both by Jan Tomasz Gross, a historian who has studied various aspects of the repression experienced by Poles during the war. But these two books deal with the aggression of Poles towards Jews. The first is *Sąsiedzi* ('Neighbors', 2001), on the pogrom that took place in the small village of Jedwabne in 1941 (the village was first occupied by Soviet troops, and from 1941 onwards by Nazis). The second is called *Strach* ('Fear', 2006), which provides an account of the pogrom mounted against Holocaust survivors in Kielce in 1946. The facts have been known ever since the events happened. In both cases, the aggressors (or at any rate some of their representatives) were identified, tried and sentenced. Nonetheless, these two books have appeared at an opportune moment in time, and in the appropriate form, to disrupt the slumbering tranquility surrounding the myth of the Pole as an immaculate, messianic sufferer.

9 From Camp to Claim

The KZ syndrome and PTSD in Scandinavia, 1945-2010

» *Ralf Futselaar*

The German invasion of Denmark and Norway on 9 April 1940 brought the phony war to an abrupt end and marked the beginning of the German conquest of Western Europe. It was also the beginning of the five year long German occupation of two Scandinavian states that were, culturally and historically, very similar. This similarity was reflected in their shared attitude towards international politics; during the 1930's neither country had shown the slightest inkling to confront Germany militarily, instead guarding the neutrality that had saved them from the carnage of World War I. But the lure of Norwegian bauxite and an open harbor for the export of Swedish iron ore, as well as hegemony in the north Atlantic, was enough for Germany to harbor aspirations for northbound expansion. With the Altmark incident as a convenient pretext, operation *Weserübung* was set in motion.

Denmark prudently but remarkably decided not to resist the vastly stronger force that streamed across its southern border and sailed for Copenhagen. The Danish government saw no realistic opportunities to ward off the invasion, and no point in aggravating the inevitable. Germany in turn expected future gains from Denmark to remain minimal. Danish realism and German disinterest together created the basis for a peculiarly gentle occupation. As an 'occupied neutral' Denmark retained considerable autonomy, as well as a considerably higher standard of living than other European countries at the time. Violence, although not quite as negligible as is sometimes claimed, remained relatively moderate. Victims of persecution were likewise few, in comparison, again, to other countries, both because little fighting took place, and because the vast majority of Danish Jews safely escaped to Sweden in 1943. All this did, however, come at a price: the Danish political, economic and cultural establishments had to accommodate to German demands and pay lip-service to National Socialism, staking both their reputations and integrity to preserve a status quo of relative peace and quiet.

The invasion of Norway, although undertaken at the same time, differed dramatically from that of Denmark. The Nazi leadership considered Norway a major strategic asset, certainly one worth fighting for. They had to, too: the Norwegians, together with British and Polish forces, made a credible, if ultimately futile, attempt to defend their country. Once defeated, Norway was occupied in a much more intrusive, and more brutal, manner than Denmark, and armed resistance continued on a relatively large scale until 1945. The five years of occupation in Norway were marked by violence and severe repression, and tens of thousands of Norwegians joined the allied war effort abroad.

Norway as a consequence suffered far greater personal losses during the war, but it was Denmark that became the cradle of research into, and recognition of, late-onset psychiatric consequences of wartime experiences. The *KZ syndrome*, one of the earliest terms for what is now PTSD, was first described and named by Danish researchers, who were mostly linked to the resistance veterans' national organization. This may seem paradoxical; the formerly occupied country which, without any doubt, had *fewest* potential victims of war trauma nevertheless pioneered its study and recognition. As will be clear from the following chapter, the strong position of a united resistance organization, the relatively low cost of generosity towards few victims, and the determination of a small group of doctors were important factors. That Danish insights found their way to Norway owed much to the linguistic and cultural closeness of both countries, but perhaps even more to the pioneering psychiatrist Leo Eitinger, who tirelessly promoted what could be called the 'Nordic' or 'somatic' interpretation of war trauma, both in his own country and around the world.

Occupation

At the time of the German invasion in 1940, both Denmark and Norway had for decades been self-perceived small European states, jealously guarding their neutrality in a dangerous Europe. While both Norway and Denmark were neutral, many considered them to lie in the *de facto* British sphere of influence. Britain was the main trading partner of both countries, and the Royal Navy was expected to act as a safeguard for at least Norwegian neutrality. In spite of this somewhat partial kind of neutrality, there existed some consensus in both countries that a German invasion was, if not impossible, at least unlikely. Germany begged to differ. Plans for the northward expansion of the Nazi empire had already been drawn up in the course of 1939.

In those plans, Norway had always been the true goal. Indeed, the initial plan had been not to invade Denmark at all, but focus exclusively on Norway. The Luftwaffe, whose need for aluminium was a primary reason for the invasion, at that time lacked planes that could fly to Norway without refueling, which necessitated the conquest of an airstrip along the way, Denmark being the obvious candidate. The German decision to conquer Denmark as a springboard for the invasion of Norway was, apparently, made with considerable reluctance. German, and British, intelligence officials believed that the Danish economy would collapse instantly when severed from Great Britain, and that the country could not contribute significantly to the German economy or war effort. Only a minority of civil servants were aware that Danish agriculture could contribute greatly to alleviating the difficult food situation in Germany, as indeed it did during the following five years. Denmark, in any event, proved Germany's greatest bargain; a breeze to conquer, cheap to occupy and profitable in the extreme.[1]

That it was such a bargain was, of course, partly a consequence of the rather remarkable Danish reaction to the invasion. While Norway waged a desperate defensive war, Denmark did not resist the invasion on 9 April 1940, and grudgingly accepted its new status as an 'occupied neutral'. King, parliament and judiciary remained in place, and life continued, to the extent possible, as normal, under uninvited German 'protection'. At least until August 1943, a Danish government of national unity actively cooperated with the occupying authorities, the so-called *Samarbejde* policy. In the course of the occupation, however, a small but vocal resistance movement developed, which opposed any such collaboration. The illegal press consistently argued against *Samarbejde*, and did not shy from calling for the liquidation of Danish politicians. Resistance fighters also attempted to sabotage the occupation by violent means, sometimes with spectacular results, albeit of negligible military significance.[2]

To the vast majority of the Danes, as is evidenced by their voting behavior both during and after the war, the decision to accommodate rather than fight the Germans seemed a wise one. Not without reason; Denmark saw very little of the violence that was the order of the day elsewhere in Europe. The country enjoyed the highest standard of living in the German-occupied area, and possibly the highest in the world outside North America. Persecution was limited, until 1943, to communists and resistance fighters, neither of whom could count on the overwhelming sympathy of most Danes. Of course the occupation brought about considerable discomforts and fear, and it hurt national pride, but not to such an extent that many Danes either actively or passively resisted it.[3]

As elsewhere in Europe, 1943 was a turning point of sorts, although again a less violent and extreme one than in other countries. After the battles of El Alamein, Stalingrad and Kursk, German fortunes appeared to be (and indeed were) turning, leading both to a greater willingness to rebel on the part of the Danes, and a greater zeal for oppression and exploitation on the part of the occupier. In August, unrest broke out, and in some parts of Copenhagen several days of rioting ensued.

1 Kirchhoff, *Samarbejde og modstand under besættelsen*, 31. Cf. Rostgaard Nissen, *Til fælles bedste*, 32; Futselaar, *Lard, lice and longevity*.

2 Bundgård Christensen et al., *Danmark besat*; Kirchhoff, *Samarbejde og modstand*.

3 Bundgård Christensen et al., *Danmark besat*.

As wartime rebellions go, August '43 was hardly an impressive display of violence, but it did mark a shift in German-Danish relations. The fiction of neutrality, which both the occupier and the Danish governments had painstakingly maintained, was shattered once and for all.[4]

Even after August '43, however, Denmark did not become an occupied nation like any other. On the contrary, after the government stepped down, its role was taken over by the various heads of department, who mostly continued the existing policy of *Samarbejde*.[5] Officially things had changed dramatically, but in actual fact they had not. Neither did the relatively comfortable life of the Danes change significantly, at least not for those willing to accept occupation as the lesser evil. The resistance movements grew somewhat after August 1943, but not immediately to such an extent that they became a significant military force. Nevertheless, 1943 saw an important change for Denmark. Until then, Denmark and the majority of the Danes had disliked but accepted German supremacy in Europe. Seen from 1943 and after, however, their initial acceptance could be reinterpreted as a mere truce between hostilities, a strategy of defense and even defiance. This had little impact on relations with Germany, but was a very meaningful change for relations within Denmark.

By then, those relations were anything but warm. In the first years of the occupation, the Danish government had persecuted communists with considerably more zeal than would have been necessary to placate the Germans. The electoral mandate that legitimized the wartime governments moreover, was disregarded by a large part of the resistance movement, which was not overwhelmingly democratic or parliamentary in its politics, and considered itself a natural ruling force for post-war Denmark. Partly in order to effectuate their influence, communist, nationalist and other resistance groups were united in the *Frihedsraad*, or Freedom Council, from September 1943. In November '43, it published the pamphlet *Naar Danmark atter er Frit* (when Denmark is free again), in which they explicitly and comprehensively denounced the participants in *Samarbejde*, and therefore almost the entire wartime and post-war political establishment.[6]

Another consequence of the new political realities was that there no longer was a bureaucratic hurdle to prevent persecution of Denmark's Jewish minority. In October 1943, deportation of the Jewish population of Denmark was finally instigated. German plans, however, were leaked, and the vast majority of Danish Jews managed to sail across the Sound in time to find refuge in Sweden. Only a

4 Kirchhoff: *Augustoprøret* 1943.

5 Hæstrup, *...til landets bedste*. vol. 1, 22; Kirchhoff, *Samarbejde og modstand*; Giltner, *In the friendliest manner*.

6 The full text is available at http://www.befrielsen1945.dk/temaer/befrielsen/retsopgoer/kilder/DKatterFrit.pdf.

few were caught, and the genocide that took place in most other occupied states had effectively been averted in Denmark.[7]

1944 brought several changes for the worse. After D-Day, the imminent collapse of the Reich was obvious to most. Politically, relations hardened as the willingness of the Danes to rebel increased. The Germans were divided. Some, like *Reichsbevollmächtigter* Werner Best, appear to have preferred, as before, to take a soft approach, not least, presumably, to save their own skin after liberation. Others were of a different mind. *Höhere ss und Polizeiführer* Günther Pancke, who had also supported the initiative to persecute the Danish Jews, proved, again, to be a serious liability to the moderate German administration headed by Best. In September 1944, Pancke, bizarrely, ordered the arrest and deportation of the entire Danish police force. This led to a collapse of the relative social order which for many Danes had been the main reason to accept German occupation. Crime rates soared. Moreover, only a few thousand policemen were deported (to Buchenwald concentration camp). A large number of them went into hiding, adding to the potential recruits for resistance activity.[8]

Finally, while the Reich was already in its death throes, the Danish resistance grew into a sizeable paramilitary organization. Not, however, the most effective one; the resistance was reasonably armed, thanks to British arms-droppings, but training and discipline were minimal. Thousands of young men and adolescents, many of them equipped with Stenguns, were ready to fight the occupier and, if need be, the Danish government. The Germans, as it turned out, were not beaten by them, or in Denmark at all. The Western *Wehrmacht* forces under General Christiansen surrendered to the Allies at the Lüneburger Heide on 4 May 1945. As allied forces marched in unopposed, the head of the Freedom Council, Mogens Fog, announced on the radio 'There was a time after the German invasion of Denmark when it seemed that we bowed before a greater power, but that was mere outer appearance. From day one, our people stood united to defend our democracy and our right to independence'.[9] These blatant lies sealed the political future of Denmark, as well as the future of treatment of trauma in Scandinavia.

An occupation of the peculiar kind that Denmark experienced was probably never really on the cards in Norway. The expected assets to be reaped in that country, and the British-supported defense against the invasion, together ruled out 'occupied neutrality' as far as the Germans were concerned. That is not to say, however, that the Norwegians would not under any circumstance have accepted such arrangements. It appears that the day after the initial invasion, when the king and most

7 Hæstrup, *...til landets bedste* vol. 1, 22; Kirchhoff, *Samarbejde og modstand*; Stræde, *Die Menschenmauer*.

8 Bundgård Christensen, 'På vagt i en lovlos tid', 91-109; Bundgård Christensen et al., *Danmark besat*, 495-501.

9 Lundbak, *Besættelsetid og frihedskamp*, 45.

of the government had been evacuated from Oslo, they had been ready to negotiate, and if necessary follow the example of the Danes. At this point, however, the leader of the Norwegian National Socialists, Quisling, had barged into a radio station and declared both German victory and his own ascendency to the position of prime minister on air. German support for Quisling's coup, if half-hearted, closed the window of opportunity for negotiation. The Norwegian government and king categorically refused to accept any arrangement in which the treacherous Quisling would take a key position.

As a consequence, Norway fought on, its army and government retreating ever further north, resisting Germany in collaboration with British and Polish troops. After the invasion of Western Europe, however, many of those forces were deployed there, and Norwegian resistance to the invasion crumbled. The royal family and the government left for Britain and the country surrendered on 10 June 1940, having held out longer than any other German-invaded country except Britain and the Soviet Union. Two months of intense fighting had caused considerable damage and many casualties on all sides. The civilian toll remained low, at under 200 lives lost. But there were thousands of military casualties.

To the disappointment of Quisling, he was not to become top dog in Norway. German doubts about him, and the great importance attached to the rule of Norway, led to the appointment of Joseph Terboven as *Reichskommissar* on 24 April 1940. When, after 62 days of war, the remaining Norwegian authorities had no choice but to negotiate with the victorious Germans, they found in him an exceptionally unpleasant man. On 25 September, he cancelled talks with the Norwegian parliament, established a *statsråd* (government) and commenced his autocratic rule of Norway, which was to last throughout the war. He banned all parties except Quisling's *Nasional Samling*, but the establishment of its leader Quisling as prime minister in 1942 was a mostly cosmetic affair – the Fascist leader was too unpopular to be of any real use.

The scope for a Danish, or *Samarbejde* style occupation was thereby reduced to zero. Unlike their Danish counterparts, who had managed to both limit the appropriation of power by German officials, and contain indigenous national socialists in a position of insignificance, Norwegian politicians had come under overwhelming National Socialist and German control. Moreover, because the Norwegian political elite had, through no real fault of their own, missed whatever chance had existed to soften the occupation by collaborating in September 1940, they also to a considerable extent escaped their Danish colleagues' dilemma of how far to go in doing so, and the need to reconcile or justify their role after liberation.[10]

10 Dahl, 'Besettelse', 386.

That is not to say, by the way, that the national conflicts that existed in Denmark were absent in Norway. Like their Danish counterparts, the Norwegian resistance was not overwhelmingly democratic, and politicians of many of the old parties may have entertained the hope to reach a Danish-style solution for a while longer than they would later have admitted. Even if the conflict between accommodation and resistance was not as clearly visible as in Denmark, it nevertheless played an important role. That such a conflict was at all possible was because Nazi ideology considered Norwegians racially equal to Germans. With the exception of the tiny Jewish community, Norwegians were therefore to be treated with a degree of consideration. They were not, like occupied peoples to the east of Germany, considered expendable *Untermenschen* whose projected fate was to serve and ultimately disappear. There was scope for friendly relations with Germany in principle, but these did not materialize in Norway in practice, and National Socialism remained unpopular.[11]

Within the limitations of racial considerations, however, Terboven proved a harsh and repressive leader. Norwegians were not very keen on their new status as 'Germanic peoples'. The attempts to Nazify Norway, which had an intensity unknown in Denmark, mostly bolstered a spirit of defiance. More generally, the occupation force was a much more prominent presence in Norway than in Denmark. Perhaps the strongest Nazi presence in everyday Norwegian life was the secret police. This organization, headed by Terboven, got a deserved reputation for ruthlessness. Several concentration camps were set up in Norway.

These were needed because, at least compared to Denmark, the number of people persecuted for political reasons was high in Norway. Several prisons and concentration camps were set up, notably the infamous Grini prison in the vicinity of Oslo. Approximately 40,000 Norwegians were interned at least part of the war, and thousands were sent on to German camps such as Sachsenhausen and Natzweiler. Both torture and executions were, if not commonplace, then at least not exceptional in occupied Norway. The systematic persecution of the Jews began earlier than in Denmark, and had a much greater impact. Many of the over 2,000 Norwegian Jews fled to Sweden and some went into hiding, but 775 were arrested and deported. Only 23 of them survived.

Not only the occupation, but also resistance was much harsher in Norway than in Denmark. Coordinated, in part, by the exiled government, the Norwegian resistance had a large military wing. The vastness of the Norwegian wilderness allowed for the formation of a sizeable guerilla army, *Milorg*, which consisted of some 44,000, mostly communist, troops. In addition, because of the slow pace of the invasion, much of the Norwegian fleet escaped the country, and some 36,000

11 Danielsen and Larsen, *Fra ide til dom*.

Norwegian sailors joined the allied war effort, many more, relatively, than their roughly 8,000 Danish colleagues. Finally, many Norwegians sought and found refuge in Sweden, where a paramilitary police force was being built up from 1943. This force consisted of about 13.000 Norwegians, many of whom took part in the fighting in 1944-45. The Norwegian civilian resistance was sizable as well, and also of a very different nature than in Denmark. In Norway, the Nazification of society was taken up with far more zeal than in Denmark, where non-Nazi authorities had, for all intents and purposes, remained in power. As a consequence, civilian resistance was stronger and more ideologically charged.[12]

At the end of the war, Norway again became a theatre of actual fighting. In 1944, the Soviet Union invaded northern Norway. The military consequences of this invasion were quite insubstantial, insofar that they did not proceed beyond the village of Kirkenes. But it did prompt the German authorities to introduce a scorched earth strategy as a safeguard against further advances. They forcibly evacuated the population and destroyed 10,400 homes in the arctic Finnmark area. Thousands of people remained, however, and had to survive the last winter of the war in difficult circumstances in a highly inhospitable environment.[13] In the end, Norway was fortunate enough not to be liberated by the USSR. On May 7, the occupying forces surrendered to a delegation of the Western Allies.

Denmark and Norway each contributed some 6,000 volunteers to the *Waffen ss*, of whom many never returned, or only after a period as Soviet POW's. Because relatively little is known about this group and because their role in the development of trauma treatment was negligible, I will by and large ignore them below.

From liberation to compensation

Norway came out of the war with an enviable reputation. The war contributions of Norwegian sailors had been widely publicized in the Allied countries, the battles of 1940 had made a lasting impact on the collective memory, and organizations like *Milorg* allowed for a martial, heroic image, as did the winter war in Finnmark. This image was not limited to the outside world; Norway itself cherished, and to a considerable extent continues to cherish, a heroic self-image of consistent and militant resistance to the German occupation.[14]

Denmark on the other hand, which had survived the occupation with enviable ease, seemed in danger of losing the peace. However prudently the Danish politi-

12 Borgen, Hofsbro et al., *Norske polititropper i Sverige/Norge*; Eitinger, Vold and Weisaeth, *Krigsskader og senvirkninger*, 283; Dahl, 'Besettelse', 392.

13 Jaklin, *Historien om Nord-Norge*.

14 Eriksen, *Det var noe annet under krigen*.

cal elite had acted during the occupation, they had evidently not been particularly heroic. It was far from certain at the time that the Allies would consider Denmark a victim of Nazi expansion, rather than a willing satellite state of the Reich. Denmark had offered no resistance to the invasion, had duly signed the Anti-COMINTERN pact and had not exactly displayed a heartfelt opposition to Nazism. That is, official Denmark had not. The small, motley band of resistance fighters, who had been widely denounced as criminals only a few months earlier, suddenly seemed a way out of trouble for the Danish political establishment. As the statement from Mogens Fog quoted above illustrates, the resistance proved willing to oblige the government with instant justification.[15]

But not for nothing. Days before the liberation, the freedom council and leading Danish politicians had engaged in a session of rather prosaic deal-brokering, and in many respects the resistance seemed to get its way. A government was to be formed which was to consist of equally large representations from the now united resistance movement and established political parties. Until new elections were held, this interim government would remain in power. (That a few months later virtually the entire Danish electorate would vote for the old parties had not at all been obvious in the spring of 1945.) Resistance fighters were given the opportunity to join the *Hjemmeværn*, an amateur volunteer army with a strong resistance identity, which even today forms a reserve army roughly equal in size to the regular Danish army. In Copenhagen, *Frihedsmuseet*, the freedom museum, was established. This sudden generosity of the Danish political elite towards the resistance movement was not inspired by PR considerations alone. Resistance fighters and fellow travelers, whose hatred of Nazism was only slightly larger than their contempt for established political parties and their *Samarbejde* policies, were celebrating throughout Denmark. Although it would go too far to describe the country as being on the brink of civil war, having thousands of disgruntled young men with firearms roaming the streets, would have been worrying under the best of circumstances.[16]

In the end, the resistance movement did not have its way after the occupation, or at least not to the expected extent. The established political parties did well in the first post-war election, and erstwhile enemies of the resistance mostly escaped lightly. Only a handful of captured Germans and Danish Nazis were ever prosecuted.[17]

The resistance, nevertheless, remained an important asset to the post-war Danish state, to ensure political legitimacy as well as foreign goodwill. Resistance veterans were in an excellent bargaining position to secure, if not political power,

15 Bryld and Warring, *Besættelsestiden som kollektiv erindring*, 84, 55-61.
16 Ibidem, compare the introduction to J.T. Lauridsen, *Samarbejde og modstand*.
17 Bryld and Warring, *Besættelsestiden som kollektiv erindring*, 84, 108.

than at least social and cultural capital. As Poulsen put it: 'We collaborated with the occupation power and achieved conditions that, in comparison with other occupied countries, were good and relatively free. We then got a resistance movement at half price, and, finally, became an Allied power without ever entering the war'.[18] For their part, the discount resistance heroes received some money, a museum and a hobby army, as well as a few commemorative stamps, numerous monuments and a great deal of attention, both at home and abroad. Finally, they received the official recognition of, and for a while the monopoly on, a newly invented psychiatric disease.

Mogens Fog, the resistance leader quoted above, was to become a key figure in the development of the diagnosing of late-onset problems as well as the help to which sufferers should be entitled. Fog (1904-1990) was a professor of neurology at Copenhagen University from 1938 to 1974. A member of the Danish Communist Party since 1924, he co-founded the *Socialistiske Læger* (Socialist Doctors) in 1932. Early in the occupation, Fog had to go into hiding, after establishing resistance organization *Frit Danmark* (Free Denmark). Later in the occupation, he was instrumental in establishing contacts between communist leader Aksel Larsen and the conservative, though resistance-minded, politician Christmas Møller (who later, in his London exile, was to become the international figurehead of the Danish resistance). The foundation of the *Frihedsraad* (Freedom Council), which developed out of these meetings, was to some degree a personal achievement of Fog. In the interim government established in May 1945 he became minister for 'special affairs' and he remained an MP for the communist party until 1950, even though he was not officially a party member after 1941. In 1958 he joined Aksel Larsen and other communists who had opposed the Hungarian invasion in the newly founded Socialist People's Party (*Socialistisk Folkeparti*). Fog was Rector of Copenhagen University from 1966 to 1972, and in that capacity actively co-operated with the student movement to democratize higher education in Denmark.[19]

On October 1, parliament passed a law Fog had drafted, *Folketingets lov nr, 475 af 1 oktober 1945 om erstatning til besættelsetidens ofre* (Law for the compensation of the victims of the occupation period). This law entitled anybody who had suffered disease as a consequence of 1) resistance work, 2) deportation or incarceration on the grounds of membership of the Danish communist party, employment in the police force or customs service, to both an annual honorary gift (*hædersgave*) in money, and compensation of damages due to discontinuation of employment, education or business. The law mainly aimed to support those who had suffered damages, primarily in terms of earnings or labor capacity, in the course of their retroactively perceived duty for the fatherland. Perhaps even more than at the sur-

18 Quoted by Sørensen, 'Narrating the Second World War', 295.
19 Kjeldsen, 'Mogens Fog'.

vivors, legislation was initially directed at the widows and children of the fallen. The number of slain heroes was of course moderate, at least in comparison with other countries. Of roughly 5,000 deportees, 540 died in or en route to camps, or shortly after their return. Of these, 291 were resistance fighters. Other resistance deaths include 71 who died in active military service for the Allies, 477 killed in action as saboteurs, and 129 executed.[20]

A compensation council (*erstatningsraad*) was established, which, until 1970, awarded full or partial compensation. It is interesting to note that, if awarded, the *hædersgave* was further administered by the state accident insurance institution (*ulykkeforsikring*, later *arbejdsskadestyrelse*). This made it possible to adjust the sums awarded to any new 'medical and social realities' that arose. Moreover, payment from the *ulykkeforsikring* did not terminate after retirement.[21] Although Fog had been adamant that 'nobody should profit from the resistance', he had laid the basis for what was to become a relatively generous system of compensation.

The fact that the Danish state actively sought to compensate the resistance fighters whom it had made the focal point of official history, did not discourage resistance organizations to set up shop themselves. The last action of the *Frihedsraad* had been to set up a Freedom Fund (*Frihedsfond*), which was to raise money for veterans and their families. With a number of fundraising operations, often linked to liberation day celebrations, they raised several millions of crowns, only to find that, at the same time, many of their perceived tasks had already been taken care of by the government, through the legislation introduced by Fog, who was, unsurprisingly, *also* a board member of the Freedom Fund.[22]

Initially, the activities of the fund had been geared more to the secondary and tertiary education of resistance orphans, the construction of student housing, and other activities not directed at veterans themselves. In so far as resistance fighters were prioritized by the Fund, they mostly received financial support, or rather loans, so they could start a business. By 1950, over 300,000 Crowns had been lent to veterans. By that time it also became clear that many of the loans would never be repaid. Businesses failed, some people died, others emigrated or simply disappeared.[23] Because of its dual nature as both a representative and a creditor of veterans, the fund was not only unable, but also unwilling to seek repayment with any firmness. By 13 March 1962, it was accepted that much of the money was irretrievably lost.[24]

20 Thygesen, *Frihedsfonden*, 32.
21 Ibidem, 34.
22 Riksarkivet (RA), *Frihedsfondens Arkiv*, Inv. No. 8.
23 RA, *Frihedsfondens Arkiv*, Inv. No. 9, board meeting of 3 March 1950.
24 RA, *Frihedsfondens Arkiv*, Inv. No 9, board meeting of 13 March 1962.

One of the most remarkable qualities of the Fund was its inclusive nature. Throughout its existence, it remained rabidly non-partisan, in spite of the outbreak of the cold war and the evident problems this posed in contacts between communist and non-communist veterans. By staunchly refusing to be divided over political issues, the fund managed to be and indeed remain the voice of the united resistance, and as such became a relatively powerful group. Board members, over time, included bishops, communist politicians, businessmen, doctors, and skilled workers, who appear to have managed to collaborate quite easily. Being a small minority, the veterans of the resistance were very keen, and apparently able, to maintain a high degree of unity.

And it was an assertive resistance; in 1951 the Fund convinced the *erstatningsraad* that the doctors appointed to investigate claimants had 'insufficient understanding' of their particular, often psychiatric, ailments, and were 'unsympathetic' to veterans. Only doctors who themselves had experienced the hardships of camp life, they argued, could be trusted to judge these cases competently. By thus excluding potentially critical doctors, the fund almost eliminated the problematic need to prove causation in cases of psychiatric illness – something that was to prove a serious problem in Norway.

In January 1970, the Freedom Fund was encapsulated by, and became part of the Danish state. It was given the responsibility to decide on matters of compensation for war victims. Resistance veterans' compensation claims were thus effectively judged by their own interest organization, albeit in the guise of a government department. Evidently, the fund had had enormous influence on the state's treatment of veterans before, and as such 1970 was the consolidation of an existing state of affairs rather than a radical break. In a sense, however, 1970 marked the definitive victory of the post-war resistance movement as the leading authority in questions of compensation. The Danish resistance may never have achieved the position of power it had aspired to in wartime, but it did have much more influence on policies regarding its veterans than resistance movements in other countries did.

That the step to become a governmental organization was necessary, had everything to do with the changing workload of the fund. During the 1960's and 50's, the fund's activities in caring for veterans had become increasingly important for three reasons. As time progressed, increasing numbers of former inmates of prisons and concentration camps developed physical and, especially, psychiatric problems. Secondly, the fund had gradually widened its criteria for help. For example, a young man arrested and deported as an 'antisocial element' during the occupation, was found in 1957 to have shown 'resistance spirit' in spite of not belonging to any group and not having undertaken any resistance action, and received help from the fund on that basis. As one board member commented during this particular meeting, 'the so-called antisocial fall outside the official work of the fund in the same way that policemen, customs officials, and the *race-persecuted* [my emphasis], but we never turn these cases down without first investigating whether practical or advisory help can be offered.'[25] Finally, the fund actively sought contact with sufferers of war-related illness and, with increasing success, admonished them to seek help and compensation.

In Norway, the problem of compensation for war victims was quantitatively greater and more pressing than in Denmark. In the course of the war, up to ten percent of the population had suffered severely, and most of those were in the productive age group needed for rebuilding the country. It also became a problem significantly earlier; the number of war casualties was already considerable at the beginning of the occupation. And since Norway had seen virtually no military action before, legislation to address problems related to war victims was not in place. On 9 December 1941 legislation on war pensions was introduced in Norway, both for military personnel and civilians. These laws were aimed at people who had become invalids, and the widows of the fallen, offering full or partial pensions, depending on the seriousness of the disability incurred. On returning to Norway, the formerly exiled, legal, government initially continued the practice introduced in 1941, with the provision that people who had committed or engaged in 'treason or spying' were excluded, and those who had suffered as a consequence of resistance or other 'patriotic activities' were now included.[26]

In December 1946, parliament passed the *krigspensjoneringslovene* or war pension laws. These were to offer compensation to those who had become disabled while on active duty for their country, and for those families that had lost their main breadwinner. The law, divided into the military and civilian laws (separated because compensation for military personnel came from the coffers of the Ministry of Defense) focused on compensating loss of income incurred as a consequence of patriotic activities. As in Denmark, pensions were not primarily meant to reward people for heroic behavior, but to repay the damages incurred in doing so. Unlike Denmark, pensions were rather low. They were not indexed, and declined as a consequence of post-war inflation. In the difficult reconstruction years, the entire budget for war pensions was set at a little over 6.2 million crowns, a sum that was to prove quite insufficient.

Within a few years, the insufficiency of the 1946 arrangements became evident, and a *dyrtidstilleg* or inflation-bonus was introduced in 1951. Inflation, however, was far from the only problem. The awarding, and especially the refusal to award, pensions became increasingly controversial throughout the 1950's, as was

25 RA, *Frihedsfondens Arkiv*, Inv. No. 9, board meeting 5 April 1957.
26 Luihn, *Men krigen er jo slutt*, 20, 24.

the setting of the degree of invalidity.[27] There were allegations that doctors were instructed to minimize the number of successful claims.[28] The thousands of Norwegian veterans were not united in a single organization, as their Danish counterparts were. Nor were they in as powerful a political position. The level of political collaboration had been less, and resistance far more common. This changed, to a degree, in 1953. In that year the vocal and particularly press-savvy *Krigsinvalideforbund* (Union of War Invalids) was founded, and began a campaign for change. They also supported individuals who felt their pensions were too low, or had been unjustly denied. Several individuals did take the authorities to court over low or refused pensions and won. Pensions were raised several times, but remained, by and large, quite difficult to get.

Moreover, it was not until 1968 that the essential problem behind the pension laws was addressed, namely that the burden of proof for causality between illness and wartime experiences lay squarely with the applicant. In the case of psychiatric problems this was problematic, and increasingly so as time passed by. As noted, in Denmark the Freedom Fund had strong-armed the government into accepting that only 'sympathetic' doctors were qualified to judge applicants' medical condition and establish causality. In Norway there was no veterans' organization with such power, and the odds remained stacked against the applicant.[29] As time progressed, causality only became more difficult to establish. Moreover, an increasing number of people were suffering psychiatric problems for which both the degree of invalidity and causality proved very problematic.

Two consecutive 'doctor commissions', the first of which had been established in 1957 to investigate the health problems of war veterans, had suggested to change this, and to make the level of stress/suffering experienced in wartime the primary criterion for awarding a pension. It took years before their suggestions finally became law. The 1968 extended law (*tillegslov*) identified groups whose wartime experience was considered to have been of such severity that there was no need to prove that their later health problems had been caused by those experiences. In theory, this made pensions more accessible in Norway than in Denmark, at least for a specific part of the victim population.[30] The groups included were:

- People who had, for a period, served actively in organized resistance in Norway.
- People who, because of their active, organized resistance work had been interned in concentration camps. (This category, interestingly, was to include Jews and hostages.)

27 Ibidem, 62.

28 Middelthon, 'Legen og invaliden'. In: Retterstøl, *'Og livet går videre...'*, 56.

29 Eitinger, *Concentration camp survivors in Norway and Israel*, 19; Eitinger and Strøm, *Mortality and morbidity after excessive stress*, 20.

30 Ibidem.

- People who had served aboard Norwegian ships at the disposal of the Norwegian government, or on foreign ships at the disposal of Allied powers, if that service was known to the Norwegian government.
- People who, as a consequence of active service, had been in enemy captivity.
- Military personnel who, under the war of 1940, had suffered abnormally severe exposure to suffering. (Six specific sections of the armed forces were identified.)
- Military Personnel stationed in or outside Norwegian territories who undertook missions within Norway, or served actively in allied operations.

By identifying these groups, and relieving them of the burden of proof of causality, Norway introduced a new way of viewing especially the psychological after effects of wartime suffering. In keeping with the research conducted in both Norway and Denmark, late-onset after effects were officially sanctioned as a *normal* consequence of severe suffering. In 1986, a commission was set up under the leadership of professor Leo Eitinger to further detail the kinds of experiences that could be presumed to lead to late-onset psychological disease. This resulted in a more detailed, and somewhat more extensive list of victims whose late-onset problems could be assumed to have been caused by their wartime experiences.[31]

As interesting as it may be to know who were included, it is at least as important who were not. Obviously, the creation of a category of very severe cases had the side effect of leaving groups out as well. People in these groups could still qualify for pensions, but had to prove the causal relation between their problems and their wartime experiences. In particular veterans of the Alta Batallion in Finnmark appear to have found their exclusion insulting and degrading. In 1997, however, an official committee declared this exclusion to have been justified. I will get back to that particular episode below.

The KZ syndrome: consensus on neurological damage

In their long struggle for higher and more readily accessible pensions, Norwegian veterans and activists consistently and explicitly used the Danish arrangements as a model. By pointing out the much more generous compensation and remuneration arrangements in the neighboring country, they not only proposed an alternative approach, but primarily tried to shame the Norwegian government into change. In comparison with other European countries discussed in this volume, Norway was far from heartless in its treatment of veterans and war victims, but Denmark was geographically, culturally, and linguistically close, and veterans

31 The Eitinger-report can be found at http://www.regjeringen.no/nn/dep/hod/Dokument/NOU-ar/1998/NOU-1998-12/26.html?id=375533 (accessed 15 March 2009).

from both countries were in relatively intensive and frequent contact. The notion that Norwegian veterans were treated considerably worse than their Danish counterparts was an embarrassment, and as such the political power of Danish veterans was an asset to their northern counterparts, who hammered the message home through outraged leaders in newspapers and tabloids.

But the importance of the Danish connection did not end there. Both the discussions about compensation, and the activities of veterans' organizations came to be dominated by problems related to late-onset psychiatric problems of former camp inmates and veterans. Because these problems were both debilitating, and very difficult to link, causally, to wartime experience, a scientific theory to explain this type of invalidity was direly needed. That theory also came from Denmark, in fact from a resistance veteran and former concentration camp inmate.

In May 1945, a young medical doctor by the name of Paul Thygesen returned to Denmark. A former resistance member, he had spent the last ten months of the war in Husum, one of the labor camps in the Neuengamme Concentration Camp system. There he had been able, albeit under the direst of circumstances, to provide a modicum of medical care for his fellow inmates. Within a year after his return, he published a book about the experience, *Læge i tyske koncentrationslejre,* ((medical) doctor in the German concentration camps). His involvement did not end there. He became a member of a team of doctors investigating erstwhile inmates, and was to remain an important figure in their treatment for decades.[32]

Early in his investigations, he linked somatic insults in the camps to the apparently psychosomatic problems he observed. A study in collaboration with Mette Hertz, *Postdiphteric nervous complications*, appeared in 1947 in the series *Acta psychiatrica et neurologica*. Around the same time, Thygesen was nominated by the *Frihedsfond* as one of the doctors with a 'proper understanding' of the needs and problems of resistance veterans. As a consequence Thygesen, and others, not only came into a position where he could offer substantial help to former inmates, and others, but also gained first-hand knowledge of many symptoms and medical problems.[33]

Paul Thygesen, Per Helweg-Larsen, and several other medical practitioners and researchers investigated camp survivors from 1947 onwards. Over a thousand repatriated prisoners were examined, mostly by survey, and it was found that three quarters of them suffered 'neurotic' problems. Initially, conclusions were disseminated mainly in Danish, to a Danish medical audience. In 1949 Helweg-Larsen et al. published 'Sultsygdommen og dens følgetilstande hos koncentrationslejrfanger' in *Ugeskrift for Læger*.[34] This was followed in 1952 by *Famine dis-*

32 Thygesen, *Læge i tyske koncentrationslejre.*

33 Hertz and Thygesen, 'Postdiphtheric nervous complications'.

34 Hellweg-Larsen et al., 'Sultsygdommen og dens følgetilstande hos koncentrationslejrfanger'.

ease in German concentration camps: complications and sequels, in which Thygesen and Kieler described the mental consequences of famine disease in six long-term consequences. 1) curtailment and brutalization of emotional and moral outlook; 2) impairment of memory; 3) diminished powers of spontaneous reaction; 4) a tendency to irritability and emotional instability; 5) absence of libido and; 6) dullness and apathy. A year later, in 1954, Thygesen and Knud Hermann published an article in which the observed problems received the name they would keep for decades: the KZ syndrome. KZ is the German abbreviation for concentration camp, and the syndrome was initially thought to be a consequence of the very particular circumstances in those camps.[35]

Thygesen, being a much respected veteran of the resistance and close to Mogens Fog, was in a strong position scientifically as well as politically. Already in 1954, a statue (!) was erected in his honor by the national society of former Neuengamme inmates – an unusual, and perhaps somewhat over-the-top honor for a man just 40 years old. His work was also very useful for, and actively promoted by, the Freedom fund. In fact, the entire team of researchers investigating the new syndrome shared the aura of resistance heroism, and because they also held a key position in judging claims for support on medical grounds, there remained little scope for opposition against their view on the somatic and psychosomatic consequences of concentration camp internment.[36] The acceptance of the KZ syndrome in Denmark went smoothly because of the overlap between cultural capital, political clout and medical consensus.

In later decades, the research tradition continued, especially in the work of Nielsen, who followed 1,354 former inmates into the 1980's. His work demonstrates the long time-gap between the physical or psychological insult and the symptoms of KZ syndrome or, as it was called by time he published, PTSD.[37] Although the acceptance of late-onset psychiatric problems of former inmates was quick and research extensive, treatment remained difficult. Recognition, however important, was not itself a cure for serious disability, and treatment remained troublesome.

As said, Norwegian veterans' organizations were acutely aware of the state of affairs in the neighboring country. Already in 1946 Axel Middelthon, a survivor of both Natzweiler and Dachau and a member of the newly founded Norwegian society of political prisoners, met Thygesen at a conference in Warsaw.[38] They

35 Hermann and Thygesen, 'KZ Syndromn'; compare: Thygesen et al., 'Concentration camp survivors in Denmark'.

36 Thygesen would (much) later write both a, rather sentimental, history of the fund and two chapters about Fog. Thygesen, *Frihedsfonden*; Idem, 'Befrielsesregeringens minister – og besættelsestidens ofre' and 'Forskeren og lægen – de følgende år'. In: Bredsdorf, *En bog om Mogens Fog.*

37 Nielsen, 'Disability during the years 1946-79'; Nielsen and Sørensen, 'KZ-syndromet i individuelle forløb'.

38 Middelthon, 'Legen og invaliden'. In: Retterstøl, *'Og livet går videre...'*, 54.

would be in repeated contact with each other in the decades to come. In 1950 Thorkild Dige, a member of the Frihedsfond board, travelled to Norway to explain Danish compensation rules, and did so again in 1955. The *Grini post*, a magazine of the organization of former political prisoners, published an article by Dige. 'The Danish people and government have understood their responsibility towards the victims of the resistance struggle' the *Post* claimed, and added that Norwegian politicians had better take notice.[39]

In 1956 the compensation council (*erstatningsraad*), a private organization primarily aimed at obtaining compensation for former inmates from Germany, organized a conference in Oslo under the title 'The health of KZ inmates in the searchlight'. This conference invited several prominent experts, including Thygesen and Fog, and the French expert Richet, to Oslo. The Norwegian government, to the irritation of the organizers, chose not to send any representatives. As the conference attendants discussed problems of long-term psychiatric damage, and the problems in establishing causality, the Norwegian state seemed to stubbornly turn its back on their efforts.[40]

Not so, however, the Norwegian medical establishment. As mentioned above, the *krigsinvalideforbund* managed to convince a number of doctors to set up an investigation into the health of erstwhile prisoners in the 1950's. The commission was to be chaired by Axel Strøm, professor of public health at Oslo university. One of his five colleagues was a young doctor by the name of Leo Eitinger, who would become both the public and the professional face of Norwegian trauma research and the KZ syndrome. Leo Eitinger had a personal history not entirely dissimilar to that of Thygesen, insofar that he, too, was a camp survivor. In 1939, Eitinger had arrived in Norway as a refugee, having left his native Czechoslovakia after the German invasion. In 1942, Eitinger was arrested and deported to Auschwitz. On his return to Norway, he found he was one of only 23 Norwegian Jews who had survived deportation.[41]

Unlike Thygesen, however, camp survivors appear not to have been the initial interest of the young psychiatrist Eitinger. No less personal, his earliest published works are about the psychiatric problems of refugees, notably his 1958 PhD thesis *Psykiatriske undersøkelser blant flyktninger i Norge*.[42] There is no doubt that the experiences of Eitinger had been at least as horrific as those of Thygesen and probably much worse, but he did not, as Thygesen did, find himself surrounded by a sizeable group of people with the same experience. Hence Eitinger was not embedded in a victims' organization like his Danish colleague, and appears to have retained

39 *Grini posten*, May 55
40 *Grini Posten*, November 1956.
41 Retterstøl, 'Leo Eitinger 70 år'.
42 Eitinger, *Psykiatriske undersøkelser blant flyktninger i Norge*.

a degree of professional detachment from any such organizations throughout his career.[43] Nevertheless, as the twentieth century progressed, Eitinger's relation with veterans' organizations became closer. As he became the main national and international protagonist of the KZ *syndrome*, he was a natural ally of those organizations pressing for recognition of late-onset consequences. On occasion, he ran afoul of various veterans' organizations and the *krigsinvalideforbund*, and he was downright harsh in his denunciation of victim culture and what he considered to be rent neurosis:

> 'It is deplorable if therapy or support groups contribute to reducing a victim to a state of permanent dependence. Being a victim means having had an unhappy fate. It is not reasonable, however, to demand that the world makes good all its past injustices. Those who have become victims have a right to reasonable help and a fitting compensation, but suffering does not entitle one to eternal protection or special treatment. To accept that type of deal, also if it happens subconsciously, is to do the sufferer a disservice – because it eventually undermines his ability to free himself of this suffering, and to take control over his own life.[44]

Eitinger accepted, more or less wholesale, the interpretation of the KZ syndrome as proposed by Thygesen and others. At the time of the *legekommisjon*, and for many years thereafter, Eitinger and his colleagues were convinced of the accuracy of Thygesen's notion that neurological damage due to somatic insults, notably undernourishment and weight loss, were the main cause of late-onset psychological problems. The Norwegian doctors were applying Danish knowledge and Danish research methods to their investigation, just as Norwegian veteran's organizations had used Denmark as a model for legislation, recognition, and financial compensation.[45]

At its inception in 1957, the doctor's commission investigated 300 people who had been selected through the Association of War Disabled, the organization that had taken the initiative to establish the commission in the first place. They were therefore not a random sample of the population of potential sufferers, as would have been preferable from a strictly scientific point of view. Compared to Danish investigations up to that time, which had focused mainly on wartime weight loss and post-war psychiatric problems, the Norwegian investigation could be very extensive. Notably, as Eitinger observed, an extensive physical and psychological investigation, in combination with a survey of their prewar health, showed that their problems did not stem from earlier psychiatric problems, an important point

43 Middelthon, 'Legen og invaliden'. In: Retterstøl, *'Og livet går videre...'*, 65.
44 '"Glemmer vi vår egen lidelse, høreer vi heller ikke andres"'.
45 Strøm, 'Purpose and scope of the investigation', 83-84.

from both the medical and the activist point of view. 'Taken jointly', he concluded as early as 1961, 'these results support the assumption that organic brain changes are basically responsible for the KZ syndrome.'[46]

A second doctors' commission began its work in 1966, again led by Axel Strøm, and with Leo Eitinger among its members. In a (semi-)random population of survivors, no less than 83% suffered late-onset consequences. In keeping with the tradition of Thygesen, Eitinger and Askevold identified two broad categories of problems, namely those with a somatic and those with a psychosomatic cause. The KZ syndrome, of course, was placed firmly in the former realm.[47]

Several member of the doctors' commission would continue to publish on the KZ syndrome, but no-one approached the subject with such zeal as Leo Eitinger. As early as 1964 he published a comparative study of former concentration camp inmates, and in 1971 a study on mortality and morbidity after extreme stress, in addition to many shorter papers and interviews. From 1966 he was head of the Oslo University Hospital psychiatric clinic, and later became Norway's first professor of catastrophe and disaster psychiatry. He pioneered the field of victimology and gained considerable international standing. Because of his activism, against racism and for human rights, he was not only a scientific heavyweight in his field, but also increasingly a public figure in Norway and the world. As Eitinger grew older, his status rose even further. In 1988 *Lege for Livet* (doctor for life) was published, an exceptionally saccharine hagiography. Since his death, a prize has been named after Eitinger and his wife Lisl, awarded for efforts for international human rights.[48]

For much of his career, Eitinger continued to emphasize the somatic nature of much of the late-onset problems that ex-inmates and others suffered. Initially, this emphasis on the physical causes of illness played a prominent role in the campaigns of the Association of War Disabled, who could claim that the KZ syndrome was no less real than an amputated leg. In the struggle for recognition, the perceived somatic nature of the KZ syndrome was a valuable asset. It fitted well, moreover, in the image of the masculine resistance hero that prevailed in the 1950's and 60's – much better, probably, than a purely psychological disease would have done.

The KZ syndrome and the realities of disease

The somatic nature of the KZ syndrome was emphasized and exploited by those seeking to emancipate sufferers of late-onset psychological illness. In Denmark, and later in Norway, this contributed to the early acceptance of such problems

46 Eitinger, 'Psychiatric post-conditions in former concentration camp inmates', 87.
47 Luihn, *Men krigen er jo slutt*, 94.
48 Consult: http://www.uio.no/om_uio/priser/eitinger/about.html.

as medically serious, as well as to claims for compensation and treatment. The emphasis on somatic causes, notably but not exclusively weight loss, also rigidly limited the number of people who could be diagnosed as having this particular type of ailment. Even if the second Norwegian doctors' commission had at least reported problems caused by psychological rather than physical stress, the KZ syndrome belonged squarely in the physical stress category. In other words, severe late-onset psychological disease had gained recognition and was an accepted diagnosis, but only insofar as it had somatic causes. While other problems were not denied, they did not enjoy the same status, a problem that was particularly pertinent in Norway, where causality between past experience and current disease had to be proven in a relatively skeptical environment.

The largest, and most prominent, group of people with serious complaints who fell outside the definition of the newly minted disease were the Danish and Norwegian *krigssejlere*, or 'war sailors'. From both Denmark and Norway, thousands of seamen had escaped to join the Allied war effort, 7-8,000 Danes and about 35,000 Norwegians. Their primary contribution had been to ferry Allied supplies across the sea, notably the Atlantic Ocean. Although their work was for the most part civilian in nature, at least insofar that they were not combatants, they were exposed to frequent and gruesome warfare, especially because German u-boats targeted convoys of ships delivering supplies and troops. From a modern perspective, frequent exposure to life-threatening danger over a period of years, combined with witnessing the destruction of other ships, often manned by friends and relatives, may seem an evident cause of psychiatric stress later on. This was not, however, evident at the time, and it took until the 1980's before the problems of the war sailors were fully recognized. However stressful, sleep-deprived and dangerous their wartime experience had been, they had neither gone hungry nor been systematically mistreated.

There were not only many more Norwegian than Danish war sailors, but they also appear, on average, to have been exposed to far more danger. A staggering 6,000 men died, against about a thousand Danes.[49] The war sailors did not, initially, enjoy the kind of medical attention that camp survivors did. In most cases, they could not initially be awarded war pensions, unless invalidity could be linked to physical injury. In Norway, with its tens of thousands of veteran war sailors, only a few hundred received a war pension until well into the 1960's. In part, this was the result of the particular type of danger to which the sailors had been exposed. Unlike the land war, where getting wounded was common, the war sailors very predominantly either died in a torpedo attack, or escaped physically unscathed. With a few exceptions, a sailor either drowned or did not.

49 Askevold, 'Krigsseilersyndromet'.

Another reason why the number of pensions awarded was very low, at least according to sailors and those who argued on their behalf, was that it was particularly difficult to obtain a civilian pension, and the contribution of the war sailors had been, officially at least, a civilian one. The reality, without doubt, was that many former sailors were in particularly bad shape, and that most of them did not receive compensation, in spite of their work during the war. In the course of the 1960's, however, the war sailors became a focal point of war memories. Especially author and journalist Per Hansson, who published *Hver tiende matte dø* (every tenth (man) had to die) in 1967, argued vehemently in favor of the forgotten sailors.[50]

The sailors for their part were not altogether unaware of their 'forgotten' status. Many who sought war pensions found themselves refused, while seeing the medical problems of many former war sailors escalate. It soon turned out that the sailors were not quite as forgotten as they may have seemed. In 1966, questions in parliament led to the establishment of the Fleischer committee, which was to investigate the possibility of separate pension arrangements for the sailors. A year later, the television program *Åpen post* brought further attention. That same year, *Krigsseilerforbundet*, the society of war sailors, was founded, and in 1968 the sailors were included in the *Tilleggslov*'s categories of 'special' war victims. With medical opinion on their side and considerable media exposure, the sailors had, belatedly, found recognition.[51]

But what were they suffering from? In 1973 Egede Nielsen published an account of his sailor patients' problems, which were remarkably similar to those of former KZ inmates.[52] In 1976, Finn Askevold published an outright comparison of KZ inmates and war sailors, and although the sailors did not suffer the high mortality of former inmates, he did not shy from the conclusion that: 'the purely clinical judgment is clearly that there exists a war sailors syndrome which appears to be identical to the KZ syndrome and which affects 90% of all war sailors to an invalidating degree.'[53] Although the suggestion of Askevold that the syndrome in question was one and the same, the term *Krigssejlersyndrom* lived on for at least another decade. By 1986, however, at a meeting in Copenhagen Paul Thygesen himself lamented the lack of attention paid to the plight of the sailors – an omission caused at least in part by the focus on somatic causes that stemmed from his own work of the 1940's.[54] The problem, however, had been mostly a Norwegian one, and more problems were to follow primarily in Norway. In Denmark, both

50 Hansson, *Hver tiende mann måtte dø*.
51 Luihn, *Men krigen er jo slutt*, 182.
52 Askevold, 'War sailor syndrome'.
53 Ibidem.
54 Sørensen et al., 'Krigssejlere 40 år efter'; Thygesen et al., 'Krigssejlernes skæbne'.

recognition and pensions had been doled out relatively liberally, within a relatively small, but certainly not rigid group of people. In Norway, however, it was to become, and to some extent remains, a battlefield in which recognition, ownership of the past and medical interpretations are hotly contested. The war sailors were not the only group that increasingly considered itself forgotten. Another challenge came from the north of the country.

During the German invasion, Norwegian military resistance in the south had crumbled relatively quickly. The troops in the south had, for the most part, been ill-equipped, often thrown together at random, under insufficient military leadership. They had been no match for the *Wehrmacht*. In the north, on the other hand, more experienced, better equipped and commanded troops awaited the Germans. Because of the war in Finland, Norway had mobilized troops months before to protect the northern border. In the high north of the country, these troops enjoyed a massive advantage thanks to their superior knowledge of, as well as experience in, the inhospitable arctic environment.[55]

In 1968, as mentioned, various groups of veterans who had fought in the south were included in the group of people who did not have to prove causality to obtain pensions, because the experience of chaotic warfare without proper supplies was considered particularly damaging. The veterans of the relatively successful northern campaign had mostly been excluded. In the best of times, northern Scandinavians have reservations against the much more densely populated and culturally dominant south, and the treatment of northern veterans was seen by many as blatant discrimination. The feeling of being discriminated as Northerners, and of 'being punished for competence' proved a potent recipe for resentment. During the late 1980's and early 1990's, northern veterans made sure their voice was heard.

The veterans of the Alta battalion, stationed in Finnmark, were particularly vocal about their grievances. They had fought much longer than southern veterans, they argued, under much harder circumstances, and many of them had later survived the winter of 1944-45 in the evacuated area. Psychiatric complaints were impossible to diagnose for want of a psychiatric infrastructure in the north. The tabloid newspaper VT eagerly published on the plight of the veterans. Eventually, the Norwegian government asked the long retired Eitinger to review the case of Alta battalion.

The 1998 report of the second Eitinger commission must have been a disappointment to the Northern veterans. A detailed study of both the epidemiology within the population of veterans, and the history of their wartime activities revealed, in the eyes of the commission at least, that the battalion should not be included among those for whom causality could be presumed. Neither the nature

55 The relevant part of the second Eitinger report is available at http://www.regjeringen.no/nb/dep/hod/dok/NOUer/1998/NOU-1998-12/9.html?id=375470.

of their wartime experiences, nor their health, when compared to a control group of Finnmark males of the same age, was deemed reason to extend the presumption principle to these men. This must have been a disappointment, but to the historian the second report is interesting for a different reason. Whereas the 1988 report mentions the existence of PTSD as a diagnosis 'highly similar to the KZ syndrome', in the 1998 report the old syndrome had disappeared altogether. Post DSMIV, the need for the term, and for a uniquely Scandinavian way of viewing late-onset psychological damage due to violent experiences, had disappeared.[56]

Treatment and outcomes

Judging by their paper heritage, Scandinavian organizations and scholars who studied and, to a degree, promoted the KZ syndrome and later PTSD, limited themselves in two ways. Firstly, they focused almost exclusively on those who had been on the resistance side during the war. Secondly, recognition of the debilitating effects of late-onset psychiatric damage was sought primarily as a means of ensuring the suffering heroes of the resistance received compensation, whereas treatment appears not to have been an initial priority. Insofar as the KZ syndrome was explicitly seen as a definitive neurological alteration, curing the disease seemed unlikely if not impossible.

Very little is known, as yet, about the treatment of sufferers of the KZ syndrome in Denmark. Because treatment, insofar as it existed, was primarily a matter for local medical practitioners, not a nationwide infrastructure specific to the treatment of KZ syndrome, little is documented. After the war, the Freedom Fund organized a few holiday trips for widows, to relieve their stress. After the first of these trips they were told to leave their children in Denmark, in order to ensure this end was met.[57] Other than relaxation and friendly advice, organizations like the Freedom Fund had little to offer in the way of treatment. Some patients are known to have visited psychiatrists and other doctors later in life, but little can be said about the kinds of measures they took, or did not take, when confronted with a war-traumatized patient.

A little more was done in, and hence is known about, Norway. Special centers for treatment, or rather relaxation, were founded specifically for veterans. The first and most famous of these, Bæreia, was established in 1959. At the occasion of its fifth anniversary, King Olav summed up the tasks of the centre:

56 Ibidem.

57 RA, *Frihedsfondens Arkiv*, Inv. No. 9, board meeting.

> 'Here [...] those who need it will find recreation. They will be among friends, and will hopefully be able to use all that has been made by man's hand, and find health improvement in the beautiful nature around the house.'[58]

As in the case of Danish widows, then, the emphasis was on relaxation rather than specific treatment. Given that little was known about how to treat victims, this was not as strange as it may seem now that psychiatric aid to the (potentially) traumatized is often standard.

Partly to develop such treatment, Norway established a chair of catastrophe psychiatry at the university of Oslo, initially occupied by Eitinger himself, and remained on the forefront of research into late-onset psychiatric problems. In Denmark, only the national centre for torture victims, about which more below, initially focused on problems encountered by foreign refugees, and thus became involved in the treatment of PTSD and related diseases via a more scenic route.

Eventually all heroes fall. One decade into the 21st century, veterans of the resistance are now mostly dead, or very old. In Denmark and Norway, their numbers have dwindled to at most a few thousand. Their erstwhile enemies, of course, are mostly dead too. Not that much acknowledgment had ever been forthcoming to them; although the KZ syndrome was explicitly considered a purely physical ailment, to be taken entirely seriously it had to be caused by specified heroic behavior, and joining the *Waffen SS* did not qualify

The somatic interpretation of trauma that long prevailed in both Denmark and Norway naturally focused purely on the people who had been personally exposed to the hardships that were believed to cause trauma. In practice, however, the KZ syndrome did turn out to be, to some extent, transferable. That is not to say, of course, that children and spouses were affected in the same way, but living or growing up with often depressed, frightened, alcoholic or violent parents proved more damaging than initially imagined – all the more so if it was combined with the social ostracism that came with a heritage of collaboration.

As heroes and villains alike started to die off in the later decades of the twentieth century, the second generation began to make itself heard. Among the initial groups were the Norwegian children of German fathers and sometimes mothers, among them the infamous *Lebensborn* children, who were left in Norway at the end of the war. The Norwegian state, it soon transpired, had treated these mostly very young children appallingly, even trying to open negotiations with Australia to have them deported en bloc to the other side of the world. (The Australians, although at the time keen to gather as much white human stock as possible, chose not to take up the offer.)[59]

58 Quoted in *Grini Posten. Organ for foreningen av politiske fanger 1940-45*, 16 (Februari 1964) 1.

59 Baard et al., *Fiendens barn?*, esp. 11.

Once in late adulthood, however, many of those who suffered, in orphanages and elsewhere, no longer accepted either their position or their past. Several groups sprang up, among them the ignominiously named *Rettferd for tapere* or 'Justice for Losers', founded in 1993. Since the mid 1990's, many of these once unwanted children have received compensation and apologies from the Norwegian state.[60]

They were not alone. In Denmark, children of German fathers likewise began to make themselves heard. They did so after a generation's worth of historical debunking, which had made the realities of *samarbejde* abundantly clear. Children of unknown German fathers began to demand co-operation from a stubbornly unwilling Danish state in identifying their fathers. Claus Bryld, professor of Modern history at Roskilde University, published the book *Hvilken Befrielse*, memoirs of his childhood as the son of a National Socialist collaborator, and the hypocrisy of Denmark in dealing with those it considered to have not so much collaborated, but collaborated a tad too much.[61] Even within the organizations that strive for recognition of those who had to grow up as children of perpetrators, mention of psychiatric illness remains relatively rare. In both Denmark and Norway, children who grew up in the chilly shadow of the war are angry, hurt and sometimes out for compensation, but they do not commonly consider themselves psychologically ill.

One of the first signs that this is changing is a recent (2008) book by Sven Arvid Birkeland, a Danish doctor who, after a career in surgery, worked as a researcher for the Danish Centre for Torture Victims. His book *Taget af Tyskere* (taken by the Germans) is based on interviews with surviving political prisoners, but also, and indeed primarily, the widows, children and even grandchildren of those who were involved in torture either as perpetrators or victims. By focusing to a considerable extent on psychological damage in the second and third generations, and by discussing the traumatic experiences on both sides of the conflict in the same book, he has broken taboos and, possibly, changed the understanding of the late after effects of World War II in Denmark. It also revealed, for the first time, that many of those traumatized either never sought or never received specialized treatment. The step from recognition to treatment was apparently not obvious to either the proponents of the KZ syndrome, nor to those who suffered from it.[62]

Conclusion

Neither Denmark nor Norway was looking for heroism as Europe descended into yet another war in 1939. Neither country had been involved in a major war in liv-

60 Ibidem; the website of *Stiftelsen Rettferd for Tapere* can be found at: http://www.taperne.no/.

61 Øland, *Horeunger og Helligdage*, 20-26; Bryld, *Hvilken befrielse*.

62 Birkeland, *Taget af Tyskerne*.

ing memory, and neither had a particularly developed martial culture. They had escaped World War I and did not regret having missed that opportunity to make their mark on the field of honor. In the end, however, the choice was not theirs, and operation Weserübung sucked them into World War II. While Denmark accepted the inevitable and meekly subjected itself to the Nazi empire, Norway unwillingly stumbled into a protracted war, and suffered through five years of oppression and bloodshed as a result.

In the euphoria of victory, and later as NATO members, both Norway and Denmark established a collective discourse of heroism to legitimize the post-war social order, to be taught to generations to come, and to be bombastically presented to the outside world. In Denmark this required successive governments to bows to the demands of the small, but unified resistance movement. That the resistance had been branded terrorists by the wartime political establishment only strengthened the bargaining position of the resistance. When it became evident that many veterans were struggling, it proved relatively easy to mobilize help. That the erstwhile resistance found its main representative in a professor of neurology, and counted several competent doctors among its ranks, provided fertile ground for the development of an entirely new diagnosis.

That the KZ syndrome came to be defined as a set of psychological symptoms stemming from somatic causes, was logical in the light of the experiences and early research of its intellectual father Thygesen. However, the somatic nature was to become a political asset as well. The presumed physical cause removed much of the stigma a psychological illness might have had. This was useful in Denmark, but little more than that. It was crucial in Norway.

Norway, which could build its martial self-image on a history of actual mass warfare, rather than a mostly imaginary image of mass resistance, was not nearly as hard pressed to placate its veterans. Neither would it have been altogether feasible to do so to the extent it had been done in Denmark. Norway had come out of World War II an impoverished country, and their veterans and victims potentially numbered in the hundreds of thousands. Although laws for compensation in case of invalidity were similar to those passed in Denmark, people suffering of late-onset psychological problems initially had little to expect from the Norwegian state.

However, the former camp inmates and resistance veterans in Norway did develop high aspirations. By pointing, firstly, to the vastly better treatment of resistance veterans in Denmark and, secondly, by emphasizing the somatic nature of late-onset psychiatric problems, they belatedly achieved the recognition they sought. To a degree, however, the Scandinavian interpretation of war trauma in its various guises became stifling later on, as in the case of the war sailors, when late-onset psychiatric problems had to be defined outside the established tradition of the KZ syndrome. And although this peculiarly Nordic syndrome is not included in manuals like DSM and its exclusively somatic (nutritional) causes have little empirical basis, to some extent it still lives on in both countries.[63]

63 Compare, for example, Birkeland, *Taget af Tyskerne*, 165.

PART II

A Comparative Approach

10 The Aftermath of World War II

A comparison

» *Annet Mooij*

The preceding nine chapters contain a wealth of information on eleven countries. Now it is time, here in part 2 of this book, to take stock. What conclusion can we draw based on the preceding studies? The answer to this question depends to a high degree on the selected points of comparison. Our decision in this respect was guided by the central subject of this book: the thinking about the psychic war consequences and the realization – or lack thereof – of war welfare policies in the decades following the war.

In order to be able to come to any conclusion, we will first address the differences and similarities in the memory cultures as they developed in the various countries. Our findings are in line with what we already know from existing literature. We nevertheless discuss them because this will also provide an outline of the political-historical background that can elucidate a number of other subjects, for instance the realization of legislation, and specifically the official tribute and financial compensation that were used to deal with the aftermath of World War II. Who was eligible for such compensation – and who was not – is then discussed in a paragraph on the different groups of war victims who made themselves heard in the various countries and who either were or were not recognized.

Chapter 11, *The Management of Victimhood. Long-term health damage from asthenia to PTSD*, explicitly addresses post-war thinking about the disruptive effect of the war on the psyche, the new terminology that was developed to discuss it – from KZ syndrome to PTSD – and the divergent popularity of the concept of trauma in relation to the aftermath of the war.

Culture of remembrance

How did people look back on the period 1940-1945 in post-war years? In this respect the most divergent European countries are remarkably similar. From Denmark to Poland, from Austria to the Netherlands – in every liberated and reconstructing nation the war years developed into an identical post-war myth. The pattern has been described before, the collective myths have been unraveled.[1] The first of these self-serving misrepresentations concerned the idea that the Germans and only the Germans were responsible for the horrors and barbarism of the war years. 'They' had to answer for these crimes; 'we' had had nothing whatsoever to do with it. As every national memory emphasized, the nation had fought back heroically on all fronts and the people had resisted the foreign occupation. Oppression and resistance – these were the key concepts used after the liberation to capture the meaning of the preceding years.

The resulting magnification and heroization of the resistance are a second recurring element in the post-war myth creation, first and foremost in countries whose status was not immediately clear after the war. Was Austria the first victim of Nazi politics or a nation of enthusiastic followers? Was Denmark a victim of Nazi expansion or a willing satellite state? What about Luxembourg and the collaboration of the Vichy regime? It was enormously important for all countries involved to end up on the right side of the line in 1945. In response, the cultivation of strong national memories centered around resistance and martyrdom everywhere. Austria successfully presented itself as the first victim of the Nazis; the resistance in Denmark, that had been considered criminal by the Danish authorities during the war, after the liberation was promoted to backbone of the nation. In Luxembourg almost the entire population had participated in the resistance, whereas in post-war France the Vichy regime was labeled an alien, externally enforced and imposed government.

So attention in this 'patriotic memories' phase (Lagrou) and in the early national commemorations focused on the former resistance and the political deportees who had fought against Nazism. However, this did not mean that these groups were also invested with any real political influence after the war. Quite the reverse: practically everywhere their political say in the reconstruction of their countries was curtailed very quickly despite promises to and hopes for the contrary. The speed and degree of this political elimination differed from country to country. On one end of the spectrum we find a country like Austria, where resistance and emigrés, despite their central position in the national memory, were rapidly marginalized, politically as well as from a societal point of view. Austria's new post-war elite was actually recruited from the circles of ex-Nazis. On the other end of the spectrum is Denmark, where the former resistance, marginal as it was during the German occupation, was an important and permanent political power factor in the post-war period and has remained so until today.

With the passage of time and as a result of the Cold War, the initial emphasis on anti-fascist militancy crumbled away in the West. In Eastern Europe, on the

1 Cf. Tony Judt in his essay 'The past is another country'; Lebow et al. (eds.), *The politics of memory*.

other hand, the battle against the fascists that the various peoples had fought side by side with the Soviet Union remained at the heart of the national memory. As long as the communists were in power there was no changing this. However, as the distance to the occupation grew, opportunities in the West for a critical review of the war years also increased. Looking back now we may conclude that in the long run the initially dominant representation, in which the 'national resistance' had stood firm against the German occupier, proved untenable everywhere and was exposed as a fraud. Instead, it was now emphasized that there had been more passivity and collaboration than active resistance. The largest Nazi crime, the persecution of the Jews, had not been one of the Germans alone. The local population, local authorities and public servants had often contributed actively.

In the background various factors played a role in this shift in perspective: societal processes (the critical questions asked by a new generation, the disrepute communism fell into in the whole Western world), international events (the Eichmann trial) and incidents and affairs at a national level (the 'Breda Three' in the Netherlands, the Waldheim Affair in Austria), or the release of films, television series and scientific studies (much talked-about books on Vichy-France by Robert Paxton and Henry Rousso; the work of Jan Blonski and Jan Gross in Poland). Events like these acted as catalysts at the national level and toppled the existing image.

This happened everywhere, but as the dates of these different events indicate: the pace at which the perception regarding the German occupation years shifted differed from country to country.[2] The Netherlands was quick off the mark in the 1970's, followed by France, whereas Austria had to wait for the Waldheim Affair (1986) before the flattering self-image as the first victim of the Nazis actually started to change. In Eastern Europe it took the revolution of 1989 for other views of the wartime years to break through and be discussed openly. Putting an exact date on it can be difficult, not only because not all countries have a clear tipping point, but also because the turnaround varied in terms of intensity. We also see changes in the national memories in Italy, Belgium and the Scandinavian countries, but their revision of the national past was less drastic than in the Netherlands, France and the former Eastern Bloc countries. It was more a shift of accent than a rift. In the Scandinavian countries the heroic self-image remained largely intact; the two relatively weak states in our collection, Italy and Belgium, were least able to integrate the diversity of experiences and memories into one coordinated, national memory after the war. The divided and fragmented culture

2 This is in line with the conclusions Lebow et al. draw in *The politics of memory in Postwar Europe*: 'All of the case studies in this volume point to the decade and a half between the late 1960's and the mid-1980's as the period in which the most profound changes in the politics of memory took place in each of the nations observed.' (p. 296).

of remembrance that emerged in these countries subsequently did not lend itself to a rigorous change in perspective.

Although the various national 'patriotic memories' crumbled at different paces and intensities, the outcome was more or less the same everywhere. The growing distance to the wartime years enabled a more critical self-reflection, which in turn meant more attention for the blots on the national escutcheon, for collaboration, silent cooperation, complicity of the authorities and the own population in German crimes. New research led to the recognition of national failure and national responsibilities, although the official expression of this recognition often was a long time coming. For example: it was not until 1995 that the French president Chirac officially acknowledged the accountability of the Vichy regime for the persecution of the Jews.

A second outcome of the shift in perspective was that the Holocaust became the central aspect of World War II. From the 1970's onwards the national memories of the war are centred around the persecution and extermination of the Jews in all Western countries, including West Germany. Instead of Dachau, Auschwitz now became the symbol par excellence of the Nazi crimes. This means that instead of the hero of the resistance or the former political prisoner, the prototype of the Nazi-victim is now the persecuted Jew. What sets him apart is not his militancy, his patriotism, or his political merit, but rather his innocence.[3] Only in Eastern Europe did all attention remain focused on the 'anti-fascist combatants' until 1989; Jews were not viewed or recognized as a specific victim category. With the fall of communism there was room for this recognition for the first time, even though they immediately had to share it with other groups that could now be discussed openly for the first time, in particular the victims of Stalinist terror.

A final aspect of the change concerns the growing acknowledgement of the lasting suffering of war victims, one element of which was the increasing susceptibility to psychic consequences of the war. The degree to which this took place varies between countries – the subject of this book – but all countries have more attention for these aspects some fifty years after the liberation than in the first post-war decades. On the whole we see an increasing compassion for the victims of the war.

The transformation of the culture of remembrance was accompanied by a demythologization of the national wartime past. The new perspective undoubtedly provides a more realistic view of events and a more realistic response to the question how these events could have happened. However, this does not alter the fact that the more recent notions are also amenable to change and improvement. Up to this day they are continually being refined and added to, based on new research.

3 Cf. Ludi, 'Who is a Nazi victim?'.

Laws

One of the many tasks waiting after 1945, was that all countries involved had to explain the catastrophe of the previous years. The fact that crimes had been committed, that unacceptable injustices had taken place, but also the fact that there had been people who in difficult and dangerous circumstances had acted with exceptional courage, had to be acknowledged in some way. This need was met in various ways in the post-war years. We can distinguish four types of satisfaction:

- legal, in the shape of post-war purges in which collaborators and profiteers were dealt with. The continuing prosecution and adjudication of war criminals also comes under this category;
- scientific, in the shape of research and historiography in which the historical truth is done the maximum justice possible;
- moral, consisting of medals, Resistance Crosses and other decorations, or in the form of special privileges, such as free travel or medical care;
- financial, in the shape of reparation payments and compensation, pensions and benefits.

The weight of these different types of satisfaction varies, both per country and over time. In general one can say that as more time passes after the war, financial compensation becomes increasingly important. Perhaps also because over the years the other types have more or less reached the limits of their effectiveness. There are few options left to express residual feelings of discontent and not being appreciated, other than in the shape of financial claims, and money is really the only possible remaining type of compensation.

We will not address the path of legal satisfaction here; many books have been written on the subject. The second type, that uses scientific research, has played a role in the way in which all the countries coped with the war years, although the former Eastern Bloc countries had to wait until after 1989. In the context of this book Denmark and Norway are particularly interesting, not because of their exceptional historiography, but because of the early scientific research in these countries in a completely different field, i.e. into the health of former concentration camp prisoners. This scientific attention was also a form of recognition that we will return to in the next chapter.

In this paragraph we address the latter two types of satisfaction, moral and financial, as laid down in (national) statutory schemes. It is not easy to bring order here; there is very little uniformity on either front.

As far as moral recognition and rewarding of heroism and courage is concerned, the different countries are all across the spectrum. On one, extremely parsimonious end is the Netherlands, where after the war prominent groups in the resistance announced it was not necessary to award separate decorations to people who had been in the resistance. The government was more than happy to agree; it was also government policy to avoid as much as possible distinguishing between groups and recognizing special merits. Moreover, in this way the need to decorate communists was also avoided. This policy was maintained for decades: a resistance medal was only introduced in 1980. Other countries, on the other hand, chose to put their heroes in the limelight after the war and to bestow symbolic honors on them. In Belgium the moral recognition took the shape of a many-branched system of 'statutes'; France and Luxembourg are strong on awarding Resistance Crosses, medals and honorary titles like 'Mort pour la Patrie'. Former combatants received a special card that entitled them to, for example, free travel. In Denmark also, the people who had participated in resistance activities after the war were very publicly endowed with prestige and authority. Up to this day there are special provisions for their descendants, such as scholarships and student housing. Honoring anti-fascist heroes became customary also in the communist regimes. In Poland they created the status of 'combatant'.

Different countries in this way developed forms of moral tribute, but the respective backgrounds varied. Countries like France and Belgium already had a strong veterans culture and a tradition of military honors and hero worship. For the design of these tributes they could fall back on World War I. The fact that the Netherlands lacked this prior experience no doubt contributed to the absence of a similar system of provisions in this country after World War II. In Denmark opportunistic motives appear to have played an important part in the post-war heroization of the resistance, whereas in Poland the communist ideology, with its strong emphasis on anti-fascist battle, was the driving force behind the hero worship.

The pendant of hero worship and rewarding courage is found in the restitution for being victimized. Financial schemes for war victims in the shape of compensation, pensions and benefits were realized in all countries, but also in this respect there is an almost chaotic diversity. This is best described based on the following aspects.

1 *The target groups of the schemes* — The laws in the different countries offer financial compensation for health damage and disablement caused in or due to the war. But who were eligible for this compensation? This question was answered in different ways in different countries. The victims themselves, or also the surviving relatives of perished soldiers and resistance fighters? Military victims or civilian victims? Victims of acts of war or victims of persecution and captivity? Political persecutees and prisoners or also those persecuted for other (racial, religious) reasons? The people who had committed active resistance or the 'passive' victims also? These considerations had a different outcome in every country.

2 *The diversity of the arrangements* — Different victim categories were eligible for compensation in every country. Not one country created one single scheme to cover all those different groups, although France came close. On the other end of the spectrum are the Netherlands, where over the years a separate scheme was created for every newly recognized group, and Belgium, with its by now completely nontransparent jumble of moral and financial recognition schemes.

3 *The criterion for awarding a pension* — In Belgium and France pensions were paid out on the basis of the applicant's degree of invalidity, as expressed in a percentage. The benefit was a fixed sum. In the majority of the other countries pensions were awarded on the basis of loss of income or loss of earning capacity, also expressed in a percentage. In this case the sum varied, depending on the salary to be made up. At some point Norway started using a third criterion, namely the degree of war stress experienced by the applicant.

4 *Additional requirements* — All countries had additional requirements that applicants had to meet. Sometimes it was not enough to be a resident of a particular country in order to qualify, the applicant also had to have citizenship of the country in question. This meant that refugees, stateless individuals and foreign nationals were excluded. The consequences could be considerable. For example: in pre-war Belgium some 95 per cent of the Jewish population did not have the Belgian nationality. After the war the law did not cover many of the Jewish survivors because Belgian citizenship was a precondition. Some countries also had requirements with regard to the severity of the health complaints. A particular degree of invalidity or a minimal loss of earning capacity was a precondition in order to qualify for a benefit. Each additional requirement excluded particular groups. The requirement, for example, that the applicant must have behaved 'with dignity' during the war, excluded black marketeers and criminals. Explicit exclusions also occurred. In France labor conscripts were not included in the law, in Poland 'enemies of communism and the Soviet Union' could not qualify, and in West Germany the communists were excluded.

Almost universal was the requirement of medical causality. If the applicant wanted to qualify for a pension, he had to demonstrate a causal link between his war experiences and his later health complaints. In every country that had this rule, the system caused problems, problems that increased as time passed. Someone who returned from the camps with TB would not have too much trouble establishing that his illness started in and because of captivity. But what about a former deportee who developed high blood pressure, cardiac complaints or a gastric ulcer? His case would require pulling out all the medical stops, not to mention the case of the resistance member who developed a depression thirty years after the war ended. The international conferences about the problems surrounding medical causality were organized for good reason.

The issue of medical causality contributed to the medical profession in all countries being assigned a key role in the pension or benefit award procedures. In Denmark the problem of the causality requirement was resolved by making clever use of this role. There the medical examiners were recruited exclusively from their own resistance circles, which ensured that applications were dealt with very leniently. Elsewhere the requirement of medical causality was mostly dropped for particular groups sooner or later, and the burden of proof was reversed: under certain conditions (such as minimum duration of imprisonment and minimum severity of the invalidity) it was simply assumed that the later health complaints were a consequence of war experiences, unless it could be demonstrated that this was *not* the case. France did away with the medical causality clause for all groups of deportees as early as 1953 (it had never applied for political prisoners); from 1965 Germany knew the 'concentration camp assumption'; Norway in 1968 decided to assume causality in specific groups, the Netherlands followed in 1971.

As the various countries made different decisions on all of these issues, there is a large variation in national laws; in addition most of the schemes were changed, modified or expanded over time. After a while particular conditions were liberalized, requirements were dropped, new groups were admitted or the burden of proof was reversed. The considerable variation that resulted does not mean, however, that the laws show no constants or similarities at all. First of all, each of the countries had complicated laws and accompanying assessment procedures and this resulted in execution problems everywhere. Sluggishness and bureaucracy were the most frequent complaints, and sometimes also the lack of sympathy for the applicants. In Austria this even led to the outrageous situation of former Nazis being appointed as medical examiners for the war laws. Only in Denmark everything went smoothly; the whole procedure was placed in the hands of the former resistance and they arranged things as they saw fit. Awarding pensions went so smoothly, that even the shortage problem was barely relevant. In all other countries the recognized hero or victim status was a scarce commodity, and one with considerable symbolic overtones. As time passed these overtones grew stronger rather than weaker. This made and makes the awarding of compensations and pensions not only complex, but also highly sensitive.

In addition to this type of problem we can identify a second constant. It is not found in the content of the laws, but in the pace of their realization: quicker for one group than for the other. A clear pattern is visible here. The first war laws in all but one of the German-occupied countries were intended to meet the needs of the former resistance (in particular those whose patriotism had led them to engage in active resistance, and former political prisoners or political deportees) and related categories (widows and children). France was the exception. In 1947 this country introduced a twofold pension law, one for the former resistance and at the same time one for all other groups of deportees. Although there is no difference in pace here, the post-war rhetoric in France also focused totally on the active resistance members and heroes of the nation. Former resistance fighters were endowed with additional honors and furthermore received preferential treatment. For example, from the start their medical complaints were attributed to the war unless there was proof to the contrary. For the other deportees the requirement of medical causality remained in force until 1953. At a later stage other countries (Belgium, Austria, Italy, Norway) similarly started to show favor to active resistance fighters and former political prisoners above other groups.

And so the laws for the former (active) resistance were realized earlier and they were generally better, i.e. more accessible and more favorable for those they covered. This state of affairs implies that other groups had to do without legislation for the time being. This was true first of all for the victims of persecution (Jews, Sinti and Roma, Jehovah's witnesses, homosexuals), but also for other groups, such as prisoners of war, persons who had been in hiding, displaced persons, forced laborers and the victims of criminal medical practices. They were excluded from the law because they did not belong to the category of active fighters against fascism. In particular the lack of legal recognition of the exceptional fate of the Jews is not only a painful, but also a very remarkable fact. It is a general pattern rather than an incident that the Jewish victims of the war became the subject of state care only at a relatively stage. How long the schemes were in the making differed from country to country. In Italy, for example, it took until 1955 (although the restrictive application of the law that was passed then means that 1980 or even 2003 are more realistic dates), in Norway until 1968, in the Netherlands it was 1973, in Poland 2002, and in Belgium 2003.

This failure to realize arrangements for Jewish victims is not only a consequence of the initial dominance of the resistance in the post-war nation building. It was also the result of the fact that it was difficult for the different countries to fit the systematic persecution and murder of the Jews into their traditional frame of reference for war, i.e. as a conflict between national states. Modern nation states define themselves in terms of citizenship rather than ethnicity. This made it difficult for them after the war to deal with persecution and victimhood on the basis of characteristics unrelated to citizenship or nationality. The resulting neglect of the 'own' Jewish war victims, which was also reflected in the legislation, applied even more to the (sometimes large) majority of the Jewish section of the population that did not have the nationality of the country in question.

To be able to understand the post-war developments regarding the war laws it is important to look in more detail at the question of which forces influenced the realization of these laws. We can distinguish three forces. The most important one, particularly in the first years after the war, was the national political agenda. Not the extent of the inflicted suffering or the degree of the inventoried needs determined which groups were eligible for financial support first, but rather the politically felt need for national rehabilitation. The perception and evaluation of the past years was colored by the need to boost the damaged national sense of self. Just as this need resulted in the culture of remembrance being dominated by patriotism and antifascist militancy, so the first war laws were almost without exception intended for the groups that were linked to those qualities: soldiers who had defended the country, active resistance members and political persecutees.

Legislation is an instrument for inclusion and exclusion. Intentionally or unintentionally the war laws answered the question: who is to be rewarded? In every country the people to be rewarded were initially those who had distinguished themselves on the basis of personal merit: those who had committed acts of resistance against the Germans, the fighters against national socialism and *not* the 'passive' victims of genocide and persecution. This changed after it began to sink in in most countries that their war history was more complex than the official narrative alleged. The resulting shift in focus from active resistance fighter to victim, which became apparent in the culture of remembrance, also had repercussions for the legislation. Sooner or later there was a second round in which the (new) compassion for the victims of persecution was expressed.

This was the pattern in the occupied countries. Were there any countries with a different political agenda? Yes there were. Switzerland, for example, did not have a self-image of national and heroic resistance, but one of strict neutrality. Here the greatest political virtue after the war was not militancy and an anti-German outlook, but rather an attitude of neutrality and passivity. The compensation laws that were introduced in 1957 for Swiss war victims rewarded mainly individuals who had taken no part and had avoided any and all political stand. Applicants who had committed active resistance, been in political opposition, had helped fugitive Jews and other people on the run – they were penalized because they were held partially responsible for their situation: 'they all faced severe cuts in their benefits for alleged self-inflicted victimization.'[4]

West Germany is also unique. It is the only country that after the war could not claim to have been victimized by the Nazis and in the period of reconstruction had to account for its perpetratorhood. Just as the countries that had been the victim of the Nazi-expansion focused on their heroes in their commemorations and post-war laws, so West Germany was more or less compelled from the start to concentrate on the Nazi victims and take responsibility as a state for the Nazi

4 Ludi, 'Who is a Nazi victim?', 17.

crimes. Apart from the (military and civilian) victims of acts of war, the laws in post-war West Germany also focused on the victims of persecution. Contrary to the situation in many other countries, in West Germany Jewish victims from the start were recognized as persecution victims, more so than the political persecutees. This was the result of the dynamic between the two Germanies, which made it impossible to recognize and openly pay tribute to political, i.e. communist persecutees in West Germany at an early stage.

In East Germany the situation developed very differently. The communist regime did not acknowledge any responsibility for the German Nazi crimes and focused only on heroes, not on victims. There was no room for Jewish victims as a separate category in the communist ideology, not only concretely but on principle. This ideology rejected the difference between Jews and non-Jews, because there was no such dichotomy in the working classes. There were fascists and antifascists and the victims of Nazism had been antifascist fighters, even if they had been persecuted for completely different reasons. So the argument was a different one than in the West, but in terms of the outcome – the disregard for the fate of the Jews – East Germany was more like the former occupied Western European countries than West Germany.

A second driving force behind the realization or modification of war laws was international pressure. The German reparation payments to Israel and the relaxation of the German laws for Nazi victims were realized under pressure from the US and Israel. In Austria something was done for the Jewish survivors in 1949; not voluntarily, but only after considerable pressure from the US and Jewish-American organizations. More indirectly the mere existence of reparation payments and financial compensation in one country meant pressure on the other. Once such schemes were in operation they set a standard for other countries to emulate and victim groups could refer to them in their claims. This was very clearly the case for the Norwegian war victims, who conducted their battle for more and better continuously referring to the more favorable schemes in neighboring Denmark. Financial compensation schemes have become an international language, the lingua franca of coming to terms with the war. They provide a model for dealing with a controversial past and increasingly are the vehicle used to redeem the suffering of the war.

Thirdly the lobbies of interest and victim groups have influenced the realization of war laws and provisions. The scale of this influence depended not only on the power of the pressure group – like the former resistance in Denmark, the political deportees in France and Belgium, the former Nazis in Austria – but also on the responsiveness of the state in question to the pressure groups. In general this responsiveness increased in post-war years, but it varied from country to country, depending on their financial scope (increased across all of Western Europe), the degree to which they recognized their own failure and accountability, and the inclination towards a national awareness of guilt. The latter are strongly developed in, for example, the Netherlands, where pressure groups played an important role. Countries like East Germany and Poland remained (at least until 1989) completely immune to them.

Victim categories

In the previous paragraph on legislation we have already touched upon victim groups, the fact that they were recognized in phases, and their interrelatedness. However, some additional observations are in order.

First of all: the answer to the question which victim categories a particular country recognized after the war does not follow automatically from that country's war history. Obviously this is not a universal truth, because the recognition of victim categories was also not based on pure coincidence or total arbitrariness. After the war there were real differences between the various countries in terms of presence and size of victim groups. Not every country had all groups and not all groups had the same numerical weight in all countries. After the war France had to contend with a huge group of returning prisoners of war; in Norway the war sailors were a separate category; annexed Luxembourg had a large group of former *Wehrmacht* conscripts; and the Danish Jews had escaped to Sweden in time, so Denmark did not have a group of returned deported Jews after the war.

These differences form the framework. Within it the recognition of specific victim groups is a question of political logic rather than a historical pattern. This recognition retroactively dictates how the national wartime past should be viewed. In other words: this recognition reveals how the countries want to see it. The fact that the former resistance was revered in post-war Denmark has nothing to do with the significance of the resistance during the occupation; it has everything to do with the reputation the country wanted to build after the war. The provisions for *Pupilles de la Nation* (war orphans) in Luxembourg are not the result of the enormous need in this group; they underline the image of Luxembourg as a nation of collective resistance, suffering and solidarity. There was little logic in the fact that in 1945 Austria was the first country to arrange a pension scheme for *Wehrmacht* and *Waffen ss* veterans and not for the Nazi victims. Like the decision in favor of other victim groups in other countries, this was a purely political choice.

The high degree to which recognition of particular victim groups was a political issue is also clearly illustrated by the example of Poland. As an immediate result of changes in the political climate the group of relatives of fallen soldiers, resistance and guerrilla fighters who qualified for recognition decreased and increased several times. As the ideological reins were tightened in 1948 the group of recognized victims decreased to the next of kin of fighters who had fallen defending the 'people's government', i.e. the Soviet regime. Fallen Roman Catholics, liberals, nationalists no longer counted. The liberalization after 1956 expanded the criteria for admission to the victim status again. But even then only the victims of the official 'enemy' were recognized. This enemy was Nazi Germany. Victims of the invasion of the Soviet Union, or of the Stalinist reign of terror did not exist. This did not change until 1989.

Secondly: there are hierarchical differences between victim groups. These were clearly reflected in the pace of introduction and the content of the pension and benefit schemes. 'Passive' victimhood, especially of the Jewish survivors, initially did not give access to these schemes, as it had a lowly status that was associated with a lack of heroism. This passive victimhood did not evoke feelings of pride and militancy, but rather of weakness and failure. In the decades following the war a shift, and in some cases even a reversal, has occurred in the relation between 'active' and 'passive' victimhood and in the hierarchy between the groups in the two categories. The increased status of 'the victim', and not only in relation to the war, was most pronounced in the Netherlands. Here victimhood developed into a new source of standing and public respect.

The hierarchical differences between the victim groups are closely related to the recurring mutual rivalries we observe everywhere. No country has escaped the phenomenon of the mutual comparison of the various categories of war victims. Who suffered most? Who receives most recognition? Who is given preferential treatment? Victim groups define their memory and experiences, and therefore themselves, in mutual comparisons – a conclusion Lagrou formulated as 'the inescapable referential character of group memories'.[5] The examples are legion. In Poland, Christians and Jews are engaged in a competition about the question who has suffered most; in Austria there is a constant rivalry between former Nazis and Nazi victims; in Belgium every arrangement for one group has to be compensated with a measure for the other; in Luxembourg the former resistance and the groups of conscripted ex-*Wehrmacht* soldiers have been opposing each other ever since the liberation; in France there is rivalry between resistance and persecutees, between deportees and prisoners of war, and between prisoners of war and forced laborers; in the Netherlands both the former resistance and the former Dutch East Indies community who lived through the Japanese camps are in competition with the Jewish war survivors; and in Germany the victims of communism have felt discriminated against in their struggle to be recognized as victims of National Socialism since the unification.

5 Lagrou, *The legacy*, 301.

In addition these sometimes intense rivalries in the area of identity politics were often complicated by international and party political conflicts in the past decades. In the 1950's and 60's the Cold War in some places intensified the division in the antifascist camp. Denmark was the only country where the former resistance managed to keep international politics out of the discussion and did not disintegrate into opposing communist and non-communist factions. Party political division also made itself felt at the national level, especially in Italy and in Belgium, where the language conflict also played a role. These countries clearly show how political division gets in the way of the development of an integrated national memory. It is no coincidence that these two countries up to this very day have a very fragmented culture of remembrance, in which different memory lines exist simultaneously and group experiences are often barely known outside their own circle.

Thirdly: over the course of time the number of victim groups striving for recognition increases in all of the studied countries. The point here is not whether this is a matter of neutralizing actual discrimination or the result of group dynamics and mutual comparison. The validity of claims is not the issue, only the finding that they have increased over time in all countries. Persecuted minorities (Jehovah's witnesses, homosexuals), persons in hiding, hidden children, civilian victims, former forced laborers, *Wehrmacht* deserters, second generation victims, children of collaborating parents – all of these groups came forward in the second, third or fourth instance. The idea that some twenty years after the liberation the file on World War II could be closed has proved a gross miscalculation.

A recent large addition took place after 1989, when, with the collapse of communism, a large number of taboos on the war history evaporated in one fell swoop and it was possible for the first time to give attention to groups that could never be discussed freely under communism. These were not only the survivors of the Soviet camps and other victims of communism, but also, for example, the ranks of nationalist, religious, Jewish or liberal anti-German resistance, the victims of forced emigration or the persecuted who now for the first time managed to throw off the antifascist yoke that was imposed upon them. A former Auschwitz prisoner could now be a Jewish survivor instead of a Polish anti-fascist.

The emergence of this type of 'new', or late, victim group is inevitably accompanied by a request for recognition. Part of the response consists of new research and new historiography that sheds light on the long obscured history of Eastern Europe, on previously concealed types of resistance and victimhood on the one hand, but just as much on formerly unmentionable forms of collaboration and complicity of the nations' own populations on the other. However, there was also the call for moral and financial compensation and, decades after the liberation, the question was still, or again, whether it was necessary to create new legislation or adapt existing arrangements.

The emergence of new victim groups was not limited to the former Eastern Bloc. Nor did new groups always originate in World War II. In the post-war period many other groups have emerged – participants in new wars, in Vietnam, Algeria or the Gulf, the veterans of peace missions, victims of kidnapping, torture or sexual violence – whose victimhood is not rooted in the war, but cannot be separated from the aftermath of war, as they clearly emulate the model of the (Jewish) war victim in terms of moral and financial claims and the recognition of psychic suffering. The Holocaust in this sense has become a paradigm, a model used by other victim groups as a basis to define their experiences and demands. This development will be discussed in more detail in the next chapter.

11 The Management of Victimhood

Long term health damage from asthenia to PTSD[1]

» *Jolande Withuis*

As we outlined in the introduction of this book: the phenomenon that soldiers did not recover even though their wounds had long healed, led to intensive debates within the field of psychiatry after World War I. The key question of this debate was always whether it was possible that a mentally healthy adult could be permanently affected by an external cause without organic consequences, so based exclusively on psychological pressure.

On the eve of World War II, neurologists and psychiatrists were generally of the opinion that a psychic disorder was the expression of a disturbance in the structure or functioning of the brain. The disorder was thought to have an organic basis, even if these defects usually proved untraceable in the brain. Physicians generally interpreted difficult to explain complaints as 'pension neurosis', 'secondary gain' or malingering, or as the result of some type of predisposition, so-called pre-morbidity. Psychoanalysts were less organically oriented in their thinking, but they too thought that a trauma could not cause permanent psychic damage in a mentally healthy adult. For this to happen the patient must have suffered a prior childhood trauma

Today physicians and the public at large in most Western countries do not question that people can be 'traumatized'. The notion that intensely emotional, negative experiences can, or even: will, produce permanent damage to our physical and mental health is so matter-of-course it is almost a fact of nature.

The aftermath of World War II has played a major role in this shift in thinking. In this chapter we will examine the thinking about the possible consequences of the war for the health of the survivors since Germany was defeated; we will trace via which routes new insights and experiences were disseminated, and how pace and approach differed between the countries studied here.

1 Where I derive information from the previous chapters on the eleven nations, the author's name is not always repeated for the sake of readability.

The early post-war years, 1945-1950

It has often been stated that there has been a 'conspiracy of silence' regarding the war and especially regarding the possible psychic consequences of the war since the liberation. This is a myth. In the countries that were occupied or from which people were deported, physicians often expressed concerns about the health prospects of the war victims immediately after, and sometimes even before the liberation. These were frequently physicians who had personally experienced the concentration camp system. The main object of their concerns were therefore the surviving *prisoners*, who had been exposed for years to starvation, cold, abuse, poor sanitary conditions, and exhaustion due to heavy and unhealthy labor, and in addition had often contracted wound infections or infectious diseases like typhus or dysentery.

Although the medical concerns initially focused first of all on the physical health of those who had returned, there was also concern about possible psychological consequences. An Italian psychiatrist, for example, who had paid for his resistance with imprisonment in Mauthausen concentration camp, in 1947 impressed upon his colleagues that he had seen people without any predisposition to mental illness develop psychiatric symptoms. With this observation he took a stand against the prevailing scientific conviction in Italy that suffering from mental disease should be explained either by predisposition or as a 'pension neurosis'.

Immediately after their return several physicians in Austria who had survived a concentration camp pointed out the possible consequences of these camps. Psychotherapist Victor Frankl, whose 1947 autobiography contained a chapter on the psychology of ex-prisoners, became famous. Later on in this chapter we will meet physician Ella Lingens, who ended up in Auschwitz for helping Jews, and who also at an early stage pointed out the consequences of imprisonment in the camps. In general, however, Austrian attention for the psychic consequences of the war was considerably more limited than after World War I.

In the Netherlands in those first post-war year disability pensions were paid out mainly to disabled persons and people with somatic diseases such as tuberculosis, but there were also physicians who immediately upon their return wrote about the psychological impact of the concentration camp. One of them suggested that the phenomenon of 'shell shock' should perhaps also be declared applicable to situations in which people perhaps did not experience any direct, classic acts of war, but had lived under an intensive threat of death for a prolonged period of time.

These messages came mainly from Jewish physicians. Their warnings and insights were definitely heard, but were lost in the tendency to declare the war a thing of the past and take up normal life again as soon as possible. Resistance circles and especially the resistance elite, which was made up predominantly of people who had not been imprisoned, were afraid of stimulating unrest and discontent. Nevertheless, former political prisoners were certainly aware that sometimes people were unable to overcome their horrific experiences. Those who had trouble functioning again in job and family sometimes got support, albeit awkwardly, from fellow prisoners who were more successful in adapting to normality. At the end of 1945 former Ravensbrück inmates used a questionnaire to interview each other about their health. Which turned out to be reasonable. The women mostly just wanted to go back to work.[2]

In France a different tone prevailed. Returnees, especially in comparison with the Netherlands, were surrounded with care and tribute, the leaders in the resistance were less imperious towards the rank and file, and also more self-confident when it came to demanding and reflecting on medical care. The Dutch concern that the former fighters would fall prey to pension neurosis and maladjustment was absent here. Whereas in the Netherlands the organizations of the former resistance and ex-prisoners acted mainly in a tempering manner, in France they took on the role of advocates.

Immediately after the war French medical magazines were filled with articles on the precarious health status of former deportees and soon dissertations appeared on this subject, generally also written by physicians who had been imprisoned themselves. The conditions of the returnees were given a true medical label already at an early stage: *Pathologie des Déportés*, a label that included the honorary title 'deportees', which in France was generally used for Jewish as well as ex-political prisoners.

One of the great men behind this quick recognition was internist and former Buchenwald inmate Charles Richet, a communist. The deportation pathology he defined comprised a broad spectrum of complaints, including mental and 'neuropsychiatric' disorders. It implied a general deterioration of health, which could last for some time and sometimes had a delayed onset.

Richet was an influential man. He held the position of professor at the medical faculty of Paris, which his father and grandfather had also held; his father was awarded the Nobel prize in 1913. Richet managed to have the French war pension laws state that former prisoners were not obliged to prove a causal link between their (possible) poor health and their wartime past. This link was simply assumed. French ex-prisoners were therefore less dependent on the understanding and cooperation of their physicians than their counterparts in many other countries. Also, because their physicians were convinced at an early stage of the existence of possible war diseases, French patients were less at risk of being humiliated. Specific research into the psychic consequences of the imprisonment, including intrusive traumatic memories, was conducted immediately after the war by French

2 Withuis, *Na het kamp*, 100-107.

psychiatrist René Targowla. It was a continuation of his research following World War I, when he studied, among other things, the effect of bombardments on the nervous system.

Targowla sought the explanation for what he referred to as the *asthénie psychique des déportés* not in psychological processes, but in an organic injury to the central nervous system. The mental strength of the prisoners was compromised by a combination of prolonged stress and traumatic experiences, and organic factors such as starvation, infections, fever, exhaustion, and injuries to the head. According to him the severity of the diseases was commensurate with the length of captivity. With this observation Targowla aspired to provide an objective measure for the camp damage, which was appealing not only from a scientific perspective but also in view of medical examinations and disability percentages.

Targowla's 'asthenia' could also have served as a label for the clinical syndrome that Danish physicians found in Danish former prisoners shortly after the war. Asthenia means lack of strength. The term is incorporated in the diagnoses of neurasthenia and psychasthenia, which around 1900 were used to classify symptoms like diminution of psychic energy, fatigue, apathy, lack of concentration and heart palpitations.

In Denmark also, the initiative for studying the health status of camp survivors was taken by a former prisoner: Paul Thygesen, who as a member of the resistance had been imprisoned in Neuengamme concentration camp where he had treated fellow inmates. Apart from a range of somatic conditions Thygesen and his fellow researchers found considerable mental problems in no less than three quarters of the surviving inmates, which they divided into six categories: 1. curtailment and brutalization of emotional and moral outlook; 2. impairment of memory; 3. diminished powers of spontaneous reaction; 4. a tendency to irritability and emotional instability; 5. absence of libido; 6. dullness and apathy.

Like Targowla, Thygesen interpreted these mental complaints as the result of the physical illnesses and hardships the inmates had endured. This could be a disease like diphtheria, which was very common in the camps, but the later lack of life energy, he thought, was caused above all by starvation and malnutrition.

The important and early Scandinavian contribution to the debate on the consequences of war explains the ample attention that initially went to the significance of malnutrition in the development of later complaints. The Norwegian Eitinger, for example, in the wake of Thygesen and his colleagues, thought he could find an objective measure for the endured suffering and the risk of permanent damage in the number of kilos of body weight lost. In Germany starvation was also initially seen as the culprit. However, this approach proved untenable. People who had not been starved developed the same complaints after a while.

The Polish doctors who immediately after the war conducted research among former inmates in large part had also been prisoners themselves, and they too studied the effects of starvation in the camps and in the Warsaw Ghetto. Furthermore, the effects of medical experiments on Ravensbrück inmates were studied, and psychological research into war consequences was initiated as early as 1947. *Undzere Kinder*, about Polish-Jewish orphans after the shoah, is an amazing film from 1948. This Yiddish-spoken Polish film, 'docudrama' and comedy at the same time, addresses the question whether it would be better for the children to be silent or to talk about their horrific memories and losses. The message of the film is that they should talk, but in reality even the children acting in the film never spoke to each other about their experiences during the war.[3] All of these projects met a premature end around 1950 under the political pressure of resurgent Stalinism.

To our knowledge, in the period immediately after the war no specific medical studies were conducted among camp survivors in the other countries under investigation: Belgium, Luxembourg, Italy, Norway, and East and West Germany. However, they did exchange data and insights with the French and the Danes. Danish findings, for example, quickly became a source of inspiration for victims and physicians in much harder hit Norway, and the Belgians were inspired by their French colleagues to make one notable exception in the Belgian compensation system.

This system, in which mental diseases were not eligible for compensation, was influenced strongly by the ideas of the respected Belgian physician/labor expert Marcel Moreau. Moreau had ample experience with legal procedures after workplace accidents. In his experience the prospect of financial compensation kept individuals sick. Why support these psychically ill persons who suffer from the 'lucrative neurosis' with money, he stated, when you don't support other mental patients?[4] However, despite Moreau, the prestige that political prisoners also enjoyed in Belgium was enough reason to acknowledge *asthénie des deportés*. Starting in 1948, based on this category derived from Targowla (later renamed KZ syndrome), anyone who had been imprisoned for more than six months was by definition eligible for a particular percentage of disability compensation without the need for any further determination of illness and causality.

These different approaches and observations bring several facts to the fore.

First, regarding the type of *symptoms*, it is certain that prisoners coming home from the camps had other health problems besides tuberculosis infections, hunger edema and untreated wounds. These other complaints preceded the recognition and nomination of these symptoms as a special syndrome and generally also preceded the opportunities for financial compensation. They did, however, gradu-

3 The film was shown and discussed with one of the actors at the 'Beyond Camps and Forced Labour' conference, London January 2009.

4 On Moreau, see Fassin and Rechtman, *The empire of trauma*, 64-66.

ally come to be viewed as *medical* complaints, especially where physicians were among the victims.

In all of the countries concerned with the post-concentration camp health complaints, the syndrome showed a loss of physical and mental energy that is strongly reminiscent of 'soldier's heart'. Not reported, not even among former soldiers were shell shock conversions like deafness, mutism, paralysis and strange, uncontrolled movements.

We found an interesting exception to this state of affairs in a report from 1961 by a doctor from Belgrade.[5] In Yugoslavia there was an epidemic between 1943 and the liberation of a phenomenon referred to by bystanders as 'assault disease' and by physicians as 'Kozara psychosis', after the region where the first cases were reported. From 1943 young partisans in Kozara, a region that had seen heavy fighting and the death of many partisans, began having strange fits: 'They would fall into a trance and in such a state they would continue acting out the fight with the enemy. They would gesticulate and imitate their attack (...), firing, throwing bombs (...).' Afterwards they had completely forgotten their strange behavior.

The reporter pointed out the differences with the post-war complaints as reported elsewhere and also with the symptoms of shell shock, which according to her expressed sheer terror (tremors, paralysis, mutism). The Kozara illness on the other hand was a 'neurosis of struggle and assault' and bore 'the imprint of its origin'. After the phenomenon disappeared in the course of 1945, nobody was willing to admit to his physician having suffered from it. Yet at the end of the war some 3,000 cases had been recorded.

Whereas in general the suffering of the patients *after* World War II was considerably less visible than the suffering after World War I and Kozara, their suffering *during* the war was also less obvious than the strain of waiting in the trenches and fighting in the mountains. Post-traumatic stress is often accompanied by 're-enactment', like, for example, the behavior in Kozara. Perhaps the *nature* of the most frightening World War II experiences – concentration camps and genocide – explains why re-enactment did not occur in the other war survivors.

Secondly, as to the *doctors* treating these victims: in the first years after the war doctors were confronted with patients who had lived through unspeakable, never before reported experiences. There was no readymade theory regarding the broad range of physical and mental complaints. Doctors had to combine the state of the medical knowledge with their own experiences, impressions and creativity. Initiatives for research, laws and medical care for sick war victims, i.e. mainly former prisoners, were almost always started by physicians who had been imprisoned themselves: members of the resistance and Jewish doctors. We have not found any

5 See Moric-Petrovic, 'Neuropsychiatric after-effects', 96-99.

systematic influence from Jewish organizations on the medical policies in those first years, but the strength of the former resistance in post-war society clearly made a difference. The larger the political influence of the resistance, the more attention for *la Maladie de la Résistance.*

Thirdly, with regard to medical *treatment*: little is known about the treatments that were given and how effective they were; it is not even clear if treatment was given at all. We did not find heavy-handed methods like the 'Kaufman Kür', a treatment with painful electric shocks used by some physicians to literally set their shell-shock patients back on their feet.

In the Dutch convalescent homes for former resistance members of the late 1940's the most important treatments were rest and supplementary nutrition. The notion that one had a mental disorder was offensive to the patients there; psychiatric 'treatment' was still quite generally associated with the old-fashioned madhouse where deranged individuals were locked up for life. Even though psychoanalysis was accepted as a medical treatment in the Netherlands before World War II, psychotherapy was still very unusual. The situation elsewhere seems to have been much the same. When the magazine of the Luxembourg political prisoners dedicated a special to asthenia in 1955, there was no reaction. In Luxembourg also, psychic complaints were considered a form of insanity. This cultural climate, not least among the war victims themselves, caused people to continue to look for a somatic cause for the observed mental problems among former inmates. In valorous Norway the KZ syndrome would not have been acceptable had it not consistently been assumed to have a somatic basis. The first Norwegian treatment centre Bæreia, founded in 1959, was recommended for its beautiful, calming nature; not surprisingly the treatment consisted mainly of relaxation. However, Futselaar discovered that many recognized traumatized patients neither sought nor received any kind of treatment. In the pioneering Scandinavian countries recognition of the KZ syndrome, and compensation, were not linked to treatment.

In a later period a few additional more or less specialized research and treatment centers were realized for 'late' World War II consequences. In Brussels and Antwerp two *Centres Medico-Psychologiques* opened their doors in 1962 specifically for Jewish clients. In Paris a research centre, named after Richet, opened on 18 July 1963 to study the *pathologie des déportés.*

Fourth, as to the *duration* of the illness: even the pioneers who recognized the harmful consequences of life in the camps early on, saw the medical problems as passing. As the victims recovered their physical strength, their mental problems were expected to evaporate.

And that is how things seemed to develop. In the 1950's we find no massive labor drop-out anywhere, nor do we see waiting lists for institutions, epidemic madness or general chaos. The few figures we managed to trace indicate a low number of new war disability benefits being awarded in the first decades after the war. Europe was engrossed in the reconstruction and the Cold War. People married, had children, worked and hoped to be spared a third world war. Outside France, Denmark and Norway, the war health consequences were not a publicly known affliction, nor one that the medical profession was very interested in.

The itineraries of the KZ syndrome, 1947-1980

Under the surface, however, all kinds of health problems existed.

Many patients never consulted a doctor about their complaints, because compulsions, anxiety, apathy, emotional dullness, fear of loud noises, insomnia, were most often viewed not as medical or treatable symptoms, but rather as personal idiosyncrasies.

Also, there were types of treatment that are not recorded in the statistics as treatment of war-related illnesses. Victims found their way into regular psychiatry or were treated for disorders like alcoholism, and in the majority of such cases no connection was made with the patients' recent past. Svenja Goltermann found patients in medical files of the early fifties who, back from Russian prisoner of war camps, developed paranoid war delusions and were treated with testosterone – a 'real' man could withstand war.[6]

In addition there were individual clinicians to whom victims referred each other because their wartime past or affinity with the problems were well-known. Some of these clinicians also dealt with the consequences of war in a more organized setting, but this was rarely or never in the context of governments, government bureaucracy or professional associations. The International Society for Traumatic Stress Studies (ISTSS) did not yet exist, nor did the European Society (ESTSS) or the national psychotrauma associations. Experience and research were also not exchanged and passed on via university networks, the UN or the brand-new WHO that was established in 1948. Other channels were used.

The ex-prisoners circuit

Unlike the research into and dissemination of knowledge on cancer, infectious or cardiovascular diseases, for example, in this branch of post World War II medicine direct involvement was decisive, and it generally consisted of having been a prisoner. The organizational context in which the war-related medical knowledge

6 Goltermann, 'Beherrschung'.

was exchanged was made up of the organizations of former resistance, prisoners and military veterans.

At a conference of the *Fédération Internationale des Anciens Prisonniers Politiques* (Fiapp) in 1947 in Warsaw, for example, the Danish physician-researcher Thygesen told a Norwegian former inmate of Natzweiler and Dachau about his work. This meeting was the reason that the Norwegian prisoners opted for the Danish medical research methods and the – generous – Danish schemes as their point of reference.

Not Denmark but France was the shining example for the handful of Dutch ex-International Brigade volunteers who set up a small volunteer organization in the late 1940's to provide social-medical care to former KZ prisoners. At a resistance conference in Paris in 1947 they saw old friends again among the doctors and nurses of the International Brigades, and they were introduced to the influential French physicians.

This major conference took place just before the Cold War caused a rift in the resistance organizations. The Cold War left neither the former resistance nor the organizations of former camp inmates untouched. On the contrary. In most countries their organizations were split, and so was the Fiapp. In 1950 the Western non-communist organizations founded the Fildir, the Fédération *libre* of deportees and resistance fighters, whereas the Fédération Internationale des Résistants (Fir), founded in 1951 in Vienna, was Moscow oriented. Just as many of the national *amicales* (clubs of former camp inmates) were, often deservedly, considered communist front organizations, so was the Fir.[7]

But the Fir not only became an international reference point for 'anti-fascist' activities focusing on the remembrance of resistance. The Fir also promoted a number of international medical meetings to discuss the pathologies and the long-term health deterioration caused by internment in Nazi concentration camps. In 1954 the Fir held conferences in Copenhagen and Paris; followed in 1955 by a meeting in Brussels, 1957 in Moscow, 1964 in Bucharest, 1970 in Paris, 1976 in Prague, 1979 in Warsaw, 1981 in East-Berlin, and 1985 in Hungary.[8]

The Fildir also organized conferences on the late consequences, for example in 1956 in Rotterdam. A second ideological counterpart of the Fir, the military World Veterans Federation (WVF), held conferences on the late consequences in Oslo in 1960 and The Hague in 1961.

The well-documented Fir meetings seem to have been the most influential vehicle to promote awareness of the 'late' consequences. Featuring the physicians Richet from France, Eitinger from Norway, and from Denmark the man who in

7 The paragraphs on the Fir are derived from research reports by Brancaccio (2009) and Mooij (1999). For more on Fir, Fildir and the *amicales*, see: Duignan, 'Communist fronts', 211-212; Withuis, *Na het kamp*.

8 Pross, *Paying for the past*, 219-221.

1954 introduced the term 'KZ syndrome': Thygesen, the Fir meetings formed the channel through which clinical studies conducted in those three countries were disseminated among resistance organizations elsewhere. These studies confirmed the view that survivors of experiences like deportation, imprisonment, prolonged starvation and violence, suffered from a 'deportation syndrome'.[9] The medical advisors of the Fir stated that former Nazi deportees showed a higher overall mortality rate than the rest of the population. Both the psychic and somatic consequences of war were discussed. The presented studies demonstrate that the conviction that the consequences would not last was being abandoned in 1954. The notion of *Spätfolgen* began to force its way in.

In Rotterdam (1956) the president of the medical committee of the Fildir reported that psychological disorders, caused by the camps, sometimes took years to come to light in former political prisoners. These disorders had 'repercussions on the environment and work of these people. Their milieu and their employers [needed] to take this into account.'[10]

The report of the 1957 Fir conference in Moscow, compiled by a physician who was also the founder of the French organization of ex-deportees, emphasized somatics, but under the heading 'réadaptation' it included articles on personality disorders and 'le psychisme et traumatisme de guerre'.[11]

The Polish researchers who in the early sixties, when the political climate had become a little more open, had gone back to their research among Auschwitz inmates, such as surgeon and former Auschwitz inmate Józef Bogusz, referred to the post-war health complaints of camp survivors as ('progressive') asthenia.

In The Hague (1961) asthenia was again mentioned as a common neuropsychological problem; based on the frequent complaints of fatigue it was concluded that former inmates of prison camps suffered from 'premature ageing'. With regard to the somatic complaints attention focused on tuberculosis, bronchitis, cardiovascular diseases, digestive disorders and rheumatoid arthritis. All in all '... the conference was of the opinion that there exist ailments and disabilities which appear long afterwards among persons who were interned or imprisoned in concentration camps. These effects can become manifest at any time after liberation, and no time limit can be set for their appearance. Similar effects can be observed among persons who have lived under dangerous and stressful conditions as a

9 The papers and proceedings of the 'Conférence Médico-Sociale Internationale sur la Pathologie des Anciens Déportés et Internés' in Copenhagen were printed in German as well as French. Max Michel (zusammenst.), *Gesundheitsschäden durch Verfolgung und Gefangenschaft*. The French edition, edited by Thygesen was entitled *La déportation dans les camps de concentration Allemands et ses séquelles.*

10 The reporter was Dr. A. Mans, general inspector of public health in Paris. Report in *Aantreden* July 1956.

11 Louis Fichez, *Autres séquelles*. Vienna, ca. 1957. See also: *Ermüdung und vorzeitiges Altern. Folge von Extrembelastungen*, publ. Fir, Leipzig 1973 [account of the 5th medical Fir-conference Paris 1970, with a foreword by Fichez].

result of their fight against Nazism. These effects can also be found among former prisoners of war who lived under exceptional conditions of stress.'[12]

Despite the controversial political nature of the Fir, the dissemination of the knowledge that was exchanged at these meetings was not limited to the communist milieu. The regular Fir-speaker Richet, for example, was a much cited authority within the Fildir and also chaired the Veterans conference in The Hague.

Although the separate conferences by the ideological opponents Fir, Fildir, and WVF demonstrate that competition existed between the two blocs also in the medical field, the double role of Richet nevertheless suggests that the Cold-War differences were bridged sooner within the medical-psychological context than in the politics of memory. In the early 1960's it was still taboo for government agencies in Western countries to go to Auschwitz or Buchenwald, as these former camps were located 'behind the Iron Curtain'. But Eastern-European experts did speak in The Hague.

In the chapter on the Netherlands we described that around 1970 the unity of the communist and non-communist resistance and the persecuted Jews, which became possible as the national Cold War ebbed away, was stimulated by the medical-psychological approach to the wartime past. Thanks to this new psychological perspective cold war political enemies came to recognize each other as possible fellow victims of the concentration camp syndrome. Apparently a similar development occurred even sooner at the international level.

The conference in The Hague confirms that the knowledge of the late consequences was initially developed and disseminated by physicians who had been imprisoned themselves. Among the participants were Eitinger and also for example Léon Boutbien, physician and president of the French *Amicale de Natzweiler,* and the Austrian Ella Lingens, one of the few experts in her own country dedicated to helping the victims of the Nazis.

Careful study of the list of participants furthermore reveals the influence of the former inmates of Natzweiler concentration camp on the dissemination of the knowledge on the late consequences. Natzweilers, among whom the WVF president, had gotten to know each other as prisoners under the worst possible circumstances. Often they had been *Nacht-und-Nebel* prisoners, the heaviest category of resistance prisoners in the German penal system. In Natzweiler, which was located in Alsace, there were many French, Luxembourg, Dutch and Norwegian prisoners. After the liberation they kept in touch through their *amicales*, and they

12 See *International conference on the later effects of imprisonment and deportation* (The Hague, 20-25 November 1961), 16. The meeting in Oslo, 'Experts Meeting on the later effects of imprisonment and deportation', took place from 29 April to 1 May 1960.

also continued to feel connected with their fellow prisoners from the communist bloc.

The finding that the Natzweilers worked for international recognition of the prolonged consequences of the concentration camp, is in line with my earlier research on the Netherlands. Their influence in the Netherlands on this issue is partly explained by the fact that there were some wealthy, successful men among these former inmates, who maintained relationships with the royal family, had access to ministers and high officials, and who had no problem maintaining international camp contacts thanks to their command of languages.[13]

Although the military and the resistance circles still viewed concentration camp imprisonment as the main cause of the disease that had by now become widely known as KZ syndrome, the conclusion of the The Hague conference opened the way to also recognize health complaints of resistance members who had *not* been imprisoned as caused by the war. Furthermore, the military veterans of the WVF also introduced being held captive as a POW as a source of prolonged health damage. In 1962 and 1964 former prisoners of war also held separate conferences on the subject.[14]

In this emphasis on resistance and the military, medical thinking on the long-term consequences of World War II paralleled war remembrance, which at the time still had a strong patriotic bias. Although the communist (Fir-associated) organizations of former prisoners on principle also admitted persecuted Jews, 'resistance' was still the unifying identity. Even the Jewish members defined themselves more in terms of resistance than in terms of being Jewish. It is revealing that the communist physicians and nurses who, inspired by Richet, organized the care for their comrades in the Netherlands, did not use the term *Pathologie des Deportés* but rather the also common *Maladie de la Résistance*. Jewish mental health complaints were rarely considered a separate subject. Maria Orwid, co-author of the chapter on Poland in this book and at the time member of Bogusz' Krakow research group, indicated that former political prisoners were the subjects of the first Polish Auschwitz studies. Jewish victims were not studied until after 1989.

Occasionally the difference in psychic consequences of imprisonment in a concentration camp or an extermination camp, a distinction made by the Dutch psychoanalyst and Auschwitz survivor De Wind as early as 1949, did receive attention. For instance a German monthly associated with the Fildir in 1963 published an interview with psychiatrist Werner Mende, who supported the 'new' notion that horrific experiences may lead to permanent, psychic damage, which should

13 See Withuis, *Na het kamp*, and *Weest manlijk*.

14 In 1962 the Confédération Internationale des Anciens Prisonniers de Guerre organized a medical conference in Brussels, which was continued in 1964 in Cologne. See Pross, *Paying for the past*, 220.

be regarded as a disease. Mende pointed out the difference that the nature and circumstances of these experiences could make. The least favorable was the situation in the extermination camps: the Jewish prisoners did not have a group to fall back on, their outlook was hopeless and they were not persecuted as a result of their own actions.

Yet this article, like others, discussed the health problems of the former prisoners as a whole, because the main motive for this interview was to challenge the notion 'that man has a virtually unlimited ability to resist psychological pressures'. The Dutch association of ex-political prisoners, that only granted membership to Jewish ex-prisoners if they had been arrested for acts of resistance, printed a translation and did not neglect to mention that this psychiatric turnaround should have consequences for the 'awarding of pensions'. For if the situation was such that one could speak of 'disease', there was also an obligation to pay compensation.[15]

Naturally the survivors of concentration and termination camps *did* often share the same problems and interests. One of the occasions when the vulnerability of both was visible, was when they testified at trials against former Nazis – a task that came with considerable stress and effort, often in a hostile environment. At the Auschwitz trials in the mid 1960's in Frankfurt, Austrian communist Hermann Langbein, president of the Fir-associated International Auschwitz Committee, arranged psychological and practical support for the witnesses. After a Polish witness collapsed, it had become clear that they did not have a *pfennig* in their pocket, did not speak German and therefore could not even book a hotel room. 'Psychosocial support' of witnesses was one of the first occasions in the Netherlands where growing care for war victims was translated into action.[16]

Wiedergutmachung

The claims and recommendations of the resistance and military organizations were aimed primarily at their own governments and medical establishment. Another path along which the mental health consequences of war became visible originated in the poor health of the *Jewish* survivors and its sights were set on Germany. This path was the medical assessment procedure for the 1956 West-German *Federal Indemnification Law* (*Wiedergutmachung*) for the Jewish camp victims. Many of these victims had moved to the United States. To become eligible they had to be examined by a physician who was licensed in the country where he practiced:

15 'Hoeveel kan de mens verdragen? Nieuwe onderzoekingen over de psychologie van de angst' [How much can man bear? New researches on the psychology of fear], in: *Aantreden* 1963, 348-9, quoted in De Ridder, *De geest*, 143. Originally published in *Freiheit und Recht*, the magazine of the Zentralverband demokratischer Widerstandskämpfer und Verfolgtenorganisationen.

16 Withuis, 'Geestelijke oorlogsschade', 420.

America, but who was also able to present his report in German. So the patients often came to be examined by psychoanalysts who had fled Germany before the war and had continued their psychoanalytic practice in their new homeland.

Goltermann demonstrates that psychiatry, initially unwilling to acknowledge the possibility of permanent or late psychic consequences, was influenced by the *Wiedergutmachung* to change its mind.[17]

German psychiatry, she writes, immediately after the war claimed the monopoly on the treatment of the victims of war. Those 'victims of war' notably were not the Jews or former resistance fighters, but German soldiers and, for example, victims of bombardments. It was also immediately decided that psychiatrists would never allow, as they did after World War I, a garrison of 'tremblers' (*Kriegszittern*) to arise, who thanks to disability pensions 'managed to escape the normal problems of life'. Health complaints that were not based on any objective organic change, like the widely observed apathy among the German population in 1945-46, were considered 'functional'. It was also deemed possible that they were the result of starvation and exhaustion. The term 'dystrophy' came into use to describe this condition. However, this explanation lost its validity when the men who had returned from the Soviet camps around 1949 still had complaints after the effects of the starvation had worn off. Again, it was the same list of symptoms: anxiety, sweating, mood changes, irritability, exhaustion, apathy.

The dogma that the capacity of the human mind to cope with mental strains is unlimited and that giving in to neurotic complaints would cause chronicity, was increasingly tampered with. The two thousand 'war returnee doctors' in particular, who worked as volunteers for the *Verband der Heimkehrer*, protested. Gradually the notion emerged that severe stress could lead to permanent damage. While psychiatry held to the explanatory concepts of predisposition and pension neurosis, internists developed the concept of a 'psychosomatic disease'. As a result soldiers who had returned from the Soviet camps often preferred to be treated by GP's and internists instead of psychiatrists.

Even more than as an effect of this professional competition, the debate gained momentum as a result of the *Wiedergutmachung*. German doctors and lawyers were confronted with foreign experts who expected them to take into account the unique nature of the persecution of the Jews: the loss of loved ones, total lack of rights, persecution for the purpose of genocide. It helped that the causality requirement was less strict under the *Indemnification Law* than under the laws for the German victims.

This was the context into which German psychiatrist Ulrich Venzlaff in 1958 introduced the concept of 'experientially determined personality change'. Golter-

17 See also Goltermann, 'Psychisches Leid'.

mann attributes the success of this concept, against the views of the conservative medical front, in part to the West German desire to get in the good graces of the Western allies. *Politics of War Trauma* indeed, especially as this motive was absent in East Germany. That country did not pay *Wiedergutmachung*, and whereas over the years, in the wake of the American psychoanalysts, there was an increasing tendency in West Germany to view *every* Jewish survivor as suffering from a 'survivor syndrome', their neighbors to the East conversely considered the late consequences a typically Western ailment.

Goltermann and Pross document how the efforts of psychoanalysts such as Kurt Eissler, Henry Krystal and William Niederland to have patients recognized as suffering from an illness caused cracks in German organicist thinking. So unlike the medical opinions of the – European – Fir on the former resistance, the insights regarding health damage among Jewish survivors were imported from the other side of the ocean, where they were developed by doctors who had not spent any time in a camp. Their engagement consisted of their having escaped the murderous racism. By emphatically designating an 'external stressor' as the sole cause of the traumatization of camp survivors, these clinicians distanced themselves from the classic analytical principles.

After their work first reached the American universities (Krystal's classic *Massive Psychic Trauma* (1968) includes the proceedings of university workshops), it eventually contributed to the 'discovery' in 1980 of PTSD. Even psychoanalysis-oriented American psychiatry had not foreseen the long-term after-effects of World War II. The first version of the DSM classification list, drawn up by the APA in 1952, contained only a category known as 'Gross Stress Reaction', which could occur in emotionally stable soldiers during action, but then usually disappeared. This category was dropped in the DSMII of 1968. Only *after* the struggle for acknowledgement of late health damage from World War II were the delayed effects of war trauma recognized in the DSMIII.[18]

At the same time that Niederland and the others in America developed their insights, their Jewish colleagues in Europe continued with their work in this area. The European resistance organizations gratefully used these doctors' strong confirmation that long-term mental damage did exist, and disseminated it through their international conferences.

18 See Shephard, *A War of nerves*, 364; Andreasen, 'Posttraumatic stress disorder'.

Increasing problems, 1960-1980

Awarding compensation

While the psychiatric perspective on the consequences of war was still being developed in medical practice as well as scientific debates, patients who saw their poor conditions as a consequence of the war were already appealing to the war pension schemes that had been implemented everywhere. The problems they encountered in their applications both to the *Wiedergutmachung* and to national laws and schemes, were an important stimulus for changes in medical thinking and medical attitudes.

The award of compensations and pensions in the case of poverty and adversity is always accompanied by definitions, limitations and examinations. Who is entitled, who is not? Who is included in the target group for which the scheme is intended, who is not?

A major difference in the background philosophies of such schemes is whether the benefit is grounded on merely having gone through a bad experience c.q. having behaved very bravely, or on the health damage caused by this experience or courageous act. To receive an indemnification or honorary pension solely on the basis of experiences or merit, all that is needed is the historical or administrative verification that one actually has these experiences or this merit. Did this person actually commit those acts of resistance and was he imprisoned in that camp?

War welfare schemes varied per country, per victim category and per period, but almost always they were benefits to compensate reduced or lost 'earning capacity' or disability. With the exception of France, suffering or heroism did not warrant indemnification.

Where illness and disability are the foundation for a benefit, physicians in the modern welfare states act as gatekeepers. In the implementation of the war schemes physicians, as objective professionals, were appointed to be the judges of whether someone was ill, and if so, whether his condition was caused by the war.[19]

These appointments were based partly on the notion that there are, at least among colleagues, undisputed criteria to declare someone ill or healthy. However, this is not the case. Such consensus is rare and it is absent in the type of conditions that are the result of the prolonged exposure to violence, threat of death and witnessing the death of comrades. In other words, to war. After 1945 the medical professionals therefore frequently re-introduced both pre-war arguments – premorbidity and secondary gain – against a causal relationship between terrifying

---

19 Only East Germany did not have this problem, because it did not have separate war benefits. There were disability benefits, regardless of whether disability was caused by illness, accident, or war, but fitting work was the preferred solution, because work was considered therapy. See Goltermann, in this book.

experiences and chronicity. Distrust towards malingerers was not absent either. Even undeniable, demonstrable and life-threatening somatic diseases yielded examination problems. In these cases the issue was not, as in psychogenic or psychiatric diseases, whether someone could be called 'sick', but whether the illness was indeed caused by the war.

What complicates the aftermath of World War II even more, as compared to the First, is that the victims are not only, and not even primarily, soldiers, but civilians. They had no employee-employer relationship to their own state. Non-military persons who had chosen to join the national resistance were often placed under national financial responsibility after the war through ingenious legal arguments like the 'notional employment contract'. However, a substantial number of victims were persecuted, punished or murdered not because their *country* was at war with Germany, but because they belonged to an imaginary category like a 'race' or some other stigmatized group. Even though they were citizens, their relation to the benefit schemes of nation states after the war was precarious to say the least.

Harshness and heartlessness

Medical examinations for a pension for illness as a result of the war could be humiliating and frightening experiences. Many victims were forced to undergo this post-war humiliation and fear.

When Polish-Jewish Mrs. A. in 1960, aged 53, applied for a German *Wiedergutmachung* pension, it was partially awarded. In one of the four concentration camps where Mrs. A. had been interned, she had been forced, under the worst imaginable medical conditions, to abort a six-month pregnancy. She had been suffering chronic abdominal infections ever since and she was no longer able to have children. Her husband, brother, and sister had died while imprisoned in the camp. The medical examiner, on the basis of 'physical and mental exhaustion', awarded her an 'MdE' of 25% for the period 1941 to 1946. An MdE is a *Minderung der Erwerbstätigkeit* (reduced earning capacity). She was therefore deemed *during her incarceration* and the year after to have been 25% less able to earn a living than a healthy person. She was not eligible for further compensation.

She appealed the decision, and an endless series of medical re-examinations followed. One of the later medical examiners acknowledged that she had indeed undergone severe stress, which could, however, be considered done with in 1949, when she had remarried and emigrated to Canada, where she had integrated well. He also felt that her complaint of feeling lonely as a result of her childlessness was understandable. But loneliness resulting from childlessness in his opinion was not a consequence of her persecution for being Jewish. For the same also applied to others who were fated to remain childless. Finally, there was the loss of self-respect she presented as a consequence of her infertility. The doctor understood that also. But infertility was only a problem until the age of menopause at the latest. After that infertility is normal. By the time this decision was made it was December 1979. At age 72, after twenty years of legal actions, medical examinations and re-examinations, Mrs. A. was awarded a minimal pension until 1962, the year she turned fifty-five and could reasonably be expected to have entered menopause.

During his five years in concentration camps Mr. O. had been hung by his arms, among other things. As a result he had sustained frostbite in his feet; in addition he had suffered a leg phlegmone, a painful, infected wound that was very common in the camps. In 1956, following an operation on his legs, he applied for a pension based on circulatory problems. Unfortunately the medical examiners determined that although the *arterial* problems were indeed a consequence of his persecution, the problem they held responsible for the highest percentage of his disability was his *venous* circulation and this was considered constitutional in his case. Result: no pension for Mr. O.

After heart surgery his physician reported that Mr. O. was no longer able to work. O. requested a reconsideration, but the court followed the negative decision of a German professor, who, unlike O.'s New York doctor, felt that O.'s illness was not related to his imprisonment. He should know: after the war this former *Luftwaffe* volunteer and ex-Nazi specialized in the harmful effects of being a prisoner of war on the cardiovascular system. In his opinion this harmful effect did not apply to imprisonment in a concentration camp. Mr. O. died in 1982, seventy years old, before his next appeal was heard.

Sadly, Mrs. A. and Mr. O. were no exceptions. In *Paying for the Past*, the book these histories were taken from, insult and injury alternate in an endless succession of lawsuits and appeal cases. With barely concealed anger the author of this study, the German doctor Christian Pross, describes who the doctors were on whose judgment persecuted persons like A. and O. depended for a decision on a *Wiedergutmachung* pension: they were frequently ex-Nazis.[20]

Our research shows that the treatment of the applicants improved over the years in most countries. The experiences of patients changed as medical insights, cultures and social relationships changed, and apart from differences per period, their experiences also differed per country and per doctor. Moreover, it mattered what group of victims one belonged to.

The above examples concerned Jewish survivors. In Germany and Austria for a long time they were very likely to be examined by a former Nazi for an assessment of the consequences of what the Nazis had done to them. Perhaps even a Nazi who as an ex-soldier enjoyed the benefits of some military pension. And things

20 See Pross, *Paying for the past*, 119-122 and 156-160 respectively.

were not always better elsewhere. In Italy the application of a Jewish survivor was rejected because she was unable to present her medical file from Auschwitz.

Pross' examples demonstrate which conflicts could occur even with respect to relatively clear-cut diseases. The patient ran the risk of being caught between a doctor who had fled to America and awarded him, sometimes without even seeing him in person, a high percentage of 'illness as a consequence of the war', and a German medical examiner who as an ex-Nazi continued his war against the Jews by awarding him a lower allowance or none at all. Pross named the heartlessness and arbitrariness of the cases he collected as 'retraumatization'. The Jewish-American lawyer Milton Kestenberg, who handled many appeal cases and in 1982 presented a host of medical examination misery in the famous volume *Generations of the Holocaust,* spoke of a 'continuation of persecution through legal channels'.[21]

Moreover, the handling of claims was characterized by bureaucracy. Even minor inaccuracies in dates concerning transports from one camp to another could lead to a refusal of indemnification; the claimant, Kestenberg states, was consequently treated like 'a liar and a cheat'. More than half of the applications for indemnification for medical damage were decided in the courtroom. There were considerable regional differences in attitude. Berlin, for example, was known as flexible and generous.

According to Kestenberg the younger generation of German doctors was infected by its predecessors. Psychoanalysts suggested more empathic explanations for the examination problems. De Wind thought that doctors, being forced to read about all the horrors the applicants had endured, were overcome by a horror so big that it generated aversion against the patient. Alexander and Margarete Mitscherlich pointed out the psychological defense by the younger generation of knowledge about the crimes of their parents. These considerations by no means diminish the assessment problems.

However, the medical examinations of resistance fighters and veterans were also not without problems in their own countries. There was good reason that in addition to their medical position, the social and legal position of the victims was also discussed at the mentioned conferences.

A medical-legal symposium in 1967 in Cologne was dedicated entirely to the assessment problems. One of the speakers was Ella Lingens. Her job at the Austrian Ministry for Social Administration was to medically evaluate appeals of application rejections on the basis of new expert opinions. In her speech she underlined the difficulty of the task to assess health impairments. At the same time she condemned the attitude of many of her colleagues, who rejected claims on bizarre

21 Kestenberg, 'Discriminatory aspects', 63; Pross and Kestenberg presented papers of similar import in Hannover 1989.

grounds, while not being up to date on the medical literature on the subject. Implementation of the laws on war victims not only called for 'the collaboration of psychiatric experts with a genuine democratic orientation and high moral scruples', she said, it also demanded that the doctors involved had 'acquired the necessary specialized knowledge in this field'.[22] According to Lingens, especially psychiatrists outside the cities lacked knowledge of recent literature; the transformation of attitudes towards the mentally ill had also passed them by.

Most medical knowledge on the psychic consequences of war was developed and disseminated by directly involved parties. But that those 'own doctors' classified mental problems as 'KZ syndrome' did not mean that such problems counted as legal grounds for a pension. In the earliest post-war years this was only the case in Denmark, France and the Netherlands (and in Belgium with regard to the asthenia of part of the political prisoners). Since the 1960's more countries accepted psychic complaints as an illness for some categories of victims; Germany and Austria since 1965, Norway since 1968.

Unfortunately such a statutory provision did not remove all assessment problems. As mentioned before, the assumption that there is professional consensus about the diagnostic criteria for diseases, and particularly mental diseases, is naïve. In addition, a doctor's ability to imagine the past of the patient can make a huge difference, especially in cases like this. The medical examiners that the applicants of resistance pensions and other schemes had to deal with, were usually not the doctors from the resistance or prisoner-of-war conferences, where the shared wartime experiences and political ideals reduced the usual distance between doctors and patients.

That the knowledge on the KZ syndrome was being developed within the limited circle of physicians who were intensely involved, caused a knowledge gap with their colleagues, resulting in friction in everyday practice. There was a reason that the Danish resistance as early as 1951 arranged that only doctors who were sympathetic towards the applicants could carry out medical examinations, and Dutch former prisoners demanded to be examined only by doctors who had themselves survived a camp. In any event, their role as medical examiners for the war welfare laws meant that the physicians stepped outside the bounds of their profession and had to make semi-legal decisions.

Causality

Also in Cologne was the medical advisor of the Dutch organization responsible for the payment of pensions, internist W.F. Noordhoek Hegt. In 1967 he noticed an

---

22 Lingens, quoted in Ecker and Embacher in this book.

increase in the number of cases in which it was difficult to prove a causal relationship. The origin of, for example, diabetes, arteriosclerosis and coronaries was difficult to establish. Physicians had no choice but to assess the link between wartime experiences and these complaints on the basis of unsubstantiated presumptions. Noordhoek Hegt was therefore quite pleased that the burden of proof, at least for part of the resistance disabled, had recently been 'reversed'.[23]

This reversal in 1967 was the outcome of a tough battle. As early as September 1948 in a consultation of several European ministers of Foreign and Social Affairs in Brussels, there was a proposal to harmonize war welfare schemes and put the burden of proof on the government in all countries, as was the case in France regarding the deportees. This proposal was rejected at that time, following objections from the Netherlands.[24] But in the mid to late 1960's, as the examination problems increased, more and more objections were lodged against the procedures in many countries. The Luxembourg and Dutch ex-political prisoners were asking for the French scheme. In Austria organizations demanded that victims entitled to a pension automatically received a 100% 'MdE'.

They were successful. In several countries the burden of proof was reversed (even if the conditions for this causal assumption varied in terms of disability percentage or the length of imprisonment). In Germany a court decided in 1965 that for the Jewish survivors 'the causal relationship between illness and persecution was accepted without proof in those survivors who had been concentration camp inmates for more than a year.' This was the so-called 'camp assumption'. In Norway the burden of proof was reversed from 1968 onwards for a defined number of groups. In the Netherlands the existing scheme was expanded in 1971, and in 1973 the reversed burden of proof was immediately included in the new Benefit Act for Victims of Persecution (WUV).

The fact that governments increasingly had to prove the absence of a causal link, was a pleasant outcome for both parties in the medical examination situation. Thanks to the reversal of the burden of proof clinicians were freed from a task many of them began to see as a burden: to reject people. The patients escaped a dependency relationship they experienced as offensive. In the case of their often vague complaints and with doctors who denied the existence of 'late consequences', the patient's personality was often subjected to examination just as much as his symptoms. This was all the more sensitive because in addition to

23 See Herberg, *Die Beurteilung von Gesundheitsschäden*, 29-33.

24 Information from Hinke Piersma, based on a missive from the Minister of Foreign Affairs to other ministers, 9 September 1948 (National Archive, nr. 96, 2.04.51 and idem 2.04.52). The meeting was a consequence of the Treaty of Brussels 17 March. This pact between France, Great Britain, Belgium, the Netherlands and Luxembourg, a first step in the direction of the EEC, was mainly a military reaction of the West to the communist coup in Prague.

financial security this pension offered the applicants the honorable recognition of their wartime past.

The flip side of this gain was that to qualify for a pension or benefit one had to accept the role of being mentally or psychosomatically ill, something earlier generations had difficulty with. That is why it was vitally important that the name of their illness expressed recognition that it was caused by the war. The label 'KZ syndrome' allowed patients to maintain their self-respect, much like half a century earlier 'shell shock' had offered an escape from the offensive label 'male hysteria'.

Both well-intentioned political policymakers and physicians who sided with the victims, presented the reversal of the burden of proof as the outcome of growing medical understanding. It was not. The question of causality in many cases is beyond medical science and it was often on the basis of harshness, arrogance and paternalism that is was answered with 'no', or on the basis of kind-heartedness or political ideology that it was answered with 'yes'.

The reversal of the burden of proof was a political decision to deal with an increasingly untenable situation as humanely as possible. As a Dutch professor of psychiatry (again an ex-inmate) said in all candor, it was not as a doctor, but as a citizen that he thought it 'an outright scandal' 'that a Jew should have to prove he is traumatized'. Such a procedure would *make* people ill.[25]

Instead of reading the previous paragraph on the discovery of the 'late sequelae' of World War II as a story of growing medical-psychological understanding we should read it as a story of changing power-balances: patients gained and doctors lost power.

And from yet another perspective with yet another conflict of interest: those who quickly after the liberation felt that that we should put the war behind us, lost power in favor of the 'rememberers'. There were doctors and patients in both camps.

The politics of war trauma and of memory were mutually reinforcing.

Shifts and changes

Before coming to conclusions, it is illuminating to return to the Netherlands. Our critical questions with regard to the current Dutch trauma culture were the original starting point for this European project. Although after completing our research we can conclude that in the field of war trauma the Netherlands are quite exceptional, the Dutch development can be of use to understand the state of war trauma in other countries.

---

25 A. van Dantzig, cited in: *Medische causaliteit*, 22.

In the 1960's a wave of democratization and anti-authoritarianism passed through Western Europe. The left came to power, youth culture was celebrated, Marxism rehabilitated. There were demonstrations against social injustice; incomes had to become more equal, universities more accessible, elites and regents had to be taken down a peg, and last but not least: doctors needed to listen more closely to their patients.

In the Netherlands this soft revolution stirred great enthusiasm. Even Dutch elites were quick to integrate the claims and protest of the young generations.[26] The international mood of change accelerated interior developments that were already in motion. Between 1945 and 1975, the Dutch mentality underwent a transformation. Especially the processes of secularization, democratization en therapeutization caused a fundamental change in culture and society. Dutch mental health care stopped being divided, as it had been, along religious lines. The use of psychotherapy grew rapidly. From being an elite treatment psychotherapy turned into a popular way of thinking about oneself and one's fellow citizens. The influence of psychiatry on how people think they should deal with difficult life experiences increased. Emotions were expressed instead of repressed; the 'culture of silence' of the post-war reconstruction era turned into the 'culture of speaking out' of the 1970's and 1980's (and subsequently into today's trauma culture).

At the same time the interest in the war developed rapidly. 'The War' became the moral touchstone *par excellence*. The creation of a Resistance Remembrance Cross compensated the parsimonious post-war decoration policy. Commemoration became more and more important. New war monuments were built, school children were being educated about the war by camp survivors, ministers and members of the royal family attended concentration camp commemorations and talked with survivors.

The discovery of the KZ syndrome stimulated all this and in turn this new way of thinking stimulated that people began to define themselves, their partners or parents as sufferers of such a war syndrome. They began to interpret the problems in their lives and health as illness resulting from the post-war silence about the war. Around 1970 survivors of World War II still found it difficult to face up to their mental problems – merely acknowledging illness would mean that Hitler had won after all – yet a decade later mental illness was no longer taboo. But only if it was 'because of the war'. The step towards the acknowledgement of mental problems could be made by this generation when doctors called their condition a real illness and the cause was external and respectable.

The idea of a cathartic letting it all get out to restore one's happiness became widespread, and the echo of that was what war victims explained to the public:

26 Kennedy, *Building New Babylon*.

'After the war nobody was willing to listen to what we had gone through. We were pressed to repress our memories and feelings.'

The assertive protest attitude that seized the Netherlands did not pass the medical professions and psychiatry by, and it also had an effect on the resistance disabled, Jewish survivors, and repatriates from the Dutch East Indies. The first were increasingly less willing to accept long waiting times and rejections in the pension procedures, the latter two groups, for whom no such pension existed, more and more openly advocated a law that would guarantee them a good income like the former resistance had. It helped that the KZ syndrome became widely known and that it became common to blame the late consequences on the lack of care and interest from the government. The war was 'repressed' after 1945. Amends were to be made here and the pensions and benefits provided the opportunity to do so. After the cool reception of the Dutch war victims, who in 1945 had returned to a nation in a mood of discipline and asceticism, and after decades of underestimating the extent of their health problems, this shift was a welcome development.

The new responsiveness to victims, which in 1972 was crucial in the decision of the Dutch Lower House not to release the infamous Three after all, also applied to medicine. Nobody wanted to be accused of a prolonged lack of attention for wartime suffering. Whereas around 1950 most doctors, the resistance elite and the public at large had assumed that attention would result in psychic weakness, in 1975 a *lack* of attention was assumed to be the cause of the problems. Concepts like 'pre-morbidity' and 'secondary gain' by now were felt to be arrogant and insensitive, as indeed they often were. As compassion for victims increased, distrust towards claimants was more and more considered inappropriate. Humiliating attitudes and procedures that patients before had viewed as inevitable, were now increasingly felt to be unacceptable. If a doctor suggested that health problems that the patient himself attributed to the war were perhaps related to work or marriage, this was experienced as a personal *and* collective insult: as a repetition of the postwar neglect of all war victims. Such lack of understanding was no longer tolerated, not by victims, and not by society either.

The fact that the Netherlands changed in such an extreme manner was partly due to the fact that the innovation of 'the sixties' coincided with other drastic changes: the critical revival of interest in World War II, the collapse of the particularly grisly Dutch cold war culture, and the rapid decline of the signifying role of religion, including pillarization as the socially binding context.

Thanks to this simultaneousness these changes reinforced each other, and moreover, World War II became the focal point where everything came together. The ideological vacuum left by the secularization was filled by the psychotherapeutic thinking; war-related mental problems changed from shameful into a source of status.

What was the effect of the sixties elsewhere?

Although the collective war memory underwent such a complete metamorphosis from political to psychological only in the Netherlands, and although the recognition of the war consequences did not lead to such a pervasive trauma culture in any of the examined countries, sooner or later this shift in mentality and social relations to a higher or lesser degree occurred there also.

In France there was less catching up to do. There the war victims had been treated with considerably more respect since the war. And so the French relationship to the 1960's is a different one. Here it was not the war victims who shared in the benefits of the mental revolution; it was the 1960's youth who decades later, once they were established as doctors, lawyers, or politicians, applied the principle of equality and expanded compassion with victims to new groups of traumatized persons, such as refugees or victims of terror attacks. In the country of the *asthénie des deportés* archaic terms like neurasthenia, hysteria and sinistrosis (a 'revenge neurosis' of someone who constantly feels he wronged and who demands compensation) were increasingly considered offensive to all victims of trauma, and were consequently banned in 1992.

In Belgium the language conflict cuts across both mentality and war memory. Whereas in Flanders a political view of the wartime past still prevails, psychology is winning ground in Walloon. Luxembourg found its own way in this maze. The government there seems to have found a solution for the war problems that discouraged medicalization and victim rivalry. In 1967 they did *not* give in to the desire of the former political prisoners to reverse the burden of proof. In Austria for a long time the attitude towards the mentally ill *and* towards Jewish victims and communists was dismissive and arrogant. In Poland, on the other hand, the willingness among the survivors to define themselves as psychiatric patients (taken by Orwid to be a resultant of democratization), came about very late. For the Eastern European countries in general the 'sixties' were less relevant than the Cold War, which did not end there until 1989.

Expansion and dissemination, 1970-2000

PTSD

At the same time that psychiatrists in America, confronted with the late consequences of World War II in Europe, developed a new way of thinking about psychic trauma, the United States was caught up in a controversial war in Vietnam.

While the war was being fought no big medical-psychological problems presented themselves. The soldiers were kept ready for their terrifying anti-guerrilla fight with rest, recreation and the new benzodiazepines. Because there was relatively little fighting and the soldiers returned to home bases where there was plenty of fun to be had, there were few cases of acute stress. But once they were home permanently they proved unable to move on. Unemployment, alcohol abuse, drugs, violence, homicide and suicide were alarmingly common.

It was a time when progressive social movements thrived like never before. These movements considered protest against the war of paramount importance. The student movement supported conscientious objectors; the civil rights movement felt that it was predominantly black men who were sent to their deaths; the women's liberation movement ensured that women would not let themselves be sent home from their new jobs as they had in 1945, nor stay out of politics like good girls.

And then there was the patients' rights movement, that opened up psychiatry – not just because patients sought publicity to protest against treatments like electroshocks, but also because more and more links were suggested between madness and evils in society. The stigmatization of psychiatric patients decreased. Novels like *One Flew over the Cuckoo's Nest* and *I Never Promised You a Rose Garden*, and studies like Goffman's *Asylums* en Szasz' *The Myth of Mental Illness* were bestsellers. *Asylums* (published in 1961), in which Goffman compared life in mental hospitals with the harsh life in 'total institutions' like prisons and army barracks, and demonstrated that the effect of institutionalization was the opposite of a cure, was reprinted annually between 1970 and 1976.

Around 1970 some psychiatrists and social workers began to discern a pattern in the many acts of violence committed by Vietnam veterans. In publications they linked their actual mental health condition to their wartime past. They supported ex-soldiers who were down on their luck, testified as expert witnesses in courts about the 'Post-Vietnam Syndrome' and explained to courts martial that alleged deserters were actually suffering from 'traumatic stress'.

Strategically decisive was that this handful of pioneers effected an alliance with the powerful antiwar movement. An interesting development, as initially the *crazy Vietnam vets* could expect to be met with hostility from all sides. They were despised by the hawks and their patriotic following because they had lost the war, and hated by the public at large that did not see worthy heroes returning, but drug addicted murderers, rapists and thieves; the anti-war movement called them *baby killers*.

The scattered initiatives and minor articles on the 'Post-Vietnam Syndrome' caught on, both among clinicians who did not know what to do with these clients, and among the multitude of patients who were not yet officially recognized as such. While the medical establishment initially did not make the connection between wartime past and alcoholism, violent behavior, depression and suicide, groups of former veterans 'rapped' about their situation and experiences on many university campuses. At the same time the new feminists revealed that rape and incest caused the same kind of long-term psychic damage that the war veterans reported. Post-traumatic amnesia and dissociation were being noticed.

Institutions that would have to bear the costs of a recognized veterans' disease, such as the War Office, opposed the recognition of a post-traumatic Vietnam Syndrome. On the other hand, for some the fight for recognition was indeed a *political* campaign: the warmongers were responsible for this mess, *they* had to bleed. Recognition was a matter of some urgency because insurance companies preferably reimburse clearly defined diseases, not vague complaints that were being interpreted in vague terms by vague therapists.

The PTSD cause was strengthened when similarities became apparent between Vietnam Syndrome, rape trauma syndrome, battered child syndrome, Stockholm syndrome (identification of hostage with hostage taker) and the conditions of the refugees from East Asia who came to the US in droves in the mid 1970's. The case was clinched when those symptoms furthermore turned out to match the data gathered in the previous two decades on World War II camp survivors. The notion that people with different traumatic experiences shared a pattern of complaints gained ground.

In 1980 the time had come: the joint lobby of pacifists, veterans, feminists and well-intentioned psychiatrists resulted in the inclusion of PTSD in the psychiatric *manual*: indeed, abnormal experiences can leave 'normal' people with a mental disorder. The invention of the new disease, that much is clear, was as much a political as a medical matter.

A third dissemination route

The DSM recognition initiated a new dynamic. People were diagnosed as suffering from PTSD, new clinics were realized and we see the emergence of professional journals, associations, information brochures, standards, conferences, and clinicians who specialized in this subject ('psychotraumatologists', 'victimologists'). The public at large became increasingly familiar with the term and started applying it to themselves or other people.

The mission to spread knowledge about this new disorder took on an international dimension. In March 1985 older pioneers and ambitious newcomers founded the Society for Traumatic Stress Studies (STSS, later ISTSS), which concentrated on the treatment of 'a wide range of victim populations', and on disseminating knowledge about the short-term and long-term consequences of all kinds of disasters, including others than the man-made ones, for example natural disasters and large-scale accidents. The ISTSS became a prominent medical-scientific organization, with representatives in the World Health Organization and the United Nations.[27] In 1993 the European Society was founded, which organized a

27 Withuis, *Erkenning*, 213-246.

series of Conferences on Traumatic Stress in England, the Netherlands, Norway and France.

Thanks to the rapid recognition of war trauma and the generous government financing of war-related care after 1972, the Netherlands, that in the early post war years had been slow in recognizing the KZ syndrome, caught up and even adopted a pioneering role. The Netherlands is important in both ISTSS and ESTSS. The first president of the ESTSS was Dutch internist W. de Loos, who had treated former resistance members for many years. In tandem with the explosive international growth of the PTSD-related trauma industry, the Netherlands could fulfill its favorite role as model country in this field. In the past decades Dutch experts have provided trauma education in many countries, including West Germany, Israel, Japan, East Germany, and post-apartheid South Africa. The importance of the route via Fir, Fildir, WVF and *Wiedergutmachung*, in which the Netherlands had no role to speak of, diminished. Of the old Great Powers of the KZ syndrome Norway maintained its position thanks to the famous Eitinger. In Denmark a combination of early research into KZ syndrome and the new PTSD approach led to the foundation of a Danish and an international expertise and treatment centre for torture victims.

The people most active in the dissemination of the new trauma message were engaged to their cause, just like the activist doctors of Fir and Fildir had been, but this new commitment was based less on personal experience. It was thoroughly professionalized, at a considerably higher social level, had more connections with the academic world and research funds, and focused on many other 'disasters' besides World War II. And so a European-American education network on PTSD and the late consequences of war travelled around the globe.

In Europe the old World War II network was expanded with new experts. A new network was formed that exchanged information about the consequences of World War II. Among the participants in an international symposium in Hannover in 1989, besides Eitinger and Orwid, were Krystal and the critical authors on the *Wiedergutmachung* medical examinations Pross and Kestenberg, and from the Netherlands a 'professionalization expert' plus psychiatrists Bastiaans, Keilson and Lansen. The latter, director of the Jewish Sinai Clinic, a few years later organized courses in Berlin with Dutch semi-governmental support.[28]

Regardless of the criticism on the trauma industry that subsequently developed in countries like America, England and the Netherlands, the official medical recognition of possibly permanent consequences of traumatic experiences undeniably opened up new avenues. In societies where democracy is absent or relatively new, PTSD proves to help victims draw attention to their fate. In the former Soviet

28 See Rossberg & Lansen, *Das Schweigen brechen*.

Union, for example, which is not discussed here, even today the victims of that other murderous totalitarian regime: the Gulag, compete with the Nazi victims. PTSD helps to bring the misery of the Gulag survivors to the attention of clinicians, at least Western ones.[29]

In Poland, sympathy for victims increased because of the more open, democratic and liberal atmosphere; thanks to the international status of PTSD it became possible to openly discuss the concept of trauma and bring it to the attention of the medical establishment. In combination with the wall coming down, the Western recognition of PTSD opened the door for Orwid (and others) to focus on the Jewish survivors, because a double taboo disappeared: the taboo on psychic consequences of war and on being Jewish.

Medical research among another concealed and stigmatized Polish victim group, the so-called 'Syberacs', was also only possible after 1989, as under communism it was officially denied that the Russians had caused carnage and deported Polish citizens during the war. Despite their high PTSD scores the Siberia-survivors do not have a victim status; a causal relationship with their past camp experiences is rarely recognized by the organizations that carry out the medical examinations.

The official existence of a disease 'PTSD' in Norway helped the late recognition of the complaints of the *krigssejlere*. Although most 'war sailors' were not combatants, Futselaar writes, 'they were exposed to frequent and gruesome warfare. German U-boats targeted convoys of ships delivering supplies and troops. From a modern perspective, frequent exposure to life-threatening danger over a period of years, combined with witnessing the destruction of other ships, often manned by friends and relatives, may seem an evident cause of psychiatric stress later on.' Initially, however, mere fear was not viewed as a potential cause of disease: 'However stressful, sleep-deprived and dangerous their wartime experience had been, they had neither gone hungry nor been systematically mistreated.'

At long last, thanks to the globalization of trauma-thinking, even Austria got its 'psychosocial centre' ESRA in 1994, and a second treatment centre in 1999. ESRA attracted mainly Jewish clients from Vienna, but in recent years has increasingly provided counseling and care to political persecutees and to clients outside the capital. As for the Netherlands: Centrum '45, which opened in 1973, offered group therapy and various types of creative therapies. Professor Bastiaans treated patients with the forbidden drug LSD. His goal was to bring about an emotional catharsis by stirring up memories during the LSD-high and having the patient go 'back to the camp' under his guidance. Although Bastiaans did get results (members of the resistance thought the world of him), his colleagues did not approve

29 See Adler, *The Gulag survivor;* Merridale, 'The collective mind'.

of his method. The risks to the patient were too high.[30] According to a prominent Dutch clinician recognition was the only medicine to relieve this suffering; a cure would never be achieved.

Shephard has denounced the dramatically poor outcome of the recognition of PTSD for the Vietnam veterans: thousands of young people in the United States were declared patients and provided with a lifelong pension, while the doctors who brought this about could not provide any effective remedies.

Today trauma treatment, regardless of the type of trauma, is part of the standard offering of psychiatric and academic institutions and it is therefore even more difficult to check the state of the care for World War II victims.

Transgenerational traumatization

The concept of PTSD (and the subsequent expansion of the key concept of 'trauma') was the culmination of a development we observed earlier: the continuous increase of populations to which the notion of the 'late consequences' supposedly applied.

The symptoms that were first referred to as asthenia and subsequently as KZ syndrome affected former inmates from the Nazi concentration camps. Soon the potential KZ syndrome population as defined by Fir and Fildir was expanded with prisoners of war and resistance members who had *not* been interned.

In the second described circuit, the *Wiedergutmachung*, the existence of a 'survivor syndrome' was argued by American psychoanalysts on the basis of the unique nature of the Holocaust. This unicity was the reason why, contrary to the biological-psychiatric discourse, traumatization through an external stressor became conceivable.

On the one hand, therefore, there were specific experiences with specific consequences that justified a new perspective. On the other, it proved possible for different experiences to have the same consequences. And so the basis of the argument was lost, whereas the notion of 'late consequences' remained.

Even before the trauma concept was expanded through PTSD, the populations of potential late war victims had already been expanded to include the post-war children, who were (young) adults by the time they developed mental health complaints.

Attention was first drawn to the phenomenon now known as 'transgenerational traumatization' in the United States in the late 1960's, where it was linked to the concept of 'second generation'. Those articles, illustrated with clinical examples, argued that children in Jewish and resistance families had frequently grown up with parents who were traumatized by the war. Because they had had to take

30 See Enning, *De oorlog van Bastiaans*.

care of their parents, they were insufficiently 'attached'. This had resulted in an inability to choose their own path in life, insufficient separation from the parents and 'their' war; the feeling of having to make up for the wartime suffering and a resulting inability to enjoy life; problems with aggression management and forming relationships.

Inspired by American-Jewish publications and by the brand-new discovery of the KZ syndrome, the Netherlands was quick to recognize the 'second generation'. The first publications stem from the early seventies. The Netherlands later played a very active role in the international dissemination of this body of thought. Psychoanalyst Han Groen-Prakken, for example, inspired Eastern-European clinicians and victims to take an interest in the Jewish second generation.[31]

In Germany the mental habitus of 'resistance children' receives attention, but selectively, as is evident from Heinz Suenker's research. He observes a sharp contrast in treatment between children of communist resistance members and the children of the heroes of the famous Operation Valkyrie of 20 July 1944, when *Wehrmacht* officers led by *Graf* von Stauffenberg attempted to assassinate Hitler. The latter are well cared for with scholarships and therapy. The former group are out of the picture, just like their parents; communist camp survivors, being 'supporters of a totalitarian regime' were not covered by the compensation schemes and were unemployed as often as their children are today. In East Germany, however, children of the communist resistance were relatively privileged.[32]

There is a tendency to talk about the various 'children' in one and the same breath. Yet there is a fundamental difference between the Jewish war orphans or hidden children and the 'second generation': the first group actually lived through the war. In 1979 in his dissertation on Jewish war orphans the Dutch-German psychoanalyst Hans Keilson coined the term 'sequential traumatization', which is now thoroughly integrated in the international trauma literature. Keilson demonstrated that it was the cumulation of successive traumatic experiences that caused the greatest damage. First the anti-Jewish measures; then persecution, deportation, and camp; and finally, after the war, while the child often lacked an affectively supportive environment, the realization of the losses.

The international scientific and medical interest in Jewish war orphans and former hidden children increased explosively after the 'Hidden Children Conferences' in New York (1991) and Amsterdam (1992) respectively. To Orwid these conferences were encouraging partly because they empowered the Polish-Jewish 'children' to start an association. In Belgium the term psychotrauma in the context

31 See on Belgrade: Stajner-Popovich, 'De "verloren" tweede generatie', 113-127.

32 Heinz Suenker (University of Wuppertal), lecture 'Children of the resistance in Germany and their relationship to politics after 1945', conference Beyond Camps and Forced Labour, London January 2009. On the exclusion of communist camp survivors from indemnification schemes, see Pross, *Paying for the past*, 52-54.

of the war is used exclusively for this group. The renewed attention in 1999 led to a Moral Statute, in which the childrens' suffering was acknowledged, and in 2003 to financial compensation. Depending on one's address, a request for such compensation can, however, have a different outcome. Applications in Walloon are practically always accepted on the basis of PTSD; in Flanders, on the other hand, they are usually rejected, because there the consensus is that no causal relationship exists between health complaints and war.

With the continuing expansion of the categories of war victims, the children of collaborators or German fathers also arrived on the victim scene. In accordance with the general psychologization of the war in the Netherlands, in this country this group presents itself first of all as psychologically damaged as a result of stigmatization by society. In Belgium there are, once again, differences between the different language regions. In interviews with Belgian historians, the Walloon 'children' did speak in psychologizing terms about the burden of their past. Children of the Flemish collaborators, in contrast, are less likely to present themselves as psychologically damaged. They view themselves primarily as the victims of political repression and they want rehabilitation rather than therapy.[33]

In Norway many of the ill-treated children of German fathers have received compensation and apologies from the Norwegian state since the mid 1990's. In Denmark the children of German fathers also made themselves heard. Initially these Norwegian and Danish children were predominantly angry and they did not define themselves as psychically damaged. This seems to be changing. A physician of the Danish Centre for Torture Victims recently interviewed widows, children and grandchildren of people who were involved in torture either as perpetrators or victims. As Futselaar writes: 'By focusing to a considerable extent on psychological damage in the second and third generations, and by discussing the traumatic experiences on both sides of the conflict in the same book, he has broken taboos and, possibly, changed the understanding of the late after effects of World War II in Denmark.'

With the inclusion of the children of war victims and perpetrators in the category of 'war victims', a fundamental boundary was crossed. After the types of experiences that could potentially cause permanent health damage had been expanded since the first tentative explorations in the area of war consequences from concentration and extermination camps to more general stressful situations, bringing in the post-war generations made it possible to be a trauma victim *without* actually having experienced the traumatic experience.

33 See Kesteloot, 'Kinderen van verzetslui of collaborateurs'.

Formulated differently: we observe more and more categories of people wanting to be part of the triumphant nation state by way of recognition of their 'war caused victimhood'.

Disease as politics

Since Vietnam the notion of 'late consequences' was expanded to such a degree that perpetrators are now also seen as victims. The concept of trauma allows perpetrators to transform themselves into victims. Veterans since 1980 are considered probable candidates for PTSD. Political expediency stimulated this expansion. Disease can function as a political escape route to leave controversial, painful issues unnamed and undecided.

This can be illustrated with both the Indonesian and the Algerian war of independence. In both cases a controversial war was initially cloaked in euphemisms and amnesia, and was later followed by a public debate on committed atrocities. In both cases 'trauma' offered the perpetrators the way out, so the country that started the war as the colonizing nation (the Netherlands, France) escaped a debate on committed crimes and the accountability of individual soldiers, the army, or the state for these crimes.

After initial resistance, veterans of the Dutch 'police actions' in Indonesia are today viewed mainly as patients, and that is what they want. Approximately a decade ago a comprehensive program was set up so the veterans could enjoy relaxing activities and entertainment together with fellow-veterans and partners. The initiative came from veterans organizations as well as the government-initiated support structure that has been in existence since the recognition of KZ syndrome. Veterans from the colonial war fall partly under the same system of care as Jewish survivors and members of the resistance.

Veterans organizations in France, in response to the revelation that soldiers were guilty of torture in Algeria, also demanded money and care – for the soldiers. Clinicians furthermore arranged that *all* persons involved were given the label of trauma, regardless of guilt or innocence, and regardless of the side they had been on in the conflict. This is comparable to the most recent developments in Denmark. It means, for example, that Algerian children whose fathers were executed by French soldiers were being declared the fellow-sufferers of their fathers' murderers. The argument is that they all suffer. 'Psychiatrists and psychoanalysts,' Brancaccio writes, 'emphasized the common denominator of suffering that linked together war experiences of different groups. The different experiences (and different responsibilities) of military or social groups that had used, witnessed, or been victimized by the violence of the war were thus redefined as a common and generalized experience of psychological trauma.'

Because of this medicalization governments do not have to choose between conflicting historical positions. Seeing victims, heroes and criminals of war all as patients helps a nation to create a certain unity. By doing so the government can escape difficult decisions as to who is guilty, who is innocent and who has suffered more. The system offers an honorable escape to perpetrators as well as to nations.

In politically unfree societies the existence of an official disease like PTSD acts as a crowbar against the denial of the possibly permanent damage of traumatic experiences such as imprisonment in a camp; in democracies PTSD turns out to invite concealment, illness and victim rivalry. Whereas the KZ syndrome played no role in the former GDR, the fall of the wall revived the debate, initiated by East-German refugees, on the psychic consequences of living in a socialist dictatorship. Recently the name of this alleged disease changed into 'Stasi syndrome', a syndrome, as Goltermann found out, that also affects people who were never persecuted by the Stasi. The Stasi-sufferers demand a legal status equal to the Jewish Nazi victims, especially with regard to the reversal of the burden of proof. Their demands are increasingly supported by psychiatrists.

Conclusions

Ever since the liberation from Nazism patients and physicians have been occupied with the long-term or late health consequences of World War II. Former political prisoners from the resistance, other resistance members, ex-POW's – at meetings they all exchanged information about their post-war health problems. Another route through which the protracted after-effects of World War II came to light, was through the Jewish applications for the German *Wiedergutmachung* payments. In nearly every case the problem was a striking loss of mental and physical energy, a syndrome that was first coined in the term asthenia, and was later named KZ syndrome. It proved difficult to distinguish between psychical and physical health damage.

Denmark, France, and Norway led the way in the acknowledgement of the late consequences, thanks in no small measure to the strong position of the resistance in those countries. In the 1960's West Germany, under pressure from the Americans, followed with the recognition of the health damage of the Jewish survivors in particular.

The implementation of the many types of national pension and disability schemes in the long run showed that medical thinking, and in particular psychiatric thinking, was not in line with the health perception of the victims and the practical experience of the clinicians. The dogma that something like the threat of death and being imprisoned in a concentration camp could only cause lasting health damage in 'pre-morbid' persons was undermined since the 1960's, especially by the medical examination problems.

Around 1970 the desire for the introduction of the so-called 'reversed burden of proof' in the law emerged almost everywhere, and for certain categories in some countries this reversal was indeed realized. The patient then no longer had to prove the link between his complaints and his wartime past, the benefits agency had to demonstrate that such a relationship did *not* exist.

The timing was no coincidence. The change in psychiatric thinking received a strong impetus from the 1960's onwards from the international social movements of those years, that in their striving for democratization also criticized the hierarchical relationship between doctors and patients and the stigma on mental disorders. The combination of increasingly assertive patients and the revival of attention for World War II caused a taboo on medical explanatory concepts like pre-morbidity, secondary gain, flight into illness and most certainly malingering. People wanted recognition that the war had caused their illness. Clients as well as society at large increasingly considered distrust regarding their stories unnecessarily offensive.

At what pace and to what degree this change occurred varied per country and sometimes even per region. The degree to which the sixties innovations were accepted proves to be a parameter for the acceptance of war trauma.

Another catalyst was the inclusion in 1980 of post-traumatic stress disorder in the psychiatric classification system DSMIII. With the disorder PTSD the debate about whether an external stressor could permanently affect a mentally healthy adult, which had been dragging on since World War I, was ended at one go. The question of pre-morbidity was placed out of order, as it were; the 'external stressor' was officially declared the principal cause.

France deserves special attention in this conclusion. Thanks to the way in which compensation was given shape there shortly after the war, former prisoners did not need to behave like patients; the legal recognition of a particular disablement was based on their *experiences* (being deported) rather than on their complaints. Nevertheless, France now also has an *Empire du Trauma,* as authors Didier Fassin and Richard Rechtman call it in their recent book. This empire is located in the support of and assistance to victims of crimes like terror attacks, and disasters such as factory explosions, in the aid to refugees, and internationally, through organizations like *Médecins du Monde* and *Médecins sans Frontières,* that provide relief after earthquakes etcetera. Started as regular medical aid organizations, today they focus completely on psychological support.

Unlike in the Netherlands, these intensive activities that are centered around the concept of 'trauma' did not emerge in the slipstream of the discovery of the *war* trauma. Whereas in the Netherlands the discovery of the late consequences of war provided the impetus for a new proliferation, also in aid to refugees for example, and in Denmark the early medical knowledge concerning the KZ syndrome is clearly linked to the actual care for the victims of torture, in France PTSD and the recently emerged large-scale trauma aid are not linked to the aftermath of World War II. Modern trauma thinking in France is predominantly applied to new groups of victims. France to some degree maintained its autonomous course by preferring the WHO classification of mental illnesses over the American DSM that is dominant elsewhere, but the new concept of 'war traumatic neurosis' included in this classification offered the same 'advantages' as PTSD: the external stressor is wholeheartedly acknowledged as the main cause of the disease and any 'predisposition' has been dropped.

With PTSD a trend that was already in motion: the trend of expansion of victim categories reached a provisional peak. After the possibility of external traumatization in adults had initially been reasoned out for a limited group with specific horrific experiences, more and more groups came forward with related health complaints.

This expansion is open to much criticism. It often hides the historical and political reality, declares victims and perpetrators equally traumatized and invites a self-definition of 'being sick'. PTSD has given ample room to the competition for the status of victim and has sacralized victims, i.e. placed them outside the normal interaction procedures of argument and criticism.

In addition the adoption of the concept of trauma has impoverished medical-psychological research. The classic distinction between 'man made' and other disasters was pushed into the background. With the banning of the suspicion or even the critical sense towards victims, important questions regarding the influence of the affective environment during and after the traumatic event, the risk of chronicity, the significance of a person's personality and medical history, also became taboo. By declaring everyone a potential PTSD-sufferer, the question of what exactly causes traumatization and for what reasons frightening situations have different outcomes in different periods and cultures and for different people, disappears from view.

Whereas the first years after the war saw the careful exploration of how and why the deportation to concentration or extermination camps had medically unforeseen consequences, in the end those 'late consequences' were all lumped together under one motto: 'People who experience something bad may be left with long-term consequences,' is the empty catchphrase now.

At the same time our research has shown that in places where a regime or medical establishment has little compassion for (certain groups of) victims, as for example behind the former Iron Curtain, PTSD can function as a vehicle for recognition of the long lasting health consequences of imprisonment, persecution and torture.

Conclusion

» *Annet Mooij and Jolande Withuis*

'It's politics, stupid' – this variation on the slogan from Bill Clinton's election campaign can be viewed as the briefest possible summary of the most important finding of this study. The primacy of politics in the realization of a national perspective on the wartime past and the development of a collective memory was already demonstrated in earlier studies. 'The politics of memory' is today an established concept in historical and social science circles. Our own research shows that political rather than medical interests and considerations were often also decisive in answering questions related to the post-war care for war victims. What victim groups should the government be concerned about? Who is first in line to qualify for a pension or some other financial arrangement? What kinds of war-related health damage should be compensated?

To name but a few striking examples of these political rather than medical considerations: in West Germany communist ex-prisoners did not qualify for benefits because they were seen as agitators against the democratic rule of law. In Poland the group of surviving relatives of fallen fighters who qualified for recognition increased or decreased with the fluctuations in the post-war political climate. German legislation for sick and disabled Jewish survivors was prompted strongly by the desire to be part of the Western alliance, just as the East German refusal to contribute to the same *Wiedergutmachung* sprang from a national self-definition as an antifascist and therefore innocent nation. Whereas from the 1960's on West Germany focused on the Jewish victims, attention in the neighboring GDR went to the former communist resistance members who had been imprisoned. Also, in the West the psychic damage was assumed to be much more extensive than in the East, where the persecution trauma was considered a primarily Western phenomenon.

The fall of the Berlin Wall in 1989 had far-reaching consequences. Not only for Germany. Jewish survivors or their children in Eastern Europe, for example, had to wait for the wall to come down before they could organize themselves as such, which could then result in the discovery of shared psychic complaints. The same applies to the victims of Soviet terror. The dissemination of the concept of PTSD, which was facilitated by the disappearance of the East-West divide resulted in new rivalries among victims and alleged victims.

After 1945 the eleven countries in this study dealt with the medical, and in particular psychic problems of the victims of World War II in very different ways.[1] This 'dealing with' comprises the attitudes of the government, the medical establishment and fellow citizens, as well as those of the victims themselves. Each country dealt with the victims differently, and each had its own timing of recognizing particular groups as 'victims'. The perception, recognition and acknowledgement of psychic war damage varied strongly, both over time and between countries.

Dealing with the consequences of World War II was filled with controversy, conflict and competition. In not one country did it follow logically from the extent of the experienced suffering or the severity of the post-war complaints. It is not possible to deduce from a country's actual wartime history (the facts regarding who were victimized) which groups received the care and attention after the war. Just like the collective memory and remembrance of the years of war are by no means a simple reflection of historical events, so the medical and psychological care for the sick did not follow automatically from the extent of the suffering during or after the war.

Although the different countries responded very differently to the post-war tasks, a pattern is still discernable here. The medical provisions and the laws for the financial support of the war victims all put soldiers, veterans, armed resistance and political prisoners first. As was the case with war remembrance, attention did not focus on the most heavily persecuted groups such as the Jews and gypsies until much later. They were persecuted on the basis of 'race' and not as citizens of an enemy nation. For this reason these groups after the war were often not included in the national legislation. The fact that genocide does not fit in the context of the nation state caused a blind spot in the legislation. Moreover, the survivors of the Holocaust did not contribute to the heroic self-image the occupied countries wanted to present after 1945. On the contrary: they were a direct reference to the horrible failure of the nation state to protect its citizens. This fact was initially ignored in the post-war reconstruction stage; to recognize this failure or even the damage the persecution had done to the survivors' health, would only undermine the desperately needed national recovery and precarious national self-confidence.

The starting point for our investigation was the Dutch situation: a trauma culture as a result of the discovery, around 1970, of the KZ syndrome. This 'trauma culture' means, among other things, the assumption that in the case of adversity those affected will develop psychiatric symptoms in the future. Our study reveals that this Dutch development is by no means matter of course.

---

1 It proves difficult to make a strict distinction between psychological and somatic complaints. There was always a broad spectrum of complaints in both areas: from fatigue and heart palpitations to apathy and lack of concentration.

Only in the Netherlands did the insight into the existence of 'late consequences' lead to such a generalized sense of trauma; here the concept stimulated new groups to define themselves as war patients. None of the other countries saw a political development comparable to the 'war welfare policy' developed since 1972 for the advancement of organizations of and for war victims. However, the Netherlands was not this generous to its heroes and victims from the start. Prior to 1970 the Netherlands had been distinctly reticent, and few war victims had come forward to report being ill or suffering psychologically. Especially in countries with a strong military tradition or strong veterans organizations the care for war victims was organized more generously and more effectively, often by the Ministry of Defense. The French resistance, for example, which had a politically strong position and proceeded with confidence, managed to successfully insert itself in the transitional structures. Partly because the French resistance, unlike their Dutch colleagues, did not hesitate to claim privileges and make illness a topic for discussion, this country led the way in the recognition of permanent health damage, especially among the deportees.

In France the concept of trauma is also very successful today, but the route to this popularity was not via the late consequences of World War II, which were recognized so early on. PTSD was introduced after terror attacks and disasters, in refugee aid, and after a more recent war, i.e. the Algerian war. In the aftermath of this war the trauma concept functions as it originally did in the US: it ignores the issue of guilt and places the varying experiences with acts of war of very different groups (military, perpetrators, victims, bystanders) in one category.

In the other pioneer of the KZ syndrome, Denmark, trauma thinking is just as little associated with World War II, but instead with the care for recent victims of human rights violations such as torture. Ultimately the countries that conceived and developed the KZ syndrome (Denmark, France, Norway) are not the countries where the PTSD diagnosis with regard to World War II was most successful. This demonstrates that psychic complaints can be acknowledged without thinking in terms of trauma. It was Thygesen who in the early 1950's introduced the term KZ syndrome. But although the disease comprised various psychological symptoms, their cause at that time was not sought in a psychological dynamic.

A wave of criticism of the trauma concept has now started in the countries with the strongest trauma cultures (US, UK, Netherlands), but in countries like Austria, Italy and Poland the general acceptance of PTSD is still a thing of the future. The issue is not necessarily the term PTSD or the related philosophy, but rather the recognition that disruptive experiences like war, persecution and imprisonment in camps can also lead to permanent damage to the health and mental balance in 'normal' adults. This recognition is what the most enlightened physicians and patients very much want, and the official international recognition of PTSD can serve as a crowbar here.

People do not survive genocide and persecution, deportations and bombardments, long-term fear of death and massive loss of loved ones unscathed. But the form in which they express their problems, or more passively: how these problems manifest themselves, is related to the forms of presentation, interpretation, and experience that the social environment offers – the models, diseases, and formulations and behaviors that circulate in society or the medical profession. Time and again the way in which people interpreted their conditions proved to be highly dependent on the interpretative possibilities they had at their disposal. Where 'trauma' is an accepted concept, it will be the context for the interpretation of complaints. In France, where the resistance confidently propounded the *pathologie des déportés*, suffering complaints after being imprisoned in the camps was not as uncommon as in the Netherlands, where 'theatrics' were not appreciated, but where the number of patients exploded when KZ syndrome became a common concept. In Scandinavia one could have a KZ syndrome, but it was not viewed as 'psychic'. Immediately after the war the patients and their families in Germany did not interpret their health problems as war complaints. This interpretation was simply not available.

An international comparison as made in this book, in which the differences and similarities between countries are central and the national state as the unit of comparison, begs the question how relevant the significance of national differences really is. In other words: how do the national forces relate to the also very clear transnational and supranational influences on the aftermath and coming to terms with World War II in Europe?

Taking into consideration the previous parade of countries and observing the powerful differences in how the war victims were approached and dealt with in the various countries, the only possible conclusion is that despite the globalization and the many transnational influences, national factors have been dominant in determining what that aftermath and coming to terms looked like. Which factors these were and which influences best explain the observed differences, is, however, not cut-and-dried. We can name several.

First of all, as mentioned before, the considerations of *memory politics* play a role. The post-war patriotism and resulting national taboos regarding World War II; the national self-image; the decisions who will be considered heroes and victims – all strongly influenced the medical policies and the recognition of war diseases.

Secondly there were the *differences in affluence*. The development of pension and compensation schemes depended partly on a country's financial scope as compared to the size of the group of potential claimants. A wealthy country like Denmark could afford a generous scheme for the relatively small Danish resistance. A poor country like Poland, had it wanted to, could not even begin to financially compensate the group of war victims. The number of potential claims would have been endless. The rich countries also had their financial limits. In the Netherlands, for example, the provisions for the second generation of children of Jewish survivors and resistance fighters were discontinued for fear that the costs would rise too fast and unchecked, as had been the case with previous schemes.

A third, very weighty influence consisted of a country's *political culture and creed*. This influence followed several paths.

The investigated countries differ in terms of their responsiveness to pressure groups, in the existence of channels and the organization possibilities for pressure groups and interest groups. There was a very distinct difference between East and West in this respect. Recognition of the sick in Poland and the GDR was not the result of pressure from the basis, it was dictated by the state. The communist regimes dictated who were heroes, who were victims and who were nothing. Western Europe knows a large variation in this respect, also over time. Most extreme, immediately after the liberation, was Denmark, where one could almost speak of a diktat of the former resistance lobby. In the Netherlands responsiveness to pressure from the side of victims increased strongly from the 1970's.

The investigated countries also differed in their degree of political stability. Weak states like Belgium and Italy after the war turned out to be least successful at developing one integrated national narrative; they remained divided and fragmented in their culture of remembrance. The extreme political discord in post-war Italy contributed to the fact that experiences and memories of different groups barely penetrated outside the circle of fellow-victims. They continued to exist separately, not integrated into one whole, one coordinating national narrative. Covering up differences, and therefore a strategy of silence, helped the construction of the new Italy. Up to this day there is very little attention in Italy for the psychic consequences of war, persecution, deportation, captivity.

A fourth distinguishing national element is found in what we may refer to as the various *cultures of care*. Here, also, different aspects can be distinguished.

The Netherlands, West Germany and the Scandinavian countries are all strongly developed welfare states. The expansion of the welfare state has generally made people in the post-war period susceptible to the idea of 'being entitled' to the achievements of the welfare state, whether they be social benefits, medical care or legal aid. Applications for many benefits and provisions started to rise in the 1970's. War victims also increasingly began to see themselves as being entitled, which in the Netherlands and Denmark was expressed in a strong rise in applications for existing schemes and arrangements, particularly in the 1970's.

It is also clear that the concept of trauma implies a way of thinking that, more than collectivistic societies, suits individualized societies, where personal suffering is no longer expressed and dealt with primarily within (extended) family, church or political party, but has become the object of state care.

With regard to the medical-psychiatric climate it is worth mentioning the absence of an unequivocal influence of World War I on the care for war victims after World War II. Experiences in World War I had demonstrated that any individual who is caught in an extreme situation for a longer period of time, regardless of how healthy he is to begin with, can break down and start exhibiting hysterical or neurotic symptoms. And yet the countries that shared this World War I experience responded differently to the new challenge after 1945. Neither the assumption that countries that participated in World War I were better prepared because of their experiences with shell shock and therefore provided more adequate care, nor the opposite assumption: that due to this (costly) experience they were afraid to acknowledge psychic consequences, is altogether true. In addition, the fear of malingering, pre-morbidity and chronic pension neurosis also existed in countries that were not touched by World War I. In these countries people were generally aware of the experiences elsewhere, and comparable debates were also held outside military psychiatry, namely in the field of social insurance medicine. This field was also acquainted with the concept of secondary gain and malingering.

The investigated countries show differences in the degree of dissemination of medical-psychiatric concepts. The Netherlands had a strong mental health movement even before the war; France has a strong psychoanalytical movement. This dominant presence affected society in a process of so-called proto-professionalization: the phenomenon that people take over insights and terminology from the professionals and interpret, formulate and present their complaints accordingly. They tend to seek professional help more quickly.[2]

This proto-professionalization was also stimulated by the democratization movement of the 1960's, which included a de-stigmatization of the psychiatric patient and an emancipation of emotions. In some countries (for example Austria) this breakthrough was not very pronounced, in others it was much more intense, as for example in the Netherlands.

In our opinion the accelerated and fairly extreme Dutch development after 1972 is based on the convergence of several historical developments, and partly on the cultural innovations of the 1960's, which were especially successful in the Netherlands. The Dutch elites that accepted or even welcomed the sixties, appear to have accepted the war syndrome in the same torrent of modernity.

The democratization and leveling that followed from the sixties touched on the essence of the problems surrounding the medical acknowledgement of the KZ syndrome, in which the question of causality and earning capacity – to be answered by the physician – was very important. As a result of the changes of the 1960's and 70's the power balance between physician and patient became more equal,

2 De Swaan, *In care of the state*, 244-246.

there was more attention for the social aspects of mental illness, and 'assessment' of the patient's personality became increasingly taboo. The arrogance of the medical establishment to assume that these were all people who were after a pension decreased, while compassion and awe for the victims increased.

At the national level, finally, *contingent factors* are also important. A particular concurrence of circumstances at the right time could strongly affect how the medical profession and the population thought about health problems. Sometimes certain individuals played an important part (Eitinger in Norway, Bastiaans in the Netherlands, Terracini in Italy), or incidents and affairs were the catalyst (the Breda Three in the Netherlands, the Waldheim affair in Austria), or the publication of books provided an impulse, like the high-profile books by Robert Paxton and Henry Rousso on Vichy-France and the work of Jan Blonski and Jan Gross in Poland.

However, national factors were not the only influence on developments after 1945. Further research is definitely required into the influence of religion on the emergence and recognition of war trauma and the potential development of a trauma culture.

One question that forces itself upon us is whether church and religion act as the opponent of, or alternative for, a psychiatric approach. One of the conclusions that can be drawn from our research is that the trauma concept is more successful in Protestant cultures than in Catholic ones (Belgium, Italy, Austria, Poland). Why this is so is not clear. Did the Catholic faith meet a need for comfort and meaning that the Protestant churches left unanswered? Did the hierarchical Catholic church offer less room for the personal suffering of the believers? Or did the stronger developed notions of guilt and individual responsibility in the protestant, and especially Calvinistic, cultures perhaps increase susceptibility to a trauma culture?

A second possibility is that the degree of secularization rather than the religious culture (Protestant or Catholic) is decisive. In the Netherlands, for example, the rapid secularization may have stimulated trauma thinking. An ideological vacuum had emerged that was filled by a rapid popularization of psychological theories, including war trauma. In this way 'trauma' may have functioned as compensation for the loss of religious signification.

Further investigation is also required regarding the significance of the existence or absence of a veteran culture, one of the characteristic differences between countries that were or were not involved in World War I.

A presently accepted explanation for the Dutch developments is that the Netherlands, unlike countries that experienced World War I, had no 'veteran tradition'. For whereas after the liberation the Netherlands emphatically waived all homage and felt that awarding separate medals to resistance fighters and former soldiers was not necessary, countries that did have such a veteran tradition – France being the best example – quickly developed various kinds of moral recognition and rewards for heroism and courage in the form of the resistance crosses, medals and honorary titles such as 'Mort pour la Patrie'.

One of the anticipated outcomes of the comparison of the different countries was that the huge increase in the number of people who were sick in the Netherlands after 1970 could be explained from the absence of recognition immediately after the war. In this hypothesis the traumas that came to light decades after the liberation were the price the Netherlands had to pay for withholding honor and recognition.

Our study shows that it was by no means true that no complaints developed in France, on the contrary: the resistance managed to incorporate the *pathologie des déportés* in an old tradition. Homage explicitly went together with the recognition of the new war disease. Belgium also paid tribute to its heroes. Contrary to the situation in France, this was not accompanied by a liberal recognition of a new disease. Nor did Belgium in later years 'catch up' the way the Netherlands did.

Further investigation must look for an explanation for these facts. Could France, like Belgium, have done without the *pathologie des déportés*? Are there alternative explanations for the absence of a trauma culture in Belgium?[3]

And then there are the transnational influences. Over the past twenty years they have undoubtedly become stronger, but they are not only recent. The reparation payments Germany started in the 1950's are a first transnational phenomenon. They created an influential model for the settlement of a painful and controversial past, and at the same time an international network was developed, for the distribution of money, but also for the dissemination of medical knowledge and ideas on the consequences of war, imprisonment, and extreme stress. The American medical profession became involved in European thinking on medical and psychological consequences of war through the reparation payments to Nazi victims who had moved to the US.

The German *Wiedergutmachung* had a huge impact on the psychiatric profession recognizing the long-term damage caused by the war, which initially had been considered impossible. Because the medical examinations of Jewish survivors were carried out by psychoanalysts who had fled to the US before the war, their medical understanding of the war trauma was exported to Germany. The same knowledge also strengthened the conviction of the international organizations of resistance, political prisoners, and prisoners of war that the war, and especially imprisonment in concentration camps, had caused permanent, predominantly psychological, damage. These – highly political – organizations had started inves-

3 Relevant to this issue is Jay Winter's suggestion, that the huge *cultural* (more than mere medical) meaning of the concept of shell shock in Great Britain (as compared to Germany and France), was related to the absence of veterans organizations in England.

tigating these consequences (and the struggle to get them acknowledged) immediately after the liberation. And they managed to bridge the Cold War differences before politics did.

Some specific events also had a clear cross-border effect. For example, the Eichmann trial in 1961 stimulated the debate on guilt and accountability with regard to the persecution of the Jews. It initiated the shift of the Holocaust from the margin to the centre of the national memory of World War II, a shift that is visible everywhere. It was furthermore strongly stimulated by another transnational influence: the European unification. From the start World War II has been defined in the European unification process as a 'foundational event' and this is especially true of the shared memory of the Holocaust, which is seen as part of the core of the European identity. That this is still the case was demonstrated in the negotiations about recent expansions, in which the new Eastern European member states were more or less forced to take stock of their past, and in particular to no longer avoid the issue of their co-responsibility for the Holocaust. The formation and expansion of the European Union therefore went hand in hand with an institutionalization and also uniformization of Holocaust memory.

At yet another level the so-called Americanization or globalization of the Holocaust is making itself felt, namely in the development, strongly influenced by the US, of the Holocaust into a universal symbol, 'the negative core event of the twentieth century'.[4]

The transnational influences have a homogenizing effect and they de-nationalize national remembrance. National differences are now less sharp than a few decades ago. The Holocaust has become a universal point of reference that refers to something terrible that should never be allowed to happen again, and a moral point of reference that urges countries to take action against the danger of genocide, mass murder and ethnic cleansing: 'The Holocaust has become a moral certainty on which action can be based (...). And it is a moral certainty that stretches across national borders and unites the West.'[5] The Holocaust can only fulfill this unifying function because as an event it has become highly abstract and separated from its original historical context, its specific perpetrators (the Nazis and their accomplices) and its specific victims (the Jews).

At the same time the globalization of the Holocaust and the international breakthrough of PTSD have enhanced each other. The 1982 film *Sophie's Choice,* which had a huge influence on the worldwide recognition of the Holocaust as a unique crime, is a poignant illustration of this process. For the theme of the film is the war trauma of Sophie, the mother who had to decide which of her two children would die in the gas chamber.

4 Diner, in Diner and Wunberg (eds.), *Restitution*, 19.

5 Sznaider, in Diner and Wunberg (eds.), *Restitution*, 57.

Bibliography

Adler, Nanci, *The Gulag survivor: Beyond the Soviet system*. New Brunswick/London, 2002.

Aerts, K., 'De Kroon ontbloot. Genadeverlening bij de doodstraf tijdens de zuiveringen na de Tweede Wereldoorlog'. *Bijdragen tot de Eigentijdse Geschiedenis*, 17 (2006), 15-47.

Ahonen, P., *After the expulsion. West Germany and Eastern Europe 1945-1990*. Oxford, 2003.

Aigner, F., 'Die Verfolgung der Zeugen Jehovas in Österreich 1938-1945'. In: R. Steininger (ed.), 2000, 9-21.

Albrich, T., *Exodus durch Österreich. Die jüdischen Flüchtlinge 1945-1948*. Innsbruck, 1987.

Amicale des Pupilles de la Nation, *D'Pupilles de la Nation erënnere sech*. Luxembourg, 2004.

Andreasen, Nancy C., 'Posttraumatic Stress Disorder: Psychology, biology and the manichaean warfare between false dichotomies'. *The American Journal of Psychiatry*, 152/7 (1995), 963-965.

Anonymous, 'Conséquences de la déportation. L'état de santé des anciens concentrationnaires'. *Rappel*, 9 (1954), 59-63.

Anonymous, 'Das muss auch einmal gesagt werden'. *Rappel*, 20 (1966), 315-317.

Anonymous, 'Exposé des motifs relatif au projet de loi ayant pour objet diverses mesures en faveur de personnes devenues victimes d'actes illégaux de l'occupant'. *Rappel*, 20 (1966), 562-565.

Anonymous, 'Statut de la Résistance (suite). Discussions à la Chambre des Députés. Chapitre IV Les dommages de guerre corporels. C) les rentes'. *Rappel*, 22 (1968), 51-59.

Apfelbaum (Kowalski), E. (ed.), *Choroba głodowa. Badania kliniczne nad głodem wykonane w getcie warszawskim w roku 1942*. Warsaw, 1946.

Askevold, F., 'Krigsseilersyndromet'. In: N. Retterstøl (ed.), 1982.

Askevold, F., 'War sailor syndrome'. *Psychotherapy and Psychosomatics*, 27 (1976/1977), 133-138.

'Atti del XXVI Congresso della Società Freniatrica Italiana (Roma, 5-8 Aprile 1923)'. *Rivista Sperimentale di Freniatria*, 48 (1924), 3-71.

August, J. (ed.), *Die Auschwitz Hefte*. Hamburg, 1994.

Aussaresses, P., *Services spéciaux, Algérie 1955-1957: mon témoignage sur la torture*. Paris, 2001.

Baard, B., P. Haave and L. Borgerund, *Fiendens barn?* Oslo, 1999.

Baeyer, W. von et al., *Psychiatrie der Verfolgten. Psychopathologische und gutachtliche Erfahrungen an Opfern der nationalsozialistischen Verfolgung und vergleichbarer Extrembelastungen*. Berlin, 1964.

Bailer, B., *Wiedergutmachung – kein Thema. Österreich und die Opfer des Nationalsozialismus*. Vienna, 1993.

Bailer-Galanda, B., *Die Entstehung der Rückstellungs- und Entschädigungsgesetzgebung. Die Republik Österreich und das in der NS-Zeit entzogene Vermögen*. (Veröffentlichungen der Historikerkommission der Republik Österreich, vol. 3). Vienna/Munich, 2003.

Bailer-Galanda, B., 'Entschädigung für seelisches Leid? Verfolgungsbedingte Gesundheitsschäden und das österreichische Opferfürsorgegesetz'. In: A. Friedmann et al. (eds.), 2004.

Bailer-Galanda, B. and E. Blimlinger, *Vermögensentzug – Rückstellung – Entschädigung. Österreich 1938/1945-2005*. Innsbruck/Vienna/Bolzano, 2005.

Balduzzi, O., 'XXIII Congresso della Società Italiana di Psichiatria (intervention)'. *Rivista Sperimentale di Freniatria*, 71-72 (1947-1948), 207.

Baley, S., 'Psychiczne wpływ drugiej wojny światowej'. *Psychologia Wychowawcza*, 12 (1948), 6-24.

Baley, S., 'Wpływ wojny na psychikę młodzieży i dorosłych w Polsce'. *Psychologia Wychowawcza*, 12 (1947), 1-11.

Bandhauer-Schöffmann, I., *Entzug und Restitution im Bereich der Katholischen Kirche*. Veröffentlichungen der Historikerkommission der Republik Österreich, vol. 22/1. Vienna/Munich, 2004.

Bankier, David (ed.), *The Jews are coming back. The return of the Jews to their countries of origin after WW II*. New York/Oxford, 2005.

Barrois, C., *Les névroses traumatiques*. Paris, 1998.

Bauerkämper, A., *Die Sozialgeschichte der DDR*. Munich, 2005.

Bauman, Z., *Nowoczesność i zagłada*. Warsaw, 1991.

Baumann, R., 'Analyse 2: Siegi Hirsch, le "Mensch" de l'année 2002'. *Regard – Revue du Centre Communautaire Laïc Juif de Belgique*, 20 February 2003. www.cclj.be/regards/web/gd_analyses.asp?year=2003.

Beauge, F., '350.000 anciens d'Algérie souffriraient de troubles psychiques liés à la guerre'. *Le Monde*, 28 December 2000.

Beauge, F., 'Je me suis résolu à la torture...moi-même procédé à des exécutions sommaires'. *Le Monde*, 23 November 2000.

Beauge, F., 'Torturée par l'armée française en Algérie. Lila cherche l'homme qui l'a sauvé'. *Le Monde*, 20 June 2000.

Beckermann, R., *Unzugehörig. Österreicher und Juden nach 1945*. Vienna, 1989.

Behrenbeck, S., 'Between pain and silence. Remembering the victims of violence in Germany after 1949'. In: R. Bessel and D. Schumann (eds.), 2003, 37-64.

Beinhauer, E.R., 'Selige Sr. Restituta. Helene Kafka – Märtyrerin in Proexistenz, Protest und Prophetie'. In: Stefan Karner and Karl Duffek (eds.), *Widerstand in Österreich*. Graz/Vienna, 2007, 88-93.

Berger, E. (ed.), *'Verfolgte Kindheit'. Kinder und Jugendliche als Opfer der NS-Sozialverwaltung*. Vienna, 2007.

Berger, J., 'Ein Drama, über das man nicht redet. Veranstaltungsreihe im Bregenzer Wald über NS-Morde an Kranken und Behinderten'. *Der Standard*, 11 April 2008, 11.

Berger, K. et al., *Der Himmel ist blau. Kann sein. Frauen im Widerstand. Österreich 1938-1945*. Vienna, 1985.
Berger, K. et al., *'Ich geb Dir einen Mantel, daß Du ihn noch in Freiheit tragen kannst'*. Vienna, 1987.
Berger, K. et al., *Vollzugspraxis des 'Opferfürsorgegesetzes'. Analyse der praktischen Vollziehung des einschlägigen Sozialrechts.* (Veröffentlichungen der Historikerkommission der Republik Österreich, vol. 29/2). Vienna/Munich, 2004.
Bergmann, M.S. and M.E. Jucovy (eds.), *Generations of the Holocaust*. New York, 1982.
Bernard, P. 'L'agonie psychique des anciens d'Algérie'. *Le Monde*, 17 October 2003.
Bessel, R. and D. Schumann (eds.), *Life after death. Approaches to a cultural and social history of Europe during the 1940s and 1950s*. Washington D.C., 2003.
Beyens, N., 'Federalisering op z'n Belgisch'. *Kleio* 43 (2002) 5, 5-9.
Bezoekersgids Het Fort van Breendonk. De nazi-terreur in België. 2003.
Biess, F., *Homecomings. Returning POW's and the legacies of defeat in postwar Germany*. Princeton, 2006.
Birkeland, S.A., *Taget af Tyskerne. Danskere i 2n Verdenskrig*. Copenhagen, 2008.
Bischof, G., 'Die Instrumentalisierung der Moskauer Erklärung nach dem 2. Weltkrieg'. *Zeitgeschichte*, 11/12 (1993), 345-366.
Bischof, G., A. Pelinka and D. Stiefel, 'The Marshall Plan in Austria'. *Contemporary Austrian Studies*, vol. 8. New Brunswick, 2000.
Bischof, G., S. Karner and B. Stelz-Marx (eds.), *Kriegsgefangene des Zweiten Weltkrieges. Gefangennahme, Lagerleben, Rückkehr*. München, 2005.
Błoński, J., 'Biedni Polacy patrzą na getto'. *Tygodnik Powszechny*, 61 (1987) 2.
Bogusz, J., 'Wojna i okupacja a medycyna'. *Międzynarodowa Sesja naukowa w Krakowie 25-26 kwietnia 1985 r. Materiały*. Krakow, 1986.
Bohlmann, F., 'Die Eingliederung der Schwerbeschädigten in den Arbeitsprozeß'. *Arbeit und Sozialfürsorge*, 1 (1946), 301-302.
Boldorf, M., 'Die Verdrängung der Kriegsbeschädigtenproblematik in der SBZ/DDR'. In: P. Erker (ed.), 2004.
Boldorf, M., 'Eingliederung der Kriegsopfer und Schwerbeschädigten Ostdeutschlands in den Arbeitsprozeß 1945-1951'. In: C. Buchheim (ed.), *Wirtschaftliche Folgelasten des Krieges in der SBZ/DDR*. Baden-Baden, 1995, 403-415.
Bonifas, L., *Le dédommagement des enrôlés de force luxembourgeois après la deuxième guerre mondiale*. Brussels, 2007.
Borgen, P.H.F. and T. Hofsbro, *Norske polititropper i Sverige/Norge 1943-1945: operasjonene i Norge 1944-1945*. Oslo, 2006.
Boszormenyi-Nagy, I. and G.M. Spark, *Invisible loyalties. Reciprocity in international family therapy*. Hagerstown (Maryland), 1973.
Botz, G., 'Eine deutsche Geschichte 1938 bis 1945?' *Zeitgeschichte*, 1 (1986), 19-38.
Botz, G., 'Methoden- und Theorieprobleme der historischen Widerstandsforschung'. In: Helmut Konrad and Herbert Steiner (eds.), *Arbeiterbewegung – Faschismus – Nationalbewusstsein*. Vienna, 1983.
Botz, G., *Nationalsozialismus in Wien. Machtübernahme, Herrschaftssicherung, Radikalisierung 1938/1939*. Vienna, 2008.

Botz, G. and G. Sprengnagel (eds.), *Kontroversen um Österreichs Zeitgeschichte. Verdrängte Vergangenheit, Österreich-Identität und die Historiker*. Frankfurt/New York, 1994.

Brainin, E. and S. Teicher, 'Die Wiener Psychoanalytische Vereinigung und der Nationalsozialismus'. In: *Tel Aviver Jahrbuch für deutsche Geschichte*. Göttingen, 2004.

Bredsdorff, E., *En bog om Mogens Fog*. Vestergaard, 1992.

Brekke, M., 'Vi intervjuer Leo Eitinger: hinsides menneskelig forstand'. *Tidsskrift for Den norske legeforening*, 115 (1995), 1402-1404.

Bronner, A., *Vienna Psychoanalytic Society – The first 100 years*. Vienna, 2008.

Bruckmüller, E. (ed.), *Wiederaufbau in Österreich 1945-1955. Rekonstruktion und Neubeginn*. Munich, 2006.

Bryld, C., *Hvilken befrielse? Fortælling fra en opvækst i nazismens og retsopgørets skygge*. Copenhagen, 1995.

Bryld, C. and A. Warring, *Besættelsestiden som kollektiv erindring*. Roskilde, 1998.

Bundgård Christensen, C., 'På vagt i en lovlos tid'. *Fortid og Nutid*, 2 (2001), 91-109.

Bundgård Christensen, C. et al., *Danmark besat. Krig og hverdag 1940-45*. Copenhagen, 2005.

Bunzl, M., *Symptoms of modernity*. Berkeley/Los Angeles/London, 2004.

Burger, H. and H. Wendelin, *Die Praxis der Vollziehung des Staatsbürgerschaftsrechts an den österreichischen Juden*. (Veröffentlichungen der Historikerkommission der Republik Österreich, vol. 7). Vienna/Munich, 2004.

Buruma, Ian, 'The joys and perils of victimhood'. *The New York Review of Books*, 8 April 1999, 4-8.

Busch, T. and B. Winhab (eds.), *Jelka, aus dem Leben einer Kärntner Partisanin. Nach Tonbandaufzeichnungen von Helene Kuhar*. Basel, 1984.

Caestecker, F., 'The reintegration of Jewish survivors into Belgian society 1943-1947'. In: D. Bankier (ed.), 2005.

Ceravolo, M., Camera dei Deputati, Legislatura II, *Atti Parlamentari*. (Discussioni, Seduta 4 dicembre 1956), 29545-29549.

Claisse, S., 'Reconnaissance et méconnaissance des espions après guerre'. In: L. Van Ypersele, E. Debruyne and Stéphanie Claisse (eds.), *De la guerre de l'ombre aux ombres de la guerre, l'espionnage en Belgique durant la guerre 1914-18*. Brussels, 2004, 87-98.

Cohen, Rita E., *Vergelijkend onderzoek naar regelingen voor oorlogsgetroffenen in het buitenland en in Nederland*. (Undergraduate thesis Dutch law, University of Amsterdam, 1987).

Comité Exécutif, 'Amnestie'. *Rappel*, 9 (1954), 129-130.

Commission spéciale pour l'étude des spoliation des biens juifs au Luxembourg pendant les années de guerre 1940-1945, *La spoliation des biens juifs au Luxembourg 1940-1945. Rapport Intermédiaire*. 2007.

Committee for Skeptical Enquiry, 'Psychics and missing children', 1997. www.csicop.org/sb/9703/belgium.html.

Congrès de la Société Franco-Algérienne de Psychiatrie, 'Souffrances et mémoires. La guerre d'Algérie 1954-1962', Paris, 2003. http://www.sfapsy.com/Divers/Congres-SFAP.htm.

Consiglio, P., 'Le anomalie nel carattere dei militari'. *Rivista Sperimentale di Freniatria*, 40 (1916), 131-172.

Cook, B. (ed.), *Europe since 1945: An encyclopedia*. New York, 2001.

COR, 'Exposé des motifs'. *Rappel*, 20 (1966), 534-539.

COR, 'Statut légal de la Résistance'. *Rappel*, 20 (1966), 255-260.

Corradini, E., *Il reinserimento dei perseguitati razziali nel secondo dopoguerra: L'itinerario della legge n. 96 del 10 marzo 1955*. (Dissertation, University of Turin, 1995).

Crocq, L., 'Les névroses traumatiques doivent être reconnues et indemnisées'. *LXXXIII Congrès de psychiatrie et neurologie de langue française*, Comptes rendus, Paris, 1985.

Crocq, L., *Les traumatismes psychiques de guerre*. Paris, 1999.

Czech, H., 'Fahnenflucht in die Krankheit? Die Militärpsychiatrie und die Behandlung der "Kriegsneurotiker" in den beiden Weltkriegen'. *Kontext XXI*, 2 (2002), 24-26.

Dachs, H., 'Von der "Sanierungspartnerschaft" zur konfliktgeladenen Unübersichtlichkeit. Über Entwicklungen und Verschiebungen der großen Koalition 1986 bis 1994'. In: Reinhard Sieder et al. (eds.), *Österreich 1945 – 1995. Gesellschaft – Politik – Kultur*. Vienna, 1995, 290-303.

Dahl, H.F., 'Besettelse, Dansk og Norsk'. *Historie/Jyske Samlinger* 2 (2001), 387-397.

Danielsen, R. and S.U. Larsen, *Fra ide til dom: Noen trekk ara atviklingen av Nasjonal Samling*. Oslo, 1976.

Dasberg, H., 'Psychiatrische und psychosoziale Folgen des Holocaust. Epidemiologische Studien in Israel'. In: H. Stoffels (ed.), 1991.

Davies, P.J., *France and the Second World War: Occupation, collaboration, and resistance*. London, 2001.

Deschamps, A., *Les maladies de l'esprit et les asthénies*. Paris, 1919.

Diehl, J.M., *German veterans after the Second World War*. Chapel Hill, 1993.

Diner, Dan and Gotthart Wunberg (eds.), *Restitution and memory. Material restoration in Europe*. New York/Oxford, 2007.

Donaggio, A., 'Orazione inaugurale al XXII congresso della Società italiana di psichiatria (1940)'. *Rivista sperimentale di Freniatria*, 63 (1940), 378-386.

Doorslaer, R. van (ed.), *Gewillig België. Overheid en Jodenvervolging tijdens de Tweede Wereldoorlog*. Antwerpen/Amsterdam, 2007.

Dopfeld, P., 'Auszüge aus S.D.-Berichten'. *Rappel*, 8 (1953), 49-52.

Dostert, P., 'Die Luxemburger im Reserve-Polizei-Bataillon 101 und der Judenmord in Polen'. *Hémecht: revue d'histoire luxembourgeoise*, 52 (2000), 81-99.

Dostert, P., 'La Résistance luxembourgeoise pendant la seconde guerre mondiale et la reprise politique de 1944/45'. In: *Les années trente: base de l'évolution économique, politique et sociale du Luxembourg d'après-guerre? Actes du Colloque de l'A.L.E.H. du 27-28 octobre 1995* (Beiheft zu *Hemecht: revue d'histoire luxembourgeoise*, 48 (1996)), 25-50.

Dostert, P., '"Vive Letzebuerg – Vive Charlotte". La résistance patriotique contre l'occupant allemand (1940-1945).' In: *Les courants politiques et la Résistance: Continuités ou ruptures? Colloque international Esch-sur-Alzette, 24-26 avril 2002*. Luxembourg, 2003, 365-383.

Duhot, E. and R. Targowla, 'Essai sur la psychose émotive des bombardements'. *Annales d'hygiène publique et de médecine légale*, 32 (1919), 21.

Duignan, P., 'Communist fronts', In: B. Cook (ed.), 2001, 211-212.

Dumoulin, M. et al., *Nieuwe geschiedenis van België. Deel II: 1905-1950*. Tielt, 2006.

Dupong, P., 'Le gouvernement en exil'. In: N. Bosseler and R. Steichen (eds.), *Livre d'or de la résistance luxembourgeoise de 1940-1945*. Luxembourg, 1952, 34-36.

Dynowska, W., *All for freedom: the Warsaw epic*. The Indo-Polish library, 1946.

Ecker, M., 'Spätes Gedenken. Richard Groher 1902 – 1943'. *Betrifft: Widerstand. Zeitschrift des Zeitgeschichtemuseums Ebensee*, November 2005.

Ecker, M., *Tales of edification and redemption? Oral/audiovisual Holocaust testimonies and American public memory 1945-2005*. Salzburg, 2006.

Eeckhout, P. van den et al., *Bronnen voor de studie van het hedendaagse België, 19e-20e eeuw*. Brussels, 1999.

Eghigian, G., 'The psychologization of the socialist self: East German forensic psychology and its deviants, 1945-1975'. *German History*, 22 (2004), 181-205.

Eghigian, G., 'Was there a communist psychiatry? Politics and East German psychiatric care, 1945-1989'. *Harvard Review of Psychiatry*, 10 (2002), 364-369.

Eitinger, L., *Concentration camp survivors in Norway and Israel*. Oslo, 1964.

Eitinger, L., 'Psychiatric post-conditions in former concentration camp inmates'. In: *Later effects of imprisonment and deportation*, 1961.

Eitinger, L., *Psykiatriske undersøkelser blant flyktninger i Norge*. Oslo, 1958.

Eitinger, L. and A. Strøm, *Mortality and morbidity after excessive stress: a follow-up investigation of Norwegian concentration camp survivors*. Oslo, 1973.

Eitinger, L., N. Retterstøl and U.F. Malt, *Psykoser og organisk betingede sinnslidelser*. Oslo, 1986.

Eitinger, L., R. Krell and M. Rieck, *The psychological and medical effects of concentration camps and related persecutions on survivors of the Holocaust: a research bibliography*. Vancouver, 1985.

Eitinger, L. et al., *Krigsskader og senvirkninger: Krigspensjonering gjennom 50 år*. Oslo, 1995.

Embacher, H., '"...daß die Ehre der Kameraden unangetastet bleiben müsse..." Die "Wehrmachtsausstellung" und das Geschichtsbild des Kameradschaftsbundes'. In: Helga Embacher, Albert Lichtblau and Günther Sandner (eds.), *Umkämpfte Erinnerung. Die Wehrmachtsausstellung in Salzburg*. Salzburg, 1999, 96-132.

Embacher, H., 'Eine Heimkehr gibt es nicht? – Remigration nach Österreich'. In: *Exilforschung. Ein internationales Jahrbuch. Jüdische Emigration*. Bd. 19, Munich, 2001, 187-209.

Embacher, H., 'Literatur der Gefühle. Die Widerspiegelung der Waldheim-Affäre in der österreichischen Literatur'. In: Moshe Zuckermann (ed.), *Deutsche Geschichte des 20. Jahrhunderts im Spiegel der deutschsprachigen Literatur*. Göttingen, 2003, 148-166.

Embacher, H., *Neubeginn ohne Illusionen. Juden in Österreich nach 1945*. Vienna, 1995.

Embacher, H., *Restitutionsverhandlungen mit Österreich aus der Sicht jüdischer Organisationen und der Israelitischen Kultusgemeinde*. (Veröffentlichungen der Historikerkommission der Republik Österreich, vol. 27). Vienna/Munich, 2003.

Embacher, H. and M. Reiter, *Gratwanderungen. Die Beziehungen zwischen Österreich und Israel im Schatten der NS-Vergangenheit*. Vienna, 1997.

Embacher, H. and M. Reiter, 'Partisanin aus christlicher Nächstenliebe. Österreichische Sloweninnen in den Konzentrationslagern'. In: Rudolf G. Ardelt and Hans Hautmann (eds.), *Arbeiterbewegung und Nationalsozialismus in Österreich*. Vienna/Zürich, 1990, 553-579.

Enning, Bram, *De oorlog van Bastiaans. De LSD-behandeling van het KZ-syndroom*. Amsterdam, 2009.

Eriksen, A., *Det var noe annet under krigen. 2. verdenskrig i norsk kollektivtradisjon*. Oslo, 1995.

Erker, P. (ed.), *Rechnung für Hitlers Krieg. Aspekte und Probleme des Lastenausgleichs*. Heidelberg, 2004.

'Erzählte Geschichte. Berichte von Widerstandskämpfern und Verfolgten'. *Dokumentationsarchiv des österreichischen Widerstandes*. Vienna/Munich, 130-162.

'Event mit "Kirtagscharakter"'. *Der Standard*, 15 December 2007.

Extreme Lebensverhältnisse und ihre Folgen (Schriftenreihe des Ärztlich-wissenschaftlichen Beirates des Verbandes der Heimkehrer Deutschlands e.V., B. 7). Bad Godesberg, 1959.

Fassin, Didier and Richard Rechtman, *The empire of trauma. An inquiry into the condition of victims*. Princeton/Oxford, 2009.

Feichtlbauer, H., *Zwangsarbeit in Österreich. 1938-1945*. Vienna, 2005.

Fejkiel W., *Choroba głodowa w obozach koncentracyjnych na podstawie własnych, 5-letnich doświadczeń*. Pamiętnik XIV zjazdu Towarzystwa Internistów Polskich we Wrocławiu w roku 1947. Wroclaw, 1948, 369-373.

Fernsebner-Kokert, B., 'Kritik an der Ehrentafel für Klinik-Chef'. *Der Standard*, 25/26 August 2007.

Forster, D., *'Wiedergutmachung' in Österreich und der BRD im Vergleich*. Innsbruck, 2001.

Francesconi, H., *Extremtraumatisierung und ihre Folgen für die nächste Generation. Die psychischen Störungen der Nachkommen ehemaliger KZ-Häftlinge*. Vienna, 1983.

Frankl, V.E., *'...Trotzdem ja zum Leben sagen'. Ein Psychologe erlebt das Konzentrationslager*. Vienna, 1947.

Franzinelli, M., *I tentacoli dell'Ovra*. Turin, 2000.

Freund, F. et al., *Vermögensentzug, Restitution und Entschädigung der Roma und Sinti*. (Veröffentlichungen der Historikerkommission der Republik Österreich, vol. 23/2). Vienna/Munich, 2003.

Freyberger H.J. et al., *Gesundheitliche Folgen politischer Haft in der DDR*, edited by the Konferenz des Landesbeauftragten für die Unterlage des Staatssicherheitsdienstes der ehemaligen DDR. Dresden, 2003.

Friedmann, Alexander et al. (eds.), *Psychotrauma. Die posttraumatische Belastungsstörung*. Vienna/New York, 2004.

Friedrich, J., *Der Brand. Deutschland im Bombenkrieg 1940-1945*. Berlin, 2002.

Fritz, M., *Essig gegen den Durst*. Vienna, 1986.

Frydman, M., *Le traumatisme de l'enfant caché. Répercussions psychologiques à court et à long termes*. Gerpinnes, 1999.

'Für Spaniens Freiheit. Österreicher an der Seite der Spanischen Republik 1936-1939. Eine Dokumentation'. *Dokumentationsarchiv des österreichischen Widerstandes*. Vienna/Munich, 1986.

Futselaar, R., *Lard, lice and longevity: a comparative study of the standard of living in occupied Denmark and the Netherlands, 1940-1945*. Amsterdam, 2008.

Gabriel, E. and W. Neugebauer (eds.), *Vorreiter der Vernichtung. Von der Zwangssterilisierung zur Ermordung. Zur Geschichte der NS-Euthanasie in Wien*, Teil II. Vienna, 2002.

Gampel, Y., *Some reflections on counter-transference in psychoanalytical work with Shoah survivors*. University of Tel Aviv, typescript, 1991.

Garscha, W., 'Entnazifizierung und gerichtliche Ahndung von NS-Verbrechen'. In: E. Tálos et al. (eds.), 2000, 852-883.

Gärtner, H. and S. Rosenberger, *Kriegerdenkmäler*. Innsbruck, 1991.

Gehler, M., '"... eine grotesk überzogene Dämonisierung eines Mannes..."' In: Michael Gehler and Hubert Sickinger (eds.), *Politische Affären und Skandale in Österreich. Von Mayerling bis Waldheim*. Vienna/Munich, 1995, 614-665.

'Genocide of European Roma (Gypsies) 1939-1945'. *Holocaust Encyclopedia*, http://www.ushmm.org/wlc/article.php?ModuleId=10005219.

Gerbl, C., Alexander Mestrjk and Reinhard Sieder, 'Die "Schlurfs". Verweigerung und Opposition von Wiener Arbeiterjugendlichen im Dritten Reich'. In: E. Tálos et al. (eds.), 1988, 243-268.

Geyer, M., '*Endkampf* 1918 and 1945. German nationalism, annihilation, and self-destruction'. In: A. Lüdtke and B. Weisbrod (eds.), *No man's land of violence. Extreme war in the 20th century*. Göttingen, 2006, 37-67.

Gherarducci, D., 'Alcune considerazioni sui quadri psichici dei prigionieri di guerra rimpatriati'. *Rivista Sperimentale di Freniatria*, 74 (1950), 19-37.

Gierowski, K., 'Ferne Nachtwirkungen einer Stressbelastung bei den Opfern des totalitären Systems in Polen'. In: T. Payk (ed.), *Perspektiven psychiatrischer Ethik*. Stuttgart/New York, 1995, 341-49.

Gierowski, K., 'Zaburzenia posttraumatyczne u ofiar totalitaryzmu w Polsce'. *Studia historyczne*, 41 (1998) 4, 577-588.

Gildea, R., *France since 1945*. Oxford, 1996.

Giltner, Ph., *In the friendliest manner: German-Danish economic cooperation during the Nazi occupation of 1940-1945*. New York, 1998.

Ginsborg, P., *A history of contemporary Italy: Society and politics 1943-1988*. New York, 2003.

'"Glemmer vi vår egen lidelse, hører vi heller ikke andres": intervju med professor Leo Eitinger'. *Dyade*, 24 (1992) 4, 12-16.

Goffman, E., *Asylums: Essays on the social situation of mental patients and other inmates*. New York, 1961.

Goltermann, Svenja, 'Die Beherrschung der Männlichkeit. Zur Deutung psychischer Leiden bei den Heimkehrern des Zweiten Weltkriegs 1945-1956'. *Feministische Studien*, 18 (2000) 2, 7-19.

Goltermann, Svenja, *Die Gesellschaft der Überlebenden: Kriegsheimkehrer und ihre Gewalterinnerungen an den Zweiten Weltkrieg*. Munich, 2009.

Goltermann, Svenja, 'Psychisches Leid und herrschende Lehre. Der Wissenschaftswandel in der westdeutschen Psychiatrie der Nachkriegszeit'. In: Bernd Weisbrod (ed.), *Akademische Vergangenheitspolitik. Beiträge zur Wissenschaftskultur der Nachkriegszeit*. Göttingen, 2002, 263-280.

Goor, J. van, *De Nederlandse koloniën*. The Hague, 1994.
Goschler, C., *Schuld und Schulden. Die Politik der Wiedergutmachung für NS-Verfolgte seit 1945*. Göttingen, 2005.
Gotovitch, J., 'Verfolgung und Vernichtung belgischer Sinti und Roma'. In: W. Dlugoborski (ed.), *Sinti und Roma im KL Auschwitz-Birkenau, 1943-44. Von dem Hintergrund ihrer Verfolgung unter der Naziherrschaft*. Auschwitz, 1998, 209-225.
Gotovitch, J. and C. Kesteloot (eds.), *Collaboration, répression. Un passé qui résiste*. Brussels, 2002.
Gouvernement du Grand-Duché de Luxembourg, *Livre d'or des victimes luxembourgeoises de la guerre de 1940 à 1945*. Luxembourg, 1972.
Grass, G., *Im Krebsgang*. Göttingen, 2002.
Gross, J.T., *Fear: Anti-Semitism in Poland after Auschwitz: an essay in historical interpretation*. New York, 2006.
Gross, J.T., *Neighbors: The destruction of the Jewish community in Jedwabne, Poland*. Princeton, 2001.
Grossmann, A., 'A question of silence: The rape of German women by occupation soldiers'. In: R.G. Moeller (ed.), *West Germany under construction: Politics, society, and culture in the Adenauer era*. Ann Arbor, 1997, 33-51.
Grubrich-Simitis, I., 'Extremtraumatisierung als kumulatives Trauma. Psychoanalytische Studien über seelische Nachwirkungen der Konzentrationslagerhaft bei Überlebenden und ihren Kindern'. In: Hans-Martin Lohmann (ed.), *Psychoanalyse und Nationalsozialismus. Beiträge zur Bearbeitung eines unbewältigten Traumas*. Frankfurt, 1984.
Gstrein, N., *Die englischen Jahre*. Frankfurt, 1999.
Haan, Ido de, *Na de ondergang. De herinnering aan de Jodenvervolging 1945-1995*. The Hague, 1997.
Haas, H., 'Der Anschluss'. In: E. Tálos et al. (eds.), 1988, 1-24.
Hackl, E., *Abschied von Sidonie*. Zürich, 1989.
Hadar, Y., 'Existentielle Erfahrung oder Krankheitssyndrom? Überlegungen zum Begriff der "Zweiten Generation"'. In: H. Stoffels (ed.), 1991.
Haesler, L. and T. Hofheim, 'Die Unmöglichkeit zu trauern und deren Bewältigung durch Identifizierung: Ein Modus transgenerationalen Transmission des Traumas'. Lecture at the conference *Psychische Schäden alternder Überlebender des Nazi-Terrors und ihrer Nachkommen*. Hannover, 11-14 October 1989.
Hæstrup, J., *... til landets bedste. Hovedtræk af departementchefsstyrets virke 1943-45*. Copenhagen, 1968.
Hanisch, E., 'Der Ort des Nationalsozialismus in der österreichischen Geschichte'. In: E. Tálos et al. (eds.), 2000.
Hansson, P., *Hver tiende mann måtte dø: fra konvoifarten under siste verdenskrig*. Oslo, 1967.
Hauch, G. (ed.), *Frauen in Oberdonau*. Vienna, 2006.
Hauch, G. (ed.), *Industrie und Zwangsarbeit im Nationalsozialismus*. Innsbruck, 2003.
Hauch, G., 'Ostarbeiterinnen. Vergessene Frauen und ihre Kinder'. In: Fritz Mayrhofer and Walter Schuster (eds.), *Nationalsozialismus in Linz*. Bd. 2. Linz, 2001, 1271-1310.

Heger, H., *Die Männer mit dem rosa Winkel. Der Bericht eines Homosexuellen über seine KZ-Haft von 1939-1945*. Hamburg, 1972.
Heim ins Reich. L'échec d'une annexation. Documentary by Claude Lahr. Luxembourg, 2004.
Helweg-Larsen, P. et al., *Famine disease in German concentration camps: complications and sequels*. Copenhagen, 1952.
Helweg-Larsen, P. et al., 'Sultsygdommen og dens følgetilstande hos koncentrationslejrfanger: foreløbig meddelelse'. *Ugeskrift for Læger*, 111 (1949), 1217-1240.
Henke, K.D., 'Deutschland – Zweierlei Kriegsende'. In: U. Herbert and A. Schildt (eds.), 1998, 337-354.
Herberg, H.J. (ed.), *Die Beurteilung von Gesundheitsschäden nach Gefangenschaft und Verfolgung*. Bielefeld, 1967.
Herbert, U. and A. Schildt (eds.), *Kriegsende in Europa. Vom Beginn des deutschen Machtzerfalls bis zur Stabilisierung der Nachkriegsordnung 1944-1948*. Essen, 1998.
Herman, Judith Lewis, *Trauma and recovery*. New York, 1992.
Hermann, K. and P. Thygesen, 'KZ-Syndrom'. *Ugeskrift for Læger*, 140 (1954), 825-836.
Hertz, M. and P. Thygesen, 'Postdiphtheric nervous complications'. *Acta Psychiatrica et Neurologica* (Supplement), 44 (1947).
Hilger, A., *Deutsche Kriegsgefangene in der Sowjetunion, 1941-1956: Kriegsgefangenenpolitik, Lageralltag und Erinnerung*. Essen, 2000.
Hinsch, F., *En politibetjents dagbog fra KZ-lejrene*. Copenhagen, 1994.
Hohengarten, A., *Wie es im Zweiten Weltkrieg (1939-1945) zur Zwangsrekrutierung Luxemburger Staatsbürger zum Nazi-Heer kam*. Luxembourg, 1974.
Holm-Sørensen, S.A., *Foråret 1945 – en dansk kz-fangers erindringer*. Copenhagen, 1995.
Holocaust Encyclopedia. United States Holocaust Memorial Museum.
Hornung, E. et al., *Zwangsarbeit in der Landwirtschaft in Niederösterreich und im nördlichen Burgenland*. (Veröffentlichung der Österreichischen Historikerkommission der Republik Österreich, vol. 26/3). Vienna/Munich, 2004.
Isastia, A.M. (ed.), *Il ritorno dei prigionieri italini tra indifferenza e rimozione*. Rome, 2006.
Jabloner, C. et al., *Schlussbericht der Historikerkommission der Republik Österreich. Vermögensentzug während der NS-Zeit sowie Rückstellungen und Entschädigungen seit 1945 in Österreich*. Vienna/Munich, 2003.
Jackowska, E., 'Psychiczne następstwa deportacji w głąb ZSRR w ocenie Sybiraków'. *Psychiatria Polska*, 39 (2005) 1.
Jackson, J., *Charles de Gaulle*. London, 1990.
Jackson, J., *France: The dark years, 1940-1944*. Oxford, 2001.
Jaklin, A., *Historien om Nord-Norge*. Oslo, 2006.
Janet, P., *Les obsessions et la psychasthénie*. Paris, 1903.
Jones, Edgar and Simon Wessely, *Shell shock to PTSD: Military psychiatry from 1900 to the Gulf War*. Hove/New York, 2005.
Joris, G., 'Erkentelijkheidceremonie Rechtvaardigen in Brussel'. *Joods Actueel*, 5 (2007), 9.
Judt, Tony, *Geschichte Europas von 1945 bis zur Gegenwart*. Munich, 2006.
Judt, Tony, 'The past is another country: Myth and memory in postwar Europe'. In: István Deák et al. (eds.), *The politics of retribution. World War II and its aftermath*. Princeton, 2000, 293-323.

Kaneda, M., (selected papers from Przegląd Leksarski – Oświęcim). Nippon Iji Schisposcha 1982.

Kansteiner, W., 'Testing the limits of trauma: The long-term psychological effects of the Holocaust on individuals and collectives'. *History of the Human Sciences*, 17 (2004), 97-123.

Karner, S. and P. Ruggenthaler, *Zwangsarbeit in der Land- und Forstwirtschaft auf dem Gebiet Österreichs 1939 bis 1945*. Vienna, 2004.

Kaufer, R., *Die psychischen und neurologischen Spätschäden nach Konzentrationslageraufenthalt*. Greifswald, 1965.

Kennedy, James, *Building New Babylon: Cultural change in the Netherlands during the nineteensixties*. New York, 1995.

Kępiński, A., 'Anus Mundi'. *Przegląd Lekarski Oświęcim*, 21 (1965) 1.

Kępiński, A., 'Dulce et decorum'. *Przegląd Lekarski Oświęcim*, 1972.

Kępiński, A., 'Genocide crimes'. *Przegląd Lekarski Oświęcim*, 1972.

Kępiński, A., 'Koszmar'. *Przegląd Lekarski Oświęcim*, 1966.

Kępiński, A., 'O wi cimskie refleksje psychiatry'. *Przegląd Lekarski Oświęcim*, 19 (1964) 1, 7-9.

Kępiński, A., 'Psychopatologia władzy'. *Przegląd Lekarski Oświęcim*, 1967.

Kępiński, A., 'Rampa. Psychopatologia decyzji'. *Przegląd Lekarski Oświęcim*, 1968.

Kępiński, A., 'Some psychosociologic problems of Nazi mass crimes during Word War II'. *Przegląd Lekarski Oświęcim*, 18 (1962), 81-83.

Kępiński, A. (1970), 'The so-called "KZ-syndrome" – An attempt at a synthesis'. In: Z.J. Ryn (ed.), 2005, 141-156.

Kępiński, A. and M. Orwid (1962), 'From psychopathology of Übermenschen'. *Archives of Psychiatry and Psychotherapy*, 9 (1970) 1-2, 79-81.

Kerschbaumer, M.Th., *Der weibliche Name des Widerstandes*. Vienna, 1980.

Kesteloot, Chantal, 'Kinderen van verzetslui of collaborateurs: Opgroeien zonder vader of moeder'. (Seminar *Trauma in Historische Context*, Rome, 2005).

Kesteloot, Chantal, 'La place de la guerre dans les sociétés nationales'. *Colloque Institut Historique Allemand de Paris*, April 2006.

Kestenberg, Milton, 'Discriminatory aspects of the German indemnification policy: A continuation of persecution'. In: M.V. Bergmann and M.E. Jucovy (eds.), 1982, 62-79.

Kirchhoff, H., *Augustoprøret 1943*. Copenhagen, 1943.

Kirchhoff, H., *Samarbejde og modstand under besættelsen. En politisk historie*. Odense, 2002.

Kirchhoff, H., J.T. Lauridsen and A. Trommer (eds.), *Gads leksikon Hvem var hvem 1940-1945*. Copenhagen, 2005.

Kjeldsen, M., 'Mogens Fog'. In: H. Kirchhoff et al., 2005.

Kochanski, A., 'Polska 1944-1991'. *Informator historyczny*. Warsaw, 1996.

Koppen, J., *Passer en Davidster. De strijd van de Duitse bezetter en de collaboratie tegen de vermeende samenzwering van vrijmetselaars en joden in België (1940-1944)*. Brussels, 2005.

Kowalczykowa, J., 'Starvation disease in the Auschwitz concentration camp.' *Przegląd Lekarski – Oświęcim*, 17 (1961), 28-31.

Kreitner, C., *Öffentliche 'Jugendfürsorge' während des Nationalsozialismus in Österreich (1938-1945)*. Klagenfurt, 2002.

Krystal, H. and W.G. Niederland, 'Clinical observations on the survivor syndrome'. In: H. Krystal (ed.), *Massive psychic trauma.* New York, 1968.

Kuch, K. and B.J. Cox, 'Symptoms of PTSD in 1243 survivors of the Holocaust'. *The American Journal of Psychiatry,* 149 (1992) 3, 337-340.

Kunzenmann, W. (ed.), *Sr. Maria Restituta Kafka. Märtyrerin aus dem Widerstand.* Innsbruck, 1998.

Kuretsidis-Haider, C. and W. Garscha, 'Nationalsozialistische Verbrechen vor Gericht. Eine Einführung'. In: Thomas Albrich, Winfried Garscha and Martin Polaschek (eds.), *Holocaust und Kriegsverbrechen vor Gericht – Der Fall Österreich.* Innsbruck, 2006, 11-25.

Lagrou, Pieter, 'Herdenken en vergeten. De politieke verwerking van verzet en vervolging in België na 1945'. *Spiegel Historiael,* 29 (1994), 116-122.

Lagrou, Pieter, *The legacy of Nazi occupation. Patriotic memory and national recovery in Western Europe, 1945-1965.* Cambridge, 2000.

Landau, H. (with Erich Hackl), *Lexikon der österreichischen Spanienkämpfer.* Vienna, 2008.

Langbein, H., *Der Auschwitz-Prozess. Eine Dokumentation.* Bd 1. Vienna/Frankfurt/Zurich, 1965.

Langbein, H., *Menschen in Auschwitz.* Frankfurt/Berlin/Vienna, 1980.

Later effects of imprisonment and deportation. International conference WVF, The Hague, 20-25 November 1961.

Lauridsen, J.T., *Samarbejde og modstand, Danmark under den Tyske besættelse 1940-45. En bibliografi.* Copenhagen, 2002.

Lebigot, F. and M.D. Colas Benayoun, 'Reconnaissance et réparation des blessures psychiques de guerre'. *Revue francophone du Stress et du Trauma,* 4 (2004), 103-111.

Lebow, Richard Ned, Wulf Kansteiner and Claudio Fogu (eds.), *The politics of memory in postwar Europe.* Durham/London, 2006.

Leeuw, A. van der, 'De ontwikkeling van de overheidszorg voor oorlogsgetroffenen'. In: A. Engelsman (ed.), *Oorlogstrauma's na 45 jaar? Politiek en psychiatrisch ongeduld.* Amsterdam, 1989, 85-104.

Lerner, Paul, *Hysterical men. War, psychiatry, and the politics of trauma in Germany, 1890-1930.* Ithaca/London, 2003.

Lerner, Paul, 'Psychiatry and casualties of war in Germany, 1914-1918'. *Journal of Contemporary History,* 35 (2000), 13-28.

Lerner, Paul and Mark S. Micale, 'Trauma, psychiatry, and history: A conceptual and historiographical introduction'. In: M.S. Micale and P. Lerner (eds.), 2001, 1-27.

Leśniak, R., 'Personality changes in former prisoners of the Auschwitz Birkenau concentration camp. A preliminary report'. *Przegląd Lekarski,* 20 (1964), 29-30.

Leśniak, R. (1965), 'Post-camp personality alterations in former prisoners of the Auschwitz-Birkenau concentration camp'. In: Z.J. Ryn (ed.), 2005, 39-56.

Leśniak, R. et al., 'Some psychiatric problems of Auschwitz concentration camp in the light of personal investigations'. *Przegląd Lekarski – Oświęcim,* 1962, 1a (special issue).

Leśniak, R. et al., 'Zagadnienia psychiatryczne obozu w Oświęcimiu'. *Przegląd Lekarski,* 6 (1960), 180-182.

'Letter to the stars: Der Fluch der guten Erinnerung'. *Der Standard*, 15 December 2007.

'Letter to the stars: Stolpersteine der Erinnerung'. *Der Standard*, 15 December 2007.

Levi, D., 'La psicoanalisi italiana e il trauma dei sopravvissuti: Il caso italiano che non c'è'. In: Bruno Maida (ed.), *1938. I bambini e le leggi razziali in Italia*. Florence, 1999.

Levi-Bianchini, M., 'Atti del XXVI congresso della Società Freniatrica Italiana'. *Rivista Sperimentale di Freniatria*, 48 (1924), 55-57.

Leys, Ruth, *Trauma: A geneaology*. Baltimore, 2000.

Lichtblau, A., 'Antisemitismus – Rahmenbedingungen und Wirkungen auf das Zusammenleben von Juden und Nichtjuden'. In: E. Tálos et al. (eds.), *Handbuch des politischen Systems Österreichs. Erste Republik 1918-1933*. Vienna, 1995, 454-471.

Liebmann, M., 'Katholischer Widerstand – Der Umgang mit Priestern, die aus den KZS zurückkamen'. In: Stefan Karner and Karl Duffek (eds.), *Widerstand in Österreich 1938-1945*. Graz/Vienna, 2007.

Lingen, Kerstin von (ed.), *Kriegserfahrung und nationale Identität in Europa nach 1945*. Paderborn/Munich/Zurich, 2009.

Lingens, E., 'Die Situation in Österreich'. In: H.J. Herberg (ed.), 1967.

Lingens, E., 'Jüdische Schicksale. Berichte von Verfolgten'. In: *Dokumentationsarchiv des österreichischen Widerstandes*. Vienna, 1992, 634.

Loesch, A., 'Les Pupilles de la Nation'. In: N. Bosseler and R. Steichen (eds.), *Livre d'or de la résistance luxembourgeoise de 1940-1945*. Luxembourg, 1952, 673-675.

'Loi du 25 février 1967 ayant pour objet diverses mesures en faveur de personnes devenues victimes d'actes illégaux de l'occupant'. *Mémorial*, 27 February 1967, A No. 12.

'Loi du 4 avril 2005 portant création a) d'un Comité directeur pour le Souvenir de l'Enrôlement forcé; b) d'un Centre de documentation et de recherche sur l'enrôlement forcé. *Mémorial*, 20 April 2005, A No. 49.

Longstaff, S.A., 'Congress for cultural freedom'. In: B. Cook (ed.), 2001.

LPPD, 'Mémoire concernant les dommages corporels et les droit des victimes, adressé par la Ligue Luxembourgeoise des Prisonniers Politiques et Déportés a Messieurs les membres du Gouvernement, de la Chambre de Députés et du Conseil d'État'. *Xe anniversaire de la libération*, special issue of *Rappel*, 10 (1955), 375-382.

LPPD, 'Mémoire concernant les rentes des patriotes invalides et des veuves des victimes politiques'. *Rappel*, *8* (1953), 286-289.

LPPD, 'XXXe anniversaire de la libération des camps: en présence de S.A.R. le Grand-Duc Jean, de M. le Ministre d'État, du Gouvernement et des Autorités Municipales, dimanche, 11 mai 1975 à Luxembourg'. *XXXe anniversaire de la libération des camps*, special issue of *Rappel*, 1975.

Ludi, Regula, 'Who is a Nazi victim? Constructing victimhood through post-war reparations in France, Germany, Switzerland'. UCLA Center for European and Eurasian Studies, 2005. http://repositories.cdlib.org/international/cees/ols/3.

Luihn, H., *Men krigen er jo slutt: om de norske krigsinvalidene fra frihetskrigen 1940-45*. Oslo, 1990.

Lundbak, H., *Besættelsetid og frihedskamp 1940-45*. Copenhagen, 1996.

Lyttelton, A., *The seizure of power: Fascism in Italy, 1919-1929*. New York, 2004.

Maas, J., 'L'identité nationale luxembourgeoise: Enjeux idéologiques et politiques dans la société de la première moitié du xx siècle'. In: *Les courants politiques et la Résistance: Continuités ou ruptures? Colloque international Esch-sur-Alzette, 24-26 avril 2002*. Luxembourg, 2003, 16-36.

Mączka, Z., 'Operacje doświadczalne przeprowadzane w obozie koncentracyjnym w Ravensbrück'. *Polski Tygodnik Lekarski*, 1946, 1, 1074-1079.

Maislinger, A., 'Andere religiöse Gruppen'. In: Dokumentationsarchiv des österreichischen Widerstandes, *Widerstand und Verfolgung in Salzburg, 1934-1945*. Vienna, 1983.

Majerus, B., 'Die Leidensgeschichte des luxemburger Volkes. Warum der Dokumentarfilm Heim ins Reich nicht überzeugen kann'. *Forum online für Politik, Gesellschaft und Kultur in Luxemburg*, 245 (2005), 48-49.

Majerus, B., 'Le débat existe bel et bien... À propos des actes du colloque "Les courants politiques et la Résistance: continuités ou ruptures?"' *Forum online für Politik, Gesellschaft und Kultur in Luxemburg*, 227 (2003), 60-63.

Majerus, B. (ed.), *Lieux de mémoire au Luxembourg*. Luxembourg, 2007.

Malina, P. and G. Spann, *Bibliographie zur österreichischen Zeitgeschichte 1918-1985. Eine Auswahl*. Vienna, 1985.

Malle, A. et al., *Vermögensentzug, Rückstellung und Entschädigung am Beispiel von Angehörigen der slowenischen Minderheit und ihrer Verbände*. (Veröffentlichungen der Historikerkommission der Republik Österreich, vol. 23/1). Vienna/Munich, 2004.

Manoschek, W., 'Österreichische Opfer der großdeutschen Krieger'. In: Hamburger Institut für Sozialforschung (ed.), *Eine Ausstellung und ihre Folgen. Zur Rezeption der Ausstellung 'Vernichtungskrieg. Verbrechen der Wehrmacht 1941 bis 1944'*. Hamburg, 1999, 87-111.

Manoschek, W. (ed.), *Opfer der Militärjustiz. Urteilspraxis – Strafvollzug – Entschädigungspolitik in Österreich*. Vienna, 2003.

Manoschek, W. and G. Sandner, 'Die Krieger als Opfer: Das Kriegsopferversorgungsgesetz (KOVG) in den Debatten des österreichischen Minister- und Nationalrates und in österreichischen Printmedien'. In: Hannes Heer et al. (eds.), *Wie Geschichte gemacht wird*. Vienna, 2003, 109-144.

Mari, A., 'Guerra e psicosi', *Note e Riviste di Psichiatria*, 48 (1948), 17-30.

Marrus, M.R., 'Vichy France and the Jews: After fifteen years'. In: Sarah Fishman et al. (eds.), *France at war: Vichy and the historians*. New York, 2000.

Marrus, M.R. and R.O. Paxton, *Vichy France and the Jews*. New York, 1995.

Martini, F., 'Polinevriti in prigionieri di guerra'. *Rassegna di Studi Psichiatrici*, 35 (1946), 466-514.

Marx, E., 'Le calvaire des Israélites du Grand-Duché de Luxembourg'. In: Nicolas Bosseler and Raymond Steichen (eds.), *Livre d'or de la résistance luxembourgeoise de 1940-1945*. Luxembourg, 1952, 569-572.

Massange, C., *Bâtir le lendemain. l'Aide aux Israélites victimes de la guerre et le Service Sociale de 1944 à nos jours*. Brussels, 2002.

Mazower, M., *Der dunkle Kontinent. Europa im 20. Jahrhundert*. Berlin, 2000.

McNally, Richard J., *Remembering trauma*. Cambridge/London, 2003.

Medische causaliteit en late oorlogsgevolgen. Utrecht, 1987.

Merridale, Catherine, 'The collective mind: Trauma and shell-shock in twentieth-century Russia'. *Journal of Contemporary History*, 35 (2000) 1, 39-55.

Micale, M. and P. Lerner (eds.), *Traumatic pasts: History, psychiatry, and trauma in the modern age, 1870-1930*. Cambridge, 2001.

Michel, M. (ed.), *Gesundheitsschäden durch Verfolgung und Gefangenschaft und ihre Spätfolgen.* (...) Frankfurt, 1955.

Middelthon, A., 'Legen og Invaliden: Loven og Rikstrygdeverket'. In: N. Retterstøl (ed.), 1982, 54-66.

Ministère des travaux publics et de la réconstruction, *Statut des prisonniers politiques et de leurs ayants droit*. Coordination par arrêté royal du 16 octobre 1954.

Mitgutsch, A., *Haus der Kindheit*. Munich, 2002.

Moeller, R.G., 'Deutsche Opfer, Opfer der Deutschen. Kriegsgefangene, Vertriebene, NS-Verfolgte: Opferausgleich als Identitätspolitik'. In: K. Naumann (ed.), *Nachkrieg in Deutschland*. Hamburg, 2001, 29-58.

Moeller, R.G., 'Germans as victims? Thoughts on a post-Cold War history of World War II's legacies'. *History & Memory*, 17 (2005), 147-194.

Moeller, R.G., 'Sinking ships, the lost Heimat and broken taboos: Günter Grass and the politics of memory in contemporary Germany'. *Contemporary European History*, 12 (2003), 1-35.

Moeller, R.G., *War stories. The search for a usable past in the Federal Republic of Germany*. Berkeley, 2001.

Monieta, A. and W. Anczurowski, 'Nasilenie objawów zespołu stresu pourazowego (ptsd) u Sybiraków z terenu północno-wschodniej Polski'. *Psychiatr. Pol.*, 38 (2004) 4, 673-683.

Mooij, Annet, 'De langste schaduw: Het denken over psychische oorlogsgevolgen'. In: Conny Kristel (ed.), *Binnenskamers: Terugkeer en opvang na de Tweede Wereldoorlog*. Amsterdam, 2002, 261-291.

Mooij, Annet, *Psychische oorlogsgevolgen* (unpublished report SOTO). Amsterdam, 1999.

Moreau, M., 'La question des névroses traumatiques et des névroses de guerre dans son état actuel'. *Journal Belge de Neurologie et de Psychiatrie*, 5/6 (1941/42), 97-124.

Moric-Petrovic, Slavka, 'Neuropsychiatric after-effects on a group of participants in the People's Liberation War of Yugoslavia'. In: *Later effects of imprisonment and deportation*, 1961, 96-99.

Morina, C., 'Instructed silence, constructed memory: The SED and the return of German prisoners of war as "war criminals" from the Soviet Union to East Germany, 1950-1956'. *Contemporary European History*, 13 (2004), 323-343.

Moritz, S., *Grüß Gott und Heil Hitler. Katholische Kirche und Nationalsozialismus in Österreich*. Vienna, 2002.

Morselli, E., *Le nevrosi traumatiche*. Turin, 1913.

Moser, J., *Demographie der jüdischen Bevölkerung Österreichs 1938-1945*. Vienna, 1999.

Müller, A. and C. Fleck, 'Unzucht wider die Natur. Gerichtliche Verfolgung der "Unzucht mit Personen gleichen Geschlechts" in Österreich von den 1930er bis zu den 1950er Jahren'. *Österreichische Zeitschrift für Geschichtswissenschaften*, 9 (1998) 3, 400-422.

Nathan, T.S., 'Children of Holocaust survivors'. Lecture at the 8th International Congress of the International Association of Child Psychiatry and Allied Professions. Philadelphia, 1974.

Nathan, T.S., 'Inter-generational impact of parental life stress'. Lecture at The Third International Conference on Psychological Stress and Adjustment in Time of War and Peace. Tel Aviv, 1983.

Neugebauer, W., *Der österreichischer Widerstand 1938-1945*. Vienna, 2008.

Neugebauer, W., 'Widerstand und Opposition'. In: E. Tálos et al. (eds.), 1988, 537-553.

Neugebauer, W., 'Widerstandsforschung in Österreich'. In: Anton Pelinka and Erika Weinzierl (eds.), *Das große Tabu. Österreichs Umgang mit seiner Vergangenheit*. Vienna, 1987, 163ff.

Neugebauer, W., 'Zwanzig Jahre Dokumentationsarchiv des österreichischen Widerstandes'. In: Helmut Konrad and Wolfgang Neugebauer (eds.), *Arbeiterbewegung – Faschismus – Nationalbewusstsein. Festschrift zum 20jährigen Bestehen des Dokumentationsarchiv des österreichischen Widerstandes und zum 60. Geburtstag von Herbert Steiner*. Vienna/Munich/Zurich, 1983.

Neugebauer, W. and P. Schwarz, *Der Wille zum aufrechten Gang. Offenlegung der Rolle des BSA bei der gesellschaftlichen Integration von ehemaligen Nationalsozialisten*. Vienna, 2005.

Neumann, V., *Nicht der Rede wert. Die Privatisierung der Kriegsfolgen in der Bundesrepublik*. Münster, 1999.

Neuner, Stephanie, 'The effects of compensation policy on the psychically war-disabled: State insurance and welfare policy for "war neurotics" in Germany after WWI, 1920-1939'. (unpublished paper Skt. Moritz, 2006.)

Niederland, W.G., 'Clinical observations on the survivor syndrome'. *International Journal of Psychoanalysis*, 49 (1968), 313-315.

Niederland, W.G., 'The problem of the survivor'. *Journal of the Hillside Hospital*, 10 (1961), 233-247.

Nielsen, H., 'Disability during the years 1946-79 among members of the Danish resistance movement deported to German concentration camps'. *Ugeskrift for Laeger*, 145 (1983), 350-355.

Nielsen, H. and H. Sørensen, 'KZ-syndromet i individuelle forløb'. *Nordisk Psykiatrisk Tidsskrift*, 38 (1984), 305-312.

Niven, B., 'The GDR and the bombing of Dresden'. In: B. Niven (ed.), *Germans as victims. Remembering the past in contemporary Germany*. New York, 2006, 109-129.

Nonnenmacher, G.G., *La grande honte de l'incorporation de force des Alsaciens-Lorrains, Eupenois-Malmédiens et Luxembourgeois dans l'armée allemande au cours de la deuxième guerre mondiale*. Colmar, 1965.

Nußbaumer, A., 'Osteuropäische Frauen als Zwangsarbeiterinnen in der Landwirtschaft des Pinzgaues'. In: Evelyn Steinthaler (ed.), *Frauen 1938. Verfolgte – Widerständige – Mitläuferinnen*. Vienna, 2008, 118-128.

Øland, A., *Horeunger og Helligdage-tyskerboerns beretninger*. Copenhagen, 2001.

Orwid, Maria, 'Remarks on adaptation to post-camp life in former prisoners of the Auschwitz concentration camp. A preliminary report'. *Przegląd Lekarski – Oświęcim*, 18 (1962), 94-97.

Orwid, Maria (1964), 'Socio-psychiatric after-effects on imprisonment in the Auschwitz-Birkenau concentration camp'. In: Z.J. Ryn (ed.), 2005, 57-68.

Orwid, Maria et al., 'Psychosocial effects of the Holocaust on survivors and the second generation in Poland: Preliminary report'. In: John Lemberger (ed.), *A global perspective on working with Holocaust survivors and the second generation.* Jerusalem, 1995, 205-242.

Orwid, Maria et al., 'Psychosoziale Folgen des Holocausts in der ersten und zweiten Generation der Holocaustopfer in Polen'. *Dialog,* 1993, 95-103.

Overmans, R., 'Die Rheinwiesenlager 1945: Ein untergeordneter Eintrag im Leidensbuch der jüngeren Geschichte?' In: G. Bischof and R. Overmans (eds.), *Kriegsgefangenschaft im Zweiten Weltkrieg. Eine vergleichende Perspektive.* Ternitz-Pottschach, 1999, 233-264.

Padovani, G., 'Esperienze e considerazioni neuropsichiatriche di guerra e di prigionia'. *Rassegna di Studi Psychiatrici,* 37 (1948), 168-201.

Padovani, G., 'Relazione morale e finanziaria dell'attività della Società italiana di psichiatria nel sessennio 1941-1946'. *Rivista sperimentale di Freniatria,* 5 (1948), 269-280.

Padovani, G. and L. Bonfiglioli, 'Le vicende storiche e statistiche dell'assistenza psichiatrica in Italia durante la 2a guerra mondiale'. *Rivista Sperimentale di Freniatria,* 52 (1948), 375-396.

Paul, H. and H.J. Herberg (eds.), *Psychische Spätschäden nach politischer Verfolgung.* Basel, 1963.

Pauley, B., *From prejudice to persecution. A history of Austrian Anti-Semitism.* Chapel Hill, 1992.

Pavan, I., 'Gli incerti percorsi della reintegrazione: Note sugli atteggiamenti della magistratura repubblicana 1945-1964'. In: Guri Schwarz (ed.), *Gli ebrei in Italia tra persecuzione e reintegrazione postbellica.* Florence, 2001.

Paxton, R.O., *Vichy France, Old Guard and New Order, 1940-1944.* New York, 1972.

Payne, S.G., *A history of fascism, 1914-1945.* London, 1995.

Pelinka, A., 'Paradigmenwechsel: Lernen aus der Geschichte. Die katholische Kirche Österreichs, der autoritäre Ständestaat und die Zweite Republik'. In: Dokumentationsarchiv des österreichischen Widerstandes, *Themen der Zeitgeschichte und der Gegenwart.* Vienna, 2004, 43-55.

Pellacani, G., 'Le neuropatie emotive e le psiconeurosi nei combattenti'. *Rivista sperimentale di Freniatria,* 60 (1920), 1-65.

Peloso, P.F., 'Psychiatry and psychiatric patients in Italy during World War II'. *International Journal of Mental Health,* 35 (2006), 66-80.

Pezzino, P., 'The Italian resistance between history and memory'. *Journal of Modern Italian Studies,* 10 (2005), 396-412.

Pfanzelter, E., 'Homosexuelle und Prostituierte'. In: R. Steininger, 2000, 75-97.

Pfeil, W., *Die Entschädigung von Opfern des Nationalsozialismus im österreichischen Recht.* (Veröffentlichungen der Historikerkommission der Republik Österreich, vol. 29/1). Vienna/Munich, 2004.

Picciotto, L., 'The Shoah in Italy: Its history and characteristics'. In: Joshua D. Zimmerman (ed.), *Jews in Italy under fascist and Nazi rule, 1922-1945.* Cambridge/New York, 2005.

Piersma, H., *De drie van Breda. Duitse oorlogsmisdadigers in Nederlandse gevangenschap 1945-1989*. Amsterdam, 2005.

Ploeg, H.M. van der and J.M.P. Weerts (eds.), *Veteranen in Nederland. Onderzoek naar de gevolgen van oorlogservaringen – Tweede Wereldoorlog –Politionele acties – Korea*. Lisse, 1995.

Poirier, J. and F. Salaün, *Médecin ou malade? La médicine en France au XIXe et XXe siècles*. Paris, 2001.

Pollard, J.F., *The fascist experience in Italy*. New York, 1998.

Ponteville, I. and C. Kesteloot, 'Kinderen van verzetslui of collaborateurs: opgroeien zonder vader of moeder' (dossier). Brussels, 2003.

Poznanski, R., 'French apprehensions, Jewish expectations: From a social imaginary to a political practice'. In: D. Bankier (ed.), 2005.

Pross, Christian, *Paying for the past. The struggle over reparations for surviving victims of the Nazi terror*. London, 1998.

Prot, K., 'Późne skutki wczesnej traumy – podobieństwa i różnice pomiędzy "dziećmi Holokaustu" a 'Sybirakami'. *Psychoterapia*, 1 (1999), 5-10.

Prusnik, K., *Gämsen auf der Lawine. Der Kärntner Partisanenkampf*. Klagenfurt, 1980.

Pulzer, P., *The rise of political antisemitism in Germany and Austria*. London, 1988.

Putkiewicz, Z., 'Próba badania wpływu wojny na psychikę młodzieży w Polsce'. *Psychologia Wychowawcza*, 14 (1949), 144-153.

Putz, E., *Ernst Jägerstätter. '...besser Hände als der Wille gefesselt...'*. Linz/Passau, 1987.

Rabinovici, D., *'Papirnik'. Stories*. Frankfurt, 1994.

Rabinovici, D., *Suche nach M*. Frankfurt, 1997.

Rammerstorfer, B., *Nein statt Ja und Amen. Leopold Engleitner: Er ging einen anderen Weg*. Linz, 1999.

Rathkolb, O. and F. Freund (eds.), *NS-Zwangsarbeit in der Elektrizitätswirtschaft der 'Ostmark' 1938-1945. Ennskraftwerke – Kaprun – Draukraftwerke – Ybbs-Persenbeug – Ernsthofen*. Vienna/Cologne/Weimar, 2002.

Reiter, M., *Die Generation danach. Der Nationalsozialismus im Familiengedächtnis*. Innsbruck/Vienna/Bolzano, 2006.

Reiter, M., *Unter Antisemitismusverdacht. Die österreichische Linke und Israel nach der Shoah*. Innsbruck/Vienna/Bolzano, 2001.

Retterstøl, Nils (ed.), *'Og livet går videre...': ekstreme påkjenninger, menneskets reaksjoner: festskrift til Leo Eitinger på 70-årsdagen 12. desember 1982*. Oslo, 1982.

Richet, Ch., 'Notes sur le typhus exanthématique observé à Buchenwald'. *Bulletin de la Société Médicale des Hôpitaux de Paris*, 15-16 (1945), 183-187.

Richet, Ch., 'Troubles neuro-psychiatriques observés à Buchenwald'. *Le Progrès Médical*, 16 (1946), 355-356.

Richet, Ch. and A. Mans, *Pathologie de la déportation*. Paris, (1956, 1958), 1962.

Richter, A., *Vergesst uns nicht – wenn auch die Tage wandern und auch die Jahre. Eine Festschrift zum 50jährigen Bestehen der Vereinigung der Opfer des Stalinismus e.V.* Berlin, 2000.

Ridder, Tom de, *De geest van het verzet. Ex-politieke gevangenen uit '40-'45*. Zutphen, 2009.

Rosen, Gerald M. (ed.), *Posttraumatic Stress Disorder. Issues and controversies*. Chichester, 2004.

Rossberg, Alexandra and Johan Lansen (eds.), *Das Schweigen brechen. Berliner Lektionen zu Spätfolgen der Schoa*. Frankfurt, 2003.

Rossi Doria, A., *Memoria e storia. Il caso della deportazione*. Catanzaro, 1998.

Rostgaard Nissen, M., *Til fælles bedste*. Copenhagen, 2003.

Rot-Weiss-Rot Buch. Gerechtigkeit für Österreich! Darstellungen, Dokumente und Nachweise zur Vorgeschichte und Geschichte der Okkupation Österreich. (Nach amtlichen Quellen). Vienna, 1946.

Rousso, H., *The Vichy syndrome. History and memory in France in 1944*. Cambridge, 1991.

Rutkowski, K., *Następstwa urazów psychicznych doznanych w dzieciństwie*. Krakow, 2006.

Ryn Z.J. (ed.), *Auschwitz survivors. Clinical-psychiatric studies from 'Medical Review – Auschwitz'*. Krakow, 2005.

Saerens, L., 'De jodenvervolging in België in cijfers'. *Bijdragen tot de eigentijdse geschiedenis (1930/1960)*, 17 (2006), 199-235.

Safrian, H. and H. Witek, *Und keiner war dabei. Dokumente des alltäglichen Antisemitismus in Wien 1938*. Vienna, 2008.

Samoy, E., *Ongeschikt of ongewenst? Een halve eeuw arbeidsmarktbeleid voor gehandicapten*. Leuven, 1998.

Sarfatti, M., 'Characteristics and objectives of the anti-Jewish racial laws in fascist Italy 1939-1943'. In: Joshua D. Zimmerman (ed.), *Jews in Italy under fascist and Nazi rule, 1922-1945*. Cambridge/New York, 2005.

Sarfatti, M., *Gli ebrei nell'Italia fascista: Vicende, identità, persecuzione*. Turin, 2000.

Sauer, W., 'Österreichs Kirchen 1938-1945'. In: E. Tálos et al. (eds.), 1988, 517-536.

Schaepdrijver, S. de, 'Een eeuwig soort heden'. *Kleio*, 43 (2002) 5, 12-17.

Schenck, E.G. and W. von Nathusius (eds.), *Handbuch der ärztlichen Erfahrungen aus der Gefangenschaft*. Bad Godesberg, 1959.

Schiller, G. and H. Weigel (eds.), *Taschenbuch der ärztlichen Begutachtungen*, Berlin (Ost), 1964.

Schindel, R., *Gebürtig*. Frankfurt, 1992.

Schindel, R., *Ohneland*. Frankfurt, 1986.

Schmidt, M.G., *Sozialpolitik der DDR*. Wiesbaden, 2004.

Schoentgen, M., 'Die Resistenzorganisationen in Luxemburg nach dem 2. Weltkrieg'. In: *Les courants politiques et la résistance: Continuités ou ruptures? Colloque internationale Esch-zur-Alzette, avril 2002*. Luxembourg, 2003, 519-551.

Schoentgen, M., 'Juden in Luxemburg, 1940-1945'. *Forum online für Politik, Gesellschaft und Kultur in Luxemburg*, 179 (1997), 17-19.

Scuto, D., 'Mémoire et histoire de la Seconde Guerre mondiale au Luxembourg. Réflexions sur une cohabitation difficile'. *Hemecht: revue d'histoire luxembourgeoise*, 58 (2006), 499-513.

Sebald, W.G., *Luftkrieg und Literatur*. Frankfurt, 2001.

Seberechts, F., *Tussen Schelde en Wolchow. Vlaanderen en het Oostfront*. Roeselaere, 2002.

Senato della Repubblica. (Prima Legislatura), *Atti Parlamentari* (Resoconti delle discussioni) XIV, 1948-50. Rome.

'Service des dommages de guerre corporels 2005'. Rapport pour le Ministère de la Santé, Grand-Duché de Luxembourg.

Shamir, H., *Economic crisis and French foreign policy 1930-1936*. Boston, 1989.
Shephard, Ben, *A war of nerves. Soldiers and psychiatrists 1914-1994*. London, 2000.
Shephard, Ben, 'Risk factors and PTSD: A historian's perspective'. In: G.M. Rosen (ed.), 2004, 39-62.
Shephard, Ben, 'Why the psychiatry of war is too important to be left to psychiatrists'. In: *War and Medicine*. London, 2009, 166-179.
'Sieg für Zeugen Jehovas. EU-Menschenrechtsgerichtshof verurteilt Österreich'. *Der Standard*, 1 August 2008, 7.
Sima, V., 'Die Deportation slowenischer Familien aus Kärnten. Rahmenbedingungen, Präludium und Vorbereitung'. In: Österreichische Liga für Menschenrechte, *Die Deportation slowenischer Familien aus Kärnten 1942*. Vienna, 2003.
Simonin, A., 'Le Comité Médical de la Résistance: un succès différé'. *Le Mouvement social*, 180 (1997), 159-178.
Skarga B., *Innego końca świata nie będzie*. Krakow, 2008.
Skjæraasen, M., *Lege for livet: en bok om Leo Eitinger – medmennesket*. Oslo, 1988.
Skocpol, Theda, *Protecting soldiers and mothers. The political origins of social policy in the United States*. Cambridge/London, 1992.
Śluzar, J., 'Wyniki badań klinicznych w obozie koncentracyjnym Gross-Rosen i Litomierzycach'. *Nowiny Lekarskie*, 52 (1945), 8-17.
Smets, E., 'De herinnering aan de nazi-genocide. De bevrijding van de kampen in de Belgische pers, september 1944-mei 1945'. *Bulletin Trimestriel de la Fondation Auschwitz*, 84 (2004), 99-112.
Smith, A.L., *Die 'vermisste Million'. Zum Schicksal deutscher Kriegsgefangener nach dem Zweiten Weltkrieg*. Munich, 1992.
Société de Médicine Mentale et Société de Neurologie, 'Séance commune du 25 juillet 1942. Discussion du rapport du Dr. Moreau: La question des névroses traumatiques et des névroses de guerre dans son état actuel'. *Journal Belge de Neurologie et de Psychiatrie*, 9/10 (1941/42), 223-274.
Société de Médicine Mentale et Société de Neurologie, 'Séance commune du 31 octobre 1942. Suite de la discussion du rapport du Dr. Moreau: La question des névroses traumatiques et des névroses de guerre dans son état actuel'. *Journal Belge de Neurologie et de Psychiatrie*, 1/2 (1943), 16-59.
Sørensen, H., O.E. Hansen and J. Worm Petersen, 'Krigssejlere 40 år efter. Psykiske og sociale følger – en pilotundersøgelse'. *Ugeskrift for Læger*, 145 (1983), 3685-3688.
Sørensen, N.A., 'Narrating the Second World War in Denmark since 1945'. *Contemporary European History*, 14 (2005), 295-315.
Śreniawa-Szypiowski, R. (ed.), *Powstanie Warszawskie 1 sierpnia – 2 października 1944*. Warsaw, 1994.
Stajner-Popovich, Tatjana, 'De "verloren" tweede generatie: fluisteringen uit Oost-Europa'. In: Joost Baneke et al. (eds.), *Trauma en identiteit*. Assen, 1998, 113-127.
Steenberge, J. van, *Schade aan de mens. Deel I Evaluatie van de arbeidsongeschiktheid in het recht*. Berchem-Antwerpen/Amsterdam, 1975.
Stein, W., 'Psychonerwice jeńców, "choroba drutów kolczastych", objawy i mechanizm'. *Lekarz Wojskowy*, 24 (1948), 49-65.

Steinberg, M., *Extermination, sauvetage et résistance des Juifs de Belgique. Hommage des Juifs de Belgique à leurs héros et sauveteurs 1940-1945.* Brussels, 1979.

Steiner, E., 'Gedenken an slowenische Nazi-Opfer. Erstmals "Erinnerungsmarsch" für hingerichtete Widerstandskämpfer in Klagenfurt'. *Der Standard,* 25 April 2008, 11.

Steiner, J.F., *Varsovie 44: l'insurrection.* Paris, 1975.

Steininger, R., *Vergessene Opfer des Nationalsozialismus.* Innsbruck/Vienna/Munich, 2000.

Steinmetz, S., *Österreichs Zigeuner im NS-Staat.* Vienna/Frankfurt/Zurich, 1966.

Stephensen, H., *Et krigsmonument – ni 4. Maj Kollegier.* Copenhagen, 1979.

Stephensen, H., *Frihedsfonden 1945-1970.* Copenhagen, 1970.

Stille, A., 'The double bind of Italian Jews: Acceptance and assimilation'. In: Joshua D. Zimmerman (ed.), *Jews in Italy under fascist and Nazi rule, 1922-1945.* Cambridge/ New York, 2005.

Stoffels, H. (ed.), *Schicksale der Verfolgten. Psychische und somatische Auswirkungen von Terrorherrschaft.* Berlin etc., 1991.

Stojka, C. and K. Berger (eds.), *Wir leben im Verborgenen. Erinnerungen einer Roma-Zigeunerin.* Vienna, 1995.

Stora, B., W.B. Quandt and J.M. Todd, *Algeria, 1830-2000: A short history.* New York, 2004.

Storeide, A., *Fortellingen om Fangeskapet.* Oslo, 2007.

Stourzh, G., *Um Einheit und Freiheit. Staatsvertrag, Neutralität und das Ende der Ost-West-Besetzung Österreichs 1945-1955.* Vienna/Cologne/Graz, 1998, 11-27.

Stræde, T., *Die Menschenmauer. Dänemark im Oktober 1943: Die Rettung der Juden vor der Vernichtung.* Copenhagen, 1997.

Strøm, A., 'Purpose and scope of the investigation'. In: *Later effects of imprisonment and deportation,* 1961.

Summerfield, Derek, 'The invention of post-traumatic stress disorder and the social usefulness of a psychiatric category'. *British Medical Journal,* 322 (2001), 95-98.

Swaan, A. de, *In care of the state. Health care, education and welfare in Europe and the USA in the modern era.* Cambridge/Oxford, 1988.

Szafran, A.W., 'Rouw zonder einde: klinische aspecten'. *Bulletin Trimestriel de la Fondation Auschwitz,* 31 (1992), 23-31.

Szasz, T., *The myth of mental illness: Foundations of a theory of personal conduct.* New York, 1961.

Szymusik, A. (1964), 'Progressive asthenia in former prisoners of the Auschwitz-Birkenau concentration camp'. In: Z.J. Ryn (ed.), 2005, 69-82.

Szymusik, A., 'Psychological disorders in former prisoners of the Auschwitz concentration camp. A preliminary report'. *Przegl d Lekarski,* 18 (1962), 98-102.

Szymusik, A., A. Piotrowski and J. Bomba, 'Psychiatry in Eastern Europe'. *American Journal of Psychiatry,* 150 (1993) 6, 988-989.

Tálos, E. and W. Neugebauer (eds.), *Austrofaschismus. Politik, Ökonomie, Kultur. 1933-1938.* Münster, 2005.

Tálos, E., E. Hanisch and W. Neugebauer (eds.), *NS-Herrschaft in Österreich 1938-1945.* Vienna, 1988.

Tálos, E. et al. (eds.), *NS-Herrschaft in Österreich 1938-1945. Ein Handbuch.* Vienna, 2000.

Tanay, E., *Passport to life. Autobiographical reflections on the Holocaust.* Ann Arbor, 2004.

Tanay, E., 'Powstanie w getcie Warszawskim'. *Psychoterapia*, 141 (2007) 2, 79-93.
Targowla, R., 'Les données de la narcose intraveineuse liminaire dans les états "neuropathiques": Le syndrome d'hypermnésie émotionnelle tardif'. *Annales de Médicine*, 51 (1950), 223.
Targowla, R., 'Pathological sequelae of deportation in German concentration camps during World War II'. *La Presse Médicale*, 62 (1954), 611-613.
Targowla, R., 'Syndrom der Asthenie der Deportierten'. In: M. Michel (ed.), 1955, 30-47.
Tas, J., 'Psychische stoornissen in concentratiekampen en bij teruggekeerden'. *Maandblad Geestelijke volksgezondheid*, 1 (1946), 143-150.
'Témoignage sur le Comité Médical de la Résistance. Notes extraites par Emmanuelle Picard du fonds AN 72 AJ 80. Témoignage de Robert Merle d'Aubigné'. 1994. http://www.histrecmed.fr/CMR.pdf.
Teutsch, A., 'An analysis of adaptation to camp conditions in prisoners during World War II in Nazi concentration camps. A preliminary report'. *Przegląd Lekarski – Oświęcim*, 18 (1962), 90-94.
Teutsch, A. (1964), 'Psychological reactions to psychosomatic stress in 100 former prisoners of the Auschwitz-Birkenau concentration camp'. In: Z.J. Ryn (ed.), 2005, 27-38.
Ther, P., *Deutsche und polnische Vertriebene. Gesellschaft und Vertriebenenpolitik in der SBZ/DDR und in Polen 1945-1956*. Göttingen, 1998.
Thurner, E., *Nationalsozialismus und Zigeuner in Österreich*. Salzburg, 1983.
Thygesen, P. 'Befrielsesregeringens minister – og besættelsestidens ofre'. In: E. Bredsdorf, 1992.
Thygesen, P., 'Forskeren og lægen – de følgende år'. In: E. Bredsdorf, 1992.
Thygesen, P., *Frihedsfonden 1945-1995*. Copenhagen, 1996.
Thygesen, P., *La déportation dans les camps de concentration allemands et ses sequelles: une analyse médicale et sociale. (par la Croix Rouge Danoise)*. Copenhagen, 1954.
Thygesen, P., *Læge i tyske koncentrationslejre*. Copenhagen, 1945.
Thygesen, P., 'The concentration camp syndrome'. *Danish Medical Bulletin*, 27 (1980), 224-228.
Thygesen, P., K. Hermann and R. Willanger, 'Concentration camp survivors in Denmark: Persecution, disease, disability, compensation. A 23-year follow-up. A survey of the long-term effects of severe environmental stress'. *Danish Medical Bulletin*, 17 (1970), 65-108.
Thygesen, P. et al., 'Krigssejlernes skæbne'. *Bibliotek for Læger*, 178 (1986), 185-204.
Tomaszewski, W., 'Następstwa przewlekłego głodzenia'. *Nowiny Lekarskie*, 35 (1945), 242-249.
Toscano, M., 'The abrogation of racial laws and the reintegration of Jews in Italian society (1943-1948)'. In: D. Bankier (ed.), 2005.
Uhl, H., '1994 – Erinnern und Vergessen. Denkmäler zur Erinnerung an die Opfer der nationalsozialistischen Gewaltherrschaft und an die Gefallenen des Zweiten Weltkriegs in Graz und in der Steiermark'. In: Stefan Riesenfellner and Heidemarie Uhl (eds.), *Todeszeichen. Zeitgeschichtliche Denkmalkultur*. Vienna/Cologne/Weimar, 1994, 111-195.

Uhl, H., *Steinernes Bewusstsein. Die öffentliche Repräsentation staatlicher und nationaler Identität in Österreich in seinen Denkmälern.* Vienna/Cologne/Weimar, 2006.

Uhl, H., 'Transformationen des österreichischen Gedächtnisses. Erinnerungspolitik und Denkmalkultur in der Zweiten Republik'. *Transit: Europäische Revue, Vom Neuschreiben der Geschichte. Erinnerungspolitik nach 1945 und 1989*, 15 (1998), 100-119.

UNRRA Inter-Allied Psychological Study Group, *Psychological problems of displaced persons.* London, 1945.

Venzlaff, U., *Die psychoreaktiven Störungen nach entschädigungspflichtigen Ereignissen.* Göttingen, 1958.

Venzlaff, U., 'Erlebnishintergrund und Dynamik seelischer Verfolgungsschäden'. In: H. Paul and H.J. Herberg (eds.), 1963, 95-109.

Venzlaff, U., 'Gutachten zur Frage des Zusammenwirkens erlebnisreaktiver, vegetativer und hormonaler Faktoren bei Verfolgungsschäden'. In: H. Paul and H.J. Herberg (eds.), 1963, 111-124.

Venzlaff, U., 'Mental disorders resulting from racial persecution outside of concentration camps'. *International Journal of Social Psychiatry*, 10 (1964), 177-183.

Vermeulen, M., *La détention dans les camps de concentration allemands: conséquences psychiques d'une situation traumatisante.* Brussels, 1987.

Vermeylen, 'Événements et psychoses'. *Journal Belge de Neurologie et de Psychiatrie*, 13 (1943-1945), 129-148.

Verri Melo, I., *La Sindrome del sopravvissuto: Le conseguenze dell'internamento nei campi di concentramento nazisti.* Florence, 1991.

Vyssoki, D., 'Im Alter wird das Langzeitgedächtnis präsenter'. *Der Standard*, 9 June 2008.

Vyssoki, D., 'Trauma bei den Opfern der NS-Verfolgung'. In: A. Friedmann et al. (eds.), 2004.

Wahl, N., *Verfolgung und Vermögensentzug Homosexueller auf dem Gebiet der Republik Österreich während der NS-Zeit sowie deren Bemühungen um Restitution, Entschädigung und Pensionen in der Zweiten Republik.* (Veröffentlichungen der Historikerkommission der Republik Österreich, vol. 25). Vienna/Munich, 2002.

Walczewska, J., J. Furgał and K. Rutkowski, 'Ocena aktualnego stanu zdrowia osób deportowanych na Syberię w latach 1940-1953'. *Gerontologia Polska*, 10 (2002) 4, 186-189.

Wallerang, M., *Luxemburg unter nationalsozialistische Besatzung. Luxemburger berichten.* (Studien zur Volkskultur in Rheinland-Pfalz 22). Mainz, 1997.

Warring, A., *Tyskerpiger – under besættelse og retsopgør.* Copenhagen, 1994.

Weber, E., *The hollow years: France in the 1930s.* New York, 1994.

Wehler, H.U., *Deutsche Gesellschaftsgeschichte, Vol. 4: Vom Beginn des Ersten Weltkrieges bis zur Gründung der beiden deutschen Staaten 1914-1949.* Munich, 2003.

Weil, P., 'The return of Jews in the nationality or in the territory of France'. In: D. Bankier (ed.), 2005.

Weinzierl, E., 'Kirchlicher Widerstand gegen den Nationalsozialismus'. In: Dokumentationsarchiv des österreichischen Widerstandes, *Themen der Zeitgeschichte und der Gegenwart.* Vienna, 2004, 76-85.

Weinzierl, E., *Prüfstand. Österreichs Katholiken und der Nationalsozialismus.* Mödling, 1988.

Weinzierl, E., *Zu wenig Gerechte. Österreicher und Judenverfolgung 1938-1945.* Vienna, 1969.

Wever, B. de, 'De collaboratie in Vlaanderen'. In: J. Gotovitch and C. Kesteloot (eds.), *Het gewicht van het oorlogsverleden*. Brussels, 2003, 39-49.

Wind, E. de (1949), 'Confrontatie met de dood'. In: Tom de Ridder and Marleen van de Ven (eds.), *Eddy de Wind. Confrontatie met de dood. Psychische gevolgen van vervolging.* Utrecht, 1993, 11-24.

Wind, E. de, 'Directe en late gevolgen van extreme belastingssituaties – het concentratiekamp'. *Maandblad Geestelijke volksgezondheid*, 21 (1966), 287-300.

Winkler, C., 'Männlichkeit und Gesundheit der deutschen Kriegsheimkehrer im Spiegel der Ärztekongresse des "Verbands der Heimkehrer"'. In: M. Dinges (ed.), *Männlichkeit und Gesundheit im historischen Wandel ca. 1800 – ca. 2000*. Stuttgart, 2007, 157-174.

Winter, Jay, 'Shell-shock and the cultural history of the Great War'. *Journal of Contemporary History*, 35 (2000) 1, 7-11.

Withuis, Jolande, 'Bestaat PTSS? Over trauma, traumacultuur en traumamisbruik'. *Icodo-Info* 18 (2001) 3/4, 5-18. Translation: 'Does PTSD really exist?'. www.niod.nl.

Withuis, Jolande, *Erkenning. Van oorlogstrauma naar klaagcultuur*. Amsterdam, 2002.

Withuis, Jolande, '"Geestelijke oorlogsschade". De oorlog in het maandblad 1945/2000'. *Maandblad Geestelijke volksgezondheid*, 2001, 5, 394-451.

Withuis, Jolande, *Na het kamp. Vriendschap en politieke strijd*. Amsterdam, 2005.

Withuis, Jolande, *Weest manlijk, zijt sterk. Pim Boellaard 1903-2001. Het leven van een verzetsheld*. Amsterdam, 2008.

Young, Allan, *The harmony of illusions. Inventing Post-traumatic Stress Disorder*. Princeton, 1995.

Zahn, C., 'Gordon'. In: *Solidarity witness. The life and death of Franz Jägerstätter*. Springfield, 1964.

'Zeugen Jehovas. Vergessene Opfer des Nationalsozialismus'. *Dokumentationsarchiv des österreichischen Widerstandes*. Vienna, 1998.

Zuccotti, S., *The Holocaust, the French, and the Jews*. New York, 1993.

Index

(A) = Austria
(B) = Belgium
(D) = Denmark
(F) = France
(G) = Germany
(I) = Italy
(L) = Luxembourg
(N) = The Netherlands
(No) = Norway
(P) = Poland

List of Contributors

Jacek Bomba (1941) is a psychiatrist and psychotherapist. He is a doctor of medical sciences, professor and director of the Department of Child and Adolescent Psychiatry, and Chairman of Psychiatry, the Jagiellonian University Collegium Medicum, Krakow. He was elected President of the Polish Psychiatric Association three times. His main research area concerns adolescent depression (*La dépression chez l'adolescent. Étude psychologique et épidémiologique*, 1988). Edited series: *Schizophrenia; various contexts, various therapies* (2000, 2002, 2004) and *The brain and the psyche* (2007).

Maria Teresa Brancaccio (1961) studied political science and history in Naples and Paris and wrote a PhD thesis on the history of ADHD (Amsterdam, 2001). Since 2006, she is affiliated to the Institut universitaire d'histoire de la médecine et de la santé publique (IUHMSP), Department of Medicine, University of Lausanne, Switzerland. Since 1997, she has been working part-time as project coordinator at the International Department of the Anne Frank House (Amsterdam). She is currently researching the history of suicide and she occasionally lectures at the University of Maynooth (Dublin).

Maria Ecker (1976) is a historian. Her dissertation: *'Tales of edification and redemption'? Oral/Audiovisual Holocaust Testimonies and American Public Memory* appeared in 2006. Fields of interest: oral history, Holocaust testimonies, reception of the Holocaust in the US, Israel, and Austria, Holocaust education. Since 2009 she has worked as a historian/educator at the Mauthausen memorial.

Helga Embacher (1959) is professor of Contemporary History at the University of Salzburg. She works in the field of Jewish history, anti-Semitism, national socialism and Muslims in Europe, and is the leader of the project '(New) Anti-Semitism and Anti-Americanism in Germany, France and Great Britain. A Comparative Study', which will be published in 2010. Since 2009 she leads the project 'Perpetrators, Victims and Beneficiaries: Provenance Research at the University Library of Salzburg'. Her publications include *Neubeginn ohne Illusionen. Juden in Österreich nach 1945* (Vienna, 1995) and *Gratwanderungen. Die Beziehungen zwischen Österreich und Israel im Schatten der Vergangenheit* (Vienna, 1998, together with Margit Reiter).

Ralf Futselaar (1976) studied economic and social history at the University of Groningen and University College Cork. He was awarded a PhD by the University of Amsterdam in 2007 for his thesis *Lard, Lice, and Longevity. The Standard of Living in Occupied Denmark and the Netherlands: 1940-1945*, which has since been published as a book by Aksant Academic Publishers. He currently holds a research fellow position at Kwansei Gakuin University, Japan, and is working on a book on the decline of tuberculosis in post-war Germany and Japan.

Svenja Goltermann (1965) teaches history at the University of Freiburg. She is the author of *Die Gesellschaft der Überlebenden. Deutsche Kriegsheimkehrer und ihre Gewalterfahrungen im Zweiten Weltkrieg* (Munich, 2009) and a number of articles, including 'The Imagination of Disaster. Death and Survival in Postwar West Germany', in Paul Betts, Alon Confino and Dirk Schumann (eds.), *Between Mass Death and Individual Loss: The Place of the Dead in Twentieth Century Germany* (Oxford, 2008, 261-274).

Sonja van 't Hof (1960) is editor-in-chief of the Dutch public mental health monthly *Maandblad Geestelijke volksgezondheid (MGv)*. After graduating in psychology, she received a PhD in sociology in 1994 (*The historical and cultural specificity of anorexia nervosa. Fallacious theories and tenacious 'facts'*. Lisse, 1994). She has published on the recent history of public mental health, child psychiatry and medicine in the Netherlands (www.sonjavanthof.nl).

Annet Mooij (1961) is a freelance researcher. She has published several books in the field of medical history. In 1999-2000 she took part in the research project of the Netherlands Institute for War Documentation on the return and reception of war victims in the Netherlands after 1945. Her publications on the aftermath of World War II include 'De langste schaduw. Het denken over psychische oorlogsgevolgen', in Conny Kristel (ed.), *Binnenskamers* (Amsterdam, 2002, 261-291) and *De strijd om de Februaristaking* (Amsterdam, 2006).

Maria Orwid (1930-2009), doctor of medical sciences, was a psychiatrist and psychotherapist. She was the founder and director of the Department of Child and Adolescent Psychiatry at the Jagiellonian University Collegium Medicum, Krakow, and co-founder of the Polish Psychiatric Association Section for Psychotherapy, and later Section for Family Therapy. The results of her research into the post-war adaptation of Auschwitz concentration camp survivors were published in *Socio-psychiatric after-effects of imprisonment in the Auschwitz-Birkenau concentration camp* (1963). Her publications include the first Polish textbook on adolescent psychiatry (1981), *To survive and what next...?* (2006) and *Trauma* (2009).

Jolande Withuis (1949), sociologist, is a senior researcher at the Netherlands Institute for War Documentation (NIOD). In her dissertation she analyzed the influence of World War II and the Cold War on the mental world of communism. She has published articles and books on Ravensbrück survivors, gender, on the historical sociology of trauma (*Erkenning. Van oorlogstrauma naar klaagcultuur*, 2002), and on the collective history of concentration camp survivors (*Na het kamp. Vriendschap en politieke strijd*, 2005). Her biography of a Dutch resistance hero and Dachau survivor (*Weest manlijk, zijt sterk*, 2008) received much acclaim. Methodologically her work combines historical, psychodynamic and sociological perspectives.